Journeys Toward Progress

STUDIES OF ECONOMIC POLICY-MAKING IN LATIN AMERICA

PAUL KLEE: Highway and Byways

Journeys
Toward Progress

STUDIES OF
ECONOMIC POLICY-MAKING
IN LATIN AMERICA

Albert O. Hirschman

THE TWENTIETH CENTURY FUND

NEW YORK · 1963

TO

Celso Furtado

AND

Carlos Lleras Restrepo

Master Reformmongers

Foreword

In 1959 the Twentieth Century Fund organized a Latin American study group which held a number of sessions and whose members contributed papers exploring some of the principal economic ideas and policy problems currently discussed in Latin America. These papers were published in 1961 by the Fund in a volume *Latin American Issues: Essays and Comments,* edited by Albert O. Hirschman who had acted as rapporteur of the group.

A recurrent theme of the group's discussions was the nature of the policy-making process in Latin America. Impressed with the difficulties of generalizing in this field, Professor Hirschman proposed to the Fund a study that would attempt to reach conclusions through painstaking observation of the sequence of policy-making around significant and protracted policy problems. The present book is the outcome of this effort. Three countries are involved: Colombia, Chile, Brazil. Land reform, inflation, and a peculiarly obdurate regional problem compose the major portion of the survey. Through these lenses the author then appraises in general the potentialities of successful economic and political decision-making.

Professor Hirschman's distinctive views on economic development are well known and have had a significant impact on theory and policy. In testing and elaborating his ideas in a new area he worked in consultation with Charles E. Lindblom, a political economist who has contributed much to our understanding of the policy-making process in the United States. The pathways which Professor Hirschman sees leading to progress are not always straight or short. The painting by Paul Klee reproduced at the author's suggestion as a frontispiece reveals perhaps better than words the manifold and often ambiguous ways in which he sees nations "journeying" toward their goals.

The Twentieth Century Fund expresses its appreciation to Professor Hirschman and his associates for carrying out the work. The efforts of the

Latin American countries to achieve progressive, just, and free societies are watched throughout the West with an awareness of how much, for all of us, depends upon the outcome. This book wants to be a help in that undertaking — a modest help, Professor Hirschman would say, but it is one in which the Fund takes satisfaction.

AUGUST HECKSCHER, Director, The Twentieth Century Fund

41 East 70th Street, New York. February 1963

Acknowledgments

In planning the present study, it became clear to me that I would be setting out on a hazardous expedition into the vast no man's land stretching between economics and other social sciences such as political science, sociology, and history. I therefore asked Charles E. Lindblom of Yale University, a veteran of such expeditions, to assist me with his counsel and criticism. This he has done, as a consultant to the project, with selfless zest and uncanny perceptiveness and I have drawn freely on the wealth of ideas and suggestions with which he supplied me in the course of our written and oral exchanges. Our collaboration had originated in the discovery that working in different areas we had reached strongly related conclusions.* Yet, Professor Lindblom is not to be held responsible for any of my statements. He has disagreed with many of them, but in these cases his willingness to do so patiently and articulately has also been invaluable to me.

The study was brought underway during the summer of 1960 when Professor Lindblom, my wife and I took an extended trip to Mexico, Colombia, Chile, Argentina, and Brazil. There we conducted interviews with numerous government officials, political, business and labor leaders, intellectuals, and economists who had special knowledge about the events which I intended to chronicle, often because they had played important roles in them. A large number of documents, published and unpublished, were also collected. I wish to record here my deepest gratitude to those, too numerous for individual mention, who, by their frank expressions of opinion and by digging deep into their memories or files, helped to satisfy our seemingly unending curiosity.

In this connection, an apology is owed to our Mexican and Argentine friends. Because of time considerations I decided to confine myself to three

---

* As explained in our joint article, "Economic Development, Research and Development, and Policy-Making: Some Converging Views," *Behavioral Science*, April 1962.

out of the five country studies originally planned; but I am hopeful that the plentiful and fascinating materials we collected on Mexico's policy toward foreign investment and on the petroleum and steel policies of Argentina will eventually be put to good use.

I returned to Brazil, Colombia, and Chile in the summer of 1962, both to check on questions that had arisen in the course of writing and library research in New York and to bring my "problem histories" up to date. Mid–1962 is their common terminal point.

Having carelessly revealed her talents during the writing of my previous book, my wife, Sarah Hirschman, was this time pressed into the labor force as research assistant from the outset. She has been most dedicated and productive; this book could not possibly have been written without her versatile help.

The study was financed by the Twentieth Century Fund. My appreciation for its support and steady, unobtrusive encouragement is the deeper as this project has been a highly experimental venture. The staff of the Fund was unfailingly helpful and remarkably flexible.

Columbia University was generous in granting me leave of absence during the academic year 1961–62 so that I could devote my full time to research and writing.

Thanks are finally due to a number of persons who made detailed comments on preliminary drafts of individual chapters. These include Stefan H. Robock and Ambassadors Roberto de Oliveira Campos and Lincoln Gordon for the chapter on Brazil; Enrique Peñalosa and Eric B. Shearer for the chapter on Colombia; and Joseph Grunwald and Aníbal Pinto for the chapter on Chile. I have also profited from discussions with David B. Truman and William Vickrey on the Digression following Chapter 5, which has appeared separately in the *Quarterly Journal of Economics*.

ALBERT O. HIRSCHMAN

Columbia University, New York. January 1963

Throughout this book passages given in translation were translated by the author unless otherwise noted.

Contents

Introduction

The essence of this volume is in the flow of the three stories told in Part One. Each story chronicles in some detail how a stubborn economic policy problem has been grappled with in Latin America over a long period of time. The subjects studied, Brazil's actions to strengthen the economic position of its drought-ridden and stagnating Northeastern provinces, attempts in Colombia to improve patterns of land use and land tenure, and Chile's experience with recurring inflation, should possess considerable intrinsic interest for the student of economic development. However, in undertaking to look concurrently at such widely differing problems, I also entertained some ulterior purposes and curiosities. Essentially they were to learn something about the problem-solving capabilities of public authorities in Latin America, about the conditions favorable to the emergence and growth of such capabilities and about characteristic ways and motions with which they assert themselves. General considerations about such matters, largely based on the country studies, make up Part Two of the book.

The basic justification for asking some probing questions in this field is easily given. At their outset and during their course, the processes of economic development and modernization confront decision-makers with a broad variety of policy problems; success in promoting development clearly depends in large measure on how these problems are attacked and handled. For the economist the point can be made plausible by comparing the emergence of a public policy problem to the rise in the price of one commodity relative to other prices. In economics the responses of private producers to such a price rise have long been studied conceptually and been subjected to careful measurement; for it is recognized that the speed, strength and direction of producers' responses (the so-called price elasticity of supply) have much to do with the ability of an economy to take advantage of newly arising opportunities, to absorb blows and to adjust

1

successfully to change. As producers react to changes in relative prices, so policy-makers react to the emergence, persistence or worsening of economic policy problems, and the speed, strength and pertinence of their reactions are of such enormous importance for "progress" that, at the risk of tackling an insoluble puzzle, it is worthwhile to ask such questions as:

When does a state of affairs become a problem? How and to whom does it become a problem — who takes action and pressures others into action? When problems are attacked with fresh energy and some success, what are the relative weights in various circumstances of stronger motivation, of new insights and of new alliances? What are characteristic first responses and can we observe typical learning processes when a problem is experienced and attacked repeatedly over a period of time? Which problems tend to be tackled seriously only in an atmosphere of crisis, and why? What is the role of imported ideas and foreign advice? Is there a specific Brazilian, Colombian, Chilean or Latin American "style" or "strategy" of problem-solving?

This list, which could easily be lengthened, suggests the kind of questions I had in mind at the inception of this study. I felt that the best method of looking for answers was to scrutinize the record of a few specific, documented, protracted, significant policy problems. Many of the cues or hints that have been gleaned are to be found only in the country chapters themselves. There they are being noted and held up briefly for the reader to see. Among them are probably some of the most suggestive points which have been encountered, but usually it is not quite clear whether they are general laws, exceptions to such laws, or just *curiosa*. In any event, at this stage of our effort, many "finds" did not warrant generalization or did not lend themselves to insertion into the more systematic observations on policy-making which are presented in Part Two.

Before taking up our inquiry, its relation to the more traditional concern of development economics should be made clear. When economists build models of growth, they typically do not give explicit independent roles to the ability or motivation to solve problems of public policy. For most existing economic theories, public decision-making either lies entirely outside the realm of economic analysis — as when certain basic decisions are relegated to the shadowy world of "pre-conditions" to economic growth — or public decision-making in appropriate quantity and quality is viewed as an automatic by-product of economic processes which are impelled by the "classic" inputs of capital, labor and natural resources, to which technical progress and education have lately been added.

Private decision-making has fared somewhat better since it has been dealt with through the concept of entrepreneurship. But the entrepreneur of formal price theory is conceived of as springing into action as soon as his calculations tell him that a profit can be made. His ability to calculate and his motivation to achieve profits are never in doubt. The actions of Schumpeter's creative entrepreneur who combines inputs in a novel fashion and produces new outputs would seem to be less rigidly determined. But upon considering this question in his later writings, Schumpeter derided the tendency of some of his disciples to consider entrepreneurs as "particularly rare birds" and he settled for a statistical theory according to which the creative ability required is distributed in some regular, if unequal, fashion among people so that entrepreneurial innovation again becomes an activity which we can expect to be secreted in a reliable flow by the economic system itself.[1]

The conviction that entrepreneurial decision-making plays a far more autonomous role in the process of economic development has recently led to the formulation of hypotheses concerning the psychological and sociological factors responsible for its *emergence*.[2] Yet, by concentrating on the earliest stage of economic expansion, these theories pay indirect homage to the traditional conception that once growth has been brought underway decision-making and problem-solving become a regular by-product of the growth process. In relation to economic growth, entrepreneurship is here granted grudgingly the same, severely limited role which Descartes' philosophy had assigned to God in relation to the world: that of getting things underway by a small initial push, a fillip (*chiquenaude*) as Pascal put it sarcastically, whereupon the world is starting to spin subject to its own rational and quantifiable laws without further divine interference.

The desire to dispense with the assumption of an initial push and the feeling that ebbs and tides of decision-making play a considerable role at *all* stages of development had led me earlier to investigate a variety of mechanisms (imbalances, linkages and the like) which make for the tides, i.e., which squeeze out extra doses of entrepreneurial and managerial decision-making in the course of the development process. This leading theme of my previous book was by no means limited to private decision-making.

---

[1] J. S. Schumpeter, *Business Cycles*, McGraw-Hill, New York, 1939, Vol. I, p. 130.
[2] David C. McClelland, *The Achieving Society*, Van Nostrand, Princeton, 1961, and Everett E. Hagen, *On the Theory of Social Change—How Economic Growth Begins*, Dorsey, Homewood, Ill., 1962.

The assertion was made that nonmarket forces, e.g., the response of public authorities to an electric power shortage, are not necessarily or intrinsically less automatic than the response of private entrepreneurs to a rise in the price of their product.[1] The desire to document this assertion leads directly to the principal concern of this book, namely, to the investigation of the behavior of public decision-makers in problem-solving situations.

The difficulties facing any scientific inquiry in this field are no doubt formidable. In attempting to explain economic policy decisions we may well be dealing with actions which because of the limited number of observations and participants and because of the importance of personalities do not lend themselves to any generalization or to any testing of hypotheses. Yet why not try if the subject is sufficiently important?

It can hardly be doubted that it is. The role of policy-making in the contemporary scene is being stressed every time we ask competent observers in Latin America about the "conditions of economic progress." The crucial part of the answers will usually be in such clauses as "provided inflation can be contained within reasonable limits" or "if only the government stopped making purely political appointments to important managerial posts" or "assuming that action on agrarian reform will be forthcoming more rapidly." In other words, key importance is attached to events in the economic life in these countries about whose determinants the literature on economic development has had remarkably little to say.

At one time, rather long ago, it was intellectually respectable to recognize the decisive and autonomous influence of public decision-making on economic growth or decay. In the fourteenth century the painter Ambrogio Lorenzetti contrasted in magnificent detail the consequences upon economic life in the city and countryside of Good and Bad Government in a series of famous frescoes at Siena's Municipal Palace. Good and bad government have long been important categories in the discussion of political and economic realities in Latin America; their continued relevance lies in the fact that they cut right across other distinctions such as those between Left- and Right-wing governments or between military and civilian rule.

At this point the question may well be asked whether our inquiry does not fall squarely into the problem area covered by political science, a discipline which, after all, has attempted, ever since Plato, to define the principal characteristics and constituent elements of "good government." I am

---

[1] *The Strategy of Economic Development*, Yale University Press, New Haven, 1958, pp. 63–65, 143.

no doubt trespassing to some extent; but political scientists typically view good government as resulting from certain institutions and capacities such as an adequate bureaucracy, public participation in the governmental process, legitimacy, ability of a political elite to mediate conflicts and so on. Hence the political scientist's advice to countries with a defective political process is to acquire these institutions and capacities much as economists advise them to step up capital formation or to generate a group of entrepreneurs. Our inquiry, on the other hand, takes the existing political framework with its defects for granted and explores whether and how the weight and urgency of certain economic policy problems can nevertheless lead to constructive action. Our basic working hypothesis must be that, within rather broad limits, the existence of defects in political structure does not constitute an absolute impediment to progress in dealing with economic policy problems; by the same token, it is likely that problem-solving will under these conditions follow quite unfamiliar paths whose possible efficiency and hidden rationality we must try to appreciate.

Returning to economics, one should point out that the laissez-faire doctrine faced the problem of good government and advocated a marvelously simple solution: assuming that public decision-making is necessarily of poorer quality than private decision-making, it proposed to improve the average quality of decision-making by reducing the weight of the public component (the role of government) in the total. Those who advocate, on the contrary, that public decision-makers assume ever new and more central tasks have usually argued their case in a negative fashion, by showing that these tasks were not being adequately performed by private decision-makers; and they have generally assumed that public authorities could carry out these tasks with some acceptable level of efficiency. The experience that this is not necessarily so has meant that the concepts of good and bad government have reappeared in a new guise: it is quite current today in Latin America to speak disparagingly of "bureaucratic interventionism" and to contrast it with "integrated planning." But such semantic inventions do not tell us much about how to achieve the latter or how to stay clear of the former. Some progress in this endeavor can perhaps be made by detailed observation of the sequence of policy-making around one particular problem, such as we have undertaken. Time and again, we shall come across certain activities of government that are particularly *failure-prone* or certain types of agencies that tend to sink into a morass of inefficiency and corruption while others with different characteristics become outposts of progress and change. In the present state of our knowledge, even isolated observations on such points may be useful steppingstones to much-needed understanding.

But our interest in policy-making goes considerably beyond the traditional concept of good government, which refers normally to the quality of public decision-making *within* a given social and institutional framework. Good government includes for us emphatically, if rather unusually, the ability to effect important changes or reforms in this framework itself. The country studies inquire specifically into the ways in which public decision-makers become aware of the need for such reforms and act to bring them about.

In the last analysis, then, we are dealing with the old paradox of change. How can good government arise out of bad, reform out of reaction and progress out of stagnation? As in my previous work on economic development, I attempt to answer these questions by avoiding the tempting device — or sleight-of-hand — which consists in discovering some "prerequisite," be it a resource base, a rate of capital formation, an elite, an ideology or a personality structure, that must allegedly be introduced before change can possibly assert itself. Rather, I am trying to show how a society can begin to move forward *as it is, in spite of what it is and because of what it is.* Such an enterprise will involve a systematic search along two, closely related lines:

> *first,* how acknowledged, well-entrenched obstacles to change can be neutralized, outflanked and left to be dealt with decisively at some later stage;
>
> *secondly,* and perhaps more fundamentally, how many among the conditions and attitudes that are widely considered as inimical to change have a hidden positive dimension and can therefore unexpectedly come to serve and nurture progress.

It must be stressed that this search does not imply by any means a systematic bias in favor of gradualism or against institutional innovations. This will become abundantly evident to anyone reading the rest of this book. Our approach is, however, open to the criticism that it is unduly tolerant of existing flaws and failings, and frequently even bestows creative virtues on them. But if one wishes to dispense with the concept of a unique and universally required pre-condition, change is once again unintelligible and inconceivable *unless* some of the very ingredients of the old order can be shown to be ambivalent and to possess some progress- and growth-promoting potential. Hence the close attention I pay to possible blessings in disguise and the collector's interest I take in constellations which permit strength to be drawn from alleged weaknesses do not spring from infatuation with paradox; rather they are dictated by the essence of the process of change as I am able to understand it.

The historical processes of retardation and decline have often been rendered more intelligible by the idea that the very forces which made for progress and success of an individual, a nation or a civilization in one period can become a hindrance in the next. If this fairly familiar notion were to be inverted it would state that the very forces that are responsible for stagnation in one period can make for progressive change in the next. In this form, I submit, the idea contributes to the understanding of the development process. More important, if it could be instilled into the policy-makers, it should sharpen their perception of the various roads available to them and enhance their resourcefulness.

Little needs to be said about the possible relevance of this book to the current Latin American scene and to United States policy. The United States government is embarked on a uniquely daring venture with its Alliance for Progress. It has become the advocate of land and other social reforms and is attempting to condition its aid on some progress in these matters. It is thus involving itself into the policy-making process of other countries to a hitherto unheard-of extent. To attain some knowledge of typical policy-making sequences and of successful reform strategies should clearly be of help in this undertaking. At the same time, Latin American leaders, especially the younger group of economic and political planners which is moving into and aspiring to positions of power, are anxiously asking themselves how thorough a transformation of their societies is needed and whether this transformation must precede or could be a concomitant and result of a variety of partial improvements. It so happens that these are to a considerable extent the kinds of questions which I had in mind upon undertaking the studies contained in this book. It is pleasant to note this convergence of a private research interest with a pressing public need. Whether the suggestions which have been gathered will be found illuminating or perplexing, encouraging or distressing by the policy-makers, remains to be seen.

I

Three Problems
in Three Countries

Chapter 1

Brazil's Northeast

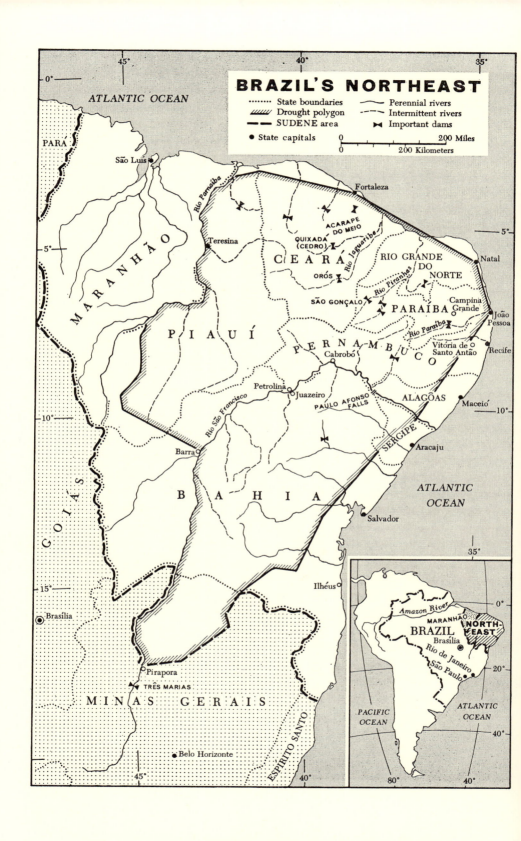

BRAZIL'S NORTHEAST

- ······· State boundaries
- ⫽⫽⫽ Drought polygon
- – – – SUDENE area
- ● State capitals
- —— Perennial rivers
- – · – Intermittent rivers
- ⋈ Important dams

0   200 Miles
0   200 Kilometers

ATLANTIC OCEAN

PARÁ

MARANHÃO

São Luís

Teresina

Rio Parnaíba

Fortaleza

ACARAPE
DO MEIO

QUIXADA
(CEDRO)

CEARÁ

ORÓS

Rio Jaguaribe

RIO GRANDE
DO
NORTE

Natal

SÃO GONÇALO

Rio Piranhas

PARAÍBA

Campina
Grande

João
Pessoa

PIAUÍ

PERNAMBUCO

Cabrobó

Rio Paraíba

Vitória de
Santo Antão

Recife

Petrolina

Juazeiro

PAULO AFONSO
FALLS

Rio São Francisco

ALAGÔAS

Maceió

Barra

SERGIPE

Aracaju

BAHIA

ATLANTIC
OCEAN

Salvador

GOIÁS

Ilhéus

Brasília

Pirapora

TRÊS MARIAS

MINAS   GERAIS

ESPÍRITO SANTO

Belo Horizonte

Inset map

35°

Amazon River

MARANHÃO

BRAZIL

Brasília

NORTH-
EAST

0°

Rio de Janeiro

São Paulo

20°

PACIFIC
OCEAN

ATLANTIC
OCEAN

40°

80°   40°

Chapter **1**

Brazil's Northeast

In the past year or two the Northeast of Brazil has become familiar to newspaper readers and even to television viewers in the United States as an area where over 20 million people, close to one-third of Brazil's population, live in great poverty and perhaps in imminent danger of take-over by Castro-Communist-inspired peasant leagues. To Brazilians, on the other hand, the Northeast has been a national problem area for at least eighty years, ever since the long and cruel drought of 1877–79. For the original problem of the Northeast, and for a long time the only one clearly perceived, was this climatic-climactic phenomenon of repeated drought. Occurring capriciously, almost at random intervals (the average works out at ten years) and of varying duration (one to three years), the droughts bring to a halt a large part of the ordinary agricultural and pastoral pursuits in the Northeast's vast interior zone which extends over almost a million square kilometers and is inhabited by 13 million people.

Recently, as we shall see, the problem of drought has been subsumed in the larger problem of underdevelopment of the entire Northeastern region, of its wide lag behind the vigorously growing Center-South of the country. It has thereby become merged, *inter alia,* with the problem of land use in the humid Northeast, a coastal strip devoted almost exclusively to the growing of sugar cane. The economy of this strip, which includes the two large cities of Recife and Salvador (Bahia), has gone through many difficult adjustments since the days, some three hundred years ago, when it was Europe's principal supplier of sugar. Among the events requiring such adjustments we need mention only the abolition of slavery in 1888, the competition from the Caribbean and indeed from the expanding sugar production of the State of São Paulo. But the resulting pressures gave rise to a variety of financial counter-measures and to decentralized, gradual responses by individuals, firms and agencies involved in the "mono-

culture" of cane. The droughts, on the other hand, were sudden, spectacular events with which individual action was wholly unable to cope.
Almost from their onset they cried out for vigorous action by the state
— the next best agency once Providence failed, as it periodically did.
State action was usually of two types: immediate relief for refugees from
the drought[1] and a new strong impulse to search for better means to deal
with the problem. We have here a situation that is particularly favorable
to the unfolding of a learning process: the policy-makers are presented
time and again with essentially the same difficulty and they accumulate a
large stock of experiences in grappling with it, and in seeking to avoid or
cushion its impact. But before tracing these successive experiences, we
must say a few words about the problem itself.[2]

General Characteristics of the Drought Problem

Insufficiency of rainfall is by no means the principal characteristic of
the Northeastern interior area, generally known as the *sertão*. True, there
is *always* a long-drawn-out dry season, lasting from about June to December, during which most of the rivers except the hardy São Francisco and
Parnaíba dry up. Ordinarily the rains come in January and reach their peak
in March and April, thus permitting one crop to be harvested in May–June.
There are also many useful drought-resistant (xerophilous) plants and
trees that can store water or are otherwise fully adapted to the dry season
and commonly survive even the drought years. In a normal year total rainfall, 90 per cent of which occurs in the first five months of the year, is about
27 inches — an amount adequate for temperate zone climates (London re-
ceives only 24 inches) but somewhat low for the tropics because of the
high rate of evaporation. Being rather dry, yet not dry enough to turn into
desert, the sertão is one of the healthier areas of the lowland tropics, with
relatively few insects and plagues that are dangerous to man, cattle or
crops. Settlement has proceeded gradually from the coast inland, absorb-
ing the nomadic aborigines, on the basis of cattle raising and the growing
of food crops and commercial plants, among which the mocó cotton tree,
a perennial, is the most important. Food crops are grown largely for sub-

---

[1] Known as *flagelados* or *retirantes*.
[2] Only information important for the understanding of the sequence of policy-making is presented here. A comprehensive survey of the economy of the Northeast will be
available in Stefan H. Robock, *Northeast Brazil: A Developing Economy,* The Brookings Institution (forthcoming).

sistence, but it is rather remarkable that the intermediate zone known as *agreste*, which lies between the humid cane-growing coastal strip (the *zona da mata*) and the sertão proper, grows most of the staple foods (corn, beans, manioc) consumed in the cane zone and the coastal cities.

The huge Northeastern zone of 950,000 square kilometers, defined as the "Drought Polygon" in Brazilian legislation, is of course by no means homogeneous. It has several drought-free elevated and mountainous areas — *chapadas* or *serras* — in which rainfall is much higher than the average for the region. In the southern part — around the São Francisco River — the periodic droughts are less pronounced, but because the average rainfall is lower, dryness is more of a permanent condition and settlement tends to be much sparser than in the states of Ceará, Rio Grande do Norte, Paraíba and Pernambuco, which are the heartland of the drought zone. It is here that the sertão supports a rather dense population — at present over twenty persons per square kilometer — except when the rains do not come. At such times the traditional recourse has been for people to move out toward the two perennial rivers, to the humid enclaves or water reservoirs in the sertão, or toward the cities in the South or on the Coast in the hope of securing non-agricultural work and assistance. The scourge being entirely unpredictable, little individual provision is made for it. Yet the risk is always kept in mind. "Everything is conditioned on the drought: business projects, private plans, weddings, trips."[1] If it does not rain sufficiently by Saint Joseph's Day (March 19) — which virtually coincides with the equinox — then, according to local folklore, it is time to act, for even if it rains thereafter, the crops will have hardly enough time to mature before the onset of the next dry season in June. While there has been a steady net emigration from the area (not enough to offset the natural increase in population), much of the refugee population that leaves during the drought returns with the first rains. All accounts agree on the attachment of the *sertanejo* to his land and his way of life;[2] moreover, the land that has gone through a bad drought spell is supposed to be particularly fertile as a result of the decomposition of certain rock salts during the drought.[3]

[1] Consêlho Nacional de Economia, *O problema nacional das sêcas,* Editora Jornal do Brasil, Rio, 1958, p. 29.

[2] According to an International Labor Office report of 1937, Northeastern migrants looking for work in São Paulo are reluctant to enter into contracts of even a year's duration. Cf. Fernand Maurette, *Some Social Aspects of Present and Future Economic Development in Brazil,* ILO, Studies and Reports, Series B, No. 25, 1937, p. 80.

[3] Sylvio Fróes Abreu, "Possíveis contribuições da tecnologia para os problemas fundamentais do nordeste," *Seminário para o Desenvolvimento do Nordeste,* Anais, 1959, Rio, Vol. 1, p. 48 (Special Edition of *Desenvolvimento e Conjuntura*).

The problem of the Northeastern sertão is therefore less its dryness than the irregularity of the dry spells. It has little in common with such well-known arid lands as Egypt, or the Peruvian Coast or large parts of our own Southwest, where irrigation is the *sine qua non* of agricultural activity and settlement. Thus it does not fit easily into the handy dichotomy of rainfall versus irrigation agriculture which is the basis of Wittfogel's theory of the tyrannical "hydraulic society."[1] Rather, one might be tempted to lump both of these categories into a single one denoting agriculture proceeding under comparatively certain climatic conditions of either sufficient or insufficient rainfall and to oppose it to an "uncertainty agriculture" of the type that is found in the Northeast. In the basic structure of its problems, the region is perhaps best compared, not to other arid zones, but to lands where an unpredictable calamity overhangs an otherwise pleasant or at least bearable existence, as in Italy or Japan where people make a living on the fertile slopes of occasionally erupting volcanos. The *nordestino* shares with these populations a refusal to concern himself too much with the possibility of disaster. If disaster comes he expects the government to step in. But in fact the government's action is shaped by the same basic situation which makes the exercise of foresight difficult or impossible for the individual: government action, as we shall see, has displayed a jerky character almost molded on the jerky behavior of nature.

It may appear strange that large masses of men should elect to live in an area where they know they will be exposed to complete loss of livelihood several times in their lifetime. Brazilian writers have explained the puzzle by opposing the risky but free life of the sertão to the oppressively organized life on the coastal sugar plantations, with its many reminders of the not-so-defunct slavery.[2] In addition, and perhaps more important, the numerous efforts of individuals and the government to stave off the destructive consequences of major droughts, while failing so far to achieve their objective, did succeed in making life more tolerable; this in turn has provided a broader basis for settlement during normal years, attracting an ever larger, ever more sedentary population, and thereby setting the stage for a catastrophe of ever larger dimensions should a bad drought strike.

It must be understood that the successful adaptation of the sertanejo to

---

[1] Karl A. Wittfogel, *Oriental Despotism*, Yale University Press, New Haven, 1957.
[2] Cf., e.g., Limeira Tejo, *Brejos e carrascaes do Nordeste*, Edições Cultura Brasileira, São Paulo, 1937, pp. 154–155.

his environment even in a normal year is no mean achievement in view of the rigorous living conditions during the seven months when the rivers dry out and the land is parched. Several important elements in this adaptation have resulted from individual spontaneous actions that were merely reinforced and oriented by State agencies:

(a) Small dams have been built wherever feasible to keep the rivers from running off to the ocean, and to retain them for use by man and cattle during the dry season.

(b) Underground water has been tapped through wells.

(c) By use of the so-called *vazantes* agriculture, a genuine Northeastern invention, food crops (cereals and vegetables) are grown right in the dried-out river beds and around the receding rims of the dams. This practice not only increases the total food supply but brings in a second harvest of fresh produce after the lands whose fertility depends on rainfall have yielded theirs.

(d) Finally, native drought-resistant plants have been increasingly utilized to produce cash income. Most important is the mocó cotton tree, which, together with cattle raising, has been the principal source of agricultural employment and settlement. Other valuable xerophilous plants are the carnauba palm (whose leaf yields wax), the oiticica tree (from whose nut drying oil is extracted) and the caroá cactus (which yields a strong textile fiber primarily used for bagging). Grass and hay have been complemented by plantings of the palma forrajeira, a spineless cactus which is successfully used as cattle feed.

Another highly significant characteristic of our problem is that it concerns a geographical region removed from the main centers of political power and active economic growth both of which have long been located in the São Paulo–Rio–Belo Horizonte triangle. The Northeastern region began to lose its economic predominance around 1700 with the development of mining in Minas Gerais; the country's capital was shifted from Bahia to Rio in 1762. Ever since then the major impulses to economic growth — coffee production, European immigration, industrialization — have occurred in the Center-South. From the point of view of political influence the Northeast has suffered from its fragmentation into numerous states of small size. A successful politician from the Northeast could never deliver as large a block of votes (nor rely on as much support from local armed forces) as one from the State of São Paulo or Minas Gerais, the two populous states which have wielded most political power since the establishment of the Republic.[1]

But the Northeast is no quiet backwater. On the contrary, it has never become quite reconciled to being out of the center of things. The presence of two large and old cities, Recife and Salvador, the region's prominent role in Brazil's history, its continuing important contribution to Brazilian cultural life, particularly in the social sciences and letters, are all elements in this attitude of resentment against the established leadership of the Center-South. The Northeasterner has long been an active claimant of "justice." Because of the lag in the region's development, ambitious and talented Northeasterners have often been attracted by political and military careers in preference to less promising ones in commerce and industry, and they have therefore constituted a rather powerful lobby at the seats of power. The region's size and large population, its historical and cultural importance, the assertive influence and pressure exerted by its elite, and, last but not least, the very depth of misery and degradation into which a large part of its people are periodically plunged, have all made for a nation-wide consciousness that the overcoming of backwardness and suffering in the Northeast is one of the principal tasks of Brazil as a nation.

A Quick View of the Sequence of Decision-Making

The long history of official attempts to grapple with the Northeast's problems is marked by a few major decisions and efforts. One of our principal interests is to identify the factors responsible for these decisions. An inspection of the dates at which they were taken and of the surrounding circumstances immediately suggests two obvious surface clues:

(1) A bad drought year usually jolts the government into a major new effort; and

(2) The presence of a Northeasterner in a key government position is most helpful in producing forceful action.

The first factor is no doubt dominant, but the second is by no means negligible. In the accompanying table we list all major drought years recorded since the "Great Drought" of 1877–79 and the principal consequential actions taken by the government. The third column indicates whether a Northeasterner was in a position to influence the government in favor of his region.

[1] *Seminário,* Celso Furtado in Vol. II, p. 217; also Charles Morazé, *Les trois âges du Brésil,* Armand Colin, Paris, 1954, p. 104.

This schematic presentation is meant to give only a preliminary, panoramic view of the extremely complex sequence of decision-making with respect to the Northeast. On the whole, it bears out our statement that traditionally a big drought has been required to spur the authorities into action. The combination of a big drought with the presence of a Northeasterner at the head of government or high up in its councils proved particularly effective in 1919 and 1932. The regularity we have detected is by no means uniform; some serious droughts (1888–89, 1900 and 1915) failed to produce immediate and important new decisions while some important decisions — the creation of the Inspetoria in 1909 and of the São Francisco River Valley Commission — were not immediately preceded by a drought. Similarly, some decisions, particularly those following the 1958 drought, were taken in favor of the Northeast without any Northeasterner lending support to them from a top governmental position. These "exceptions" to our first tentative generalization are themselves significant and will be explained in due course. In the process we hope to arrive at a more sophisticated understanding of the course of events than is supplied by the rather primitive two-factor theory reflected in the table.

However primitive, the table draws attention to a phenomenon which will also have to be explained. Frequently a recurrence of drought brings with it not only a resumption and expansion of an activity (such as public works spending) undertaken in the previous phase, but the establishment of an entirely new institution, such as the Bank of the Northeast in 1952 or SUDENE in 1959. What are the reasons for this institution-building? Is it motivated by the failure of existing institutions to fulfill their assigned objectives or rather by the discovery of new objectives, new tasks and new approaches to the problem? These are also questions to which we will attempt to find answers.

Before starting on a more detailed account of the sequence of events, a word should be said about the economics of droughts in relation to public works spending. Dam and road construction received a strong stimulus during each drought not only because of a suddenly reawakened desire to help the Northeast and to cushion the impact of future disasters, but simply because, with crops failing, large masses of labor became available for non-agricultural activities. Thus, from the point of view of economic development, the drought is not a wholly negative force. It causes a considerable part of the population to switch from production of consumer goods for subsistence to capital formation while consumption requirements are more or less adequately assured by relief shipments from the rest of the country.

Whether this opportunity to push capital formation is fully exploited depends on the existence of investment projects ready to be undertaken when the emergency strikes. The difficulties in having such a "shelf" available are well known; they have been much in evidence even in advanced industrial countries where the shelf idea has long been proposed in connection with business cycle policy. In the Northeast these difficulties have led to much wasted opportunity and to many false starts. Nevertheless, if the

CHRONOLOGY OF MAJOR DROUGHTS AND IMPORTANT GOVERNMENTAL DECISIONS

MAJOR DROUGHT YEARS	IMPORTANT DECISIONS AND ACTIONS[a]	INFLUENTIAL POSITIONS HELD BY NORTHEASTERNERS AT TIME OF DECISION
1877–79	Dec. 1877: First National Commission of Inquiry established. Engineering Survey in 1889. First large dam (Quixadá) started in 1884, then stopped in 1886.	
1888–89	[1888: New Commission to resume Quixadá Dam organized.]	
1900	[Oct. 1900: Special relief funds, to be spent primarily on public works, decreed.]	While economy-minded President Campos Salles is on state visit in Argentina, measure is issued by Vice-President *Rosa e Silva* and *Epitacio Pessôa*, then Minister of Justice.
	1909: Establishment of Inspetoria of Works against Droughts, a Federal agency later known as DNOCS, subordinate to Minister of Transportation and Public Works.	*Francisco Sá*, Minister of Transportation and Public Works in Nilo Peçanha administration.
1915	[New agency reaches highest rate of expenditures of 1909–19 period.]	
1919	1920–22: New financing secured for Inspetoria and large-scale public works contracted for and undertaken. Almost entirely suspended in 1923–24 under Bernardes administration.	1919–22: Administration of *Epitacio Pessôa*, only Northeasterner ever to hold Presidential office.

area is today comparatively well endowed with highways and dotted with dams, it is largely due to this mechanism whose uses have not been adequately understood. It has become traditional, whenever a new policy is being advocated for the Northeast, to oppose the economic development objectives of that policy to the "mere relief" activities of the past, though relief shipments during droughts can contribute powerfully and have in fact contributed respectably to capital formation, as will be shown.

MAJOR DROUGHT YEARS	IMPORTANT DECISIONS AND ACTIONS[a]	INFLUENTIAL POSITIONS HELD BY NORTHEASTERNERS AT TIME OF DECISION
1930–32	1932–37: Second period of large-scale public works. 1933: Establishment of Agricultural Stations by Inspetoria.	*José Américo de Almeida,* Minister of Public Works, 1931–34, of first Vargas Administration.
	1934: Insertion of article into new Constitution reserving minimum of 4% of total tax revenue for anti-drought defense in Northeast. (Not reinserted into 1937 Constitution.)	
	1946: Reinsertion of special earmarking into new Constitution.	
	1948: Establishment of São Francisco Valley Commission and of São Francisco Hydroelectric Company.	
1951–53	1952: Establishment of Bank of Northeast of Brazil (BNB).	*Rômulo de Almeida,* special adviser to Vargas and first President of BNB.
1958	1958: Considerable step-up in public works spending.	
	1959: Creation of Superintendency for the Development of the Northeast (SUDENE).	*Celso Furtado,* planner of SUDENE and its first Superintendent.

[a] Actions that are direct consequences of a drought but cannot qualify as "important" are shown in brackets.

From the Big Drought of 1877–79 to the Creation
of the Inspetoria (1909)

The history of serious official concern with the conditions of the North-east starts with the "big drought" of 1877–79, whose horrors have been chronicled in vivid detail by Rodolpho Theophilo.[1] It came after an exceptionally long period of adequate rainfall — the last drought prior to it dates back thirty years to 1845. Population and economic activity increased rapidly in the interval, so much so that the growth of Ceará, according to a contemporary observer, was paralleled only by that of São Paulo.[2] Therefore, the failure of the rains to come in 1877, or in the next two years, had all the effectiveness of a surprise attack. Of the one million inhabitants of Ceará a half were estimated to have perished as a consequence of the disaster. In the interior many died of hunger and thirst, or because they took to eating poisonous roots. Even larger numbers who reached the cities perished there from exhaustion or from epidemic diseases as smallpox, yellow fever and typhoid swept the improvised encampments. Banditry and crime were rife and several instances of cannibalism were reported.

Because of poor communications, the local, provincial and federal authorities were at first slow to react. People who reached the cities received relief payments or food and clothing. Some emigrants were taken by boat northwestward to the Amazon region; most were employed in improvised public works — among which church, prison and cemetery construction predominated, though some thirty-six dams, mostly small structures, were built or started.[3]

However, these emergency relief measures were woefully inadequate, and were moreover frequently accompanied by arbitrary and corrupt practices. Once the scope of disaster was realized, nation-wide concern and alarm arose. Late in 1877 the Conde d'Eu, the Emperor's son-in-law, presided over "memorable sessions"[4] and discussions among scientists and engineers at the Polytechnic Institute of Rio, which were followed up by the establishment of an Imperial Commission of Inquiry to look into ways of preventing similar disasters in the future.[5] The commission's principal

---

[1] Rodolpho Theophilo, *Historia da secca do Ceará (1877 a 1880)*, Imprensa Ingleza, Rio, 1922.

[2] *Ibid.*, p. 72.

[3] *Ibid.*, pp. 143–148.

[4] This term is used by Euclides de Cunha in *Rebellion in the Backlands (Os sertões)*, 1902, English translation 1944, University of Chicago Press, p. 47.

[5] The Commission's terms of reference are given in Theophilo, *Secca do Ceará*, pp. 141–143.

recommendations called for improvement of transportation in the zone by building harbor installations and several railroad lines and the construction of some twenty dams, both small and large. Detailed study of the large dams was entrusted two years later, in 1880, to a British engineer. One of the three dams he recommended was started by the government in 1884. This was the famous Quixadá Dam (capacity: 128 million cubic meters), whose construction went through so many stoppages and changes in design as a result of both erratic appropriations and technical difficulties that when it was finally completed in 1906, its very name had become a byword of governmental inefficiency and waste. President Penna, who inaugurated it, cited Quixadá in one of his yearly messages to Congress as the horrible example to be avoided in the future,[1] as did President Epitacio Pessôa in 1920 to justify his calling in of foreign engineering firms.[2]

Here we have one important reason for the creation, in 1909, of the first federal agency, the "Inspetoria of Works against the Droughts," which has remained in operation ever since with slight changes in name.[3] The desire for an end to improvisation and fitful decision-making, for careful professional study in advance of projects, for maintenance of dams, wells and roads once they were completed had been strongly stimulated by the first experiences with larger-scale public works undertaken on an *ad hoc* basis by the federal government. The Inspetoria thus was created not so much as a *direct* response to the droughts as because of dissatisfaction with the way in which the fight against them had been conducted since 1877. This dissatisfaction had led from 1904 onward to the establishment of a variety of temporary federal commissions (Commission of Dams and Irrigation, Commission of Studies and Works against the Effects of Droughts, Commission of Perforation of Wells) located in one or the other of the Northeastern states. These commissions were in turn untidy and inefficient and gave way in 1909 to a unified permanent agency, the Inspetoria, with headquarters in Rio, which was to operate under the authority of the Minister of Public Works. This portfolio was then held, in the Nilo Peçanha administration, by Francisco Sá, long-time Senator from Ceará and advocate of Northeastern causes.

---

[1] *Mensagens Presidenciaes (Documentos Parlamentares)*, Rio, 1912, Vol. I, p. 591.

[2] *Ibid.*, 1922, Vol. IV, p. 277. In 1923, José Américo de Almeida wrote: "The experience of Quixadá discouraged new initiatives" (in *A Parahyba e seus problemas*, second edition, Livraria do Globo, Port Alegre, 1937, p. 190).

[3] From Inspetoria de Obras Contra as Sêcas to Inspetoria Federal . . . . (IFOCS) and then, in 1945, to Departamento Nacional de Obras Contra as Sêcas (DNOCS). We shall use here the term Inspetoria and, for the later period, the initials DNOCS.

Poor administration and lack of continuity and professional expertise were only some of the defects the new Inspetoria was expected to cure. At least equally disturbing had been the abuses that invariably accompanied the distribution of relief funds and their use for individual enrichment and political advantage. Already during the great drought of 1877–79 cases of personal and political profiteering had been reported with such frequency that a special commission of inquiry was dispatched to Fortaleza by the Minister of Finance.[1]

Most of the irregularities occurred in distributing relief funds and goods handed over by the federal government to the state authorities. During the drought of 1888–89, which coincided with the abolition of slavery (1888) and the demise of the Empire (1889), the central government was in no position to do more than to resume some public works and extend some relief funds. A contemporary report on these operations in the State of Rio Grande do Norte states:

> If the drought has been a calamity, an even greater one has come with the relief funds either because of the fabulous sums that were misspent or because of lack of patriotism on the part of the administrators of this service. These public relief funds became a means of political deals . . . commissions were established in all points of the state formed by special friends of the government and they distributed large amounts of money and of manioc flour as they pleased.[2]

In addition to outright misappropriation and politically oriented distribution of relief funds, the undertaking of public works was also a powerful political weapon and was so used. Dams and roads were built "to benefit properties of friends or to consolidate the political influence of some political chief of the interior." This result was frequently achieved also through the federal government turning over works it had constructed to the states or municipalities, which in turn let favored individuals take them over.[3]

In evaluating these and monotonously similar later reports of abuses it must of course be realized first that considerable political capital could also be made — by the opposition — by simply claiming that such abuses

---

[1] Thomaz Pompeu Sobrinho, *História das sêcas,* Batista Fontenelle, Fortaleza, 1958, Vol. II, pp. 180–209, 280–282.

[2] Excerpt from report of the Governor of Rio Grande do Norte quoted in R. Pereira da Silva, *Trabalhos relativos aos estudos de Parahyba e Rio Grande do Norte,* Inspetoria de Obras Contra as Sêcas, Publication No. 12, Imprensa Nacional, Rio, 1910, p. 33.

[3] Pereira da Silva, *Trabalhos,* pp. 9–10.

had taken place; secondly, that ordinary moral standards are likely to be in jeopardy when the lives of large masses of men have been disrupted and when hunger, disease and violence are in the air; and finally, that it takes considerable naïveté (or hypocrisy) to hold that such processes as public works spending could or should be entirely insulated from politics.

In any event, there was considerable room for improvement in performance and continuity, and the desire for such improvement, for better maintenance, for a "systematic plan" and scientific studies, as well as the belief that federally distributed funds would be less scandalously misspent, inspired the creation of the Inspetoria in 1909.[1] The ground was well prepared for this decision not only as a result of the negative experiences thus far recounted; Euclides da Cunha's powerful book *Os sertões*, published in 1902, did much to arouse guilt feelings among the Brazilian elites about their neglect of the hardy inhabitants of the sertão and their cruelty toward them during the Canudos Rebellion of 1896–97. At the same time, the hope became firmer that modern science and engineering would have much to contribute toward solving the problems of the Northeast. Thus, the establishment of the United States Bureau of Reclamation in 1902 and the first successes of large-scale irrigation in our arid Southwest became well known and were much admired.[2] In Brazil itself, the achievement of the Alves administration (1902–6) in eradicating, under the leadership of Oswaldo Cruz, yellow fever and other epidemic diseases in Rio led to increased confidence that the scourges of the tropics could be conquered. In fact, President Alves, during whose terms only a minor drought (1903) is reported, was the first one to proclaim the need for continuity and foresight. In his 1906 message the President said: "We persisted in the works against the effects of the droughts, convinced as we were that it is no longer permissible to wait for the arrival of these terrible crises before combatting them, since their periodicity is already well known."[3]

A contemporary observer notes that the Alves administration, which finished the Quixadá Dam and established the above-mentioned commissions that were the direct forerunners of the Inspetoria, could not decently refuse to do something for the Northeast when it was at the same time

---

[1] The absence of such a plan is deplored in *ibid.*, p. 8, and by President Penna in his message of 1907.

[2] See, for example, José Américo de Almeida, *A Parahyba*, p. 188. Also Coelho Lisbôa, *Problemas urgentes*, Imprensa Nacional, Rio, 1909, pp. 134–137.

[3] *Mensagens*, Vol. I, p. 395.

spending rather lavishly on cleaning up and embellishing the capital — an interesting remark to which we shall come back.[1] Alves' actions and attitudes were indeed far removed from those of his immediate predecessor, President Campos Salles, who, guided by his Finance Minister Joaquim Murtinho, was singlemindedly striving to restore Brazil's credit abroad and the stability of its currency, both badly shaken after the first decade of Republican rule. During the serious drought of 1900 it took a temporary absence of the President from Rio for the partisans of help to the stricken Northeast — such as Epitacio Pessôa, later President and then a young Minister of Justice — to rush through a measure providing some relief funds.[2] The scanty public works that were undertaken or reactivated as a result were stopped as soon as the 1901 rainy season arrived. Thus Campos Salles himself proudly reports in his annual message of that year: "Fortunately abundant rains came, putting an end to the calamity and reducing the size of the sacrifices imposed upon the Federal Treasury . . ."[3]

Little wonder that Northeasterners acquired a durable mistrust of the soulless canons of financial orthodoxy!

What was the concept behind the setting up of the Inspetoria, which was to launch the first systematic attempt at attacking the problem of the Northeast? Did the clamor for continuity cover up a lack of clarity about what it was that was to be done with continuity? Perhaps. Yet there was also much underlying agreement about the basic approach to be followed. In the first place, the principal role in the solution of the problem was to be played by natural scientists and engineers. The latter were to occupy all the top positions in the Inspetoria according to its statute. This was in part a reflection of the elite status enjoyed by the engineer in Brazil since the latter part of the nineteenth century, as a result of the influence of French positivism and the prestige of the engineering schools of Rio, São Paulo and Minas Gerais. But there was also widespread conviction that the particular solution at hand was principally one of engineering: the construction of storage reservoirs, or açudes.[4] To retain the precious rain water for the dry season — what could be more obviously useful? Moreover, the configuration of the terrain virtually invites dam construction in much

---

[1] Naylor Bastos Villas-Bôas, "As obras contra as seccas no imperio e no primeiro periodo republicano," *Boletim da Inspetoria Federal de Obras Contra as Sêcas*, Fortaleza, April–June 1937, p. 95. Also Luiz Carlos Martins Pinheiro, "Notas sôbre as sêcas," *Boletim do Departamento Nacional de Obras Contra as Sêcas*, Nov. 1959, p. 70.

[2] Pompeu Sobrinho, *História*, Vol. II, p. 114.

[3] *Mensagens*, Vol. I, p. 256.

[4] The term *açude* is used to indicate both dam and reservoir.

of Ceará, Paraíba and Rio Grande do Norte where the intermittent rivers frequently descend through narrow gorges (*boqueirões*).[1] Theophilo, the chronicler of the 1877–79 drought, pointed out repeatedly in his work how the açudes provided a veritable oasis in the midst of the general desolation. One argument for the açudes is indeed that rain falls even in the driest year; while the rains may come too late and in too concentrated a fashion to be of use for rainfall agriculture, they still fill up the reservoirs.

The primary function of the açude was conceived to be retention of water, not only in case of drought, but also for the ordinary dry season. To store water for people and cattle was all that was expected from the very small açudes that were being built in many places by the landowners themselves. To subsidize such construction to the extent of 50 per cent of the total cost — up to 70 per cent in the case of municipally or state-built dams — has been one of the Inspetoria's principal functions ever since the start of its operations. The costly construction of the larger dams, on the other hand, made economic sense only if they were used for irrigation, and the Quixadá Dam was duly provided with a small network of irrigation canals. Drainage being inadequate, the soils in the irrigated basin became in part sterile because of excessive salinity, and thus Quixadá came into disrepute on yet another count.[2] But the unhappy Quixadá experience did not lead to any doubt as to the value of the açude solution as such.

From the beginning, the larger açudes were meant to serve as "strong points" of resistance against drought in the sertão itself, thus making the exhausting and humiliating migrations to the coast unnecessary for the sertanejos and sparing the cities contact with the miserable and occasionally mutinous flagelados.[3]

In addition to dams, the digging of wells was of obvious utility and was included among the works to be undertaken by the Inspetoria, along with construction of railroads and roads, establishment of meteorological and pluviometric stations, geological and botanical surveys, and so on.[4] But the açude was clearly the kingpin of the contemplated solution, and the establishment of the Inspetoria did not mean a change in that conception but merely the decision to pursue it more systematically, scientifically and with greater continuity and more independence from "politics."

---

[1] José Américo, *A Parahyba*, p. 189.
[2] Pompeu Sobrinho, *História*, p. 107.
[3] Miguel Arrojado Lisboa and Epitacio Pessôa, *As obras do Nordeste* (Resposta ao Senador Sampaio Corrêa), Rio, 1925, p. 52.
[4] Decree No. 7619 of Oct. 21, 1909.

Were any other possible solutions perceived at the time? One fairly obvious response was in evidence during each drought: emigration. Moreover, as early as in 1877 the government made free coastwise transportation available, particularly toward the "empty" northern provinces of Maranhão and Pará. With the rubber boom of 1890–1910, large numbers of Northeasterners were tempted to try their luck even farther in the Amazon Basin. This solution, favored, for example, by the Campos Salles administration during the 1900 drought,[1] was anathema to the group of militant Northeastern regionalists who were convinced that a few basic investments would convert their land into one of Brazil's most fertile provinces. It happens that both emigration and the transformation of the sertão require better communications with the interior. Railroads and roads make it easier for people to leave the sertão, and permit relief shipments, construction materials and equipment to be brought in. They also permit people to move about within the sertão in search of the more humid highlands, the perennial rivers and the reservoirs. Thus, an important area of agreement on means existed here among partisans of different and even opposing solutions to the problem. This is perhaps one reason why road construction has always been one of the most successful elements of the public works program in the Northeast.

The Inspetoria: From Solid Beginnings to Feast and Famine in the Twenties

The new agency started out most hopefully. Its first Director, Arrojado Lisboa, was a prominent mining engineer, a man of experience, dedication and intelligence.[2] He put together a team of qualified engineers and scientists, including several foreign technicians, with whom he set out to organize systematic studies of the region's geography, geology, rainfall, hydrology, flora and so on. In addition, he had the political savvy to realize that public opinion would not be impressed by studies alone, however valuable, but required visible progress in the form of public works.[3] He therefore undertook to study larger-scale works, particularly dams, in the

---

[1] Thomaz Pompeu Sobrinho, "As seccas do Nordeste, 1825–1925," *Livro do Nordeste*, Commemorative issue of first centenary of *Diário de Pernambuco, 1825–1925*, Recife, 1925, p. 51. Also Martins Pinheiro, "Notas sôbre as sêcas," *DNOCS Boletim*, Nov. 1959, p. 70.

[2] His paper "O problema das sêcas," written in 1913 and republished in *DNOCS Boletim*, Nov. 1959, remains an excellent analysis of the drought problem.

[3] Pompeu Sobrinho, *História*, pp. 249, 275.

states of Ceará, Paraíba and Rio Grande do Norte. He even felt that a show of "real" activity was immediately required and ordered construction work on some dams to be begun on the basis of previous and sometimes incomplete studies. This activity, however, was strictly limited since the early years of the agency coincided with a period of financial stringency resulting from the bust of the rubber boom and a decline in coffee prices.

Arrojado Lisboa resigned in 1912. The revised regulation of the Inspetoria which was issued under the new Hermes administration at the end of 1911 definitely conveys the impression that bureaucracy was beginning to assert itself vigorously in the new agency. The regulation, after reproducing more or less the earlier provisions on the agency's functions and attributions, devotes sixteen pages of finely printed text to a detailed description of the positions, responsibilities, rights and duties of the personnel.[1]

The creation of the agency in itself did not bring the sought-after stability and continuity of even the small resources that were placed at its disposal. For example, having reached a level of 6.9 million milreis in 1913, expenditures were slashed to 2.0 million in 1914, a year of financial crisis, as though the Inspetoria catered to some entirely non-essential function. A serious drought hit the Northeast in 1915 and while relief funds were made available as usual, it turned out that the area was not much better prepared to face the emergency with the agency than it had been before.

The largest dam undertaken (Acarape do Meio) went through almost as many changes in design, interruptions and difficulties as the Quixadá Dam had experienced prior to the establishment of the Inspetoria.[2] In particular, recurrent shortages of funds led to irregular and delayed payments not only to suppliers but also to workers and, in 1915, to drought refugees. Started in 1910, the dam remained unfinished for many years. A detailed account of its history comes to the following conclusion: "Without doubt, the picture which the public administration of this undertaking presented is quite dark and reveals the incapacity of the Government of the Republic to carry out great undertakings under its own immediate responsibility."[3]

The principal contribution of the agency during the first ten years of its

---

[1] Decree No. 9256 of Dec. 28, 1911.
[2] See case history of this dam in Pompeu Sobrinho, *História*, pp. 281–289 and 387–388.
[3] *Ibid.*, p. 289.

existence was the preparation of a number of scientific studies of the region and the organization of data collection through the setting up of flood control stations and the like. In the longer run, however, an agency that became part and parcel of the "Cartorial (i.e., bureaucratic, paper-shuffling, parasitic) State" could not provide the ideal atmosphere for a group of scientists, and the team that had been put together by Arrojado Lisboa dispersed after a few years. The geological and botanical studies were entirely dropped and even the collection of data on river flow, a most valuable type of information for several purposes, was discontinued for unknown reasons in 1916.[1] Although earlier the undertaking of construction "without adequate previous studies" had been much criticized, it turned out that there was even less public acceptance of basic research without immediate practical follow-up. Impatience with "eternal studies" was voiced and a feeling arose that, with all these fine studies now surely completed, the time was ripe for forceful action.[2]

With a severe drought coming along in 1919 and, for the first and only time in Brazil's history, with a Northeasterner, Epitacio Pessôa, newly installed as President of the Republic, such action was indeed forthcoming. Moreover, the President assumed office at the crest of the postwar boom which brought unprecedented foreign exchange income to Brazil and opened up good prospects of foreign borrowing.

There followed what is perhaps the most extraordinary episode in our story. Epitacio Pessôa had the Inspetoria contract for numerous large-scale works with foreign engineering firms, and spending on these works reached a level relative to the country's total revenue (around 15 per cent in 1921–22) that has never since been equalled. The total amount spent during the period 1919–23 on Northeastern public works was 378 million milreis, equivalent to about $150 million of current purchasing power. The results of this extraordinary fling were disconcertingly meager since most of the works were suspended by Pessôa's successor, Artur Bernardes, before they could be completed.[3] As between these two Presidents we have

---

[1] Epitacio Pessôa, *Pela verdade*, Livraria Francisco Alves, Rio, 1925, pp. 362–363.

[2] *Ibid.*

[3] Epitacio Pessôa had been forewarned that this would happen by the São Paulo deputy and economist Cincinato Braga. When the program was first presented Braga criticized both its direction and size: "The greatest error would be to begin large-scale works, completely beyond the resources of the Nation, because if they were started with this original flaw they will tomorrow be suspended as fatally as night follows day. This suspension will [make for] . . . a feeling of demoralization about these works in the future. And the very region of the Northeast will be most injured, just as it has already been injured through the original mistake of the Quixadá Dam." *Seccas do*

clearly decision-making at its most baffling, to say the least; it is therefore worth while to look into this episode in some detail.

A first question will occur to the student of economic development, steeped in the notions of "absorptive capacity" or "ability to invest": How was the Pessôa administration able to step up Inspetoria spending from an average of 4 million milreis in 1916–19 to an average of 142 million in 1921–22? The answer is relatively easy. It had become possible to undertake large-scale projects as a result of the studies carried out by the Inspetoria during the first decade of its existence.[1] To head the agency, President Pessôa called back Arrojado Lisboa, who had the best grasp of the Northeastern region and of available plans and personnel. Interestingly enough, the agency which had been created to impart some continuity to public works spending in the Northeast made possible, on the contrary, fluctuations in spending on a truly grandiose scale, because of the preliminary studies it had organized. In considering the large sums that the Inspetoria suddenly managed to spend, it must also be mentioned that a vast quantity of transportation and earth-moving equipment was brought into Brazil by the foreign engineering firms with which the works were contracted. According to Epitacio Pessôa's own account, the cost of this equipment was 188 million milreis, i.e., just about one-half of the total amount spent, and this does not include the payments to the foreign contractors for their services.[2]

Granted that, thanks to the spadework of the Inspetoria, there was no shortage of projects, what of technical skills and funds? To take the latter first, the budgetary position which Pessôa encountered upon taking office was far from brilliant. But with the influx of foreign exchange in 1919 he did not find it difficult to borrow from the banks and in 1921–22 he was able to contract sizable loans in New York ($75 million in all). In an attempt to insure permanent financial support for the Inspetoria, he also created a "Special Fund for Irrigation Works and Cultivable Lands of the Northeast." This was to receive, besides the proceeds of special loans, 2 per cent of the annual federal revenue, similarly regular contributions from the Northeastern states, as well as the proceeds accruing from the in-

---

Nordeste e reorganização económica, Imprensa Nacional, Rio de Janeiro, 1919, p. 9. Braga advocated giving priority to railroad and road construction, more for the purpose of assuring mobility of population and cattle within the sertão than to facilitate emigration to the Coast or the South.

[1] All the dams whose construction was commissioned in 1920 had been the object of studies in 1909–19. (Pompeu Sobrinho, *História,* pp. 357 ff.)

[2] Epitacio Pessôa, *Pela verdade,* p. 375.

come-earning activities of the public works once they would be completed and in use.[1]

The most serious potential bottleneck was the lack of skilled personnel and management. It was broken by turning the major projects over to three foreign engineering firms: one American (Dwight P. Robinson of New York) and two British (Norton Griffiths and C. H. Walker & Co.). This decision was defended by Epitacio Pessôa against his critics on the ground that the Brazilian state had proved its incompetence in building large-scale structures with the Quixadá and Acarape do Meio Dams and that no Brazilian firms experienced in large dam construction were available.[2]

If it can thus be understood how the President managed to achieve the remarkable volume of spending of 1921–22, the question remains why he insisted on so big a push, why he undertook to have built simultaneously about a dozen large dams (including such major undertakings as the 4 billion cubic meter Orós reservoir[3]), as well as many smaller ones, hundreds of miles of roads and railroads, not to mention important harbor improvement works at Fortaleza and two other ports. One answer is that, as it would be a long time before a Northeasterner would return to Catete Palace, he was determined to get under way, and if possible finish, as many projects as possible during his term of office.[4] But more fundamentally, it becomes quite clear upon reading his speeches that he really believed that the problem could be licked, that droughts or their consequences could be stamped out just as had been done with yellow fever in Rio. In fact, the term he constantly used to designate his objective was "extinction of the droughts" and he meant this literally since he thought of the Northeast area as a new Egypt or Mesopotamia whose dry lands would bloom as a result of the irrigation made possible by big reservoirs.

He drew a sharp distinction between the small and big açudes; while

---

[1] Decree No. 14,102 of March 17, 1920; cf. also Decree No. 3965 of December 25, 1919.

[2] Epitacio Pessôa, *Pela verdade*, pp. 328–329.

[3] This is approximately one-third the capacity of the Grand Coulee Dam whose reservoir holds 9.6 million acre-feet (one acre-foot = 1,233 cubic meters).

[4] "I see that there exists . . . an exaggerated appetite for the immediate and rapid construction of dams: I suspect that this is due to the fear that once the illustrious Northeasterner will have left the Presidency . . ., other officials who will succeed his government may stop the program . . ." Braga, *Seccas e reorganização*, p. 28. The fear turned out to be justified and thus the feeling was confirmed that each President has to get his own pet projects "over the hump" during his own term of office lest his successor discontinue them. A recent expression of this feeling was the single-minded determination with which Kubitschek pushed the construction of Brasília.

conceding that the small ones were useful in mitigating the evil, he asserted strongly that only the big ones could achieve a fundamental transformation of the agricultural economy through large-scale year-round irrigation downstream from the large reservoirs.[1]

Fired by this vision of a radical and comprehensive solution, the President was impatient with any criticism that pointed out to him that some elements of his plan could possibly be delayed until its principal components were in place. When the Brazilian currency depreciated rapidly and severely in 1920–21 and the President's expenditure policies came increasingly under public attack, he requested the famous explorer Rondon to head a mission to the Northeast and make an independent report about the probity, progress and value of the public works that were being undertaken there. The mission was quite impressed on the first two counts, but expressed doubts about the need to proceed with a large program of port, railroad and road construction simultaneously with the building of the açudes. With respect to the ports, for example, "whose construction increases considerably the volume of expenditures and thus endangers the normal prosecution of the principal works," the mission felt that "there would be no harm in waiting until *the beginning of economic development, consequent upon irrigation,* would require these improvements."[2] To this suggestion of a sequential solution Epitacio Pessôa replied that a simultaneous, "balanced-growth" solution was indispensable because "the works in progress in the Northeast — reservoirs, roads, railroads, ports — are different but harmonious elements of a single system, of a single plan: to eliminate any one is to leave the plan incomplete, to hinder the progress of the other elements and to make the objective unattainable." He also castigated on a different ground the suggestion of a partial postponement of some works: "Always the idea of postponement, in a country in which lack of continuity . . . is the characteristic note of all governments."[3]

These are revealing statements, for they explain the nature and size of Epitacio Pessôa's program as the direct response to what were widely believed to have been the mistakes and failings of governmental action in general and in the Northeast in particular. The lack of systematic planning, so frequently lamented, is to be overcome by putting together a vast complex of projects, all of them "interdependent" in some sense. Moreover,

---

[1] Epitacio Pessôa, *Pela verdade,* p. 320. Also *Mensagens,* Vol. IV, p. 393.
[2] Quoted in Epitacio Pessôa, *Pela verdade,* pp. 360–361.
[3] *Ibid.,* p. 361.

since there is lack of continuity, a government setting out to build such a complex cannot trust the next government to carry it on. Therefore, it cannot afford to postpone any of its components. At least it must get them all *started*, as a succeeding government can at best be trusted to finish what is already well under way.

Little wonder that an approach conceived in this uncompromising state of mind led not merely to the postponement of some works but to the interruption of virtually the whole program, not to all-round, harmonious accomplishments, but to all-round paralysis! For this is what happened. When Artur Bernardes, a Mineiro representative of the traditional power groups, succeeded Epitacio Pessôa in November 1922, he immediately undertook to "moderate the dispersed activity and to make it fit within the limits of the resources which can still be made available for it."[1] In March 1923, the Special Fund set up by Epitacio Pessôa in 1920 was abolished and with it the requirement that 2 per cent of the federal revenue be earmarked for the Inspetoria. In the course of 1923 and 1924, most of the larger projects were stopped and work was haltingly continued in the face of severe shortages of funds on only a few açudes. At the end of 1924, the government was authorized to sell all the equipment acquired for the Northeast at a 20 per cent discount from the purchase price. (This was practically a giveaway since the Brazilian currency had depreciated considerably since the original acquisition.) The final blow came in a terse decree of January 7, 1925:

> . . . Considering that the situation of the Treasury with whose difficulties the present Government has been fighting since the first days of its existence, obliges it to an extreme rigor in the policy of economy which it has adopted . . .
>
> Art. 1. During the fiscal year of 1925, all public works that are being carried out by the various ministries are suspended.[2]

And the public works in the Northeast *stayed* suspended during the next six years, during which the appropriations for the Inspetoria fell below even the very low level of the pre-Epitacio period.

Once again we face a riddle: Why this complete reversal? Why not finish at least some works which were fairly well advanced, such as the São Gonçalo Dam in Paraíba?[3]

It must be granted that Bernardes inherited many financial difficulties.

---

[1] *Mensagens,* Vol. V, p. 96.

[2] Fiscal year coincides with calendar year. Decree No. 16,769 of Jan. 7, 1925.

[3] José Américo, *A Parahyba,* p. 199.

Epitacio Pessôa had been an easy spender, and not only in the Northeast. Perhaps to placate opinion in the Center-South, he pushed railroad construction in São Paulo, Minas Gerais and Rio Grande do Sul and actually spent on these programs alone about twice as much as on the Northeast, as he pointed out later in self-justification.[1] In 1922 the deficit hit a record high; within the preceding two years the milreis had lost 50 per cent of its value.[2] Bernardes' Finance Minister drew a frightening picture of the state of the Treasury upon assuming office and the new government went on a course of financial austerity of which the works in the Northeast were the first victim. In 1924, a serious military revolt, aimed at regenerating Brazil's politics and society, was staged in São Paulo by a young officer group. Coming only two years after the Copacabana revolt, it further contributed to the decision to hold "unnecessary" expenditures in the Northeast to a minimum.

The Bernardes government was rather successful in achieving its financial objectives. The budget reached virtual balance in 1925, the circulation declined and the exchange rate strengthened from 1923 to 1926. The spectacle of the ruinous German inflation and the schemes of financial reconstruction in Europe may well have influenced Brazilian policies at the time. In 1923 the Banco do Brasil was given the exclusive right of note issue and the reformed Bank's first director, the São Paulo deputy and economist Cincinato Braga, an outspoken and intelligent critic of Epitacio Pessôa's Northeastern policies, inaugurated a deflationary credit policy. Early in 1924, a mission of British experts, headed by Sir Edwin Montagu, the former Secretary of State for India, made a report to the Brazilian government and naturally advised strict economy and retrenchment.[3]

But granted that in 1922 the time had come for Brazil, after a bout of inflationary spending, to absorb some deflationary medicine, why was it decided to bear down so brutally on the Northeastern projects (Inspetoria spending decreased from 15 per cent of total expenditures to less than 1 per cent in 1924 and to less than 0.5 per cent in 1925)? First, it should per-

---

[1] Epitacio Pessôa, *Pela verdade*, p. 374. Public criticism centered, not on these investments, but on the lavishness with which he entertained the Belgian royal couple in 1920 and celebrated the hundredth anniversary of Brazil's independence in 1922.

[2] J. F. Normano, *Brazil: A Study of Economic Types*, University of North Carolina Press, Chapel Hill, 1935, p. 201.

[3] "The fundamental point to which we desire to call Your Excellency's attention is the urgent necessity that your Budget should balance." *Report submitted to his Excellency the President of the United States of Brazil* by Edwin S. Montagu et al., February 23, 1924 (printed: no publisher), p. 8. See also *The (London) Economist*, July 5, 1924, p. 9.

haps be mentioned that nature was not helpful to any renewal of public works spending; adequate to overabundant rains fell in the Northeast throughout these years. Secondly, the fact that the contracts were all with foreign firms may have made interruption politically easier than if Brazilian firms had been involved as was the case with railroad construction in the Center-South.

But basically the Pessôa-Bernardes episode illustrates perhaps a general principle: in a country with one area that is rich and growing and another that is poor and stagnant, the latter is likely to be the stepchild of public investment for a prolonged period.[1] The need to provide the growing area with essential transportation services and utilities is so commanding that the poorer area is able to squeeze in only during periods of extraordinary prosperity and "inflationary excess"; it is likely to be cut out as soon as "sound finance" takes over. Paradoxically, *public spending on the poor area thus is likely to display the features usually associated with private spending on luxuries.* This behavior of the public authorities is in evidence not only during the Pessôa-Bernardes period; we encountered it earlier during the austere Campos Salles regime at the turn of the century, when even emergency drought relief for the Northeast was hard to come by, and we shall notice the association of inflationary spending with a greater readiness to help the Northeast again during the first Vargas and the Kubitschek regimes. The pattern is broken only when the backward region begins to show substantial growth or when the promotion of such growth has become a matter of paramount national urgency.

The likelihood that aid to the backward area will frequently be accompanied by inflation is reinforced by a related observation: for political reasons, programs of public spending in the backward area and in the rapidly growing advanced area are likely to be complementary, not substitutes for each other. As the matter was put in relation to the renewed interest in the Northeast shown by the Alves government in 1903: "When there were funds available for the rebuilding of the national capital, any economies with respect to the palpitating needs of that region [the Northeast] would be indefensible."[2] Fifty-five years later a similar complementarity appeared between the building of Brasília and the still "palpitating" needs of the Northeast.[3] With Epitacio Pessôa the complementary relationship worked the other way round: he was primarily interested in the

---

[1] As I have argued in *The Strategy of Economic Development,* pp. 192–193.
[2] Naylor Bastos, "Obras," *IFOCS Boletim,* April–June 1937, p. 95.
[3] Cf. p. 86.

Northeast but reconciled the Center-South to his plans through large-scale railroad construction there. In other words, while substitution may be possible among projects *within* the Center-South or *within* the Northeast, public spending in the Northeast tends to come on top of, rather than in lieu of, spending in the Center-South. Like any poor relative, the Northeast gets taken only to those parties at which the rich relatives are also present — to the real big, inflationary parties.

Achievement in the Thirties

The massive expenditures of Epitacio Pessôa naturally stimulated public discussion of the Northeastern problem, its causes and solutions. To Pessôa's optimistic belief in the ability of the reservoirs joined with irrigation to transform the region, critics opposed doubts based on the large volume of evaporation to which the dammed-up waters would be subject in the hot Northeastern climate. Rapid evaporation would not only greatly reduce the water available for irrigation but also heighten the danger that the irrigated soils would become saline. Cincinato Braga held, further, that the reservoirs might run dry during a severe drought and suggested that better transportation facilities within the region and between it and the rest of the country were more certainly useful. He was violently controverted by José Américo de Almeida, the future Minister of Public Works under Vargas, who, like most good Northeasterners, held emigration in horror and wished for an end to the "gypsy existence" of the sertanejo.[1]

But, with all the big dams left uncompleted, these contrasting opinions had not been put to a test in the twenties. The next large-scale effort, during the thirties, was therefore inspired essentially by the same vision which had inspired Epitacio Pessôa. The Pessôa-Bernardes sequence accredited the idea that the Northeast's problems were perhaps less to be blamed on malevolent nature than on political and administrative ineptness and instability. Thus, in his "Liberal Alliance" platform for the 1930 elections, Vargas advocated specifically a return to the ideas of Epitacio Pessôa and pledged renewal of large-scale public works in the Northeast which had been victimized by the "Dantesque combination of adverse climate and our disgraceful improvidence."[2]

For several reasons, the 1930 revolution which brought Vargas to power

[1] Braga, *Seccas e reorganização*. Also José Américo, *A Parahyba*, pp. 194–197.
[2] Getúlio Vargas, *A nova política do Brasil*, José Olympio, Rio, 1938, Vol. I, p. 42.

was to lead to a determined renewal of efforts to tackle the Northeastern problem. In the first place, while Vargas had been able to seize power in October primarily as a result of support from Minas, Rio Grande do Sul and an important group of army officers, some Northern states, particularly Paraíba with its President João Pessôa, had provided valuable help in the first half of that troubled year.[1] João Pessôa, a popular reformer, was Vargas' running mate as vice-presidential candidate in 1930. At the same time, he had to contend with a rebellion against his state government in the sertão town of Princesa; the evidence of federal support for the rebels and João Pessôa's assassination in July 1930, which was attributed to the "oligarchy," contributed importantly to the feeling that the end of the regime, later to be called the First Republic, could come none too soon. Thus, when Vargas had taken over the Presidency (after having been defeated in an election which was widely regarded as fraudulent), the Northeast wielded more political power than at any time since Epitacio Pessôa. This power was duly recognized by the appointment of José Américo de Almeida, essayist, novelist and political lieutenant of João Pessôa, to the crucial post of Minister of Transport and Public Works.

But the help extended to the Northeast by the Vargas regime was more than a repayment of a political debt. For one thing, it was part of the search for new sources of economic strength after the collapse of coffee prices during the Great Depression. More important, it was in line with the "reform," "anti-oligarchic" character of the first years of the Vargas regime and with its professed desire to improve the fate of the underprivileged, be they social classes or geographic regions. The movement to redress the regional balance, to "repay the nation's debt to the North" (a saying of Euclides da Cunha which Vargas liked to quote),[2] was thus far more broadly based than the drive of Epitacio Pessôa, whose somewhat frantic efforts are perhaps best explained by the fact that the election of a Northeasterner to the Presidency was felt as a freakish and non-renewable event; for according to an unwritten law of the First Republic, the Presidency was to alternate between a Paulista and a Mineiro. During the early thirties, the new concern with the Northeast was consonant with the origins, nature and inclinations of the new political regime; it was also supported by a broad current of the national mood which found expression in

---

[1] The chief executive officer of state governments frequently carried the title of President during the First Republic.

[2] Vargas, A nova política, Vol. II, p. 163.

— or was fostered by — the sociological and social protest novels of José Lins do Rego, Jorge Amado, Graciliano Ramos, Rachel de Queiroz and José Américo, a gifted and influential group of writers who came to dominate the Brazilian literary scene in the early thirties.[1]

Yet, these favorable factors may not by themselves have led to a new, large-scale governmental effort in favor of the Northeast since, at the same time, the Great Depression had of course swollen the traditional deficit of the Brazilian Treasury. Vargas' writings and speeches do not give any evidence that he was ahead of his time in understanding the principles of compensatory finance; in 1931 he invoked the austere Campos Salles as his guiding light and vowed the return to a balanced budget "as an inflexible norm."[2] Under these circumstances, the Northeast may well have had to be satisfied with expressions of sympathy had it not suffered, in 1930–32, severe and prolonged droughts that compelled action.

Both 1930 and 1931 were dry years, but because of the desire to restrain expenditures, the Inspetoria resources were hardly increased. In 1932, however, the drought was particularly severe and affected an unusually wide area. Special appropriations had been granted from late 1931 on to finance relief and emergency public works on which 220,000 flagelados came to be employed. In 1932 expenditures of the Inspetoria amounted to almost 10 per cent of the federal revenue (as against less than 1 per cent in previous years). In real terms the 1932 expenditures did not fully equal Epitacio Pessôa's peak of 1921–22, but the expenditures of those years included a very large foreign exchange component for payment of equipment and engineering services. Once the acute crisis caused by the 1932 drought had passed, expenditures dropped, but not nearly as steeply as they had risen; throughout the thirties they remained at a level which permitted some dam and road construction to continue, whereas in the second half of the twenties all new investment had come to a halt.

The thirties — particularly the first half — were in many ways a period of major achievements for the agency. A number of comparatively large dams were completed, including some that had been started under Epitacio Pessôa as well as some entirely new projects. In 1930, total storage capacity in 92 public dams amounted to 625 million cubic meters. In the thirties this capacity, mostly in small reservoirs, was quadrupled as 31 new

---

[1] For an excellent survey see Fred P. Ellison, *Brazil's New Novel*, University of California Press, Berkeley, 1954, particularly Chapter 1.

[2] Vargas, *A nova política*, Vol. I, pp. 161–163.

dams with a capacity of 1,952 million cubic meters were brought in.[1] Among these new dams were 18 with over 10 million cubic meters and 7 with over 50 million cubic meters storage capacity, as opposed to 11 and 3, respectively, before 1930. The average construction time of public reservoirs with over 10 million cubic meters capacity was 2½ years in the thirties, whereas prior to that time it was over 7 years.

Solid achievement could also be claimed in highway construction as approximately two thousand kilometers of main highways and one thousand kilometers of secondary roads were built. About one-half of this mileage was built during the drought year 1932, as it was far easier to absorb large numbers of drought refugees in road construction than in the building of dams where engineering frequently remained the critical bottleneck. No foreign firms were employed this time.

In view of the unhappy record established during previous as well as subsequent droughts, perhaps the most remarkable achievement of the thirties was a negative one: the absence of large-scale corruption in the distribution of relief funds during the 1931–32 drought. During the later phases of the Vargas regime (after the Communist-inspired military revolt of 1935 and after the proclamation of the Estado Novo in 1937) lack of public outcries over scandals may not have meant that there were none, but in 1931–32 restrictions on the freedom of expression were moderate so that the absence of attacks and criticism on that familiar score can be taken at face value.

One contemporary observer has called the government's action in the Northeast during the early thirties the "best revolutionary and human expression" of the 1930 revolution.[2] What were the ingredients of this success? The first, and probably the most important, was the infusion of new vital energies, enthusiasm and drive for achievement into the work of the Inspetoria as a result of the revolution. José Américo represented at its best the yearning for a change in the incompetent, unimaginative, yet arrogant, way in which the country had long been run by a small "oligarchy." He was himself very knowledgable about the Northeast, having written, besides a path-breaking sociological novel, a comprehensive monograph

---

[1] This figure includes one large dam (Estevão Marinho) which was started in 1935 but completed only in 1943; it belongs to the cycle of work of the thirties. The summary data given in the text have been compiled from the detailed historical figures on dam construction available in the following publications of DNOCS: Relatório de 1959, Publ. No. 194, Serie II M; Planificação e principais realizações, Publ. No. 183, Série IE; Boletim, No. 3, Vol. 19, Feb. 1959, pp. 149–194.

[2] Orris Barbosa, Secca de 32, Adersen, Rio, 1935, p. 193.

about the natural, human and economic aspects of his own state, Paraíba.[1] To head the Inspetoria, he selected a competent and active engineer, Luiz Vieira, who remained in this position for ten years, thus outlasting José Américo who resigned in 1934. In a lecture he gave in Recife in 1938 on the work accomplished by the Inspetoria, Vieira said that in 1930 the agency was "demoralized, mistrusted, without credit, almost without value" and that then "this group of young, sincere, patriotic, hard-working, honest professionals which you all know succeeded in changing a bureaucratic stagnant organization into a 'school of engineering and of civic virtue' as one of our most eminent engineers has said."[2] This was certainly true in the first five years, although at the moment at which Vieira spoke the agency was once again on the decline. In any event, it is worth underlining here that the agency, discredited though it apparently was in 1930, was not then considered hopeless, but became, after changes in personnel, the chosen instrument of the new drive to help the Northeast.

Another element making for the achievements of the thirties was the concentration of reservoir work on four intermittent river basins and of highway construction on a few principal trunk lines. José Américo felt so strongly the need to avoid dispersions of effort that he included this restriction on the work program in the agency's new statute itself, thus giving the Inspetoria some protection against incessant pressure from all sides.[3] Here we have a reaction against the excessively "comprehensive" plans of Epitacio Pessôa. In fact, José Américo wanted to relieve the agency of responsibility for road construction so it could devote itself entirely to its principal business: water.[4] While, for the time being, the agency found it impossible to relinquish responsibility for road construction, its work was given, for once, a clear direction. It is ironical that this single-mindedness in pushing dam construction, which resulted from the costly lesson learned during the Epitacio Pessôa episode, was later attacked by the agency's critics as narrow "açudomania" and lack of vision.

Actually, while the agency remained essentially an engineer's domain, José Américo looked beyond the purely engineering aspect of its work toward irrigation, the next phase which was expected to become reality as

---

[1] *A Parahyba e seus problémas.*

[2] Luiz Augusto de Silva Vieira, "Obras do Nordeste," *IFOCS Boletim,* Jan.–March 1939, p. 103.

[3] Decree No. 19,726 of February 20, 1931 approved the new statute of the agency. Articles 9 and 14 of this statute spell out the dam and road construction program.

[4] José Américo de Almeida, *O ciclo revolucionário do Ministério da Viação,* Imprensa Nacional, Rio, 1934, p. 379.

soon as the larger reservoirs would have been built. Thus the agency's new 1931 statute provided for the so-called *postos agrícolos,* i.e., agricultural research and extension services, to be established alongside the large reservoirs. In 1933 a new subdivision of the agency, the Office of Complementary Services (later renamed more descriptively Agro-Industrial Service), was established to organize and coordinate the work of these stations.[1]

Perception of New Difficulties: Irrigation and Expropriation

It was this office which gradually discovered hitherto unsuspected or only dimly perceived difficulties and problems as it attempted to bring to the Northeastern agricultural economy the full benefits of the new reservoirs through irrigation. It may seem strange that reservoirs were built at all without full provision having been made in advance for irrigation. But this splitting of the task into two stages is easily explained, first by the temptations of nature which, with its *boqueirões,* provided ideal sites for dams and thus presented the civil engineers of the Inspetoria with a far more attractive and challenging task than the laying out of irrigation canals; secondly, by the desire to allocate all available funds to the immediate job at hand; and, most important, by the fact that it could be claimed that reservoirs would have quite some usefulness *as such,* even without any irrigation, because of the amenities and the security against drought they would provide to the population, both human and animal, already established in the general area.

The situation was quite different from that in totally arid zones. There irrigation is a prerequisite for settlement and hence dam construction and laying out of the irrigation network go necessarily and naturally hand in hand. In the Northeast, settlement was an established fact and while completion of a large açude without simultaneous preparation of the irrigation network might represent a highly uneconomic use of resources, it was by no means wholly nonsensical.[2] Moreover, the fact of prior settlement

---

[1] Art. 1 of IFOCS Statute issued with Decree No. 19,726 of Feb. 20, 1931.

[2] Even Epitacio Pessôa, who made so much of the "extinction of the drought" through irrigation, defended his primary attention to dam construction in these terms: "The advantage of the açudes does not consist only in irrigation and in fishing. Certainly, irrigation is the principal economic objective; but as soon as it begins to store water . . . the açude begins to lend invaluable services . . . by supplying people and cattle with water and by permitting crops to be grown on its margins." Epitacio Pessôa and Arrojado Lisboa, *As obras do Nordeste,* pp. 25–26.
    This argument can be carried even further. Guimarães Duque claims plausibly that

created special institutional difficulties for irrigation. The lands downstream from the reservoir, including the periodically dry river beds, had already been appropriated in patterns of land tenure that were likely to be quite different from those advisable with irrigation. The socio-political difficulties involved in changing these patterns made açude construction *without* simultaneous provision for irrigation not only non-nonsensical but perhaps outright advisable lest powerful opposition be aroused against doing anything. This is intimated by the politically astute Arrojado Lisboa, Director of the Inspetoria in 1909–12 and again under Epitacio Pessôa:

> I had assistants, more theoretically than practically minded, who insisted strongly that irrigation work should be begun simultaneously with the projects [of dam construction] . . . I opposed their wishes gently but tenaciously . . . What is most important is to satisfy the immediate aspirations of the Northeast; irrigation through canals will come as an inevitable consequence. *In its own time, it will become an extreme political necessity.*[1]

Arrojado Lisboa here advocated a sequential solution; clearly he was well aware of the resistance to irrigation and counted on the açudes, once in place, to overcome this resistance.

Events were to show that his assessment of the difficulties standing in the way of irrigation was, if anything, an underestimate. The melancholy or, if one wishes, "scandalous" fact is that even today the area irrigated by the reservoirs amounts to only 7,000 hectares.[2]

The principal difficulties surrounding irrigation were perceived shortly after the large açudes of the thirties had been built. The classic statement about them is a 1940 article by José Augusto Trindade, the first Director of the Inspetoria's agricultural research and extension work.[3] Trindade first

---

the açudes made an important contribution to agriculture in the surrounding sertão. The mere proximity of an açude made life in the sertão more pleasant and secure and, even if the lands it irrigated were strictly limited in size, they could still be used for research and production of selected seeds to be planted in the sertão. "The açude permits the exploration of the dry land; the xerophilous plants are not appropriate for the irrigation basin since they can manage with whatever rains fall, but their area of cultivation is extended by the reservoir without a drop of its water being spent . . . The area of productive influence of the açude has no limits and it will never be possible to measure it." *Solo e água no polígono das sêcas*, Minerva, Fortaleza, 1953, pp. 216–217.

[1] Epitacio Pessôa and Arrojado Lisboa, *As obras do Nordeste*, pp. 53–54. (My italics.)

[2] SUDENE, *Revisão da política de açudagem e irrigação das bacias dos açudes*, Recife, 1961, mimeo., p. 1.

[3] J. A. Trindade, "Os postos agrícolas da Inspetoria de Sêcas," *IFOCS Boletim*, April–June 1940.

underlines that in the absence of a "climatic imperative" Northeasterners have acquired no tradition of, no experience with, and no particularly favorable disposition toward, irrigation. Thus the state has an all-embracing role to play, in accumulating knowledge through research, in modifying attitudes *and* in reshaping established property relations.

While advocating continued help to the large landowner through subsidy payments for small dam construction, Trindade then took a strong stand in favor of expropriation of large private holdings in the irrigable basins of the public reservoirs. He argues not so much that by retaining their land with its much increased potential yield the owners would enrich themselves at the taxpayers' expense, but rather stresses that the traditional *fazendeiro* does not believe in or take to irrigation. "With his authoritarian mentality, the habit of command and financial independence, he would not adapt himself to the requirements of an interdependent life."[1] The same observation had been made somewhat earlier by Guimarães Duque, who was to succeed Trindade as Director of the Agro-Industrial Service: "Our experience has already shown that the well-to-do landowner, the *coronel*, with his egoism, dogmatism and stubbornness, accustomed to exploit the poor in a sprawling, badly managed territory, does not possess the moral qualities needed for irrigation."[2] Trindade buttresses his argument by observing that the one irrigated crop to which the *fazendeiros* take easily is sugar cane for the production of *rapadura* (brown sugar cake) and *aguardente* (an alcoholic drink). Sugar cane, once established together with the requisite refining and distilling machinery, makes it impossible ever again to use the irrigated lands for their true social purpose, the growing of foodstuffs in time of drought. The purpose of irrigation, so says Trindade, is to correct the social balance in favor of the small landowner and sharecropper in the Northeast; they are the principal victims of the periodic droughts. The large landowner, though he may suffer serious losses in livestock, frequently profits, for example by making use of abundant cheap refugee labor to build a dam in the country (most private dams were built during the droughts) or a villa in the city. The function of irrigation is to help settle at least part of the agricultural population in such a way that it does not have to emigrate during the drought and, more important, to insure intensive yet *flexible* land use through such *annual* crops as can be in part exported to the cities in good years and will help to sustain life in the sertão during drought years.

---

[1] *Ibid.*, p. 108.
[2] José Guimarães Duque, "O fomento da produção agricola," *IFOCS Boletim*, April–June 1939, p. 156.

These ideas are simple and convincing; they have ever since been repeated and elaborated in various forms by most serious students of irrigation in the Northeast. Their enunciation in 1940 marks the end of an epoch. Up to then solutions to the Northeast's problems had been sought through public works, such as reservoirs, wells and highways, that were thought to be non-controversial or "nonantagonistic." Because they were expected to profit everyone in the region, they would hardly be likely to lead to major group conflicts in the Northeast itself. With the completion of the first large reservoirs it came to be understood that their benefits would not be at all equally divided and would moreover not be fully realized unless existing property relationships were changed or seriously interfered with at loss to some. Thus, it was the very achievement of the Inspetoria, during the thirties, in building engineering works that brought it face to face with a new problem far more difficult to solve: the attainment of conditions which would permit potential gains from these works to be fully realized and fairly distributed.

Little has been added over the last twenty years to the basic points Trindade made in 1940, but his arguments came to be accepted by important sectors of public opinion. In 1950, Vinicius Berredo, the Director of the Inspetoria, now renamed DNOCS (Departamento Nacional de Obras Contra as Sêcas), reiterated many of Trindade's ideas, insisting rather more on the scandalous enrichment which resulted from the expenditures of public monies on dam construction, when existing owners of land in the irrigated basins were not expropriated. He also showed how research and extension services would benefit primarily the large landowners. And he found strict public control of irrigated lands desirable, not only on social equity grounds or because perennial industrial crops ought to be excluded, but also in the interests of maintaining soil fertility.[1]

In 1958, the National Economic Council, a consultative body named by the President with anything but revolutionary tendencies, issued a well-documented report on the drought problem. Quoting Trindade at length, it fully supported both the need for expropriation of irrigated lands and the desirability of devoting these lands to basic food crops as a form of insurance against the risk of drought.[2]

The observation that droughts and the traditional way of fighting them

---

[1] Guimarães Duque, *Solo e água*, pp. 188–192.

[2] Consêlho Nacional de Economia, *O problema nacional das sêcas*, pp. 51–58. Trindade's ideas are also endorsed and elaborated in the reports by Thomas Pompeu Accioly Borges and José Arthur Rios in *Seminário para o desenvolvimento*, Vol. II, pp. 241–387.

through engineering works had highly *differential* effects on the position of various social groups in the Northeast was explored in depth by Celso Furtado in 1959, in the basic analytical document which played an important role in the establishment of SUDENE, the new agency for the development of the Northeast.

The principal differential effects noted by Furtado are the following:

(a) The drought itself does not affect all parts of the economy of the sertão equally. Dividing this economy into three principal sectors (1) cattle grazing, (2) the growing of mocó cotton and other xerophilous, industrial plants and cash crops, and (3) the growing of subsistence crops, he shows that drought affects the last sector far more than the other two. Thus it affects the small landowner, sharecropper and laborer in their livelihood while leaving the well-to-do owner of cattle herds or of cotton or carnauba palm plantations comparatively unscathed.

(b) Similarly, the reservoirs, as long as they do not lead to increased food production in their irrigated basins, are useful primarily in keeping cattle alive during droughts. Thus they strengthen rather than neutralize the differential impact of nature on the three principal activities.

(c) Finally, large governmental spending on public works during droughts, on dams and other structures, has the effect of retaining in the area a population that would otherwise emigrate. Thus it assures an abundant and cheap labor supply for the large landowners in normal years and prevents the introduction of more rational capital- or research-oriented methods in their cattle, cotton and other operations.[1]

While the train of thought originated by Trindade in 1940 won important adepts over the years, the only action it produced was the introduction of various irrigation and agrarian reform bills into Congress. However, these attempts to obtain legislation proved abortive and the next time a large-scale dam construction program got under way in the Northeast, in the fifties, the pattern of the thirties was repeated: dams were built without any prior planning for irrigation or for expropriation of irrigable lands. Objectively the government acted once again in the same fashion which

---

[1] Grupo de Trabalho para o Desenvolvimento do Nordeste, *Uma política de desenvolvimento econômico para o Nordeste*, Imprensa Nacional, Rio, 1959, particularly pp. 65–72. (This report, published as an official document, was drafted by Celso Furtado. It will be referred to hereafter as the Furtado Report.)

Arrojado Lisboa claimed to have consciously adopted as the only possible strategy: to build the dams first and once built let them exert the requisite pressure toward irrigation. The argument is put quite simply in the message President Kubitschek sent to Congress in 1959 in support of an irrigation law then proposed by SUDENE (but not adopted by the Congress):

> ... the great achievement realized in the past and intensified in the last three years in providing the Northeast with a network of dams ... must now be complemented by a decided effort to utilize the dammed-up waters. What has been accomplished up to now has been of the highest importance. Yet the policy of works against the effects of droughts in which we are engaged for over half a century would fail if we did not succeed in completing this effort of accumulation of waters by a program of works aiming at their integral utilization according to economic and social criteria.[1]

Fail indeed! While understandable in the thirties because of lack of experience with the problem, absence of the "complementary effort" had become the butt of jokes by the fifties: the preamble of one of the numerous irrigation bills declared that "the large açudes of the Northeast serve even today mostly to reflect poetically the beauties of the moonlit nights of the sertão."[2]

In our own country, we are by no means unfamiliar with situations that are felt to be absurd and whose correction has long been advocated by wide and influential sectors of public opinion — to no avail. It is never easy to account for the lengthy persistence of such situations. Before undertaking the attempt in our particular case, we must return to the chronological path from which we have momentarily strayed.

Constitutional Earmarking of Funds for the Northeast

Besides the considerable achievements in dam, road and railroad construction, the decade of the thirties witnessed an important attempt to place federal aid to the Northeast on a solid financial basis. The Constitution of 1934 contains an article (No. 177) which makes it mandatory that 4 per cent of Federal tax revenues be regularly allocated to "defense against the effects of the droughts" in the Northeast: 3 per cent to be spent

---

[1] Consêlho de Desenvolvimento do Nordeste, *Projeto de lei de irrigação,* Setor de Documentação, Sept. 1959, Recife, mimeo., pp. 1–2.
[2] Congresso Nacional, *Veto presidencial,* Mensagem No. 192 de 1959, Imprensa Nacional, Rio, 1959, p. 7.

in accordance with a "systematic plan," 1 per cent to be left in a special account to be used for relief purposes in case of a drought.

The idea of inserting such a provision in the Constitution arose of course largely because of the previous experience, particularly the feast-and-famine cycle of the twenties.[1] It will be recalled that Epitacio Pessôa had in part financed his Special Fund for Irrigation Works by allocating to it 2 per cent of the country's annual tax revenue. But this special earmarking lapsed when the Fund was abrogated by Pessôa's successor. Thus ordinary legislation did not seem to provide enough assurance. The insertion of a special article in the new Constitution was promoted by scientific and intellectual groups such as the Society of Geography of Rio de Janeiro, the Brazilian Society of Botany and, principally, the Society of Friends of Alberto Torres.[2] A vigorous press campaign supported the initiative. The proposed article was approved unanimously by the Constituent Assembly.

This success showed the strength both of the various Northeastern pressure groups and of the guilt feelings of the rest of the country about the Northeast, which had only recently passed through one of its periodic sufferings.

The principle of unity of the budget has always been honored in the breach in Latin America; but to violate it by constitutional provision is unusual and indicates the extent to which the Northeast's plight had become a national problem. In a sense, carving up federal revenue along regional lines can be considered a step dangerously weakening the federal tie. No concern on this score was voiced, however; on the contrary, special efforts for the Northeast have always been justified on the ground that they were required to cement national union.[3]

Yet, when the 1934 Constitution was superseded three years later by the Constitution of Vargas' *Estado Novo*, the special provision in favor of the Northeast was dropped, in line with the strongly centralistic tendencies of that authoritarian document. The earmarking was reintroduced, in some-

---

[1] Alcides Bezerra, *As seccas na futura constituição*, Archivo Nacional, Rio, 1936, p. 8. This little brochure contains a number of documents on the origin of the initiative, its supporters and its adoption by the Constituent Assembly.

[2] Cf. Alberto Torres, *A organização nacional*, Primeira Parte: *A constituição*, Imprensa Nacional, Rio, 1914. Torres, an influential writer on Brazil's political and social problems and perhaps the father of modern Brazilian nationalism, had been a strong advocate of adapting the Constitution to Brazilian "reality" and of using it as a means of introducing needed structural changes.

[3] Bezerra, *As seccas*, reports on some "discordant voices" which were primarily concerned with the question whether the Constitution should provide in detail for the various tasks facing the Brazilian government.

what altered and reduced form — 3 per cent of tax revenue was ordered set aside instead of 4 — in the Constitution of 1946 (Art. 198) which is presently in force.[1]

Once the 1934 Constitution had established the dry Northeast as a kind of permanent rentier, it was necessary to delimit precisely which area was to be the recipient of the yearly payments. For this purpose a Drought Polygon (*Polígono das Sêcas*) was defined in 1936.[2] Since it was a privilege to lie within the area of the Polygon, there was much pressure from neighboring areas in subsequent years to be admitted to the calamity club. The borders of the Drought Polygon were enlarged twice, in 1947 and again in 1951.

Both the special earmarking of federal funds for regional development and the delimitation, through law, of the region eligible for the spending of these funds were invented in the thirties; both remained important devices of policy-making in the forties and fifties. The earmarking device was used in connection with development efforts in favor of the Amazon Valley. Closer to our area of interest, it was invoked by three agencies created within the last fifteen years to deal with the Northeast: the São Francisco River Valley Commission (1948), the Bank of the Northeast of Brazil (1952) and the Superintendency for the Development of the Northeast (1959). Every time also, the geographical area in which each successive agency was to operate was exactly defined.

It would be a gross mistake to think that earmarking by law or even by constitution results in automatic transfer of funds from the Treasury to the beneficiary agencies. On the contrary, particularly with multiplication of the earmarkings, a Minister of Finance beset by financial difficulties will find many ways of "forgetting," delaying or denying the release of the funds that are "due" the various spending agencies, each of which maintains a staff in the capital to pry the funds loose from the Treasury.

Nevertheless, the special earmarking has facilitated the task of the Inspetoria and other agencies in the battle over apportionment of the budget. But there is a real question whether this has been in their own best interests. Sure of their rights and status as a rentier, they may well have felt less compulsion to turn in a good performance record and to justify their claims by carefully prepared projects. It is at least suggestive that the

---

[1] The reduction from 4 to 3 per cent is explained by the earmarking, in 1946, of one per cent for the development of the São Francisco Valley, a large part of which overlaps with the Northeast. See p. 52.

[2] Decree No. 175 of Jan. 7, 1936.

deterioration of the Inspetoria occurred after that agency had obtained the relative security implied in the constitutional provision of 1946 and that the São Francisco Valley Commission, which had an assured income from its inception, has led a rather phlegmatic and mediocre existence.

The Forties: Focus on the São Francisco River

The forties were uneventful for the Northeast. Like the twenties, the decade was free of severe droughts (a comparatively mild one occurred in 1942). The inflation of the war and postwar years eroded the real value of the yearly appropriations of the Inspetoria — which in 1945 was renamed Departamento Nacional de Obras Contra as Sêcas and will henceforth be referred to as DNOCS. Only two large dams were completed; both had been started in the active thirties.[1]

The special characteristic of the forties, in conjunction with this languishing activity of DNOCS, was a shift of interest from the northern "heartland" of the semi-arid Northeast toward the southern part of the area, traversed by the middle and lower reaches of the São Francisco River. Two entirely new agencies were created: broad tasks of river valley development were given to the São Francisco Valley Commission (CVSF), while the São Francisco Hydroelectric Company (CHESF) was put in charge of harnessing the considerable power potential of the falls of the river at Paulo Afonso.

This shift of interest became noticeable even in the late thirties when the Inspetoria prepared to turn its energies toward surveys of the middle São Francisco River Valley.[2] The task in this area was markedly different from that in the region where the Inspetoria had primarily operated. Although they are traversed by the voluminous waters of the São Francisco, the surrounding lands are poorer in soil and rainfall is lower. By the same token they are less subject to severe losses in farm output from haphazard droughts than the sertão of the three states — Ceará, Rio Grande do Norte and Paraíba — where most of the dam and road construction had been concentrated. As a result the São Francisco area is far less populated, and its economic life is more primitive than that of the northern part with its

---

[1] Estevão Marinho in the State of Paraíba with a capacity of 720 million cubic meters in 1943 and Caldeirão in the State of Piauí with 55 million in 1945.

[2] Luiz Augusto da Silva Vieira, "Obras do Nordeste" (lecture given in November 1938), *IFOCS Boletim*, Jan.–March 1939, pp. 101 ff.

xerophilous cash crops and its fertile *serras* and *chapadas*. Economic development here did not mean a precise task, such as the removal of a single, fairly well-circumscribed obstacle or handicap, but the total transformation of an environment that had proved hostile to large-scale human settlement, let alone to a satisfactory level of income for its sparse settlers.

Why was so complex a task being tackled when the more concrete job of fighting the effects of the droughts was still unfinished? A number of suggestions may be advanced. The Northeast as usually understood and as defined by the Drought Polygon includes the area traversed by the São Francisco River, approximately from the town of Barra downstream to a point 50 miles short of the mouth of the river, a stretch of over 500 miles. An agency whose very existence was grounded in the claim to distributive justice in the geographical sense could not very well violate this principle permanently within its own area of jurisdiction. In addition, with several of the larger dams completed, the agency found, as we have seen, that it now had, in connection with irrigation, socio-economic rather than purely engineering problems to solve and the reluctance to face up to this task may have been a factor in the shift of interest toward something else.

The fact that the São Francisco, Brazil's largest river next to the Amazon, flows for much of its course through Northeastern territory was bound to lead to various suggestions and attempts to marshal its water resources in the fight against the climatic emergency afflicting the areas north of it. An early grandiose suggestion was to divert some of its waters northward from its northernmost points at Cabrobó and feed them into the Jaguaribe basin, thereby curing the intermittent condition of that river.[1] Later on, in the thirties, there was much talk of making the São Francisco, through irrigation, a place of refuge for the flagelados during droughts. But lack of knowledge of the terrain and soils made for postponement. In fact, not only was the river not put to new uses, but difficulties arose regarding the service it had performed for centuries: that of supplying an artery of transportation between the Northeast and the Center-South.[2] This function was in jeopardy not only because of the completion of other modes of transport but because river traffic tended to become more hazardous as runoff

---

[1] Friedrich W. Freise, "The Drought Region of Northeast Brazil," *Geographical Review*, Volume XXVIII, July 1938, p. 377.

[2] The river is navigable in its middle course for about 1,300 kilometers from Pirapora in Minas Gerais to Petrolina in Pernambuco, from which point rapids culminating in the Paulo Afonso Falls close it to traffic.

was stepped up with the loss of forest cover in much of the catchment basin. The results were eroding river banks and sharper variation in the river's discharge.[1]

The neglect of the river came suddenly to the nation's attention during the Second World War when coastwise shipping was hampered by German submarines. In mid-1944 a special appropriation of 48.5 million cruzeiros was set aside for improvement in river navigation.[2] This rather limited objective was considerably expanded after the war when a somewhat fortuitous circumstance gave rise to a new campaign in favor of "doing something" for the river and its valley: the discussion of a new Constitution after the downfall of Vargas' Estado Novo. Taking a cue from the Northeast's success in 1934, interest groups for all of the country's underprivileged regions now were bent on staking out claims on the national budget and having them sanctioned by the new national charter. In the case of the Northeast a sizable program of public works was being carried out and more were constantly being planned by an existing agency, the Inspetoria, when the idea of constitutional earmarking first arose in 1934. For the Amazon region and the São Francisco Valley, the two additional claimants that appeared in 1946, the sequence was reversed: they first obtained by parliamentary means and logrolling assigned shares of the Federal revenue, and only then did the successful promoters begin to consider what to do with the conquered share. In the case of the São Francisco Valley, the Constituent Assembly voted in September 1946 an article obliging the government to spend at least one per cent of its fiscal revenue during twenty years on the Valley's development, after the most general kind of oratory which stressed mostly the historic role of the river as a link between North and South and the importance of invigorating the economy of the river basin to preserve the unity of Brazil.[3] Only after the constitutional provision had been voted was a parliamentary committee set up to take testimony on possible lines of action, desirable projects, priorities and so on.[4] It took another two years before Congress voted a law creating the São Francisco Valley Commission as an autonomous agency[5] within the executive branch and two more years before the commission itself presented a general plan, which was to orient its work. Since 1947, funds had

---

[1] Comissão do Vale do São Francisco, *Antecedentes do plano geral para o aproveitamento econômico do vale do S. Francisco,* Imprensa Nacional, Rio, 1953, pp. 13, 26.
[2] Decree Law No. 6643 of June 29, 1944.
[3] CVSF, *Antecedentes,* p. 14.
[4] *Ibid.,* p. 19.
[5] Law No. 541 of Dec. 15, 1948.

been made available, in accordance with the new constitutional provision, for an "emergency plan."[1]

The assurance of funds, on the one hand, and the lack of any clear idea what to do with them, on the other, led from the beginning to a predictable result: dispersal of the funds over the huge area "belonging" to the commission and over many small projects that were relatively easy to undertake, and a large degree of political influence on the pattern of these dispersed expenditures. In the latter respect, it was an open secret that from the beginning the principal power within the agency was held by a well-entrenched federal deputy from the rural parts of the State of Bahia, Manuel Novais, who, with his motto "politics is favor," epitomizes the "clientelistic" traditions of Brazilian politics.[2] His influence, extending over appointments in the agency and projects to be undertaken, remained unbroken through several administrations until the 1960 presidential campaign, when the stand he took antagonized the Kubitschek administration and Kubitschek in reprisal fired the director of the commission, a long-time Novais protégé.[3]

The commission's basic task was, of course, the regulation of river flow for purposes of navigation, flood control, irrigation, and generation of electric power. During the parliamentary debates of 1946–48, one precedent was continually invoked as justification for the project in general and the administrative autonomy of the proposed agency in particular: the Tennessee Valley Authority and its multi-purpose operations. The originators of the São Francisco project were, if anything, more multi-purposeful than the TVA; since large stretches of the São Francisco Valley lacked roads, schools, health facilities, agricultural credit, industry and even people, they felt that their project should cover all of these facets.

Within the agency, it was soon realized that regularization of river flow would first of all require heavy investment in one or two upstream dams, but the forces that had taken command were far more interested in a series of small projects which would offer a chance to reward friends and influence people.[4] Thus the commission engaged in what was officially called "a great policy of small services" such as access roads, building of infirma-

---

[1] Law No. 2599 of Sept. 13, 1955.

[2] Nelson de Souza Sampaio, *O diálogo democrático na Bahia*, Revista Brasileira de Estudos Políticos, Rio, 1960, p. 85.

[3] The *Jornal da Bahia* of Sept. 2, 1960 had a cartoon showing a tearful Manuel Novais overlooking the São Francisco Valley sprouting trees marked "jobs," "appointments," "employment," with the legend "How Green Was My Valley."

[4] Comissão do Vale do São Francisco, *Plano geral*, pp. 46–55.

ries and small hospitals, provision of water and power supply in small towns, and so on.[1] Apart from useful studies of the region, many of the projects sponsored were not really net additions to the activities already in progress, but represented merely a shift to the commission of activities previously carried on by other federal or state agencies. With respect to DNOCS, for example, there never arose any dispute about overlapping responsibilities. Chronically short of funds for its projects, DNOCS was only too glad to clear out of the São Francisco area even though so much of it was included in the Drought Polygon. It is interesting to note, incidentally, that the evident overlap in the geographical areas of responsibility went entirely unnoticed during the lengthy parliamentary debates.[2] Only a 1951 statute of the commission addresses itself tersely to the problem: its last article simply orders DNOCS to coordinate those of its projects located in the valley with the CVSF.[3]

The dispersion of CVSF's work was noted disapprovingly by Vargas after he had returned to the presidency.[4] He attributed it to the "emergency plan" which antedated the completion of the "general plan" in 1950, but by then the pattern of the commission's activities had become well ingrained, plan or no plan.

In 1956 the commission was temporarily jolted out of its quiet existence. President Kubitschek, with his unfailing eye for the dramatic key project, decided to push a major multi-purpose dam at the Três Marias site of the upper São Francisco River, in the State of Minas Gerais.[5] The project had indeed long been recognized as fundamental for regulation of the river's discharge, hence for improved navigation and large-scale irrigation along the middle and for flood control along the lower river. It will also serve to generate up to 520,000 kilowatts, and, more important for the Northeast, it

---

[1] Salomão Serebrenick, "A comissão do vale do São Francisco — objetivos e realizações," *Revista Brasileira de Geografia*, April–June 1960, Rio, p. 260. A complete survey of the activities of the agency is in the same author's *O desenvolvimento econômico do São Francisco — Um planejamento regional em marcha*, Comissão do Vale do São Francisco, Rio, 1961.

[2] CVSF, *Antecedentes.*

[3] Art. 56 of Decree No. 2599 of Sept. 13, 1958.

[4] Getúlio Vargas, "Mensagem No. 377-A ao Congresso Nacional, de 29 de outubro de 1951," *Contribuição do govêrno do Presidente Getúlio Vargas à recuperação econômica do vale do São Francisco*, Rio, 1951, p. 6.

[5] The dam is "2,700 meters long and about 70 meters high from the foundation, will impound some 120 billion cubic meters of water creating a reservoir 150 kilometers long in the main river and 60 kilometers up the Paraopeba, its main tributary in the upper basin." "The Três Marias Project in Brazil," *Water Power*, Dec. 1959, p. 4.

increases considerably the firm power capacity of the river at the Paulo Afonso Falls.

Since the Três Marias project was clearly a crucial step toward realization of CVSF's objectives, it was agreed that the commission would devote part of its resources to financing the Três Marias Dam. However, the planning and organization of this project was not entrusted to the commission but to a far more efficient and less "political" organization, the state power utility company Centrais Elétricas de Minas Gerais (CEMIG).[1] In other words, the commission became a mere sleeping partner in an operation that was central to its task. That it had failed to develop the managerial and technical competence to undertake or direct complex engineering tasks had been strongly intimated by the fact that a small dam it had built in conjunction with locks at Sobradinho to improve conditions of navigation collapsed in December 1954, fifteen days after its inauguration.[2]

Thus, the CVSF, created in 1948 as a brave new agency that would transform the São Francisco Valley, has led a wholly undistinguished existence. Unlike DNOCS, it has not had its ups and downs, nor has it been responsible for large-scale failures or rocked by scandals; instead, it fitted itself quickly and snugly into the existing bureaucratic structure, intent perhaps mainly on not being noticed. The history of the CVSF proves conclusively that, in regional development, the organ does not necessarily create the function.

There is no more striking and instructive contrast than between the activities, styles and performances of the CVSF and the agency which was created almost simultaneously with it and as its complement: the Hydroelectric Company of the São Francisco (CHESF). Both were creatures of the federal government; even though CHESF was set up as a so-called "mixed company," the federal government always owned the overwhelming majority of the share capital. The difference in performance cannot

---

[1] The CVSF was to finance all hydraulic structures, including not only the dam itself but also the intake and the penstocks, while CEMIG was financially responsible for power generation and transmission; but "CEMIG would be responsible for the supervision of design and construction of all works." ("The Três Marias Project," *Water Power*, p. 15.)

[2] "Brésil, Rapport de la mission française dans la vallée du rio São Francisco," April–May 1956, Mission Française d'Assistance Technique, Ministère des Affaires Etrangères, Paris, mimeo., p. 99. The dam has never been rebuilt even though the locks were completed.

therefore be explained by supposed differences between private and public ownership and management. Rather it must be understood in terms of differences in the nature of the tasks tackled by the two agencies. The task of the CVSF was enormous and amorphous: to promote the settlement and development of a river basin of 630,000 square kilometers; that of CHESF was precise, limited and strongly structured: to develop the hydroelectric power potential of the Paulo Afonso Falls of the same river. The task of the CVSF could be divided into numerous mutually independent subtasks, each of which could claim a high priority rating; many of these subtasks did not require a high degree of technical competence (e.g., building of a country road), and it was toward them that the CVSF, sure of its earmarked funds, irresistibly gravitated. The task of the CHESF, on the other hand, consisted of one highly interdependent group of operations which was centered around complex engineering problems and whose sequence was virtually imposed by the nature of the task itself.

Methods of financing provide another contrast. The CVSF had an assured source of income which in (poor) theory might have given it the ability to plan ahead but in fact designated it as a choice target for appetites on the loose. The CHESF was started with a wholly insufficient capital of 400 million cruzeiros and repeatedly had to request supplementary resources from the national and state governments, from Brazil's National Bank for Economic Development (BNDE), and also from the International Bank for Reconstruction and Development (loan of $15 million in 1950) and the Export-Import Bank (loan of $15 million in 1957). Each time it had to prove the soundness of its projects, progress and management.

These basic differences in the nature of the task and in methods of financing had no doubt much to do with differences in organization and performance. From its organization in 1948[1] CHESF was directed by a technically highly qualified nucleus of engineers and Army officers who stayed on for many years and kept the agency "out of politics," while the CVSF was dominated by "clientelistic" political forces from the start and soon lost some of the more qualified technicians it at first attracted.[2]

The performance of CHESF has been widely acclaimed as remarkable in all essential respects: engineering, planning and management. Planned

---

[1] The organization of a mixed company was authorized by Decree Law No. 8031 of Oct. 3, 1945 and the company was established on March 15, 1948.

[2] Lucas Lopes, a highly respected engineer-economist-executive who was principally responsible for the 1950 "General Plan" of the CVSF, soon left with a number of associates for the more promising CEMIG, the Minas Gerais utility company which resembles CHESF in many ways.

and designed by Brazilian engineers who overcame a series of complex technical problems, the first stage of the hydroelectric station was completed virtually on schedule in 1955 when three 60,000-kilowatt generating units went into operation.[1] The principal markets for the energy generated at the plant were at first the cities of Recife and Salvador, both about 400 kilometers away from the Paulo Afonso Falls; both cities had up to then been supplied inadequately by thermal plants. CHESF was in charge of long-distance transmission as well as generation of energy and was skillful in synchronizing these two tasks. With the rapid increase in electric power consumption (in large part because the old thermal generating units were discarded) CHESF drew up timely plans for continuous expansion of its operations. A second powerhouse provides for progressive installation of six units of 65,000 kilowatts, two of which went on line in 1961. Since 1955 the transmission network has been continually extended throughout the Northeast. The potential, experience and prestige of the utility company resulted during the fifties in other agencies traditionally operating in the Northeastern region (the Ministry of Agriculture, DNOCS, CVSF and Petrobrás) turning over to it their responsibilities in the field of electric power generation and transmission, along with the resources they had earmarked for this purpose.[2]

An efficient agency in an underdeveloped — i.e., generally inefficient — region will frequently find that it is being burdened with a variety of more or less extraneous tasks (sometimes until its level of efficiency comes down to the average). Something of this sort could be observed in the case of CHESF. The company had to run its affairs from the beginning along a completely paternalistic pattern. At the main construction site, where it built a small town, it not only had to provide all housing and access roads but also was entrusted with administering schools, hospitals and all community services. Moreover, in 1959 it was put in charge of managing the power company supplying the city of Fortaleza, which had long suffered from shortages and breakdowns.[3] It thus broke definitely out of the 450-

---

[1] U.S. engineering firms were brought in at various times, but purely as consultants. The most difficult technical problem encountered in course of construction — the building and closing of a cofferdam in the main arm of the river — was successfully solved through a device which was proposed by the technical director of the Company and opposed by U.S. consulting engineers. Cf. Companhia Hidro Elétrica do São Francisco (CHESF), *Relatório*, 1954, p. 3.

[2] Cf. CHESF, *Relatório de 1959.*

[3] SUDENE, *Primeiro plano diretor de desenvolvimento do Nordeste*, Recife, 1960, mimeo., Vol. I, p. 95.

kilometer perimeter (centered at Paulo Afonso) within which it was supposed to confine its activity according to its original statute. Its present
plans, worked out in collaboration with SUDENE, call for several transmission lines reaching to points, such as Natal and Fortaleza, beyond this
perimeter. Secure in its unassailable position, CHESF was alone among
the agencies operating in the Northeast in lending full cooperation to
SUDENE when that fledgling agency, which is supposed to coordinate development planning in the Northeast, worked out its first "Guiding Plan"
in 1960.

The 1951 Drought and the Bank of the Northeast

The initiatives of the forties, as we have seen, were none too closely related to the traditional core problem of the Northeast — the drought. It
would be incorrect to say that CVSF and CHESF were created expressly
to attack this problem from a new angle; an essentially autonomous interest had arisen in exploring the potential of the São Francisco Valley. So far
as this interest was at all related to the traditional centers of the periodic
droughts to the north, it arose as much from the feeling that enough had
been done for these areas as from the intent of helping them indirectly.

Nevertheless, the creation of the two new agencies had a considerable
influence on the evolution of the problem in the stormy fifties: CHESF, by
creating the tangible prospect of cheap and abundant power for all of the
Northeast, pointed toward industrialization as a major new avenue of development, while the integrated-river-basin-development ambitions of
CVSF suggested that the time-honored attack on the droughts through
dam construction and the like was somewhat passé.

These factors combined with others to produce a novel reaction when a
new drought — the first major one in nineteen years — hit the Northeast in
1951: the creation of an entirely new agency, the Bank of the Northeast of
Brazil (BNB). Vargas, who had won the Presidential elections of 1950
twenty years after his first accession to power, once again was confronted
upon assuming office with an emergency situation in the Northeast; again
large numbers of flagelados had to be given relief or temporary work on
highways and dams. This fact alone might have induced the President to
try out some other course of action than the one he and José Américo had
pushed so strongly and so hopefully in the thirties and which apparently
had not achieved its objective.

The active discussions which were held once again in the press, among experts, in Congress and in the President's office show a considerable shift of emphasis. This time hardly any voices were raised in favor of bigger and better dams and other public works in the drought area. On the contrary, the government's concentration on dams was now criticized as a narrow, strictly engineering approach to the problem which ought to be replaced by a real plan of broader economic and social planning for the Polygon. Much was made of the semantic debating point that a "positive" approach ought to replace the negative "fight-against-the-drought" approach which had held sway until then.

An important factor in the new situation was the deterioration and loss of prestige which DNOCS had suffered since its heyday in the thirties. Many of its best engineers had left for better-paying jobs in the fast-developing Center-South. The remaining professional staff consisted, in the words of a report to President Vargas by his economic adviser, Rômulo de Almeida, of "those with a spirit of sacrifice, those who don't have the courage to try a new career and those who have other 'compensations.' "[1] As a result of the last element the agency had lost its good name by 1952. Charges of irregularities in emergency relief operations were brought against it and a parliamentary commission of inquiry was appointed in 1951.[2] A large portion of the government's emergency relief and public works program was handed over, in part for this reason, to an *ad hoc* temporary agency, the Commission of Supply for the Northeast (CAN), which functioned for six months in 1951–52. The above-cited report to President Vargas recommended "removal of suspect chiefs and technicians . . . with the intention of restoring a climate of confidence (this applies to technicians with fortunes of doubtful origin, with relatives among the contractors, and to those who permitted inhuman exploitation of . . . the flagelados)."[3]

Once DNOCS was tainted with these gross faults, the government could either attempt to root them out and to regenerate the agency (it had done so in the 1930's even though the process of deterioration had not then gone nearly as far) or try out a new approach. It chose the latter course, partly because it was politically easier but partly also because real doubts had arisen about the value of the "hydraulic solution" through dams and irrigation which had thus far monopolized the attention of the authorities.

---

[1] Banco do Nordeste do Brasil, *Planejamento do combate às sêcas,* Nov. 1953, p. 15.
[2] Comissão de Abastecimento do Nordeste (CAN), *O que foi a CAN,* Rio, 1953, p. 56.
[3] BNB, *Planejamento,* p. 21.

Guimarães Duque, the widely respected Director of DNOCS's Agro-Industrial Service, had found, by comparing a given watershed's volume of rainfall with the amount of water accumulated in its reservoir, that one square kilometer (100 hectares) of terrain yields 73,000 cubic meters of dammed-up water; in turn he found that this is almost exactly the volume of water needed to irrigate one hectare of land for one year.[1] Thus, because of evaporation on the way to the reservoir, in the reservoir, and on the way to the irrigated land as well as for other reasons, the efficiency of rainfall utilization through the dam-irrigation complex is quite low (one per cent). Given the original Polygon area of 800,000 square kilometers, this calculation sets the irrigable area at a maximum of 800,000 hectares, quite apart from topographical difficulties, which, of course, cut deeply into this theoretical ceiling. Perhaps, then, seduced by the *boqueirões* and giving in to the engineers' mania for concrete structures, had one been chasing a will o' the wisp during all these years of açude-building?

This conclusion was not drawn by Guimarães Duque, who saw many uses for the reservoirs,[2] but it was intimated by the well-known Brazilian geographer Hilgard O'Reilly Sternberg in a series of articles, the first and most extensive one dating from 1951.[3] There he exposed the weaknesses and limitations of the solutions to the drought problem through hydraulic works and through reforestation, which is clearly impractical in a densely settled region. Instead, he came out in favor of a third "conservationist" solution which would conserve both soil and water. Through contour plowing and other practices, it would aim at "retaining the rainwater where it falls," particularly in those upstream zones climatically and agriculturally well endowed for feeding plant life and for simply storing water.

While these ideas are far from easy to put into practice for subsistence agriculture, the usual culprit of erosion, they served to focus attention and applause on the so-called *lavouras sêcas*, i.e., agricultural activities utilizing the native species which were well adapted to the climate, made the best of whatever rain fell, and which, being pluriennial, helped to fix the

---

[1] Guimarães Duque, *Solo e água*, p. 229. The first edition of Duque's book appeared in 1949.

[2] Cf. p. 42, note 2.

[3] Hilgard O'Reilly Sternberg, "Aspectos da sêca de 1951, no Ceará," *Revista Brasileira de Geografia*, July–Sept. 1951. Also "Geography's Contribution to the Better Use of Resources" in *The Future of Arid Lands*, American Association for the Advancement of Science, Washington, D. C., 1956; "Não existe ainda um plano para o problema das sêcas," *Boletim Geográfico*, May–June 1958; and "Sêca: causas e soluções," *Boletim Geográfico*, Sept.–Oct. 1958. The first article reproduces Sternberg's statement before a special Congressional Committee of Inquiry and has been widely quoted.

soil. It happens that almost all these xerophilous plants are for non-food, industrial uses; in the order of their importance in the Northeast they are the mocó cotton tree, the carnauba palm, the oiticica tree as well as various cactus plants among which the caroà and the palma forrageira have predominated.[1] In addition, since the mid-forties, a sisal "boom" has made the Northeast a substantial factor in the world supply of that fiber. Since all these plants take several years to mature, their cultivation requires capital and can be stimulated by making credit available.[2]

The 1952 decision to fight the drought by founding a regional banking institution is now becoming less of a puzzle. It had its direct origin in a visit to the drought area by Vargas' Minister of Finance, Horacio Lafer, in April 1951. In the brief report to the President in which Lafer suggested, upon his return, the creation of the new Bank, the need for credit to expand and improve the mocó cotton cultivation was stressed in some detail. The importance of the other xerophilous plants was mentioned in a subsequent memorandum.[3] To some extent, then, creation of the Bank was a response to a real shift in the analysis of the area's problems. Another reason for establishing the Bank, occasionally mentioned by the government and the press, was the then imminent completion of the Paulo Afonso hydroelectric station and the need for ample credit if the resultant industrial opportunities were to be fully utilized.[4]

Yet it must be observed that the idea of establishing a regional Bank, however rational it may have been or may look in retrospect, was entirely the invention, one might almost say the brainstorm, of Minister Lafer, himself not a Northeasterner, but a São Paulo banker and industrialist. Creation of the Bank had not been preceded by any public clamor for such an institution nor had there been, as in the case of the Inspetoria or even the São Francisco Valley Commission, partial measures leading up to it.[5] Essentially the ingredients of this decision were: (1) a new drought and a

---

[1] Guimarães Duque, *Solo e água*, Chapter III.

[2] The oiticica tree is not cultivated; it grows wild and its nuts are collected and sold to factories that extract and refine their drying oil.

[3] Banco do Nordeste, *Origens*, Borsoi, Rio, 1958, pp. 3–4 and 38–39. Lafer argued that the deplorable practice of growing ordinary annual cotton in between the mocó cotton trees which results in a deterioration of the mocó seed is in part due to the lack of credit.

[4] *Ibid.*, pp. 146, 172, 433.

[5] Of course, once the Bank was proposed, a large majority of commentators expatiated on the long-standing need for just that initiative. The Finance Commission of the Chamber of Deputies even went so far as to state in its report on the Bank project that lack of credit was a worse evil in the Northeast than lack of rain since the latter was only intermittent whereas the former was permanent! *Ibid.*, p. 277.

consequent impulse to "do something"; (2) loss of faith in the efficacy of the previous methods of reacting because of loss of confidence both in the "engineering approach" and in the agency (DNOCS) that had it in its charge.

The rapid search for an alternative course of action fastened on a banking institution, first, for the trivial reason that the originator of the idea came from the world of finance; second, because *fomento* corporations and development banks were then becoming fashionable and were being founded in increasing numbers in the less developed countries;[1] thirdly, and perhaps most important, some funds were readily available as a result of the above-noted provision of the 1946 Constitution which had ordered a portion of the country's revenue to be set aside for "drought defense." One-third of the total 3 per cent of fiscal revenue reserved for this purpose by the Constitution was to be earmarked in a special fund to be available in case of a drought emergency, but could meanwhile be in part invested in loans to farmers and industrialists of the drought area.[2] The purpose had been to create an emergency fund whose resources would either be kept liquid or could be readily mobilized through rediscounting, a far handier financing device than new budgetary appropriations. A subsequent law regulating this article provided for this "Special Drought Fund" to be established within the Bank of Brazil, which has a nation-wide net of branches and engages in all forms of lending.[3] Hence, all that needed to be done to endow a special regional bank with a regular flow of resources was to lift this Fund, or its loanable portion, from the Bank of Brazil.[4]

Even though rather indirectly this time, the Constitution had once again stimulated or facilitated institution building and, once again, funds were available to an agency before it had a clear concept of its task. The results bear a certain likeness to those we noted in discussing the São Francisco Valley Commission.

However, one significant difference from previous agencies sponsored by the federal authorities and established to improve the Northeastern region's economy should be noted first. While DNOCS, CVSF and CHESF

---

[1] The examples of Chile, Venezuela and Mexico are specifically quoted in the Presidential Message. *Ibid.*, p. 155.

[2] Cf. Art. 198, paragraph 2 of the 1946 Constitution; DNOCS has claims on the remaining 2 per cent.

[3] Law No. 1004 of Dec. 24, 1949. Eighty per cent of the Fund was to be available for lending operations.

[4] Cf. Art. 4 and 6 of Law No. 1649 of July 19, 1952 and Art. 1 of Decree No. 33,643 of Aug. 24, 1953. As a result of these texts the Bank's claim on the Treasury amount *grosso modo* to an annual deposit of 0.8 per cent of the expected Federal revenue.

all had their headquarters in Rio de Janeiro, it was decided that the new agency's head office should be located within the Northeast.[1] In fact, one of the principal and probably most valid arguments used by the government to justify the establishment of a new bank which would duplicate to some extent the existing facilities of the Bank of Brazil was the attraction invariably exercised by the "big branch offices of the South" on Bank of Brazil personnel.[2] A person joining a bank entirely restricted to the Northeast would be prepared to make his career in the region and would be more likely to become involved with its problems and aspirations. For this purpose it was important that the Bank's head office also be located in the region. After considerable debate and lobbying the choice fell on Fortaleza as the capital of the state most affected by the droughts. Unfortunately, Fortaleza was also, in spite of a population of 400,000, the least industrialized and least "pushy" of the three major Northeastern cities. It had remained primarily a regional administrative and distribution center, and the subsequent performance of the Bank has sometimes been traced to this character of the city within which its top management functioned.

What was this performance and what was it expected to be at its creation? The original emphasis was, as we have seen, on credit for agriculture, particularly for mocó cotton and other xerophilous plants. But as the project took shape, a host of other functions were added. In the end, there was hardly any banking operation which the Bank was not authorized to undertake, but the parliamentary debates on its establishment, the press comments and the permissible operations listed in the basic statute leave little doubt that it was expected to act primarily as an investment and development bank, with some emphasis on slow-yielding agricultural improvements.[3] Once established, however, the Bank found that the only way of committing funds rapidly was by investing heavily in short-term operations. Just as a considerable part of the resources of the São Francisco Valley Commission was used up in taking over functions from governmental agencies operating in the region, so the BNB spent a good part of its funds on short-term credit operations that had been rather satisfactorily attended to by the Northeastern branches of the Bank of Brazil. The theory was that the Bank would slowly expand its development and investment operations

---

[1] José Américo intended to move DNOCS's headquarters to the Northeast (cf. José Américo, *Ciclo revolucionario*, pp. 380 ff.) and CVSF was also originally scheduled to have its head office within the São Francisco River Valley (*Antecedentes*, p. 315), but the arguments for, and the attractions of, Rio won out.

[2] BNB, *Origens*, p. 152.

[3] BNB, *Origens, passim,* and Art. 8 of Law No. 1649 of 1952.

and that, as these expanded, the so-called "general credit" portfolio of short-term commercial credit would be made to shrink. Actually, however, this "general credit" has dominated the Bank's lending throughout the fifties: at the end of 1959 it still amounted to three-quarters of total outstanding loans.[1] While the Bank explained, frequently and correctly, in its annual reports and on other occasions that this credit aided both industry and agriculture directly and indirectly, the reality of the Bank's preponderant role as a commercial bank rather clashed with the image that had originally been built up of a developmental institution which would initiate new productive activities in industry and agriculture. The specialized agricultural and industrial credit sections of the Bank were set up for these purposes, but were slow in expanding the volume of their operations, largely because of difficulties encountered in locating industrial investment opportunities or in organizing supervised agricultural credit to operators of small farms.

A number of officials and economists who had joined the Bank in its early days left it after a few years, in part because of disappointment over the routine character of the bulk of its operations. The feeling that the Bank needed to be nudged into adopting a more active developmental policy is clearly reflected in an article of the law setting up SUDENE which orders the Bank to devote at least 70 per cent of its resources to specialized medium- and long-term credits.[2]

A sudden expansion in such specialized operations was achieved from 1960 on and in two years, from the end of 1959 to the end of 1961, their share in the Bank's total lending increased from one quarter to one half.[3] By that time, it was hard to establish to what extent the sudden change in the composition of the Bank's portfolio was the fruition of its own past efforts or the response to outside pressures and newly emerging opportunities.

It must be granted that the origin of the Bank contributed powerfully to

---

[1] See BNB, *Relatório de 1960*, p. 91. In the Bank's annual reports its lending is broken down by purpose and here it appears that, in 1959 for example, lending to agriculture and industry amounted to as much as 70 per cent of the total (BNB, *Relatório de 1959*, p. 90). However, this presentation results from the allocation of the short-term "general credit" portfolio to various economic activities and appears to be an effort at window-dressing, especially since the more routine breakdown according to agricultural, industrial and general portfolio, which corresponds to the administrative subdivision of the Bank's operations, was discontinued with the 1957 annual report and was resumed only with the report for 1960 when a sharp increase in non-short-term lending was achieved.

[2] Art. 28 of Law No. 3692 of Dec. 15, 1959.

[3] BNB, *Relatório de 1960*, p. 91, and *Relatório de 1961*, p. 29.

confusion about its task. On the one hand, the Bank's principal source of funds consisted of the Treasury deposits which were originally (i.e., in the Constitution) meant to be readily available at any time to fight drought emergencies; on the other, the Bank was expected to perform as a development institution making longer-term and risky investments. A regulatory decree attempted to resolve this conflict by ordering the Bank to invest at least 30 per cent of Treasury deposits in short-term paper.[1] (Actually, as we have seen, short-term paper occupied a far higher percentage in the Bank's portfolio.) The SUDENE law reversed this provision by stipulating that at least 70 per cent of the Bank's resources were to be held in paper other than short-term. One reason for this change was the government's decision not to use its "deposits" at the BNB for emergency expenditures during the drought of 1958, largely because needs caused by the drought far exceeded what the Bank could make available. This experience strongly intimated that the Bank should have no qualms about "immobilizing" government deposits through developmental loans in the future.

While there are some similarities between the São Francisco Valley Commission and the Bank of the Northeast, the differences between the two agencies are even greater. Unlike the CVSF, the BNB did not become the fief of one political group. During the 1952 Congressional debates opponents of the Bank made dire predictions that it would become "a source of jobs, of rewards for partisan dedication, a weapon of corruption and demoralization."[2] Yet the number of purely political appointees appears to have been quite limited. The Bank made considerable efforts to form a qualified staff, strove to improve its performance, and was receptive to new tasks. It requested and used to advantage foreign experts, made available by technical assistance agencies. An economic research office functioned within the Bank with a certain amount of autonomy and made a series of highly useful monographic studies of the region.

Thus, the Bank's performance is curiously ambiguous. It went to considerable pains to avoid taking on the look of an old-fashioned government agency with its well-known parasitic and clientelistic features. It is even possible that it was drawn for this very reason to concentrate on short-term finance: the discounting of warehouse receipts can proceed on the basis of more clear-cut, objective criteria than the financing of new industrial ventures, which allows considerably greater room for the play of pressures, influences, connections — and for malpractices.

---

[1] Art. 2 of Decree No. 33,643 of Aug. 24, 1953.
[2] BNB, *Origens,* p. 318.

Perhaps the fear of becoming infected with the clientelistic virus which had proved so damaging to the reputation and efficacy, though not to the existence, of DNOCS and CVSF was a determining factor in shaping the Bank's cautious, "reasonable," and almost ostentatiously virtuous personality and actions, with its emphasis on personnel training and management science.

Going about its task in a methodical way the Bank introduced a healthy new element of orderliness and reliability into the Northeastern scene, but it lacked the willingness to plunge ahead and the crusading reform spirit that were once again felt to be required when a new and unusually severe drought calamity hit the Northeast in 1958.

The 1958 Drought and the Creation of SUDENE

When the creation of the Bank of the Northeast was justified by the need to shift from the "narrow engineering" approach to a "broad economic" one, the meaning of this phrase was not much more than: what else can we do for the drought region besides building dams and roads? The government showed itself aware of the fact that it had set up something of an empty box; for in its 1951 message to Congress, it presented the Bank as an advance installment on a comprehensive plan that was to follow.[1] This clearly implied that, for the time being, there was no such plan.

But empty boxes are usually set up where there is a reasonable prospect that they will be filled. The feeling that the economist may have something to contribute to the analysis and solution of the problem of the Northeast was a natural one to arise in the early fifties when the art or technique of development planning came to be widely practiced. A decisive tool which permits the art to take on some characteristics of a technique is national income accounting. Estimates of Brazil's national income and product became available in 1951–52.[2] The regional breakdown of the national totals made it possible to give a quantitative expression to what was evident to any observer of the Brazilian economic scene: the disparity in levels of economic development between the Center-South and the Northeast was wide and it had been widening particularly since the nineteen thirties when industrialization centered in the São Paulo–Rio–Belo

---

[1] BNB, *Origens*, pp. 149–150.
[2] Cf. *Revista Brasileira de Economia* of September 1951. The first breakdown by states was published for the years 1947 to 1951 in the December 1952 issue of the same journal.

Horizonte triangle gathered the impressive momentum which has been steadily maintained up to the present day. The newly gained ability to summarize the disparity by one simple set of figures — per capita income estimates by states and regions — served to dramatize the situation and thereby stimulated the desire to remedy it.

Every serious study of the Northeast had from now on as its starting point a presentation of this gap and a discussion of the ways of narrowing it.[1] This approach implied several important differences from the previous focus of attention. First, instead of searching primarily for means to prevent or cushion the impact of the drought, i.e., instead of attempting to prevent a sudden catastrophic decline in income during the drought years, attention was now directed to means of stepping up income generation on a steady basis. Secondly, the data on comparative economic development of the Center-South and the Northeast made it possible to base a claim for national attention and regular subsidy to the Northeast, not on the occasional natural calamity which hits the region periodically, but on the permanent disparity in per capita incomes that had been revealed. Or, if the principle of regional "fair shares" should be deemed unconvincing, it became possible to inquire whether the disparity was due merely to superior resource endowment, entrepreneurship, thrift and virtue of the Center-South, or perhaps also to transfers of income and wealth from the Northeast to the South, i.e., to "exploitation": findings to this effect would clearly strengthen the case for a reverse flow. Finally, since the national income statistics were broken down by states, the data for the Northeastern region included the humid coastal strip and the coastal cities as well as the drought zone. Therefore, the improvement of agriculture in the zone traditionally dominated by sugar cane plantations and the strengthening of economic activity in the cities through industrialization were brought automatically within the horizon of the search.

Some of these themes can be found already in the report written for President Vargas in 1953 by his economic adviser, Rômulo de Almeida.[2] During that same year the technique of deriving investment requirements through the combined use of national income estimates and an assumed

---

[1] H. W. Singer, *Economic Development of North-Eastern Brazil*, U. N. Technical Assistance Program, Nov. 19, 1953, reissued Aug. 15, 1956, pp. 4 ff.; Stefan H. Robock, *Economic Development in North-East Brazil*, U. N. Technical Assistance Program, Feb. 7, 1957, pp. 12, 13; Furtado Report, pp. 13–22. Even the bishops of the Northeast would soon preface their program of action by a reference to the famous disparity; see p. 85, note 1.

[2] BNB, *Planejamento*, pp. 7 ff.

capital-output ratio was displayed with considerable virtuosity by a well-known economist, Hans Singer, who had surveyed the Northeast as a United Nations Technical Assistance expert.[1] Yet it took several more years and the drought of 1958 for a full-fledged regional economic development program to take shape. Thus we arrive at the last act of our story.

THE DROUGHT, DNOCS AND THE 1958 ELECTIONS

The 1958 drought was one of the most severe ever experienced by the Northeast, particularly in Ceará, Paraíba and Rio Grande do Norte. It brought in its wake a record exodus from the rural areas where crops were failing. Up to that time, the largest number of workers on the DNOCS payroll had been 200,000 during the 1932 drought. During the 1951 and 1953 emergencies, about 60,000 were recorded. In 1958 DNOCS employed at times almost 400,000 persons and the Federal Highway Bureau another 140,000.[2] In addition, there was much emigration, particularly toward Brasília; it is quite possible that the new capital would not have been completed with such speed had it not been for the spontaneous influx of Northeastern labor. At the worst time of the disaster, which hit with un-expected suddenness, an airlift of foodstuffs, medicines and other relief shipments was organized. Considerable attention was also given to the procurement of picks, shovels, wheelbarrows and similar items which per-mitted the useful employment of the flagelados.[3] With a number of large dams under construction, DNOCS could put additional labor to good use, and many smaller private dams, to which DNOCS contributed, as usual, half the construction cost, were also built. The record number of refugees that had to be assisted in 1958 has since been frequently quoted as incon-trovertible proof that all the previous attacks on the drought had been ut-terly futile. There is some injustice in this verdict since the size of the exodus was due in part at least to the density of the road network and to the advances in motor transportation. Nobody any longer stayed behind to die of starvation, thirst or root poisoning. Thus what was taken as evidence

---

[1] Singer calculated what he called backlog investment for the Northeast, i.e., in one of his definitions, the investment needed to bring the per capita income level of the Northeast up to the national average. He then showed the increase over the current rate of investment that would be required if the backlog were to be eliminated within a period of, say, twenty years. To carry out such estimates Singer assumed a constant capital-output ratio of 2.4. In his specific comments on various forms of investment he stressed, however, the extent to which better utilization of existing capital is possible.

[2] DNOCS, *Boletim*, Nov. 1959, pp. 126–127.

[3] Presidência da República, *Síntese Cronológica, Rio, 1958*, 1959, Vol. I, p. 232. See also DNOCS, *Boletim*, Nov. 1959, pp. 120–121.

of failure could also be interpreted as a partial success of one type of remedial action; but it clearly was the kind of partial success that increases
rather than dampens the pressures for further action.

In any event, the first reaction to the emergency was the usual one:
emergency credits were voted, relief shipments were sent and as many of
the flagelados as possible were employed on "work fronts." The principal
agency in all of these activities was once again DNOCS; neither the São
Francisco Valley Commission nor the Bank of the Northeast had much to
contribute at this testing time. Not many changes had come to DNOCS
since its rather decadent state had been pointed out to President Vargas
in 1953. The housecleaning then recommended had not taken place, turnover of personnel remained high (the agency had five different directors
within the five-year period 1951–1956), and morale low.[1]

Nevertheless, the droughts of 1951 and 1953 had increased DNOCS's
resources and had permitted it to activate construction work which was
continued in subsequent years. Thus it came about that from 1956 on a
substantial number of new public dams were completed. With the additional push given by the 1958 drought, total capacity of the public reservoirs rose at the end of 1959 to 6.4 billion cubic meters from 2.7 billion at
the end of 1953. Moreover, in 1958, with so much manpower available and
with the desire to do something spectacular for the suffering Northeast,
President Kubitschek ordered work resumed on construction of the largest
reservoir project of the whole Northeastern area, the 4 billion cubic meter
Orós Dam, key to the irrigation of perhaps 100,000 hectares in the Jaguaribe Valley. An old aspiration of the region and especially of Ceará State,
the dam had been among Epitacio Pessôa's ill-fated projects, but had not
been tackled since. With modern earth-moving machinery and plenty of
manpower, the construction of the dam was not expected to present major
difficulties and Kubitschek ordered it completed by 1960, his last year of
office. Together with other dams in construction, the total reservoir capacity was thus expected to double once again — to 12 million cubic meters —
by 1960–61. DNOCS also developed considerable activity in its other programs, such as lending assistance in the construction of small private reservoirs, using the public reservoirs for electric power generation, well perforation and water supply. Moreover, even though responsibility for road

---

[1] "During the [last] Administration of President Vargas DNOCS was in an entirely
disorganized state because of the abandon to which it was relegated during the previous Administration." Lúcio Meira, Minister of Public Works under Kubitschek, in a
Senate speech on the 1958 drought reprinted in DNOCS, *Boletim*, Nov. 1958, p. 20.

construction in the Northeast had passed increasingly to a separate agency established in 1945, the Departamento Nacional de Estradas de Rodagem or DNER, Kubitschek entrusted DNOCS in 1958 with construction of a highway more than 1,000 miles long from Fortaleza to Brasília.

Thus, flush with appropriations and activity, and ostensibly enjoying the President's confidence, DNOCS in 1958 could be taken by the outside observer for a purposeful and efficient agency that was recovering the vigor of its heydays under Arrojado Lisboa or José Américo. Yet no drought had ever proved so devastating for public confidence in the agency as that of 1958. Once large-scale relief operations were under way, cases of corrupt handling of funds, of padding of payrolls and similar fraudulent practices were soon widely reported. In part these practices had their origin in the difficulties DNOCS experienced in having budgetary appropriations translated into actual cash in the face of the obstacles and delays dutifully interposed by a hard-pressed Minister of Finance (who came, moreover, from the Center-South). As a result, DNOCS had to borrow funds and supplies in the Northeast and in this process became closely tied to the local drought profiteers.

Kubitschek acknowledged the reports of graft and corruption in June 1958 in a letter to his Minister of Public Works, Lúcio Meira, and requested him to have such abuses stamped out.[1] The Minister himself presented a lengthy defense in Congress in July.[2] It was around this time that the term *industriais da sêca,* i.e., "drought industrialists" or drought profiteers, gained currency. It acquired a wide range of meanings, being applied equally to vulgar thieves of relief shipments or corrupt officials in charge of emergency public works and to those who had merely adjusted their economic activity to the dry climate and thus had acquired a vested interest in it and were hostile to irrigation; this was said to be the case, for example, with some owners of carnauba palm plantations — which thrive under dry conditions — in the irrigable part of the Jaguaribe Valley. DNOCS's connection with the "drought industry" was considered to be manifold: some of the outright abuses were the work of agency officials; there was much political influence at work in determining where dams and roads were to be built; and DNOCS favored the larger economic operators by taking over their labor as soon as a drought struck.[3]

---

[1] *Síntese Cronológica 1958,* Vol. I, p. 302.

[2] Reprinted with subsequent discussion in DNOCS, *Boletim,* Nov. 1958, pp. 4–70.

[3] Antônio Callado, *Os industriais da sêca e os 'Galileus' de Pernambuco,* Edit. Civilização Brasileira, Rio, 1960, p. 29.

Thus the stepped-up activity and considerable financial resources of DNOCS actually boomeranged against the prestige of the agency. This was so particularly because of the role the agency came to play in the October 1958 elections during which a number of important governorships were at stake. In a situation full of political and social tensions the power DNOCS held over jobs and lives was frequently used to the hilt by the hard-pressed ruling political groups. The following is quoted from an analysis of the elections which appeared in a highly regarded political science journal:

> In Ceará, DNOCS and DNER became powerful forces of electoral corruption. The drought undoubtedly became a political instrument. Those who did not work for the PSD or PTB were denied assistance. In these Federal agencies relief funds were advanced up to the end of October to those who promised to vote for the candidates of these parties.[1]

In spite of these attempts at influencing the outcome of the vote, the entrenched political groups and power-holders suffered serious defeats in several Northeastern states. Among the most severe setbacks for the government were the victories in the important states of Pernambuco and Bahia of Cid Sampaio and Juracy Magalhães, both members of the UDN, the strongest opposition party. While in Pernambuco the governmental candidate retained the majority of the sertão vote, Cid Sampaio won a narrow majority through strong support in the coastal areas and the city of Recife.[2] Although he was a refinery owner and industrialist, his "reform" platform brought him the endorsement of the Communist Party and the "peasant leagues" which had sprung up since 1955 in some localities of the interior with a variety of demands.

The public outcry over the malpractices and the electoral setback suf-

---

[1] Abelardo F. Montenegro, "Tentativa de interpretação das eleições de 1958 no Ceará," *Revista Brasileira de Estudos Políticos*, April 1960, pp. 43–44. Some further details on the techniques of influencing voting behavior, quoted from another source, are given on p. 46 of this article: "The first stage of the fraudulent voting procedure is largely characterized . . . by the abuses of party discrimination in hiring and granting relief payments. The second stage is marked by the direct action of the engineers . . . and of the pretorian guard of DNOCS created especially to frighten the voters of the sertão, whether or not they are connected with DNOCS. The third stage takes place during the 48 hours preceding the election and is marked by the following events: (a) utilization of 300 DNOCS trucks to provide transportation to all voters within the radius of Federal projects; (b) the buying of election officials; (c) the direct purchase of votes by means of money and new clothing; (d) intimidation by engineers: who does not vote properly will lose his job."

[2] The elections are analyzed in considerable detail by Glaucio Veiga *et al.*, "Geografia electoral de Pernambuco" in *Revista Brasileira de Estudos Políticos*, April 1960, pp. 50–85.

fered caused President Kubitschek to send a member of his military staff, Colonel Orlando Ramagem, on a confidential mission to the Northeast. In his report, which was kept confidential by Kubitschek but released to the public by President Quadros in February 1961,[1] the Colonel painted an extraordinarily vivid, somber and alarming picture of economic, social and administrative disintegration and concluded by stating that the crisis endangered Brazil's national security. To raise in this fashion the specter of separatism or revolution was by no means new.[2] But under the double impact of natural and political calamity the credibility of the threat had suddenly increased.

THE FURTADO REPORT

The crisis atmosphere generated by the drought emergency, electoral defeat and discredit of DNOCS made the government receptive to the idea of a radically new attack. Already in May 1958 Kubitschek had re-

[1] Cf. *Correio da Manhã*, Rio, Feb. 11, 1961.

[2] Innumerable statements have been made over the years to the effect that the Northeastern problem must be resolved in the interests of national unity and integration. It is much harder to find evidence of an actual concern that national unity could be lost should the problem *not* be solved. This is a matter of the greatest sensitivity to every country, but perhaps particularly to Brazil, which has taken much pride in contrasting its success in preserving the political unity of Portuguese America with the corresponding failure of Spanish America. The following quotations take us from a comment on the 1900 drought to the time of the establishment of SUDENE, in 1959:

"Our immense country is usually considered as a geographic unit . . . We live under the same law . . . [Yet] in the life of a nation the geographic differences become more pronounced as economic development takes place . . . While the feeling of national unity is sufficiently strong today to prevent the growth of any idea of dismemberment — it may well be that tomorrow this will no longer be the case. A strategy must be drafted now which is capable of neutralizing the effects of anthropogeographic differences and which will be able to prevent the clash of two opposing economic interests — in the last analysis, the problem of the droughts is therefore the very problem of maintenance of our national unity." Miguel Arrojado Lisboa, "O problema das sêcas," 1913 Conference reprinted in *Boletim*, Nov. 1959, p. 55.

Describing the drought of 1900, one observer wrote: "The central government, deaf to the demands of those who died of hunger, smallpox and other consequences of the drought . . . gave rise to a profound movement of revolt so intense and understandable in this climate of misery that a desire for secession became more apparent every day." Thomaz Pompeu Sobrinho, "As seccas do Nordeste (1825–1925)," *Livro do Nordeste*, Diário de Pernambuco, Recife, 1925, p. 51.

"There is not . . . a single Brazilian who does not recoil indignantly at the idea of the dismemberment of our beautiful fatherland. Only a person entirely deprived of political sense could think even for a single instant of creating prejudices and antagonisms between the main geographic regions of the Republic. But it is up to the central government to make its own action more equitable and thus to eliminate the motives for grievances . . ." 1917 Speech of Epitacio Pessôa, printed in his *Pela verdade*, F. Alves, Rio, 1925, p. 314.

"The 'solution' to the problem of the drought by depopulating the region subject to the disaster was shown to be unacceptable . . . Politically, if such a measure were to be

quested the assistance of the President of the National Bank for Economic Development in his search for new "solutions" for the Northeast.[1]

Since its foundation in 1952 this official bank had become an active center of investment and development planning for such strategic sectors of the economy as electric power, transportation and basic industry. The Bank became the natural home for a group of economists who were convinced that economic development required various "structural" changes and needed to be firmly guided by the state, but by a new, managerial and efficient state rather than the old, clientelistic, parasitic "Cartorial State."[2] The intellectual leader of this group was Celso Furtado, an outstandingly able economist and economic historian, who, after some years with the Economic Commission for Latin America and a year at the University of Cambridge, returned to Brazil in 1958 as a director of the Bank. A native of the Northeast, he had already given much thought to the region's problems[3] and, on the basis of data collected by an otherwise rather sluggish working group on the Northeast that had functioned within the Bank since 1956, he prepared in record time a basic analysis of the region's problems and a plan for action which were submitted to Kubitschek early in 1959.

The Furtado Report, published as an official paper under the title "A Policy of Economic Development for the Northeast," is a highly skillful document.[4] In its opening paragraph, statistics are used effectively to convey overwhelming moral indignation:

---

advanced by the present representatives of the people, it could result in the breaking up of the Federal tie because of the violent reaction of that fourth of the Nation's population which lives in the states subject to periodic droughts." Confidential report to Vargas by his economic adviser, Rômulo de Almeida, later released as *Planejamento do combate às sêcas*, Banco do Nordeste do Brasil, Nov. 1953, p. 5, mimeo.

"National economic disequilibrium brings with it the menace of separatism as well as that of social unrest. We shall not be able to avert these dangers as long as there are in our country regions of wealth on the one hand and of misery on the other; of hunger and of luxury; of neglect and of privilege." Josué de Castro, *Documentário do Nordeste*, Edit. Brasilense, São Paulo, 1957, p. 114.

Finally, in 1959, Celso Furtado described at some length the conditions under which "in Brazil, a country of considerable geographic area, the formation of antagonistic regional groups could endanger the most important achievement of our past: our national unity." *A Operação Nordeste*, Textos Brasileiros de Economia, Rio, 1959, p. 16.

[1] *Síntese Cronológica 1958*, Vol. I, p. 291.

[2] See, for these concepts, Hélio Jaguaribe, *O nacionalismo na atualidade brasileira*, Instituto Superior de Estudos Brasileiros, Rio, 1958, pp. 37 ff.

[3] See Lecture VII on "regional disparity" in a series of lectures by Furtado in 1957 on Brazil's economic development, published by the Instituto Superior de Estudos Brasileiros in 1958 under the title *Perspectivas da economia brasileira*.

[4] A useful, more informal companion volume is Celso Furtado, *A Operação Nordeste*, Instituto Superior de Estudos Brasileiros, Rio, 1959, which consists of a lecture and subsequent discussions (to be referred to as *Openo*).

> The disparity of income levels between the Northeast and the Center-South is without any doubt the most serious problem to be faced in the present stage of our national economic development. This disparity is greater than that between Brazil's Center-South and the industrial countries of Western Europe. The Brazilian Northeast stands out in the Western Hemisphere as the most extended and populous zone where income per capita is below 100 dollars. The average income of the Northeasterner is less than one-third that of the inhabitant of the Center-South. Since income is far more concentrated in the Northeast, the disparity in living levels of the mass of the population is even greater.[1]

In explaining the disparity Furtado calls attention to various institutional mechanisms which in recent years have, unwittingly, contributed to the pauperization of the Northeastern region. In particular he shows that the Northeast, which is a net importer from the Center-South but a net exporter to foreign markets, has seen its terms of trade deteriorate as inflation at home was combined with an overvalued exchange rate, so that the cruzeiro yield of the Northeast's exports did not rise as fast as the cost of its imports. Moreover, with foreign currency values and hence the price of imported capital goods being low, a special stimulus to industrial modernization was imparted to areas where wages were comparatively high, i.e., to the Center-South; in any event, the system of exchange allocation permitted the dynamic and influential Center-South to capture more than its share of the common foreign exchange "pot."[2]

In the face of this picture of disparity, injustice and institutional bias, what did Furtado propose? In tune with the times and the dominant phraseology, he advocated a comprehensive development program embracing infrastructure, agriculture, industry and so on. Significantly, however, and in spite of his ECLA past, his principal interest did not lie in the "technique of programming," i.e., in evaluating the volume of investment required for a certain rate of per capita income growth and its apportionment among various economic sectors. His was a particularly difficult task since it could clearly not be limited to programming the kind of investment that usually provides fairly plausible and useful outlets for available public investment funds in development programs. Decades of public works during and between droughts had provided the Northeast with considerable, if poorly articulated and maintained, highway mileage, and

---

[1] Furtado Report, p. 7.
[2] Ibid., pp. 22–31 and 56–58.

abundant electric power supplies were due to become increasingly available as a result of the scheduled expansion in the generating capacity and transmission lines of CHESF. Hence, Furtado had to do better than take the easy course of merely planning for "infrastructure" investment and hoping for economic progress to graft itself onto it.

He did. His principal interest was in fact to develop a few specific lines of economic policy for the Northeast. His basic reasoning ran as follows: The Northeast needs a new dynamic center of growth and reinvestment. What growth has taken place has been due to export crops such as sugar and cotton, and the free access to the rapidly growing Center-South makes the appearance of new dynamic "exports" conceivable. But to take advantage of these opportunities, the Northeast must rely on its principal comparative advantage, i.e., cheap labor. The full use of this "asset" through industrialization à la Japan or Puerto Rico is held back by the high price of food. The latter is caused in turn by a supply of locally grown foodstuffs which is not only unstable because of the droughts but is inadequate, inelastic, and burdened with unnecessarily high transport and other costs, even in normal times.

The general nature of this diagnosis then permitted Furtado to strike out in three directions. First, of course, the dammed-up waters of the açudes should be used for irrigation in such a way that the irrigated basins will become a permanent food reserve for the sertão; secondly, organized colonization should be undertaken in the humid lands and tropical rain forests of the neighboring State of Maranhão; and, finally, to the east, a major effort should be made at achieving better utilization of the richest lands of the Northeast, the zona da mata along the Atlantic Coast.

With every one of these proposals, Furtado raised — and meant to raise — highly delicate issues. We have already discussed the strange failure of DNOCS to utilize at all adequately the waters stored in the public reservoirs for irrigation. As in the thirties, dams were built in the fifties without prior expropriation of the irrigable lands downstream, in spite of the admonitions not only of the agronomists but also of at least one long-time DNOCS Director.[1] A number of bills had been introduced in Congress to regulate the matter, but none had been voted. This excuse is not satisfactory, however, for existing legislation appears to grant the DNOCS ade-

---

[1] See p. 45.

quate authority.[1] A real difficulty was the prescription of the 1946 Constitution which permitted expropriation for reasons of public utility or "social interest," but required "prior and just compensation in money," i.e., presumably in cash.[2] DNOCS was always reluctant to spend its money on buying land; there was much local pressure for building this or that dam; and dam building remained the principal concern of engineers and directors, who had come to measure their performance by the number of cubic meters of storage capacity added to the total during their tenure. Moreover, the DNOCS bureaucracy had developed close ties over the years with the political and economic power-holders of the Northeast and was not at all anxious to antagonize more of the large or small landowners than absolutely necessary; the agency found it hard enough to expropriate and pay those who owned the sometimes sizable and valuable lands which were to be submerged by the new reservoirs.

Thus DNOCS continued to concentrate on the popular, spectacular and non-controversial job of building dams and to neglect the grubby, conflict-ridden job of irrigation. However, with dam construction spurting in the fifties almost spontaneously because of the droughts and consequent abundance of flagelado labor, the policy of storing more and more water without putting it to use took on an increasingly absurd, if not sinister, look; and the point was being reached where an increase in storage capacity without any change in the area under irrigation resulted in a loss rather than a gain of prestige for DNOCS. Taking advantage of this situation, Furtado affirmed the need to recast DNOCS's investment policy, and, following the reform proposals of Trindade, Guimarães Duque and others, advocated expropriation and controlled cultivation in the irrigable basins.[3]

Striking out in other directions, Furtado addressed himself to the issue of land use in the zona da mata. There has been no lack of lament over the appropriation of the best lands of the Northeast for the cultivation of sugar in large estates, to the exclusion of almost any other crop or eco-

---

[1] Article 19 of the Inspetoria Statute issued by Decree No. 19,726 of Feb. 20, 1931 declares: "The irrigable lands shall be expropriated when this shall be judged necessary for the establishment of agricultural settlements, or for construction and service purposes, or when their owners fail to cultivate them in accordance with the special instructions issued by the Inspetoria. The amount of the indemnity shall be determined by the value the lands had before the projects relating to the reservoir and the consequent irrigation system were approved."

[2] Art. 141, para. 16.

[3] Furtado Report, pp. 71–72; also Furtado, *Openo*, pp. 63 ff., and CODENO, *Projeto de lei de irrigação*, Recife, Sept. 1959, mimeo.

nomic activity. In the thirties Gilberto Freyre described exhaustively and almost lovingly the physiological, social and cultural faults of what he called *monocultura latifundiária e escravocrata* (the monoculture-latifundio-slavery complex).[1] Somewhat later Josué de Castro wrote in his *Geography of Hunger:*

> The Brazilian northeast . . . once had one of the few really fertile tropical soils. It had a climate favorable to agriculture, and it was originally covered with a forest growth extremely rich in fruit trees. Today, the all-absorbing, self-destructive sugar industry has stripped all the available land and covered it completely with sugar cane; as a result, this is one of the starvation areas of the continent. The failure to grow fruits, greens and vegetables, or to raise cattle in the region, has created an extremely difficult food problem in an area where diversified farming could produce an infinite variety of foods.[2]

This passage is representative of the thinking of a large group of writers and social or agrarian reformers who regard the existing pattern of land use as an abominable survival of colonial exploitation and slavery. By applying to it the term of opprobrium *monocultura latifundiária* they convey their opinion that the patterns of land use and of ownership are indissolubly linked and that it is hopeless to attempt to change the one without the other. In particular, change of land use can come only with the revolutionary break-up of the latifundio.

In spite of some feelings of uneasiness,[3] the plantation and refinery owners stoutly defended the status quo, pointing out that a land use pattern that has lasted for four hundred years and resisted innumerable crises cannot be wrong, that erosion threatens if cane is replaced by annual crops, that work on the plantations in the zona da mata is finely integrated with that in the nearby agreste zone where cropping ends just before the cane-cutting season opens, and that the large investments in refinery installations must be safeguarded.

It was perhaps this total and unbridgeable conflict that barred the issue from the realm of practical policy-making, except for numerous unen-

---

[1] Cf. in particular his *Nordeste,* 2nd ed., José Olympio, Rio, 1951.
[2] Little Brown and Co., Boston, 1952, pp. 97–98.
[3] H. W. Hutchinson in *Village and Plantation Life in Northeastern Brazil* quotes the diary of a plantation owner, a woman, who is deeply disturbed about her own tradition-bound behavior, but writes, "We lack the courage to stop planting sugar cane and to plant corn or coffee or anything else." Univ. of Washington Press, Seattle, 1957, p. 62.

forced official edicts which, from the 17th century on, ordered landowners to set aside stated percentages of their lands for growing foodstuffs.[1]

The proposal made by Furtado was an attempt to break through the deadlock and the immobility of opposing contentions and interests. It took cognizance of the interests of the *usineiros* (refinery owners) by making a diversion of some land to non-cane uses conditional upon the attainment of increased cane yields through irrigation elsewhere. When questioned about the need for land reform, Furtado was noncommittal and reserved.[2] Clearly his principal objective was to draw firmly into the discussion, for the first time, the question of land use in the Northeast's richest lands. In this way the debate was widened, a new front on which successes could be achieved was discovered and an additional *raison d'être* for a new agency was established.

Essentially the same can be said about another part of Furtado's program: colonization of the tropical rain forest lands of Maranhão. This again was an emotion-laden issue, because of the traditional reluctance of Northeastern spokesmen to conceive of emigration even as a partial solution; and indeed, during the parliamentary debates, this part of the program was attacked as though it were an effort at re-enacting the ill-equipped and ill-fated expeditions of flagelados to the Amazon region during the 1877–79 and 1899 droughts. Actually the Furtado Report could point out that spontaneous emigration to Maranhão was already in progress. The emigrants were ordinarily drifting into isolated subsistence farming. It was clearly desirable to help them become efficient food producers who would remain in commercial contact with their native provinces.

THE BATTLE FOR SUDENE

The competence, freshness and vigor of the Furtado Report and the promise of its many new approaches made a profound impression. Its inescapable conclusion was not only that agencies working in the Northeast had failed to carry out satisfactorily their assigned tasks, but that a number of crucial policy lines had yet to be tried and mapped out. Thus began to take shape a new agency, which was to have the dual task of coordinating existing agencies and of initiating entirely new policies under its own authority. A projected law creating a Superintendency for the Develop-

---

[1] Manuel Diégues Júnior, *População e açúcar no Nordeste do Brasil,* Comissão Nacional de Alimentação, Rio, 1954, pp. 158–161.
[2] Furtado, *Openo,* pp. 62–63.

ment of the Northeast (SUDENE) was sent to Congress in February 1959. As an interim measure, President Kubitschek instituted at the same time a Development Council for the Northeast (CODENO). It had purely advisory and research functions, but its existence provided Furtado and his group with an invaluable base of operations until December when the bill was passed.[1]

Almost everything about the SUDENE law was "different" and vastly ambitious. It was a new federal agency, but on its Board of Directors sat not only representatives of the economic ministries and of such to-be-co-ordinated agencies as DNOCS, CVSF and BNB, but also the Governors of the nine Northeastern states. By including in its planning area the State of Maranhão, SUDENE widened the traditional definition of the North-east.[2] Recife, in many respects a regional capital for the Northeast, was picked as the new agency's headquarters. The Superintendent was given wide authority to hire and fire.

The powers of SUDENE were sweeping. It was to supplement and to exercise full control over the activities and investments of agencies already operating in the Northeast, particularly DNOCS and CVSF, and to some extent also BNB. It was also to be principally responsible for public works and relief operations during drought emergencies.

Finally, the resources granted directly to SUDENE were substantial. The time-honored device of earmarking a portion of total fiscal revenue was used once again — SUDENE was to receive 2 per cent over and above the 3 per cent of DNOCS, 1 per cent of CVSF and 0.8 per cent of BNB — but actual appropriation was to be subject to the approval by the Congress of a Guiding Plan with detailed breakdown of proposed expenditures. In addition, the agency was to administer a number of novel privileges granted to the Northeast, such as income tax and customs duty exemptions for industries and certain preferential treatments in the allocation of for-eign exchange and in the application of preferential exchange rates. The law thus contains a variety of instruments for the promotion of industries in the Northeast except the one most used in the industrialization of back-ward areas: protective tariffs. The use of this instrument is both taboo and impractical in the industrialization of *regions* as opposed to *countries*. It is

---

[1] CODENO was established by Decree No. 45,445 of Feb. 20, 1959, and SUDENE by Law No. 3692 of Dec. 15, 1959.

[2] This can be interpreted as an attempt to take the sting out of the proposed coloni-zation of the Maranhão rain forest areas by people from the sertão. Annexation of Maranhão to the Northeast would convert into internal migration what had previously been decried as emigration.

in part for this reason that the industrialization of regions requires more direct intervention of official agencies through subsidies and direct management and capitalization than might otherwise be necessary.

Altogether, then, the proposed SUDENE law represented the most ambitious effort thus far made in and for the Northeast. Furtado's program, in general, justified its claim to represent comprehensive planning by proposing solutions to both old and new problems and by forging links between problems that up to then had led independent lives. The problems of the semi-arid Northeast had been dealt with either by building roads and dams in the central drought area (Inspetoria-DNOCS) or by attempting to develop the resources of the São Francisco Valley (CVSF and CHESF), and later again by giving greater attention to the xerophilous plants and to industrialization (BNB). Now all of these alternative attacks were to be pursued simultaneously, and agricultural diversification of the zona da mata and colonization of Maranhão were added to the list.

The feat of combining all these tasks and of stating that the solution of each was conditioned on that of the others is less remarkable perhaps as an intellectual breakthrough — a number of authorities had previously advocated a "composite" solution — than as a tactical gamble that paid off. Frequently the linking of two reforms is not good politics since it is likely to multiply the number of the reformer's enemies. One interest group may well favor a reform that does not hurt it as being "in the general interest" *provided* it is not linked with the one that hurts. But in a serious crisis, this group may feel, out of conviction or for public relations reasons, that it should not oppose the passage of the measure it favors even if this means passage of the one it opposes; and in such a situation it may therefore be good politics to link a variety of controversial issues together, through a "comprehensive" plan.[1]

A related situation is also highly relevant to the SUDENE case. Linking several issues is good politics when opponents of measure A are so discredited in public opinion that opponents of measure B would rather vote for B than be seen in the company of the opponents of A. It is then clearly advantageous, if there is a majority for A, to tie B to A. When agreement is widespread that one particularly glaring abuse needs to be corrected, a favorable opportunity exists for slipping in reform measures on which opinion is far less crystallized. This may have been Furtado's tactic when he raised the issue of diversification of zona da mata agriculture along

---

[1] This point is discussed in some detail in the Digression following Chapter 5.

with that of DNOCS operations. The sugar interests were not particularly anxious to stand up and be counted alongside the DNOCS forces; also, of course, they may have discounted the ability of SUDENE to succeed in doing away with cane monoculture, a reform undertaking in which everyone since the Dutch occupiers of Recife in the seventeenth century had failed.

These considerations bring out what was most characteristic of Furtado's proposals as compared to previous efforts. They were based not only on new ways and means of channeling aid and investment funds *into* the Northeast, but they advocated, or could be expected to lead to, changes in power positions of administrative agencies and social groups *within* the Northeast. Unlike most previous proposals, therefore, they could not count on the undivided support of all Northeastern forces, and, in fact, the passing of the SUDENE law required a major fight and involved a number of subtle bargains and alliances.

Thus far, the various agencies in the Northeast had coexisted peacefully. The coming in of the São Francisco Valley Commission had relieved rather than annoyed DNOCS, and the Bank of the Northeast even cooperated with DNOCS in one area, the financing of private, small reservoirs. But SUDENE, with its pretension to coordinate and reorient on-going activities, was something quite different. The idea was bound to be resisted strongly by existing agencies, particularly by DNOCS, which was the principal target of "coordination" and was at the same time both financially powerful and politically well entrenched. In addition to its local support, DNOCS was still a subdivision of the Ministry of Public Works, and the Minister, always an influential member of the Cabinet, happened to be in 1959 Ernani de Amaral Peixoto, son-in-law of Getúlio Vargas and head of the PSD, Kubitschek's Social Democratic Party, while the brother of the Director of DNOCS was an influential PSD deputy.

The issue was joined in the summer and fall of 1959 when the SUDENE law was before Congress. In September 1959 the respected Rio newspaper *Correio da Manhã* published a series of reports from the Northeast by the journalist and writer Antônio Callado which denounced many abuses of the "drought industrialists" and of DNOCS.[1] In addition to their sensational accusations against the DNOCS hierarchy, the articles also extolled the achievements of the peasant leagues, which had taken over some

---

[1] These reports were later republished, together with some of the ensuing "letters to the editor," parliamentary speeches and so on, in Antônio Callado, *Os industriais da sêca e os 'Galileus' de Pernambuco.*

poorly run properties in the zona da mata. Callado's views were widely held to be close to those of SUDENE. The DNOCS forces fought back hard. They engaged in character assassination of Furtado, whom they accused of a number of crimes, such as being an economic theorist, a Communist, etc.[1] They opposed the motion that the SUDENE bill be discussed on an "urgent" basis and introduced an amendment exempting DNOCS from SUDENE's authority. At the same time, to forestall debate on an irrigation bill sent to Congress by Kubitschek and proposed by the interim agency CODENO, they brought to a vote and passed a far less stringent irrigation bill which had long lain dormant in Congress. This bill was vetoed by Kubitschek, but meanwhile the CODENO project was not acted upon. While this incident showed the strength of the DNOCS forces, they were beaten on the principal issue: the SUDENE bill was passed without crippling amendments. The bill became law on December 15th, when Kubitschek signed it and hailed it in a speech which contained the following significant passage:

> I well know the interests that are being antagonized by initiatives such as the Operation Northeast . . . I am obliged to confess with sadness that I encountered obstacles to the new development policy for the Northeast because the very state of chronic wretchedness of a part of the Brazilian family gave rise to a kind of industry, i.e., to the permanent establishment of avid *clientelas* whose interests are frequently in conflict with the real needs of the people.[2]

This victory of SUDENE and Furtado was a remarkable feat. Furtado's technicianship, however brilliantly demonstrated in his report, certainly would not have been able to assure it had he not also been a good politician. What was the nature of the coalition that he put together?

First, he had the support of the newly elected "reform" governors who had come to power precisely over the opposition of the DNOCS-supported official political forces. In fact, the presence of the governors on CODENO's and SUDENE's Board of Directors, a unique feature for a *federal* agency, was a direct outcome of the 1958 elections and of the separatist fears they had stirred. Since the ministries that were sitting on the Board were usually represented in meetings at Recife, not by the Minister himself, but by some subordinate official, the state governors outranked the other Board members. With the states being granted some influence within SUDENE, administration of aid to the Northeast had come full cir-

---

[1] *Diário do Congresso Nacional*, Rio, Vol. 14, Seção II, Nov. 12, 1959, p. 2777.
[2] Juscelino Kubitschek, *Discursos, 1959*, Rio, Imprensa Nacional, 1960, pp. 350–351.

cle. Before the establishment of the Inspetoria in 1909 relief funds had usually been handed over to the state authorities for distribution, and the faults and abuses encountered with this system led to the establishment of federal agencies, such as the Inspetoria and CVSF. By 1959 it had become clear that the federal label was by no means sufficient to protect an agency from contamination by local politics and *clientelismo*. By bringing the state governors into the board of SUDENE the chances of the new agency preserving a non-partisan, professional "purity" were enhanced; for the governors, as elected officials, were bound to be representative of widely different power groups and parties. In other words, the likelihood that the agency would become a mere appendage — or shock-brigade — of some political machine was reduced by the composition of its Board of Directors.

Did Furtado's projects receive indirect help from peasant unrest that flared up in the Northeast during the second half of the fifties? Much has been written in the United States since 1960 about the peasant leagues, their leader Francisco Julião, his ominous travels to China and Cuba. The United States' sudden overwhelming interest in the Northeast and its readiness to support SUDENE are no doubt motivated in part by the threat of a Castro-type movement among the landless peasants and the impoverished slum dwellers of Recife and other coastal cities.[1] But in the Northeast sporadic outbreaks of unrest, violence, banditry and religious fanaticism have been so common, especially in the sertão,[2] that little attention

---

[1] The United States public was first informed in detail about the grave emergency existing in the Northeast in two front-page *New York Times* articles by Tad Szulc on October 31 and November 1, 1960. These alarm-ringing articles put the Northeast "on the map" for the United States public. Thereafter the Northeast became a compulsory stopover point for touring dignitaries and journalists. In the summer of 1961 President Kennedy received Furtado in the White House and indicated U. S. support for the SUDENE program.

[2] Ever since colonial times groups of Northeasterners have pitted themselves against the central authorities of the country when an attractive opportunity arose. While the wealthy, politically powerful families ruled in their fiefs as independent lords, the sertanejos eagerly rallied to powerful protectors, religious leaders and bandit chiefs.

In the middle of the nineteenth century João Santos, an obscure nordestino, led a group of men in quest of a hidden treasure in the State of Pernambuco. His followers engaged in numerous excesses, including human sacrifice. After fierce resistance they were overwhelmed by governmental forces.

In the last two decades of the century, Antônio Conselheiro (the Counselor) became known for his miracles and led worshippers to the encampment of Canudos where he reigned supreme for a number of years. The fierce successive campaigns of governmental forces and the final wiping out of the population of Canudos in 1897 is the subject of *Os sertões*, Euclides da Cunha's famous epic.

At the beginning of the twentieth century, Padre Cícero of Juazeiro became the ab-was paid to the peasant leagues in their early years. The origin and adoption of the SUDENE project can be traced to concern over them only to a very minor extent.

In 1955 peasant cultivators discontinued rent payments to the owner of one latifundio in the agreste zone of Pernambuco and successfully resisted threatened expulsion from the lands they occupied by forming a league and engaging in litigation; in subsequent years peasant leagues pursuing various grievances sprang up in several other localities. As already mentioned, these leagues had a certain influence on the election of Cid Sampaio as "reform" Governor of Pernambuco in 1958; and inasmuch as Sampaio was, together with Governor Juracy Magalhães of Bahia, one of the staunchest advocates of SUDENE, at least in 1959, a link exists between the peasant leagues and the establishment of Furtado's agency. Little more than this indirect connection can be established. The formation and spread of the peasant leagues may have entered to some extent into the awareness of danger and emergency which no doubt was an essential element of the situation that produced SUDENE. But the 1958 drought, and the discredit it brought to existing agencies, the generalized discontent shown by the 1958 elections and the purported separatist dangers appear to have loomed larger in the consciousness of the government and the members of Congress than any fears of generalized agrarian unrest or revolution.

---

solute ruler of a large group in Ceará. His political influence in the sertão was powerful and was fully acknowledged by state and Federal authorities.

All of these religious leaders enlisted fanatically devoted followers who were ready and eager to defy the "forces of order." This exclusive allegiance to a chief and to an own code of law was also characteristic of the *cangaço*, i.e., backland gang banditry, the Brazilian equivalent of Indian and Burmese dacoity. Famous bandit-leaders wielded authority over a numerous following. Lampeão, the best known of the Northeastern bandit chiefs, played important political roles during the first decades of our century; he is reputed to have helped Padre Cícero in 1914 with his drive on the state capital of Fortaleza and to have joined forces with the government in the twenties to resist the march of the Prestes Column.

It was with Prestes that seditious activities in the interior took on for the first time an outspokenly political flavor. With his eight hundred men, Prestes, a rebellious Army captain who later became Brazil's leading Communist, criss-crossed Brazil's interior, including much of the Northeast, from 1925 to 1927. His feat in eluding and fighting off the army units that were sent to exterminate his column would have been impossible had his message of justice for the poor and of punishment for the rich and powerful in their coastal cities not awakened wide sympathies.

Cf. T. Lynn Smith, *Brazil*, Louisiana State University Press, Baton Rouge, 1954, pp. 607–615; Djacir Menezes, *O outro Nordeste*, Livraria Olympio Edit., Rio, 1937, pp. 187–188; Robert J. Alexander, *Communism in Latin America*, Rutgers University Press, New Brunswick, 1957, pp. 100–101, and "Brazilian 'Tenentismo,'" *Hispanic American Historical Review*, May 1956.

One further indirect link should, however, be noted. Furtado's projects did receive the active support of Catholic bishops in the Northeast, who had displayed considerable initiative in ameliorating economic and social conditions on the local level. In 1956, after a special first Conference of the Northeastern Bishops in Campina Grande, they received the sanction of the Presidency for undertaking various community projects by means of *ad hoc* working groups consisting of representatives of different agencies, such as DNOCS, CVSF and BNB. These working groups concerned themselves with projects ranging from water supply and purification for the sertão town of Campina Grande to better utilization of certain reservoirs and agricultural resettlement projects. A second Conference of the Bishops in mid–1959 enthusiastically endorsed "Operation Northeast,"[1] and the Archbishop of Rio, Dom Helder Câmara, himself a Northeasterner, provided most valuable support for the SUDENE proposal. It may well be that this active support of the bishops for Furtado's avant-garde reform group was forthcoming because the Church, with its permanent and close contacts with the people, sensed that a mood of defiance — evidenced by the outcropping of peasant leagues — was spreading in the Northeast.

Finally, a decisive margin of political support in Congress was forthcoming from São Paulo and other Southern Congressmen to whom the SUDENE project held out the hope that the large-scale funds traditionally appropriated for the Northeast would no longer be spent just on relief, or, worse, "wasted" and "stolen" as, according to widespread opinion, was the case under existing arrangements. Furtado's project had more supporters in São Paulo and Rio than among the Fortaleza and Recife elites — for the good reason, already known to us, that it proposed as much, or more, social and economic reform as aid. It is likely that if the Northeast were a sovereign country, so reform-minded an agency as SUDENE could not

---

[1] The following is the text of the first two resolutions voted by the Conference:

"1. We declare that we the Bishops of the Holy Church are well aware of the supranatural and eternal mission that God has entrusted to us; but since it is necessary to work not only with pure spirits but also with human beings of flesh and soul, one must not forget that all that touches the flesh has its repercussion on the soul; we therefore affirm our right and duty to concern ourselves with the temporal well being of the people, especially in the underdeveloped region of the Northeast.

"Coming from us this interest shows our love for the flock which has been entrusted to us by Providence and helps save the social peace which has been endangered by the serious economic disparity between our region and the Center-South.

"2. We rejoice at the emergence of Operation Northeast, which applies within our frontiers the principles guiding the timely and auspicious Operation Pan-America whose flag has been unfurled by Brazil." *Segundo encontro dos bispos do Nordeste* (Natal, May 1959), Presidência de República, Rio, 1959, pp. 17–18.

have been established without a major socio-political upheaval. But, as shown also by the history of land reform in Southern Italy and desegregation in the United States South, the chances of evolutionary change in a non-sovereign region are better than in a sovereign country for a very simple reason: the required decisions can be taken by enlisting behind them political forces from other regions.

The final riddle is why Kubitschek gave his full support to SUDENE when he must have realized that, in the Northeast at least, SUDENE was being pushed by his political enemies or at least by the enemies of some of his political allies. One reason was that "Operation Northeast," as he liked to call it, corresponded exactly to the image he wanted to project of his administration's work and style. It fitted his passion for modernity and rounded out the other large-scale, ambitious "operations" that he had previously launched, such as the "Target Program" (*Programa de Metas*), "Operation Panamerica" and construction of Brasília. Brasília arose out of the President's aspiration to escape from the climatic and political miasma of Rio to a new, clean, cool and well-planned capital. Similarly, with SUDENE he affirmed his faith in a group of young, idealistic, nationalistic, yet "technical," planner-knights who would slay the dragons of inefficiency, larceny and backwardness which had so long cast their evil spell over the Northeast.

Yet, with Brasília being Kubitschek's principal concern during the last two years of his administration, it may appear even more strange that, in the midst of a severe inflationary spiral, he should have taken on another project that would presumably call for large-scale expenditures. But here we must invoke the complementarity effect of certain public expenditures which we noted earlier. To secure financing for the ever-mounting needs of Brasília, the President had to promise support for projects elsewhere. Moreover, when in mid–1959 he pushed aside those of his advisers who counseled a change in fiscal policy and an accommodation with the International Monetary Fund, he found that it was precisely Furtado's group of economists that remained at his side during this serious crisis and he was consequently in debt to them.

SUDENE IN ACTION

Still, Kubitschek could not go all the way against the interests of his own party in the Northeast. He did appoint Furtado as Superintendent after the SUDENE law had been approved, yet he did not touch the top management of DNOCS which had waged so bitter a fight against both

SUDENE and Furtado. This was not too serious for SUDENE since throughout 1960, an election year, the fledgling agency was busy enough building up its staff and laying its plans. The awkward "coexistence" was resolved only a year later when Jânio Quadros appointed a former member of the SUDENE staff as Director of DNOCS. Quadros in general gave SUDENE his full support, confirmed Furtado as Director of the agency and, in one of his many surprise moves, even raised him to Cabinet rank. Quadros thus made it clear that the anti-inflationary policies on which he laid great stress did not contemplate retrenchment in the Northeast, and he thereby broke with the tradition — established by earlier economy-minded Presidents such as Campos Salles and Bernardes — that the Northeast is "expendable" and is made to bear the brunt of "sound money" policies. Development of the Northeast had finally become a task of the highest priority for Brazil, one which would be vigorously prosecuted even during the periodic attempts at fiscal austerity.

After Quadros resigned in September 1961 Vice-President Goulart assumed the Presidency with Tancredo Neves in the newly created position of Prime Minister. Goulart, as the leader of the PTB, and Neves, as one of the leaders of the PSD, had close political ties with the forces in the Northeast which had done battle against SUDENE and for the continued autonomy of DNOCS. For a few days in the turmoil of the political crisis these forces were hopeful of dislodging Furtado from his position, but they were unsuccessful, largely because of the momentum and public support that SUDENE had gathered by then.

This public support became impressively evident at the end of the year when the final passage of the first large-scale appropriations bill for SUDENE was discussed in the Congress. In mid–1960, the agency had submitted its Guiding Plan with a detailed breakdown of proposed expenditures, but Congressional action had been delayed time and again, so that in 1960–61 the agency had just enough funds to build up its staff, elaborate projects and start some on an experimental scale. When the House-approved Guiding Plan finally came before the Senate in November 1961, the Northeastern elements led by Senator Argemiro Figuereido, who had originally opposed SUDENE and particularly the extension of its authority over DNOCS, attempted a comeback and introduced several crippling or harassing amendments to the Plan which largely restored the autonomy of DNOCS and forbade SUDENE to engage in any activity potentially involving the movement of Northeasterners from one state to another.

The acceptance by the Senate of these amendments led to an unexpectedly strong reaction. SUDENE was not only defended, as in 1959, by the most respected Rio and São Paulo daily papers, but was now able to marshal considerable "grass-roots" support in the Northeast. Protests against the Senate's action and petitions to the House to restore the original version of the law[1] were sent by a wide variety of groups — Governors, Chamber of Commerce, Small Farmers Federation — and the movement was climaxed on December 6, 1961 by a one-hour strike of all commercial and industrial establishments and a mass meeting in Recife. University students were perhaps the most active group in the protest movement — the only one, to the writer's knowledge, ever to have been staged in support of an economic planning agency! The House of Representatives took due notice of the popular feelings and overrode the Senate's version within a few days.

Supplied with a budgetary appropriation of 9.9 billion cruzeiros, about $30 million, SUDENE was now definitively in business. While the Guiding Plan was being voted on in the Congress, a special United States mission arrived in the Northeast to consider possible forms of U.S. assistance for the area under the Alliance for Progress. The mission, which had been agreed upon during a visit Furtado made to Washington in August 1961, reported early in 1962, and a framework agreement providing for a United States contribution of $131 million over a four-year period was signed in April 1962. The first specific commitment of United States funds was arranged in June 1962, for the construction of aqueducts in Northeastern towns. In the meantime, the Inter-American Development Bank had already made several loans to the Northeast, in agreement with SUDENE.

With Brazil passing through a serious and protracted institutional crisis at precisely the time when the United States became ready for a substantial increase in its economic assistance to Latin America under the Alliance for Progress, SUDENE offered by far the most solid anchor for the newly contemplated programs. Thanks to SUDENE, the Northeast had turned from the stepchild into the pet of both national and international development agencies.

Considerable activity was also displayed in promoting industrial expansion and modernization. One of the most important incentives of the original SUDENE law — the ability to obtain foreign exchange at a preferential

---

[1] According to the Brazilian Constitution, any change introduced by the Senate into a House-approved bill can be eliminated by a majority of the House voting a second time in favor of the original version.

rate for machinery imports destined to Northeastern industries — was annulled by the unification of exchange rates carried out under the exchange reform of Jânio Quadros, but the 1961 law approving the Guiding Plan of SUDENE contained a novel and powerful incentive: any enterprise could reduce its income tax liability by 50 per cent by investing an amount equal to twice the amount saved on taxes in a Northeastern industry approved by SUDENE.[1] Even before this extraordinary privilege came into force, industrialization made considerable strides in the Northeast during 1960–61. This development must be credited not only to SUDENE but also to the activities of the Bank of the Northeast and to the promotional efforts of special development agencies which were operating at the state level in Recife (Pernambuco) and Salvador (Bahia).

As a result of its various successes, the immediate operations of SU-DENE were now concentrated in such "non-antagonistic" fields as highway transportation, electric power and water supply, and industrialization. But the agency was not ready to forsake the reform star under which it had been born. True, even in agriculture it gave primary attention to Maranhão colonization and to experiments on the *taboleiro,* an extensive and hitherto neglected land area between the Atlantic coast and the zona da mata which it was hoped to convert to agricultural uses through the application of fertilizers.

Nevertheless, Furtado asserted on several occasions that fundamental changes in land use and institutions, in the sertão and in the zona da mata, remained one of the principal developmental tasks for the Northeast.[2] For the time being, SUDENE did not undertake any concrete move in this direction, both because it had its hands full and because it was waiting for a national agrarian reform law to be passed by the Congress. But the mere existence of an increasingly powerful agency known to advocate deep changes in traditional power and property relationships and operating right out of Recife, the capital of the zona da mata and traditional

---

[1] Art. 34 of Law No. 3995 of December 14, 1961 and Regulatory Decree No. 1166 of June 8, 1962. The somewhat ambiguous language of the original article seemed to permit a 100 per cent tax saving, and the reduction to 50 per cent through the regulatory decree is said to have been the result of pressures exerted by Northeastern industrialists who were afraid of a sudden rush to the Northeast of branch plants set up by São Paulo industries to take advantage of the tax privilege.

[2] See, e.g., his lecture, delivered at São Paulo in January 1962, "Considerações sôbre a pré-revolução brasileira," *Revista Brasileira de Ciências Sociais,* March 1962, pp. 40–56, in which he argued that the evolution of Brazil into a modern integrated society was held back, with consequent dangers of violent revolution, by the rigidity of its agrarian structure. A revised version of this lecture, under the title "Brazil: What Kind of Revolution?," has appeared in *Foreign Affairs,* April 1963, pp. 526–535.

preserve of its cane planters and refiners, led to increasingly violent attacks and accusations. The fact that Furtado had among his close collaborators various professionals who had more or less pronounced left-wing sympathies made it easy to present SUDENE as Communist-infiltrated and its plans as Communist-inspired.[1]

Furtado himself made it repeatedly clear that while he was, as he said, "a man of the Left," he worked for a "controlled" social transformation, not for a revolution with its unpredictable consequences and huge costs in terms of human lives and liberties.[2] At the same time, he was careful not to take the initiative of cutting himself off from any quarter willing to support his programs: only in this fashion was he in fact able to retain the confidence of those who, time and again, were giving SUDENE such valuable support, notably in December 1961. The fact that he accepted and welcomed United States aid probably made him suspect to some of his more extremist followers; but being the obvious target of the traditional and still quite powerful Northeastern "establishment," he had nothing at all to gain from starting a fight within the ranks of the pro-reform forces.

The fury of SUDENE's enemies, combined with SUDENE's tendency to confine itself to programmatic declarations about the need for deep structural changes in Northeastern agriculture, seemed increasingly to rule out any peaceful, gradual and collaborative transformation such as could be read into the original Furtado proposals.[3] Yet the very stiffening of attitudes, which coincided with the rise in social tensions throughout Brazil in 1961–62, led various third parties to search for new ways of breaking the threatening deadlock. In addition to revolutionary peasant leagues, peasant trade unions were established in several cane plantations with the active support of some Catholic priests. The States of Pernambuco and Rio Grande do Norte carried out some limited settlement schemes on lands which they had obtained through purchases or through expropriations. Even the Institute of Sugar and Alcohol, a traditional stronghold of the Northeastern sugar interests with price-fixing and other regulatory powers, began to exert pressure on the cane growers and refiners to lay plans for improving the efficiency of their operations and thereby to liberate lands

---

[1] Cf., for example, the articles "Os Cossacos do Capibaribe" and "Nordeste Vermelho" in *O Cruzeiro* of June 9 and June 30, 1962, respectively.

[2] In his above-cited article and in a statement before the National Economic Council, *Revista do Consêlho Nacional de Economia*, July–August 1962, pp. 376–377.

[3] See p. 78.

for the growing of food crops by newly established farm owner-operators very much along the lines of the original SUDENE plan.[1]

Thus, toward the middle of 1962, the Northeast exhibited a highly improbable conjunction of circumstances. On the one hand, an upsurge in public investment and private industrial activity was definitely underway. On the other, the region's traditional elites were subjected to a wide range of pressures, from revolutionary threats and direct local actions to gentle, face-saving persuasion and advice. Investment boom and profound social transformation were seemingly both in the making, and both were promoted and "administered" in various ways by the same agency, SUDENE. The two-pronged undertaking was by no means assured of success, yet the chances for substantial economic and social progress of the region looked brighter than at any previous time in this century.

---

[1] An agreement between the Institute and the Bank of Brazil, concluded in June 1962, made the Bank responsible for the assessment, purchase from the owners and resale to the settlers of whatever lands would become available under this program. Institute of Sugar and Alcohol, "Agreement between the Institute of Sugar and Alcohol and the Bank of Brazil (Colonization Department) to promote the improved use of lands in the cane-producing zones and the increase of diversified food crop production," unpublished document.

Chapter **2**

Land Use and Land Reform

in Colombia

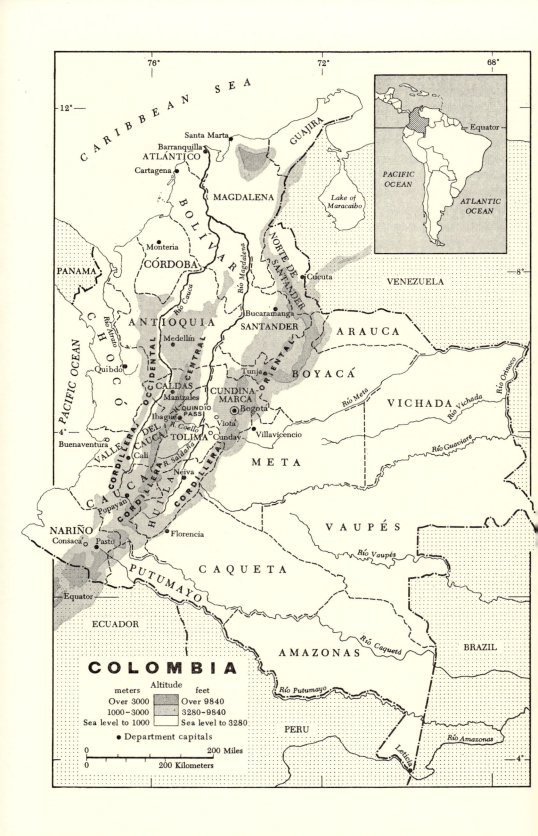

CARIBBEAN SEA

12° —

Santa Marta
Barranquilla
ATLÁNTICO
Cartagena

GUAJIRA

Lake of
Maracaibo

MAGDALENA

BOLÍVAR

Monteria
CÓRDOBA

PANAMA

NORTE DE SANTANDER

Cúcuta

VENEZUELA

— 8°

Río Atrato

Río Cauca

ANTIOQUIA

Medellín

SANTANDER
Bucaramanga

ARAUCA

Quibdó

BOYACÁ

CALDAS
Manizales
QUINDÍO
PASS
Ibagué
R. Coello

CUNDINA-
MARCA

Tunja

Bogota

Río Meta

VICHADA

Río Vichada

Río Orinoco

4° —

Buenaventura

Cali

TOLIMA

Viota
Cunday

Villavicencio

Río Guaviare

Neiva

META

HUILA

Popayán

Florencia

VAUPÉS

NARIÑO
Consaca
Pasto

Río Vaupés

PUTUMAYO

CAQUETA

Equator

ECUADOR

Río Caquetá

AMAZONAS

BRAZIL

COLOMBIA

Altitude
meters   feet
Over 3000   Over 9840
1000–3000   3280–9840
Sea level to 1000   Sea level to 3280

● Department capitals

0   200 Miles
0   200 Kilometers

PERU

Río Putumayo

Río Amazonas

Leticia

— 4°

PACIFIC OCEAN

ATLANTIC OCEAN

Equator

Land Use and
Land Reform in Colombia

Those who systematically doubt or deny the possibility of significant social and economic progress without *prior* fundamental, and usually violent, changes in power relationships among social classes frequently cite the history of land reforms in support of their point of view.[1] It is easy to show that land reforms which have been enacted in the context and as a consequence of a spectacular crisis situation, such as revolution or war, outnumber those brought about as a result of a victory of the land reform party at the polls or, more naïvely, because of some international expert's advice. In Latin America in particular, the Mexican, Bolivian and Cuban land reforms all occurred in the wake of drastic political and social change. While the available evidence indicates that improvements in the health, education or living standards of the urban masses hardly require social revolution as a "pre-condition," certain agrarian structures appear to be endowed with a special rigidity and have thereby provided the "pre-condition" theorists with an attractive line of defense for their views. Yet, even here, signs have appeared in various countries that change short of prior revolution (though far from smooth and peaceful) can no longer be ruled out once a society moves away from the stage at which it can properly be regarded as being essentially split into large landowners on one side and landless peons on the other.

The extent to which this area of the class struggle lends itself to infiltration, attrition, shifting alliances with other emerging social groups and similar complex tactics on the part of all the contestants is well brought out by the history of land tenure and land reform in Colombia.

---

[1] See Chapter 5.

While the outcome of this history is still in doubt, the record that has been written so far is sufficiently rich in moves and countermoves, in contrived change, in failures and successes that, by examining it, we will be able to learn much about the forces at work and the variety of routes available to a modernizing society in the highly explosive area of land policies.

FIRST PHASE: USE OF LEGAL WEAPONS

The modern history of land reform in Colombia starts in the late twenties and early thirties when widespread rural unrest led to the adoption of a new "land law" — Law 200 of 1936 — during the progressive administration of Alfonso López. Basically this law attempted two distinct tasks:

(1) to clear up prevailing uncertainty about existing land ownership and titles, through realistic systems of presumptions, documentary evidence and judicial procedure;

(2) to give legal strength to the often affirmed notion that ownership of land carries with it the obligation to utilize the land productively.

Both these aspects of the law have a protracted and closely interrelated history throughout Latin America virtually since the Spanish Conquest, and to understand the specific and novel nature of Law 200 some knowledge of this historical background is useful.

Historical Background

Almost from the beginning of the Conquest, the Spanish Crown, intent on bringing the sprawling territory of the New World under its control, became concerned about large land grants that failed to lead to effective occupation and agricultural production on the part of the grantees. Thus, transfer from the Crown to private ownership was made conditional on *morada y labor,* also known as *casa y labranza* (habitation and work), as early as 1513 by Ferdinand the Catholic, it being of course understood that the work was to be carried out by the Indians under the supervision of the owner or his employees.[1]

This requirement was later confirmed in considerable detail at the end of the 16th century, under Philip II. By that time the best lands in the valleys and highlands had been taken up and huge properties had been rap-

---

[1] Mardonio Salazar, *Proceso histórico de la propiedad en Colombia,* Editorial ABC, Bogotá, 1948, p. 216.

idly formed with or without valid titles. Philip's various proclamations insisted that those who received lands "will lose them if they do not work them or put cattle on them within given terms." Moreover he called for a general redistribution of improperly and illegally held lands, for the benefit both of the Indian communities or *resguardos* (reservations) which were then being given legal status and of new settlers arriving from Spain.[1] However, de facto owners were also given a way out: through the *composición,* i.e., by paying an agreed sum of money, they could obtain valid title to their lands and thereby a new term within which to satisfy the obligation of *morada y labor.*

It is highly unlikely that much land reverted to the Crown in the wake of these measures. Many of the laws dictated in Madrid were already then received in Lima, Mexico and Bogotá with the refrain: "One obeys, but one does not carry out." Yet the efforts made over the centuries by the Spanish authorities to avoid the private appropriation of idle lands should not be dismissed as so much shadowboxing. They reflected the security interests of the Spanish Crown, the desire to avoid unnecessary conflict with the Indian population and the interests of new settlers, both from Spain and from within the conquered territories.

An interesting document from the last period of Spanish rule confirms the continuity of concern about these matters. In a *cédula* (proclamation) issued in 1780 the viceroy of Sante Fé — today's Bogotá — stipulated that existing owners, even though they were squatters without title, should not be molested, but that new public lands should be granted only to settlers who would commit themselves to clean, seed, and cultivate the lands within a given time limit "with the penalty that if they did not comply they would lose the right to these lands and taking care not to grant more to each settler than he could work." Clearly we are not far from our own Homestead Acts. Moreover, the *cédula* went on to say: "Finally I have resolved that you shall see to it, but by mild measures, that the present legitimate owners of idle lands make them yield their fruit, either by themselves, or by renting them out, or by selling them to others."[2]

This resolve summarizes masterfully the objectives of peaceful land reform. How much was accomplished of these avowed objectives? Probably

---

[1] Indalecio Liévano Aguirre, *Los grandes conflictos sociales y económicos de nuestra historia,* Ediciones Nueva Prensa, Bogotá, 1962, Vol. I, Chapter VII.

[2] Royal decree (*cédula*) of 1780 quoted in: Guillermo Amaya Ramírez, *Curso sintético de legislación agraria,* Facultad Nacional de Derecho, Bogotá, 1938, mimeo., pp. 28–29, from *Diario Oficial,* No. 8752 of March 28, 1892.

very little, in view of the increasing power of the *criollo* (native-born of Spanish origin) landed elite which was soon to dislodge Spanish control altogether.

In the 19th century, many latifundios expanded further, partly through further encroachment on Indian lands (most remaining reservations were abolished in 1810), and, more importantly, by appropriation in 1861 of church-held lands, which were largely bought by powerful private interests. At the same time, nothing further was heard of attempts to coax existing property owners into making better use of their lands.

Nevertheless, important contrasting trends were at work. As early as in the 18th century a rapidly growing number of *mestizos* and new settlers from Spain began exerting pressure on the lands both of the large landowners and of the Indian communities.[1] This pressure resulted even then in the liquidation of many resguardos and in a "land tenure revolution,"[2] half a century or so before the general measure taken in 1810. The moving of an agrarian middle class into the interstices of the bi-polar feudal system laid the basis for the eventual subdivision of much of the Colombian highlands in the East (Santander and Boyacá) and the Southwest (Nariño) into small holdings.

A development of still greater magnitude and effect on Colombia's economic position was the large-scale internal colonization that got underway in the second half of the 19th century in the central cordillera province of Antioquia. New immigrants, disappointed miners and farmers in search of better lands began to open up systematically the vast and hitherto largely unpopulated mountainous and hilly lands to the south of Medellín, Antioquia's capital. What started out as typical "slash and burn" agriculture was soon converted into permanent settlements in small mountainside holdings as coffee was successfully introduced as a cash crop, particularly toward the end of the 19th century.

Claims to this area, dating from colonial grants of land, were freely disregarded by the settlers. When the holders of these claims suddenly realized the value of their long-neglected properties and asserted their rights to them in lawsuits, a variety of responses occurred. While some would-be settlers were deterred by the legal uncertainties, others decided to seek their luck by moving farther away from the centers of settlement.[3] Most

---

[1] Orlando Fals Borda, *El hombre y la tierra en Boyacá*, Documentos Colombianos, Bogotá, 1957, p. 84.
[2] *Ibid.*, p. 89.
[3] James J. Parsons, "*Antioqueño Colonization in Western Colombia*," *Ibero-Americana* 32, University of California Press, Berkeley, 1949, p. 76 and footnote 20, p. 194.

frequently, however, some compromise was reached after prolonged litigation, occasionally punctuated by violence. Since new towns and villages were founded at a rapid rate in the area, the negotiations were often three-cornered, with the public interest of the new *municipios* rather close to those of the settlers. The heirs of the old grantees were typically given an indemnity which was not particularly burdensome to the settlers but constituted a handsome windfall for the claimants.[1]

Much of the land that was being occupied was owned by the state. Here the Spanish tradition that required — theoretically — *morada y labor* as a condition for transfer of land from public to private hands was reaffirmed by a series of decrees and laws issued during the 19th century.[2] Ownership was to return to the state in case the new settlers did not comply with the freely assumed obligation to cultivate their land and to establish their residence on it. This provision was to become operative within a period of four, five or ten years in the various legal instruments, but the ten-year term tended to predominate. Attempts were made to define more concretely the term "cultivation" by specifying the proportion of the land that had to be cropped.

Antioqueño colonization covered much of the central cordillera including the fertile slopes of the Quindío, where it resulted in the creation of a new territorial unit, the Department of Caldas (1905). It spilled over both to the eastern slopes of the western cordillera bordering the Cauca Valley and to the eastern slopes of the central cordillera. In its southward push, this "homesteading frontier," as Parsons called it in a classic study, reached points 300 miles from Medellín.[3]

Colombia's temperate-climate slopes (lying at an altitude of 3,000 to 8,000 feet) thus turned into an extensive, multi-pronged "small man's frontier." And this frontier was far from "hollow" since it did not interfere with permanent settlement behind the advancing frontier.[4] It created many

---

[1] This is well detailed in *ibid.*, particularly Chapters VI and VII.

[2] Amaya Ramírez, *Curso*, pp. 32–35.

[3] Parsons, *Colonization*, p. 7. Another account, written with patriotic fervor and reformist zeal, is in Otto Morales Benítez, *Testimonio de un pueblo*, 2d ed., Banco de la República, Bogotá, 1962.

[4] Bryan Fitzpatrick, in the *British Empire in Australian Economic History, 1834–1939*, Melbourne University Press, 1941, p. 188, distinguishes the United States' "small man's frontier" from Australia's "big man's frontier." The term "hollow frontier" was coined by Preston James to denote the Brazilian pattern of internal migration (*Latin America*, The Odyssey Press, New York, 1959, p. 459). Benjamin Higgins, quoting the foregoing sources, contends that settlement in Latin America is characterized by both the "hollow" and the "big man's" frontier ("Enterprise and Development in the Latin American Setting," unpublished manuscript, June 1960). This is clearly not the case in Colombia.

problems of its own, particularly of health because of malaria and water pollution, and of fluctuating earnings, because of the settlers' eventual dependence on coffee as the principal source of cash income. But here we have a vast zone of Colombia where the traditional land problem was solved through spontaneous migration and occupation over a period of more than half a century. It may be noted by way of contrast that this same period saw the concentration of land ownership in a small number of huge latifundios in Porfirio Díaz' Mexico.

Public opinion was favorably disposed toward these settlers who opened up new lands under arduous conditions. The expression *hacer patria*, to make (or hack out) the fatherland, goes back to their labors and has retained this meaning of decentralized, individually motivated but socially useful activity. Pioneer settlers opening up public lands and squatters on privately held or claimed lands are both designated in Colombia as *colonos*, a term which connotes social approval.[1]

In the meantime the traditional hacienda system with cattle raising as the principal economic activity remained characteristic of other parts of the country. Large estates predominated in the tropical flatlands where Indian populations had never settled in large numbers and in the cool and fertile savannas from which they had been progressively driven by the Spaniards. Certain mountainous areas, particularly the fertile tropical slopes of Cundinamarca between Bogotá and the Magdalena River, were also predominantly owned in large blocks, and had mostly been converted into large coffee plantations by 1920.

So much for the historical background of the contemporary scene. It differs from the generally held notions about "feudal land patterns" in Latin America in several important respects. First, through liquidation of many Indian communities and the formation of mestizo and new immigrant groups of farmers large portions of the highlands were broken up into small holdings. Secondly, virgin lands, many of which were only nominally held by grantees of the Spanish Crown, were occupied by Antioqueño settlers and squatters, primarily in potential coffee-growing areas.

---

[1] Some of the expeditions of the colonos became legendary: thus the *Expedición de los Veinte* in 1848 assembled twenty families who made their way through canyons and trails impassable to pack animals to found the town of Manizales, which later became the capital of the department of Caldas. Parsons, *Colonization*, p. 73. Public lands were freely granted to settlers by the authorities, in recognition "that the establishment of new parishes on good lands contributes directly to the public welfare, giving value to the land which it did not have before and at the same time facilitating the support of a growing number of families who have no lands or occupations to secure the necessities of life . . ." *Ibid.*, p. 83.

Finally, a strong, though inadequately enforced, legal tradition made the acquisition of property rights on public lands conditional on their effective economic use.

Rural Unrest around 1930

In Colombia, therefore, land reform is by no means an aspiration that arose abruptly in recent years, as a result of a sudden yearning for social justice or in response to outside pressure. Rather, it has long been a developing reality. Moreover, the beginning of the contemporary debate must be dated back at least to the thirties and to the "Land Law" or Law 200 of 1936.

It has in fact become usual in brief surveys of the land tenure problem of Colombia to make a perfunctory reference to this law, to recognize the good intentions that animated its framers and then to state as a universally recognized fact that the law failed to accomplish its objectives. This presents us with an interesting riddle, for the law, widely hailed or advertised as "land reform" when passed, was years in the making and was not one of those intuitive or "lyrical" laws unrelated to reality: it was instead a response to urgent everyday situations and difficulties and was molded by them.

Rural unrest of a new kind became noticeable toward the late twenties. In 1928, a strike broke out in the banana zone owned by the United Fruit Company south of the port of Santa Marta. Police fired on demonstrating strikers, causing close to a hundred deaths.[1] This was an isolated event, but it served to draw attention to the plight of the land laborer. (Jorge Eliécer Gaitán, the populist Liberal leader, visited and reported on the zone at length after the strike.) The depression of 1929 had immediate and pervasive effects. With the budget in difficulties and, even more important, foreign loans no longer obtainable, public works were severely retrenched and the unemployed drifted back to their families in the country; but with coffee prices declining precipitously, farm income shrank at the same time. Given this double squeeze on per capita farm income, intensification of in-

---

[1] Robert J. Alexander in *Communism in Latin America*, Rutgers University Press, New Brunswick, N.J., 1957, p. 245, gives the number as 86, while V. L. Fluharty in *Dance of the Millions*, University of Pittsburgh Press, 1957, p. 37, speaks of 1,400 dead and 7,000 wounded. Such are the difficulties of historical research in Colombia even for a relatively recent period. Much the same margin of error affects all estimates of deaths as a result of guerrilla warfare in recent years. After a check through the daily press, it appears that Alexander's figures are approximately correct.

ternal migration and settlement was to be expected. However, most of the public lands with an acceptable and familiar climate in the central portions of the national territory had been taken up by this time; worse, some of these lands had lost their fertility through erosion. As a result, settlers increasingly occupied lands which they knew to be privately owned.

Engaging in other "mutinous" practices, many peasants stopped rent payments on the ground that the land they cultivated did not legitimately belong to those who claimed it as their property. Here they were exploiting a 1926 decision of Colombia's Supreme Court (subsequently reinforced by another decision in 1934) which required the claimant to a piece of land to exhibit the original title through which the disputed property had left the national patrimony. Since it was usually impossible to produce this "diabolical proof," as it came to be called, these decisions were shaking the very foundations of the established order. The hard-pressed tenant farmers were not slow in attempting to take advantage of this judicial windfall.[1]

Conflicts became particularly numerous and often violent in the coffee zone of Cundinamarca, on the Western slopes of the eastern cordillera, between Bogotá and the Magdalena River. This area was the only one in the country where most of the coffee lands were held in large plantations. Work was carried out by peons in traditional semi-feudal fashion: they were given a plot on which to live and grow subsistence crops and in lieu of paying rent they worked regularly on the plantations. Conflicts arose in the twenties over the seemingly trivial demand of these peons to be allowed to plant coffee trees on their plots in addition to the traditional corn, beans, yucca, plantain, etc. This demand was strongly opposed by the plantation owners, who sensed that once the peons owned coffee trees they would cease to be peons. With a cash income of their own they might turn into a less reliable labor force. As owners of the coffee trees, they could be fired and dislodged only after they were reimbursed for the value of the trees. In general, their bargaining power and status would vastly increase.[2]

---

[1] T. Lynn Smith, "Conflicto de teorías sobre la propiedad de la tierra en Colombia," *Revista Mexicana de Sociología,* May–August 1958, pp. 376–377.

[2] That the desire to move up in the social scale is still today an important factor in the peasant's decision to plant coffee in lieu of subsistence crops is stressed in a recent anthropological study of a Colombian village: "Cash-cropping is regarded as a 'Spanish' activity, a 'civilized' kind of work, in contrast to subsistence or maintenance agriculture. Many people turn their fields into coffee plantations, thus seriously limiting their food supply, but gaining prestige in the village. Coffee means ready cash, it means new clothes, money for travel and recreation. That at the same time the individual food supply diminishes is a fact which few people seem to correlate with cash-cropping." Gerardo and Alicia Reichel-Dolmatoff, *The People of Aritama,* University of Chicago Press, 1961, p. 223.

In some areas, the peons simply took the coveted right; after all, the planting of coffee tree seedlings is not easily detected. According to one document, a peasant league — the apparent predecessor of the Communist-led organization which has dominated some coffee growing areas near Viotá for the past twenty-five or thirty years — passed the word to all its members to plant coffee trees on their subsistence plots.[1] At the same time, in 1933, the Minister of Industry, Francisco José Chaux, eloquently urged the landowners to allow the peons to grow their own coffee. He argued that the extension of coffee *fincas* (small to medium-sized farms) such as ex-isted in other parts of the country could only be beneficial, and described the present regime as socially dangerous: "This torment of Tantalus which consists in always harvesting the coffee of someone else without ever be-ing able to look forward to having one's own trees is bound gradually to affect the psychology of the peasants. Generation after generation, the pos-sibility of improving their own and their children's economic and social po-sition through profitable seedling plantings has been before their eyes, but has been foreclosed by a prohibition which their conscience is unable to understand and which makes their life and that of their families insecure."[2]

The Minister's plea aroused a furious controversy in which he was ac-cused by the plantation owners of wishing to subvert the existing social order. In this they were probably right: The Minister hardly attempted to hide his opinion that social peace would be better guaranteed if the family coffee finca of Western Colombia were to be the rule also in the Cundi-namarca area, and he probably realized that the planting of coffee trees by the peons on their subsistence plots would be the first step in the breakup of the large coffee plantations.

To a considerable extent, this is what happened. From 1932 to 1955–56 the number of coffee farms in Cundinamarca and Tolima more than dou-bled as a result of the liquidation of many of the plantations while in the other principal coffee growing departments (Antioquia, Caldas and Valle) the number of farms increased by only 10 per cent.[3] A revolution occurred

---

[1] *Boletín de la Oficina Nacional del Trabajo*, July–Sept. 1933, p. 1301. The official agency dealing with the distribution of public lands and conflicts over lands was lo-cated from 1929 to 1934 in the Ministry of Labor and the *Boletín* is a rich source of information on all aspects of the land problem during this period.

[2] *Ibid.*, p. 1284.

[3] *Coffee in Latin America*, Vol. I. Colombia and El Salvador, FAO, United Nations, New York, 1958, p. 23, Table 12. The extraordinary multiplication of coffee farms in Cundinamarca appears to have occurred in the eight years following the 1932 census, according to Ernesto Guhl, "La seguridad social campesina en Colombia," *Economía Colombiana*, Nov. 1954, p. 20.

which hardly deserves the name "peaceful," for it was the result of a series of actions that ranged all the way from settlements with landowners who gave in to the peasants' pressure to open rebellion and seizure as in the case of some of the large plantations of the Viotá area.

But violence was by no means the monopoly of one class. While the peons were attempting to change their status by the "aggressive" action of planting their own coffee trees, and while many tenants decided they really were settlers and stopped paying rents, and squatters moved in on public and not-so-public lands, the landowners were not slow in striking back and were frequently the ones to strike first. The record from the late twenties through the mid-thirties is full of attempts by landowners to evict tenants, settlers and squatters. Many of these attempts were successful since they were staged with the full support of the local officialdom and police. Frequently they gave rise to full-scale battles, with casualties on both sides. On occasion, the landowners organized private bands of *"fieles"* ("faithfuls") consisting of laborers who were aspiring to replace the existing tenants or squatters.[1] It has even been alleged that in some instances the owners of uncultivated lands and slopes tricked colonos into taking over their land (presumably by lying low for some time) and appeared, armed with court orders and backed by police, only when the colono had uprooted the primeval vegetation and had proved the soil to be fertile.[2] However, there is no need for quite so diabolical an interpretation of the landlords' behavior. It is natural that they went to the trouble of asserting their rights only when these rights were worth something; frequently, it is reported, the attempts at eviction took place in the wake of new road construction which made colono-occupied lands more accessible and valuable.[3]

The fact that, according to the law, improvements had to be paid for was of little use to the colono, for once an order of eviction had been obtained, his bargaining power was gone and he had to accept virtually whatever compensation was offered to him. He then was chased from the land which he had considered his own, and frequently his home was immediately torn down or burned in an attempt — not always successful — to prevent any re-occupation or re-infiltration.

---

[1] "Informe del Tribunal Superior de Bogotá," *Boletín*, Oct.–Dec. 1933, pp. 1636–1638; "Memorandum de las arbitrariedades cometidas por el inspector de policía departamental de Sumapaz contra colonos de la región," *ibid.*, pp. 1665 ff.

[2] T. Lynn Smith, "Some Observations on Land Tenure in Colombia," *Foreign Agriculture*, June 1952, p. 122.

[3] Justo Díaz Rodríguez, "Economía Agraria de Colombia," *Colombia*, Contraloría General de la República, Imprenta Nacional, Bogotá, Jan.–May 1944, p. 236.

This kind of violent action and assertion of property rights had not occurred during the earlier period of Antioqueño colonization; at that time the claimants, living far away from the disputed lands, had chosen the method of protracted litigation to extract some monetary advantage from the settlers. During the twenties and early thirties, direct action to dislodge settlers became more frequent, probably because the lands then being occupied were closer to the "core" of the haciendas over which the owners maintained effective control. Evictions also took place for a variety of other reasons: because tenants had planted coffee trees against the owners' will; because tenants gave signs of becoming disaffected, unionized or otherwise subversive; and simply, as President López was to put it in one of his eloquent speeches, "because the owners felt like it (*les viene en gana*)," because they wanted to reaffirm their "supreme and feudal rights" to do as they pleased on their property.[1]

The owner's unrestricted right of eviction regardless of whether or not a squatter was acting in good faith, i.e., was unaware of the existence of private property rights on the land he was occupying, had been most bluntly affirmed in a law dating back to 1905: "When a *finca* [farm] has been occupied without rent contract or consent of the owner, the Chief of Police to whom the complaint is made will go to the farm within 48 hours of the deposit of the written complaint; and if the occupants hide or are unable to show the rent contract, he will issue the eviction order without permitting any recourse nor any other delay."[2] Thus the landowners had a legal instrument perfectly adapted to evicting the colonos, while at the same time tenant farmers had been handed by the Supreme Court an invitation to impugn the property rights of the landowners!

The authorities could not fail to take notice of the spreading insecurity and unrest. Already, in the late twenties, under the Conservative government of Abadía Méndez, an attempt was made to circumscribe strictly the right of the putative owners to evict.[3] A decree provided that the eviction proceedings had to start within thirty days of the act of occupation *or* of the day on which the occupation became known to the owner. Since the owner could always allege that he had just heard of the occupation, this decree remained ineffective and in the early thirties a large number of po-

---

[1] Marco A. Martínez E., *Régimen de tierras en Colombia*, Gráficos Mundo al Día, Bogotá, 1939, Vol. I, p. 17.

[2] Article 15 of Law 57 of 1905. Quoted in Julio García Idrobo, *Algunos aspectos de la Ley 200*, Editorial Aguila, Bogotá, 1940, p. 75.

[3] Decree 992 of 1930 in *Boletín*, June 1930, p. 445.

lice actions took place, particularly in Tolima, Cundinamarca and in the Cauca Valley[1] — all areas which in the troubled years following the elections of 1946 and the Bogotá riots of 1948 were to become principal foci of guerrilla warfare and banditry.[2] And it was precisely the reluctance of successive governments to allow police and army forces to get involved in these disputes as the exclusive and overt tools of the landowners that was a principal motive behind the search for a better system. In 1929 we read in a circular letter of the Minister of Labor:

> The idea is prevalent among the hacienda owners that the Government must give them police protection for the solution of the problem. It is clear that above all the danger of revolt must be avoided . . . and that the rights of the owner must be guaranteed in the legitimate contracts that exist. But it is also necessary that the landowners become convinced that this is not the solution of the problem, for, as we believe to have shown, the communist propaganda is not the only cause of the malaise whose existence nobody can any longer deny.[3]

As usual President López expressed this attitude best, in an important message to a group of landowners who had asked him for army units to protect their "rights":

> The government . . . will try to protect the owners who are unjustly attacked . . . but it is not ready to choke off all aspirations of the campesino to economic improvements by the bloody application of such juridical concepts which permit the unlimited abuse of the right to own land without exploiting it, and which at times authorize expropriation without indemnization when colonos and tenants are concerned.[4]

He reiterated this thought in his annual message to Congress of 1935:

> Some landowners . . . asked the State to use the weapons of public order for ridding titles to the land and the land itself of all dangerous ideas . . . The eviction procedure was to be followed by the machine gun . . . My government advised that such was not its attitude . . . toward the colono who invaded a piece of land which he believed in good faith to belong to the public domain.[5]

---

[1] *Boletín,* Oct.–Dec. 1933, pp. 1678 ff.

[2] The first thorough survey of these phenomena, usually referred to in Colombia as *la violencia,* is in Monseñor Germán Guzmán, Orlando Fals Borda and Eduardo Umaña Luna, *La violencia en Colombia,* Monografías Sociológicas No. 12, Universidad Nacional, Bogotá, 1962.

[3] *Boletín,* Aug. 1929, pp. 10–11.

[4] President Alfonso López. Answer of Sept. 6, 1934 to a letter signed by a group of landowners in *La política oficial,* Imprenta Nacional, Bogotá, 1935, Vol. I, p. 71.

[5] *Mensaje del Presidente de la República al Congreso de 1935,* Imprenta Nacional, Bogotá, p. 86.

The Land Law of 1936 (Law 200) and Its Alleged Failure

Law 200 must be read and understood against the background of this vast social upheaval, of the unceasing war of position and attrition that took place during those years between owners and peasants, of this "salutary agitation" as Minister Chaux actually put it at one time.[1]

The first move toward the land law was taken during 1933, toward the end of President Olaya Herrera's term. A special junta was set up in May and was given the task of suggesting new formulas and legislative proposals. The sense of urgency with which this junta worked must have been great, for only three months later the government was able to introduce a bill into Congress which contained many of the provisions eventually incorporated into the law. Congress, however, took its time and debated this and subsequent drafts of the law at length before passing it more than three years later, in December 1936.

As the landowning interests were always generously represented in Congress, it may be surprising that the law was passed at all. Two elements conspired to force action. One was the anarchic situation in the countryside and the fear of the owners that they would entirely lose control over their properties. The Supreme Court decisions of 1926 and 1934 which cast doubt on the validity of virtually all land titles were only one element in this fear. It was in the years 1934–36 that some of the large coffee haciendas of Cundinamarca in the Viotá area were effectively taken over by the tenants — who have run them as cooperatives ever since with the active assistance and guidance of Communist functionaries. Where matters did not reach this extreme, the prolonged conflict sometimes led to a stalemate in which the possibility or the need of mutual accommodation was perceived. In 1934, compromise settlements were entered into by various owners with tenants and settlers according to which tenants were permitted to buy the land they were occupying. In one of these agreements the owners committed themselves to "provide the best possible conditions for the widows and relatives of the tenants who lost their lives in the last regrettable incident that took place in the hacienda."[2] With the advent of the López administration the owners realized that they could no longer count on unconditional police support and became ready for settlement.

Another factor in the final passage of the law was the vigorous personality of President López and the decided reform character of his administra-

---

[1] Martínez, *Régimen de tierras*, Vol. I, p. 45.
[2] *Boletín*, July, Dec. 1934, p. 312.

tion. The Land Law was only one of a series of reform measures that López was able to push through a Congress which, while predominantly Liberal, contained many members who were far from being social reformers. Labor and social security laws, recognition of unions and of the right to strike, introduction of progressive income taxes, reform of the Constitution, which declared private property to be "a social function which involves obligations" — all were conceived and enacted in a climate of intellectual excitement by a group of highly intelligent members of the traditional ruling families who were attempting to modernize their country's economic and social structure. López was immensely enjoying his own radicalism and the way in which he shocked Bogotá society (of which he was a prominent member) by siding with striking workers and squatting peasants. Left-wing writers later accused him of "revolutionary exhibitionism" and deceitful demagoguery, but he seems rather to have had a realistic understanding of the combination of pressures and promises needed to push through measures that went against the class or immediate pecuniary interests of those who were called upon to vote for them.

Viewed against the background of this intensive struggle, the purposes of Law 200 of 1936 become clear: it attempted primarily to bring security of tenure to squatters with uncertain titles, to increase the bargaining power of the lower rural classes, and to reduce the number and intensity of conflicts in the countryside.

The very first article of the law established the fundamental principle that a presumption of private property exists in favor of those who occupy the land and make "economic use" of it. This provision was intended to remove in one stroke the tremendous uncertainty about ownership that resulted from the vagueness and dubious validity of most titles. It identified an area of interest common to two quite different groups: the colonos who had taken up lands in the public domain and the large landowners who cultivated their lands but whose titles had come under a shadow as a result of the Supreme Court decisions.

The most serious difficulties had, however, arisen over cases where squatters had moved in on lands which were claimed to be private property by absentee landowners. For these cases, the law had some rather intricate provisions. It first defined the circumstances in which lands could be held privately even though they were not in "economic use." Interestingly, these conditions were made to depend on whether the lands had been invaded. In the latter case, the documentary requirements were far more stringent. If the land was free of squatters and was not in "economic use," title could be obtained through documentary proof that the property had been transferred to or purchased by the present owner twenty years prior to the issuance of the law (Art. 3). But if there were squatters (Art. 4) the claimant had to prove that the property belonged to him as a result of a sale that had taken place *prior to the year 1821.*[1] Even then he could not evict a squatter, established for over two years, if he let 90 days go by after Law 200 had been issued or if he did not pay the squatter for his improvements within 30 days after he had had his right to the land confirmed in court. If the owner let these deadlines pass, then the squatter had the right to stay put and to acquire title to the property by paying the former owner for the value of the property over a period of five years.

The provisions of Article 4, not much noticed by later commentators since its operation was limited in time, were among the most important of the law. In effect, they legalized the status quo for most situations in which disputes were currently raging.[2] Four new obstacles were placed in the way of eviction: (1) the proof of title was made most difficult; (2) the colono was to receive full value in cash for the improvements he had made, and this included both the increase in the value of the land *and* the value of the house, plantations, fences, etc., whereas previously only one of these two components was taken into consideration; (3) the claimant was given a short time limit within which to act; and (4) the law was to be administered by special "land judges" instead of ordinary judges; these "judges on muleback" were to go in person to the disputed areas instead of leaving administration to the police, who had shown considerable partiality in favor of the landowners.[3]

As a result of these provisions, most of the existing squatters were left in possession of the lands they had occupied and acquired secure title to them. The importance of Article 4 is brought out by the following comment of a highly knowledgeable observer:

------

[1] In both cases title could also be obtained through an original and still valid land grant of the Spanish Crown. The year 1821 was taken as a cut-off point because a law issued in that year permitted the wholesale transfer of public lands into private ownership.

[2] The earliest draft of the law, prepared under the Olaya Herrera Administration, had a section specifically entitled "Status Quo" which called for a sort of general ceasefire between colonos and owners, freezing the *situaciones de hecho* (de facto situations) until they were resolved in accordance with the remainder of the proposed law. Martínez, *Régimen de tierras*, Vol. I, p. 32.

[3] "The antecedents of the law prove that the legislator created the land judges with the objective to take away from the police authorities the role that had become theirs as a result of their knowledge of the procedure of eviction . . ." Amaya Ramírez, *Curso*, p. 68.

There were hardly any owners who put forward their claims within the 90-day limit imposed by the law; as a result, the measure adopted helped solve in an equitable and lawful way the most thorny land problems, namely, those in which the legitimate and opposing claims of the owners and the workers are invoked, the one setting forth their rights as lawful owners, the others the tangible fact of work done in good faith . . .[1]

In many cases, the owners of lands that had been occupied knew they could not recover them without further violence. In this situation, the law supplied them with a graceful face-saving way of bowing to the inevitable.

The principal and substantial achievement of Law 200 was then to have consummated and legalized the breaking up of certain large estates and plantations which had been in process during earlier years. This effect of the law is well described in the following statement:

> The so-called *colonos* considered as theirs some lands belonging to others when they had exercised certain acts of appropriation such as the cutting of timber and clearing of the land in general, without the authorization of the owner. Since the land law has been promulgated it seems that these social conflicts have diminished very notoriously as the situations were resolved in accordance with the prescriptions of the Law.[2]

The sociologist Fals Borda cited specific evidence to the same effect from the Department of Boyacá: "The subdivision of private properties apparently received a new impetus after Law 200 was promulgated; the conflicts with the tenants and illegal squatters forced many owners to subdivide their lands."[3]

The mere expectation that the law would take effect had similar repercussions. According to a report in the daily press: "Owners have begun to show more understanding and are dividing large territories which belonged to them, turning over, on very easy terms, the land to those who work it."[4]

Naturally Law 200 did not confine itself to regularizing "de facto situations," but also provided for future contingencies. It attempted in various ways to reduce the uncertainties that had traditionally beset the country-

---

[1] *Ibid.*, p. 60.
[2] Jorge Enrique Gutiérrez Anzola, *Delitos contra la propiedad*, Bogotá, 1944, p. 174.
[3] Fals Borda, *El hombre y la tierra*, p. 158. This statement contrasts with the appraisal elsewhere in his study in which he joined the critics whose opinions will be reviewed presently: "Law 200 has not worked . . . it has added to the insecurity in the tenure and life of the rural workers." *Ibid.*, p. 105.
[4] *El Tiempo*, Bogotá, December 18, 1936.

Law aimed at agric stability

side with its highly mobile peasant population. Thus, it provided that farmers who in good faith occupied and cultivated privately owned lands would acquire legitimate title within the short span of five years (Art. 12). Similarly, occupants could be forcibly evicted only if the legitimate owners acted within 120 days from the date of occupation (Art. 18). The owner was thereby informed that unless he were vigilant and acted with dispatch to assert his rights the colono would speedily acquire rights of his own and it would be difficult and expensive to dislodge him.

The root cause of the conflicts had long been the existence of privately owned lands that were left uncultivated and unused and represented a permanent invitation to occupation by landless farmers. In its most revolutionary provision, Article 6, the law made a heroic attempt to get at this root cause: all privately owned lands that remained uncultivated for ten consecutive years were to revert to the public domain (exceptions to this rule included, among others, properties of less than 300 hectares). Thus, after ten years, in 1946, all privately owned lands were to be either cultivated or nationalized and ready to be distributed to would-be settlers.

Needless to say, this article of the law was the one that drew most attention and least application. It amounted to a promissory note to stage an agrarian revolution in ten years' time. Such a note is not easily, and was not, honored at maturity, quite aside from the fact that an attempt at honoring it would have been made extremely laborious and time-consuming by the appeals and other procedural provisions inserted into the law during its passage through Congress (Art. 8).

Article 6 can perhaps best be understood as the programmatic, theoretical, "lyrical" portion of the law, the purest expression of the reform spirit that inspired its framers and without which it could scarcely have assembled the energies and support that assured its passage. At the same time, the lack of application of this utopian article made it possible later on, when the conflicts of the early thirties were forgotten, to cast discredit on the whole measure and to dismiss it as an empty gesture by people ignorant of the harsh realities of the class struggle.[1]

In part, this reputation for ineffectiveness derives from the idea that the law ought to have solved the whole agrarian problem once and for all. Many thought that the law should not "merely" attack one aspect of an existing situation but should not leave anything untouched that could somehow be related to the land problem. As one critic put it:

---

[1] J. A. Osorio Lizarazo, *Gaitán*, Buenos Aires, 1952, p. 182.

> If the land law has a defect it is that it does not solve juridically and economically all the land problems. No provision is made for farm credit, rural labor contracts, social security for the peons, hygiene of rural dwellings, the breaking up of the Indian reservations and of the latifundios, the consolidation of the minifundios, protection of forests and watersheds, irrigation, water control, reforestation, the fight against erosion or other fundamental problems of a real agrarian statute.[1]

Similarly, the law was held up to contempt because it dealt remedially with the consequences of existing or future conflicts, instead of scientifically extirpating the root cause of these conflicts:

> The statute is a law of repercussion. To come into operation it needs to be preceded by a conflict, and it is obviously anti-scientific, anti-social and anti-economic to create norms of retort and of counterstroke.[2]

But far more serious charges were later leveled against Law 200. Writers have not only tagged it as incomplete and ineffective, but as counter-productive, i.e., as having perversely compounded, rather than merely left unsolved, the rural problems of the country. In this connection one particular train of events must be mentioned. Prior to the law's enactment the colono or squatter was on the lowest rung of the social ladder since he could easily be evicted with a minimum payment for the labor put into the plot of land he had ephemerally occupied. The tenant farmers or sharecroppers were better off since they had the right to their plots as long as they performed the required services for the landowner or turned part of the crop over to him. But Law 200 raised the colono from his lowly and insecure position by making it much harder to expel him and by requiring that he be fully paid for any improvements in case of expulsion. Thus his condition became suddenly desirable in the eyes of the tenant farmer or sharecropper, who was now tempted to contest the ownership rights of the *patrón* and to claim the status of colono. Whether or not this actually happened, some landowners, so it is said, *believed that it would happen* and were therefore intent on forestalling such action by getting rid of as many of their tenants as fast as possible. It is this unforeseen effect of the law which has been described everywhere in the subsequent literature on the subject: how the landowners expelled tenants, burned their houses, replaced labor-intensive crops by cattle-grazing, hired only unmarried laborers for short periods and housed

---

[1] Hernán Alzate Avendaño, *El contrato de aparcería*, Imprenta Departamental, Manizales, 1943, p. 14.

[2] Mardonio Salazar, *Proceso histórico*, pp. 304–305.

them communally instead of giving them individual plots, and so on.[1]

These events may well have occurred in some places, but the writer has not been able to find any specific evidence as to their time and place of occurrence and therefore doubts that they were nearly as pervasive as reported. This lack of evidence is the more significant since the continual violence which took place *until* Law 200 was enacted is amply documented in official sources with the names of the localities where colonos invaded private lands, or clashed in violent battles with the police who were evicting them on behalf of the owners. Until a modicum of corroborating data becomes available, it must be concluded that the view as to the alleged counter-productive effect of Law 200 has become accredited primarily through sheer repetition and successive embellishment of events which were among the possible and even plausible consequences of the law. The image of failure was readily accepted by conservative and revolutionary critics of the law as well as by those who consider the fact that life and its problems continue sufficient evidence of the failure of previous human efforts.

Developments Subsequent to Law 200

To criticize the detractors of Law 200 is not to deny that the law led to *some* reaction on the part of the landowners. But it seems likely that, on the whole, this reaction consisted, not in furthering conversion of farm land to pastures as alleged, but in delaying the reverse process — the much needed conversion of grazing lands to cropping.

---

[1] These occurrences have been reported in almost identical terms by writers of widely different political beliefs. The socialist Antonio García stated: "The large landowners 'cleaned up' their lands of colonos and were enabled to register titles which they had never had before . . . The application of the law led to the expulsion of tenants who had created the haciendas out of the wilderness and who were now paid for the 'improvements.'" *La democracia en la teoría y en la práctica*, Bogotá, 1951, pp. 37–38.

The conservative Samuel Hoyos Arango repeated the charge: "The land law constitutes one of the most serious errors committed in the country . . . because of the propaganda which was made at its enactment and because of the political and juridical demagoguery to which it gave rise; . . . a death struggle began between landowner and rural worker; the houses of the mayordomos and of the peasant families were torn down by the owners out of fear of permanent occupancy by the colonos; the worker who considered himself owner of improvements drove out the owner of the land, or else the latter expelled the worker out of fear of permanent occupation . . . Stable workers became migratory, work barracks replaced family dwellings." "Parcelación y crédito agrícola," *Economía Colombiana*, Nov. 1954, Bogotá, pp. 105–106.

Or, as Mardonio Salazar wrote: In the face of the "rude attempts against the right

The evidence about actual mass evictions of tenants and sharecroppers is neither massive nor conclusive, but it does seem likely that after the law was passed the hacienda owners were more convinced than ever that cattle raising was the only sound use for their lands and that cropping brought nothing but trouble.[1] Thus, the law had resourcefully attacked the problem of unutilized land at the cost of making that of the *under*utilized hacienda more untractable: the best lands of the country remained firmly devoted to extensive cattle grazing.

In the late thirties and early forties social unrest in the countryside subsided. The reform fervor of the first López administration gave way to the more staid, business-as-usual Liberal administration of Eduardo Santos (1938–42), and to a second term for López (1942–45) which totally lacked the luster of the first. Industrialization and wartime inflationary and supply difficulties directed the government's attention increasingly to the problem of agricultural production. Within the existing property structure, the fastest and most obvious way to increase production seemed to be to counteract the reluctance of the landowners to engage tenants or sharecroppers, i.e., to transact the unfinished business that Law 200 had left in its wake.

This was the intention of Law 100 of 1944. It defined and aimed at rendering safe for the landlord the tenancy or sharecropping contracts which were declared in the first article of the new law to be of "public utility."

---

of property . . . the owner defended himself; he became half-livestockman. He fenced in his property, converted it into a vast pasture and put one to two hundred heads of cattle on a property of a thousand or two thousand hectares." *Proceso histórico,* pp. 352–353.

Lately the same judgment, in a somewhat more temperate form, has found its way into the authoritative foreign expert's report: "Law 200 of 1936, which was intended to bring more land under production by giving title to small parcels of land to those people who actually cultivate it, but who are unable either to rent or to buy it, has proven ineffectual, to a large extent as a result of amendments. It has had the unintended effect of retarding improvements and production. Since under certain circumstances permanent improvements, such as the planting of trees, could give occupants claims to ownership or at least to compensation, many owners preferred not to permit occupancy by tenants or squatters, or to prohibit tenants and farm workers from making any permanent improvements or even from occupying the same parcel of land for several consecutive years." *The Agricultural Development of Colombia,* International Bank for Reconstruction and Development, Washington, 1956, p. 55. See also Raleigh Barlowe, "Land, Taxes, and Rural Economic Development in Colombia," Michigan State University, paper presented at the Agricultural Economics Seminar, Feb. 11, 1960, mimeo., pp. 8–9, and "Informe al gobierno de Colombia sobre tenencia de la tierra," Eduardo Llovet, FAO, Rome, 1957, mimeo., p. 10.

[1] In the Valle del Cauca, one of Colombia's most fertile provinces, it used to be said that only three lines of business promise success: (1) well-administered cattle-ranching, (2) poorly administered cattle-ranching, and (3) cattle-ranching without administration.

An important concession was made to a long-disputed claim of the land-owners: the tenant was told that, in the absence of explicit permission, he had no right to grow tree crops or other perennials on his plot but only annual plants; if he grew such forbidden fruit he made himself subject to immediate eviction (Arts. 5–6).

Another incentive granted to the landowner was a lengthening of the ten-year term during which he was to bring his uncultivated land into use, by an additional five years provided he engaged tenants or sharecroppers for this purpose (Art. 10).

These were clear signals that times and power relationships had changed. The government was now trying to enlist the collaboration of the hacendados instead of coercing them by threats. Actually these threats — the famous proposal for reversion to the public domain of lands still uncultivated in 1946 — lost further in credibility as a result of the second chapter of Law 100. This dealt with "parcelization" — the purchase of privately owned properties by the state and the resale of such properties to settlers — another invention of the authorities to conjure with open class conflict in the countryside. Parcelization was usually performed in areas where de facto occupations already had taken place. The principle followed in such transactions was that once the value of the property had been set by land appraisers the owner was to be paid in cash while the new occupants had, of course, to be granted long-term credit through agricultural credit banks, the Banco Agrícola Hipotecario and the Caja Agraria, founded in 1924 and 1932, respectively. While the resulting cost of the program severely limited its scope, parcelization represented an *ad hoc*, piecemeal way of giving in to the continued pressure on land where it became strongest, of accommodating it in a genteel way. A state that acts in this way is unlikely to go on an expropriating spree; and, in fact, when the ten years were up, not a word was heard about the enforcement of the old expropriation threat of Article 6 of Law 200.

Law 100 of 1944 is mainly of interest because of the changed political and social climate it reflected. It does not seem to have had very substantial results nor to have aroused much controversy. While it may have rehabilitated tenancy contracts to some extent, it certainly did not lead to any major changes in land use patterns. In effect, it was the last step in one line of policy-making that attempted to deal with aspects of the land problem through legislation concerning titles, squatters' rights, and tenancy contracts.

The ten-year anniversary of Law 200 in December 1946, when in principle unutilized privately held lands became expropriable, passed unnoticed in part because of the changed political situation. With the Liberals divided into two hostile factions, the Conservatives won the 1946 elections. Though the reform zeal of López' first administration had long since disappeared, it was clear that the Conservative government presided over by Mariano Ospina Pérez would be even less likely to administer vigorously the expropriation provisions of Law 200 than the Liberal administrations which had preceded it. Serious problems of public order arose after the elections and, after the convulsive Bogotá riots of 1948, an open power struggle between Liberals and Conservatives broke out in the provinces and turned into armed assault, guerrilla warfare and banditry. Important sections of the countryside in the central and mountainous departments of Huila, Tolima, Antioquia, Caldas and Valle became intermittently the scene of *violencia* which, to this day, has not been brought completely under control. This unrest, serious as it was, did not interfere with the rapid pace of economic growth experienced by Colombia during most of the postwar period. It is even possible that, much as did the enclosure movement in 17th and 18th century England, the violent conflicts in the countryside and small towns fed industrialization and the growth of the larger urban centers. Not only was the labor force in the cities swelled by refugees, but the traditional preferences for sinking savings into land were somewhat weakened.

SECOND PHASE: USE OF FISCAL WEAPONS

Economic advance in the thirties and forties was largely a matter of strides made by the manufacturing and construction industries. As the modern sector of the economy expanded rapidly, the comparative lag of agriculture and the use of antiquated techniques in growing foodstuffs and grazing cattle became ever more apparent. Thus originated another line of policy-making around the land problem, one that was inspired by the need for increasing the food supply and for making more rational use of the available land resources. Fiscal measures became the chosen instruments of this type of policy for various reasons: social reform, or the restoration of law and order through reform, was no longer an explicit high-priority objective. The legislation of reform via measures such as Law 200 had run its course and had been adjudged a "failure." Perhaps the idea arose that change could more effectively be brought about through incentives and penalties than through legislative fiat and administrative decisions. Moreover, the post-war period saw the arrival of foreign advisers and missions who felt no qualms about recommending tax measures that might incidentally or insidiously produce changes in the country's social structure, but were understandably reluctant to recommend such changes directly, particularly to a Conservative government.

The Land Tax Proposal of the World Bank Mission of 1949

The idea of using taxation for bringing pressure on landowners to cultivate their holdings was briefly discussed in the early days of the first López administration;[1] nothing came of it, however, and no further mention of the tax instrument appears until the publication some fifteen years later of the International Bank's survey *The Basis of a Development Program for Colombia.*[2]

Clearly the mission, headed by Lauchlin Currie, felt that the way in which agricultural activities were carried on in Colombia was both absurd and unjust: ". . . land use follows an unusual pattern. As a rule, the fertile level valleys are used mostly for grazing, while the steep mountainside slopes are cultivated. . . . the cattle fatten on the plains while the people often have to struggle for a bare existence in the hills."[3]

The sharpness of this indictment is a good example of both the advantages and the limitations of the "fresh look" at a problem by a foreign mission. The advantage lies in the very fact that the outsider is not familiar with nor used to the local situation, does not grasp it in its "historical necessity," and has therefore the ability to be surprised and shocked by what he sees to a greater extent than even the most determined local social reformer. The failings of the visiting expert, on the other hand, are his readiness to label as absurd any order that is unfamiliar to him, and, perhaps more important, his inability to perceive the processes of change already at work in the society which he attempts to comprehend. Thus the land use pattern of the central Colombian provinces lent itself well to the striking generalization of the Currie report, but this was so because the picture

---

[1] "The existence of large unutilized properties which could be cultivated must be curtailed. To this end, in addition to short terms at the end of which property rights are forfeited, a progressive and differential tax should be imposed so as to tax idle lands more severely than cultivated lands." Statement on agrarian policy of April 11, 1935 in A. López, *La política oficial,* Vol. II, p. 60.

[2] International Bank for Reconstruction and Development, Washington, 1950 (Chapters 5 and 18).

[3] *Ibid.,* pp. 62–63.

drawn by the mission was taken at a very peculiar moment in a continuing process of change. The long-drawn-out occupation of the mountainous and hilly lands by settlers in the central parts of Colombia had been virtually completed and most large estates in these areas had been broken up; on the other hand, the process of introducing mechanized agriculture in the flatlands had not yet started in earnest. Had the mission looked at Colombian agriculture only twenty years earlier, it would have found large estates on the mountain slopes as well; and if the tendencies of the last ten years are projected for another decade, the growing of food and industrial crops will have largely replaced cattle grazing on the most fertile plains within twenty years after the publication of the report.

The obvious conclusion to be drawn from so "uneconomic and paradoxical"[1] a land use pattern as was denounced in the Currie report is to effect a revolutionary switch: let the peasants laboring on the slopes take over the fertile lands of the valleys and drive the cattle to graze in the hills.

Naturally a report submitted by the International Bank can hardly propose an agrarian revolution to a member government; hence the therapy advocated by the Currie report was mild in comparison to the revolutionary potential of its diagnosis. It proposed a tax on land that would penalize underutilization. The existing land tax (*impuesto predial*) of 4 per thousand of assessed value would apply to lands bringing a "normal" return or more (10 and 14 per cent were given as illustrative normal yields for two varieties of fertile areas); if the return were subnormal the land tax was to be raised progressively until it would reach 4 *per cent* of assessed value in the case of zero return.[2] In addition to providing a direct stimulus to more intensive farming, the proposal was also made with the idea that the increased tax load would make absentee landlords more willing to sell out to small holders and that land prices would come down. Better land utilization and more widely distributed ownership were stated to be twin objectives.

The report's scathing comments on Colombia's agrarian structure combined with the seemingly paradoxical nature of the proposal — at given land values, taxes would *rise* as income fell below a certain level — made a considerable impact on public opinion. Since the report was believed to be the forerunner of large-scale financial aid from the International Bank, all of its proposals were at least given the benefit of the doubt. Nevertheless,

---

[1] *Ibid.*, p. 383.
[2] *Ibid.*, p. 385.

in the case of the land tax proposal, the immediate reaction was angry criticism, not only on the part of the landowning interests,[1] but also on the part of domestic fiscal experts and administrators. It was easy to show that the proposal was an administrative nightmare: Different "normal" returns would have to be set for different types of land, all kinds of exceptions would have to be granted, e.g., for land undergoing reforestation. Moreover, according to the proposal, the tax should be assessed on the basis of the "current market value," but how this value was to be set remained unclear. The existing 4 per thousand real estate tax was assessed on the basis of cadastral surveys conducted by the Geographical Institute, but as usual the values resulting from these slow surveys were far below the real values of the properties, especially after a decade of wartime and postwar inflation. Moreover, many parts of the country are not reached by the surveys and here the values declared by the owners serve as the tax base.

Thus the proposal was wide open to the comment which so frequently greets the foreign expert's advice. "His ideas are excellent, but they are impractical, they wouldn't work in *our* milieu." While hidden chauvinism and xenophobia no doubt have something to do with this judgment, foreign advisers often seem to make an all-out effort to deserve it. One reason is that they are not aware of the political restraints under which policy-making operates in the country which they advise; another is that they wish to "épater" the native with the latest policy gadget. In this connection, we may note that engineers would never advocate the introduction in an underdeveloped country of a production process which has not been proven to be free of "bugs" in an industrially advanced country, but the exercise of such restraint is unusual on the part of advisers in economic or social policies.

From a somewhat Olympian point of view the penchant of foreign advisers for impractical measures is perhaps not altogether lamentable, for this foible makes it possible for the native policy-makers to modify the expert's proposal and to make it *their own* in the process. Such an attempt to carve a workable measure out of the land tax proposal of the Currie report marks the next stages of policy-making on land use in Colombia.

After the report was issued, the Colombian government, in agreement with the International Bank, set up a committee of its own to consider the recommendations of the report. This "Committee of Economic Development" consisted of six respected Colombian citizens (three Conservatives

---

[1] *Revista Nacional de Agricultura,* Jan. 1951, pp. 8 ff.

and three Liberals). Although the committee retained Currie as its adviser, it pronounced itself against any immediate application of the tax and advised instead that the Geographical Institute be strengthened and its cadastral survey work accelerated.[1] Actually Currie had submitted to the committee a considerably revised version of his original tax proposal.[2] He limited the scheme to the fertile level lands which would be designated as such by the Institute and cut by one-half the rate of progression envisaged in the Bank report. Furthermore, he now faced the problem of how to get a realistic appraisal of land values and proposed that assessments be based on the owners' own declaration; to ensure truthful declarations he stipulated that the state could purchase any property at 140 per cent of its declared value. But even though in general Currie's advice carried considerable weight with the committee, the whole idea was shelved for the time being and the committee recommended the usual mixed bag of *fomento agropecuario* (agricultural and livestock development) measures: land surveys, agricultural credit, technical assistance, storage and distribution as well as tax *incentives* for increased cultivation of level lands. Only as a last resort, if all of these programs were to fail, then "the government shall consider the possibility to establish a tax on under-utilized agricultural land."[3]

The Bank mission episode was thus finished. Should it stand condemned as one of the many instances of unsuccessful technical assistance, of expert advice that went unheeded precisely because it was impractical or because it ignored "the weakness, if not the complete absence, of social and political forces that could induce the necessary concessions on the part of the ruling coalition?"[4]

In the light of later evidence, such a verdict would be too harsh. The Bank report had various merits: (1) it kept alive the discussion of improvements in the agrarian structure and in land use under highly adverse political conditions; (2) it deflected attention from the purely legal approach that had long held undisputed sway, to the possibility of promoting change through financial incentives and penalties; and (3) by formulating a con-

---

[1] Comité de Desarrollo Económico, *Informe final*, Sept. 1950–Aug. 1951, Imprenta Banco de la República, Bogotá, pp. 114–116.

[2] Unpublished document supplied to the author by Lauchlin Currie.

[3] Comité, *Informe*, pp. 116–117.

[4] P. Baran, "On the Political Economy of Backwardness," *The Manchester School*, January 1952, reprinted in A. N. Agarwala and S. P. Singh, eds., *The Economics of Underdevelopment*, Oxford University Press, Bombay, 1958, p. 89.

crete proposal it led to an awareness of the principal practical difficulties facing an attempt to use the tax instrument for purposes of agrarian reform.

Attempts to Achieve Realistic Land Assessment

Discussion of the tax proposal had made it clear that the principal stumbling block to the effective and equitable use of fiscal policy was the assessment problem. In Colombia land is subject to taxation not only through the previously mentioned real estate tax of 4 per thousand, whose proceeds are the mainstay of municipal finance; in addition, federal taxation provides for a patrimony (net worth) tax with a mild progression from 1.35 per thousand to 15 per thousand in the case of taxable property in excess of one million pesos so that many large landed properties are theoretically taxed at close to 2 per cent a year, a rate that should be sufficient to exert that pressure toward either utilization, lease or sale that was aimed at by the Currie proposal. Such was also the conclusion of two United Nations experts who surveyed the country's fiscal system in 1951:

> . . . the Committee on Economic Development was asked to advocate a special land tax on under-cultivated land. The authors of the present report feel that the Committee made a wise decision in not recommending such a very complicated tax which could not possibly be levied without giving excessive discretionary powers to the Public Administration. Under normal circumstances the patrimony tax, if well enforced and based on realistic valuations of land, provides sufficiently for incentives to proper cultivation of land and especially so in the case of those wealthy landowners against whom the special land tax was intended to operate.[1]

This recommendation reflects the rationality of the British and Dutch authors of the United Nations report. But it ceases to appear so rational once the difficulties besetting the realistic assessment of land are realized.

First, the technical obstacles in cadastral survey work are huge in a mountainous country with poor communications and capricious weather: on account of irregular downpours even in the so-called dry season roads are frequently and unpredictably impassable. While aerial photography is a technical achievement of considerable value, its usefulness has been restricted in Colombia because of the almost permanent cloud cover over

---

[1] "Report and Recommendations on the Tax System of Colombia with a Short Chapter on Budget Presentation and Procedure," *United Nations Technical Assistance Programme*, New York, 1952, p. 52.

large and important areas of the country. A further technical advance, in-fra-red photography from high altitudes, has partially overcome this diffi-culty as it enables the camera to take ground pictures from the air even through haze and light clouds. Technical assistance in mapping the coun-try from the air has been extended by the United States but only on a small scale, and progress has been slow.

Good cadastral surveys have, of course, been carried out in some coun-tries even before the advent of aerial photography. But the task of making such a survey and of estimating the fair market value of every farm is a most difficult one for an underdeveloped country where land is privately owned. It presupposes a large corps of well-trained surveyors who are in-corruptible and courageous and a legislature that is willing to make ade-quate appropriations for this work. Moreover, it requires either an absence of inflation or frequent revisions through resurveys or escalator devices. Rapid economic development and urbanization also affect land values pro-foundly and differentially. Thus, in Colombia, a country with powerful landowners (including not only the hacendados but the numerous and po-litically influential owners of middle-sized and small coffee farms), weak local administration, considerable inflation and rapid economic develop-ment, the establishment of realistic land values for the whole country through cadastral surveys has long been unattainable.

This is a most serious conclusion for it appears to rule out the use of taxa-tion as a means of coaxing landowners into making full use of their land and therewith the gradual, peaceful solution of the problem of under-utilized latifundios. This situation is behind T. Lynn Smith's remark that it is much easier to have a revolution in Latin America than a really effective land tax.[1]

Whether or not it is easier than reform, revolution is always *easier to visualize;* for revolution requires "only" the violent overthrow of certain ruling groups, a head-on clash, whereas reform requires a special combina-tion of circumstances, a sequence of moves in the course of which the rul-ing groups acquiesce to, or even connive in, the nibbling away of their own privileges.

Viewed in this fashion, reform is a feat of contriving which has a chance of being accomplished only if liberal use is made of some of the more wily arts of bargaining — intimidation, threats, professed willingness to resort to

---

[1] As reported by Solon Barraclough in "Major Land Tenure Problems of Latin America" in *Latin American USOM's Seminar on Agrarian Reform,* Feb. 21–24, 1961, International Cooperation Administration, Washington, p. 41.

violence, use of surprise and deception, etc. Some of these arts received abundant, if somewhat erratic, application in the next period of Colombia's history — the dictatorship of General Gustavo Rojas Pinilla.

The General came to power as a result of the increasing tendency of the ruling Conservative faction to establish a sectarian dictatorship of its own. It began to persecute not only Liberals but even certain dissident Conservative groups, and it was increasingly unable to deal with rural unrest: for example, the large tropical flatlands (Llanos) east of Bogotá came to be largely controlled by guerrilla forces. General Rojas Pinilla promised an end to party strife and political persecution and persuaded some, though not all, guerrilla forces to lay down their arms. After a brief honeymoon during which some previously suppressed liberties, particularly of the press, were restored, it became clear that the new regime was bent on perpetuating itself in power. It developed a vaguely populist, anti-oligarchic, pro-underdog ideology of the Perón type. It was clearly animated by considerable resentment against the traditionally privileged circles of Colombian society. While its policy-making was frequently inept, it did have a highly resourceful, if irresponsible, protagonist in the Minister of Finance, Carlos Villaveces, who soon became famous for the many surprise decrees he issued, ranging from serious assaults on the financial position of the propertied classes to minor pinpricks. Only too willing to impose a heavier tax burden on the landlords, he brushed aside the U. N. recommendation that the cadastral survey be improved by enlarging the staff of the Geographical Institute. With typical impatience, and intent on finding shortcuts, he issued two decrees. First, in September 1953, he ordered the automatic upward valuation of all assessments in accordance with the rise in the cost of living from the date of the last assessment.[1] Before the storm of protest against this edict had died down, he virtually countermanded it by providing, early in 1954, that the values of landed properties were to be set from now on by declarations of the owners themselves to municipal cadastral committees (*juntas municipales de catastro*). The decree contained the threat that the value declared by the owner would be the basis for payment by the state should the property at any time come to be expropriated. Here was the shortcut sought by Villaveces. Why bother with the endless, frustrating work of surveying the whole country, piece by piece, if the owner himself can be intimidated into telling us about the real value of his land?

---

[1] Art. 20 of Decree 2317 of 1953.

We noted earlier that Currie had advocated the same shortcut in 1951, but he proposed that the state would have the right to acquire properties at 140 per cent of the self-declared value. Villaveces radicalized this suggestion and decided that 100 per cent was good enough.

This idea of enforcing honesty through the threat of expropriation at the self-assessed value is ancient.[1] But, like the threat of future expropriation of Law 200, it did not work, in both cases because of what our atomic strategists call the lack of credibility of the threat. When, as had long been the rule in Colombia, the state has to pay cash for expropriated property, its ability to acquire large tracts of land even at bargain prices is strictly limited and it is naïve to suppose that the landowners do not know this. Moreover, the individual landowner is likely to rate as low the probability that the government will single *him* out — and, anyway, he has a good, well-connected lawyer friend in Bogotá — so why worry?

Nevertheless, opinion about the effect of Villaveces' measure is divided. Reportedly, in some areas it did have the desired effect of raising valuations to more realistic levels. On the whole, however, much damage was wrought by disrupting the work of the Geographical Institute and there is evidence that the largest latifundios were as undervalued at the end of the Rojas Pinilla regime as at its start. Thus, in spite of occasional talk about land reform and the threat implied in Villaveces' decrees, the landed "oligarchs" did not suffer during the General's tenure while the country's industrialists and investors in corporate assets were badly hit by the abrogation in 1953 of a cherished and lucrative privilege — the exclusion of dividend income from the income tax. This differential treatment was perhaps due to the fact that the Rojas Pinilla clique bore far greater resentment against the impenetrable and haughty world of Antioqueño industrial and banking wealth than against the old-fashioned hacendado. Moreover, many among this clique — originally members of the lower middle class — were themselves consumed by the ambition to become landowners, and, needless to say, this ambition was abundantly realized, most conspicuously in the case of Rojas Pinilla himself. That they went slow in imposing tax burdens on themselves is not too surprising.

The point is more than anecdotal, for it reveals a fundamental change that had taken place with the vigorous economic development Colombia experienced since the thirties: land ownership became a popular invest-

---

[1] In a memorandum which was given to the writer by the director of Colombia's cadastral survey, Dr. Alberto Pardo Pardo, it is traced back to the Roman king Servius Tullius!

ment among the expanding middle class and the hacendado thus acquired important allies in the defense of his own interests. Land and cattle ownership, still prized for the prestige it gave and for the protection it promised against currency depreciation and against the saver's own propensity to engage in wasteful spending,[1] became attractive also on other more "modern" grounds. Just because effective taxation on land and on income from it had lagged behind the comparatively heavy and progressive taxation on industrial and commercial income, land ownership and cattle operations became newly attractive to investors. Losses could easily be claimed in cattle operations and could be used by persons with large taxable profits from nonfarm operations to reduce total tax liabilities. Thus the progressive industrialization and urbanization of the Colombian economy, while of course creating a need for higher agricultural productivity, led to types of individual action that interfered with the fulfillment of this need.[2]

This lag in productivity did not matter too much as long as the country had a large and steadily increasing foreign exchange income as a result of sharply rising coffee prices: the necessary foodstuffs and agricultural raw materials could easily enough be acquired abroad. But when the coffee market broke in 1954 and foreign exchange once again became a scarce commodity whose allocation was subject to sharp scrutiny, the question inevitably was asked: why is it not possible for Colombia to satisfy its own needs in such products as cotton, oil seeds, barley, cacao and even cattle? Why in 1956, for example, did it have to spend $100 million or one sixth of its total import bill on agricultural imports?[3]

Decree 290 of 1957 and Its Alleged Failure

It was this desire for an expansion in food production that led to the next major legislative step, Decree 290 of 1957, issued by the military junta which governed the country for over a year after the overthrow of Rojas Pinilla. The decree was principally the work of Jorge Mejía Salazar, Minis-

---

[1] Alejandro López, "El retorno a la tierra," *Revista Nacional de Agricultura*, Aug. 1939, pp. 524–525.

[2] The quantitative importance of these actions in the total picture of Colombian agriculture cannot be ascertained. There were strong market forces working in the direction of better utilization of land. However, the awareness was widespread that land was being acquired by the rising middle class and that land and cattle operations were engaged in by industrialists for purposes of tax avoidance; and this fact is of importance in our context.

[3] Ministerio de Agricultura, *Memoria al Congreso Nacional 1957–58*, Imprenta Banco de la República, Bogotá, Vol. I, p. 18.

ter of Agriculture, who was assisted by an adviser loaned by the International Bank.

The approach followed by the decree was foreshadowed by a special report on Colombia's agriculture prepared by a new International Bank mission in 1956. This mission had been requested by General Rojas Pinilla's first Minister of Agriculture. Since the report was rendered when the Minister had long been replaced and at a time (1956) when the regime was disintegrating rapidly, its immediate impact was minimal. Confirming the Currie diagnosis, the report adjudged land use patterns to be "uneconomical and illogical"[1] although it noted some progress "in very recent years" in cultivating the good level lands both in the tropics (rice, cotton) and in the highlands (wheat, barley, potatoes).[2] As a remedial measure the report again principally proposed tax measures, and recommended that the responsibility for land assessments be returned to an invigorated Geographical Institute and that assessments be made on the basis of "optimal potential use which the quality and location of the land warrants, not on the land's current use."[3] It appears from this phrasing that the report aimed at a value different from current market value. The latter will reflect the potential use of the land if this potential use is well known and clearly established by similar nearby properties. But then, why not use the market value as a first approximation to "potential use value"? To get directly at the latter poses a virtually insoluble task for the land survey teams of an underdeveloped country — but then foreign missions seem to have a penchant for saddling the countries they advise with such tasks!

Another recommendation of the Bank report was more practical and represented a simplification as well as an improvement of the discredited Currie proposal. To encourage cultivation or the leasing or selling of idle lands, landowners were to include into their taxable income a notional income from their lands on the basis of a "presumptive return equal to 3–5% of the value of land, cattle and fixed farm capital."[4] Clearly the efficiency of such a measure would again depend on the reliability of the cadastral survey. But it would have the advantage over the Currie proposal of avoiding the need to ascertain separately the actual income from the land; it would make it impossible to claim losses in land or cattle operations which would

---

[1] International Bank for Reconstruction and Development, *The Agricultural Development of Colombia,* Washington, D. C., 1956, p. 5.
[2] *Ibid.,* p. 56.
[3] *Ibid.,* pp. 66–67.
[4] *Ibid.,* p. 67.

serve to reduce taxable income from non-farm sources and, provided again that assessments were realistic, it would reduce the attractiveness of investment in land for the rich.

This proposal was to be placed under active consideration by the Lleras government in 1960, some four years after the Bank report was issued. Why, in 1957, the infinitely more complex scheme of Decree 290 was drawn up instead is a real mystery, the more so as several of the Bank's recommendations were followed. Thus the self-assessment decree of Villaveces was duly repealed and the Geographical Institute was given a more autonomous status. Also, the report's suggestion that incentives in the form of land tax exemptions for specified periods should be given to landowners carrying out irrigation and drainage works was fully incorporated into the decree. Finally, the Bank report had classified land into three qualities: Type I: good level land, suitable for mechanized intensive agriculture; Type II: hilly and rolling land suitable for certain types of labor-intensive agriculture, and for cattle grazing; Type III: land unsuitable for agriculture though widely used for this purpose at present, to be used for grazing or to revert to forest. This subdivision had been made only for purposes of analysis, but Decree 290 made it into law adding one more category to the three, namely, land that is potentially usable but requires large-scale investment in means of communication, clearing, irrigation or drainage. The heart of the decree was the requirement that certain minimum percentages of these lands were to be cultivated. In other words the decree took it upon itself to define precisely the "economic use of land" which had been made into the condition of ownership by Law 200 of 1936.[1] It laid down the rule (Art. 5 and 6) that at least 25 per cent of Type I land and 15 per cent of Type II land had to be under cultivation once a year.[2] Those who would be found to default on this obligation were to pay a supplemental real estate tax which increased from year to year. Starting with 2 per cent of the value of the property in 1958, this penalty tax was to reach 10 per cent after four years.

Application of Decree 290 thus required first a classification of all farmlands and farms into the four land categories and, secondly, a yearly inspection to ascertain whether the various percentage requirements of the decree were satisfied. The measure was obviously and utterly unworkable, far more so than the Currie proposal which had been extensively criticized

---

[1] Ministerio de Agricultura, *Memoria*, Vol. I, p. 21.
[2] Artificial pastures were to be considered "cultivation" provided they were "technically cultivated" and used for "intensive livestock raising duly proved."

for its lack of attention to the "ambiente." Clearly the occasional passing of unworkable laws is very much part and parcel of the ambiente, and perhaps the foreign expert only shows he is becoming assimilated when he takes part in the game!

Our task being to understand, we may suggest two reasons for the decree:

The military junta had appointed a Cabinet of technician caretakers as Ministers. For example, the Minister of Agriculture was a civil engineer, who had previously worked for petroleum and construction companies. After the restless, willful and often vexatious improvisations of Villaveces, the affairs of state were to be handled in a competent and technical fashion. It is possible that the highly complex arrangement of Decree 290 recommended itself to the policy-makers because with its land classification, percentages and other intricacies it had an impressive air of engineering technocracy.

Another explanation is that the decree was cast in general terms but that it was really meant to be applied only to a few well-defined zones with fertile, level, inadequately utilized land, close to the centers of population, and owned in fairly large blocks. Since the decree could not be applied until lands were classified into the four types, and since the principal purpose of the law was to increase rapidly the production of certain foodstuffs and agricultural raw materials that were being imported or whose scarcity contributed to inflationary pressures, the zones with greatest immediate potential would clearly be the first to be surveyed. Moreover, a decree which is clearly utopian for the whole breadth of the national territory can conceivably be made to work in strictly limited areas whose economic and property characteristics are already well known, and where the available qualified personnel would be concentrated. This was indeed the direction Minister Mejía took: he started pilot projects for the application of the decree in four small areas (about 10,000 hectares) in each of the four most notoriously fertile and underutilized flatland areas of the country (Sabana of Bogotá, Cauca Valley, Tolima Llanos, and Caribbean coast). The application of the decree never went beyond this pilot stage; for after a new minister (Augusto Espinosa Valderrama) was appointed in 1958 to the first Cabinet of President Lleras nothing further was done to bring it to life.

As a result it is possible to assert — as was of course widely done — that Decree 290 represents one more spectacular failure in the history of attempts at dealing with Colombia's land problems. But such an assertion must be reconciled with the fact that considerable progress was in fact made in the late fifties in achieving the principal objective of the decree, namely, increased agricultural production in a variety of important lines (cotton, rice, barley, sugar cane, oil seeds). Imports of barley dwindled to a negligible figure and from a substantial importer of cotton Colombia became a net exporter. Increasingly, enterprising middle- or upper-class operators rented or acquired tracts of good flat land in the Sabana of Bogotá, the Cauca Valley and the Tolima plains close to the Magdalena River and sowed them to commercial cash crops.

These developments must in part be credited to Decree 290. It is conceivable that even though unenforced the threat of penalties, coming as it did after the recommendations of the various foreign missions which had received wide publicity, had some psychological effect on the owners. But the decree also contained some fat financial incentives to cultivation. Going considerably beyond the recommendations of the International Bank, it made a wide variety of agricultural investments deductible for income tax purposes.[1] Moreover, it cut in half income and patrimony tax liabilities for a wide variety of agricultural activities, with the sole exception of beef cattle operations on level lands.[2] The decree aimed particularly at promoting the formation of partnerships or corporations that would lease lands from large landowners and grow commercial crops on them.

These incentive provisions were of course immediately taken advantage of: to become effective they only needed to be invoked by the taxpayers, who can always be relied upon in such matters.[3]

Agricultural entrepreneurs taking advantage of these incentives received further timely help by concurrent legislation aiming at channeling larger bank credit resources into commercialized agriculture. In 1957 commercial banks were directed to reserve 15 per cent of their deposits for loans to agricultural activities[4] and while selective credit regulations of this kind

---

[1] Article 18.

[2] Article 19 and 20.

[3] The provisions of Decree 290 on tenancy contracts may also have been of help. To avoid the famous disputes about improvements, which had such a long and tortuous history and which made landowners reluctant to rent out their lands, the contracting parties were permitted to stipulate which crops were to be grown and to exclude the landowner's liability for any improvements unwanted by him (Art. 26). Decree 291, issued together with Decree 290, supplemented these provisions by simplifying the procedure for evicting tenants who violated tenancy contracts.

[4] Decree 198 of 1957, later confirmed by Law 26 of 1959.

had frequently been of dubious effectiveness it appears that this measure played an important role in orienting investment activity toward the raising of cash crops.

The modernization of Colombia's agriculture along capitalistic lines thus made rapid advances in the late fifties. A number of basic economic forces were also at work, such as the growth of markets as a result of industrial expansion and urbanization. Price supports and technical assistance supplied by official agencies or directly by industry were of importance in the more spectacular cases of barley and cotton.

It would probably be premature to attribute these changes to a new capitalistic mentality of the landowners. Rather, it could be argued that the continuing widespread desire to hold land, for prestige reasons, as an inflation hedge, or as a tax avoidance device, was a factor in the development of production because it led to a rise in land prices. Frequently one hears it said by landowners that with their land having risen so much in value, they cannot "afford" any longer to leave it in cattle, even though land taxation has not caught up with the increase in land values. This statement implies that the landowner, instead of maximizing income, behaves in such a way as to maintain some "normal" relationship between income from the land and its value. In other words, the potential maximum income would actually be earned only if this is required to restore the ratio between earned income and land value to its "normal" level.[1] The reasons for such behavior could be several: a loss of face could be felt and a suspicion of being incompetent could be aroused if one failed to achieve a certain earnings ratio; it is also possible that landowners who lack knowledge about market conditions or who, as a result of experience, doubt the ability of the market to absorb large additional quantities at constant prices, take an increase in land values as a more reliable signal that demand for agricultural products has expanded than a rise in prices, which may be ephemeral. The very propensity to hoard land may thus have indirectly stimulated crop production.

Viewing the agricultural progress of the fifties, one observer of the Colombian scene, Lauchlin Currie, completely reversed his earlier stand about the scandalous underutilization of Colombia's best lands and spoke of an "agrarian revolution" that had taken place silently and generally unnoticed. And he even candidly avowed that the tax proposal of the Interna-

---

[1] Such behavior would be a counterpart to the Pigou effect according to which the propensity to consume increases with larger asset holdings. Here it is the propensity to produce that would be so influenced.

tional Bank mission he had headed "would not have been advanced if the mission had arrived a few years later."[1] Currie's renunciation of his earlier views went much too far, for the problem of the idle or underutilized latifundio was still a long way from being solved. But as a result of the advances which Currie noted, the agricultural problem which policy-makers had to deal with was changing its face once again: inadequate production and unnecessary agricultural imports came to be gradually superseded as a principal cause for concern by the continued low income, depressed social status and unrest of the large mass of Colombia's campesino population. Nevertheless, the next phase of policy-making, from 1958 to mid–1960, was marked by a somewhat hectic attempt to avoid facing this problem or dealing directly with it.

New Tax Proposals under the Lleras Administration

In mid–1958, after one year of caretaker government by the military junta, Colombia started a novel political experiment, in accordance with the Liberal-Conservative pact which had given the impulse to the overthrow of Rojas Pinilla's dictatorship. Liberal President Lleras, duly elected by both parties (the Presidency was to alternate between representatives of each during four terms of four years each), formed a strictly bi-partisan cabinet, while each party held one-half of the parliamentary seats. Clearly such a political arrangement was not ideally suited to forceful action. Yet President Lleras was aware that his government had to be something more than a continuous, skillful balancing act. High expectations of an all-round better life had been raised and popular energies and pressures would once again be felt frequently and openly, rather than sporadically and in the form of backland guerrilla strife as during the preceding decade of military and "strong man" government. President Lleras thus had a doubly difficult task: his government had to play to popular galleries and at the same time it was hamstrung in its actions by its own split personality and by the suddenly restored power and assertiveness of Congress. The moves of the next period are difficult to understand if one does not keep in mind the particular tensions under which the government operated.

As previously mentioned, Espinosa Valderrama, the new, young and enterprising Minister of Agriculture, was unwilling to become the administra-

---

[1] *Programa de desarrollo económico del Valle del Magdalena y Norte de Colombia,* Informe de una Misión dirigida por Lauchlin Currie, Edt. Argra, Bogotá, 1960, p. 32.

tor of Decree 290. However, while he criticized the decree for the complex land classification system it required, he proposed a bill that would maintain this system intact, and would merely increase the cultivation requirements as well as the penalties imposed for non-compliance. The bill never got over its first parliamentary hurdle, but its introduction had two consequences: (1) it definitely buried Decree 290 insofar as the application of its penalty features was concerned; and (2) it led to a veritable free-for-all of proposals and counterproposals in and out of Congress and to widespread public discussion. Some projects that were seriously introduced appear to have been specifically designed to confuse the debate; for example, a project of the Sociedad de Agricultores (the pressure group of the large landowners and cattlemen) proposed yet another variant of Decree 290 featuring simultaneously two land classification systems, one the fourfold system of Decree 290 itself and the other the eightfold system used by the Geographical Institute!

With Decree 290 clearly no longer in operation, the whole attempt started by the Currie report to coax owners into cultivating their lands through monetary penalties had proven abortive. Yet it was to be expected that the collapse of this attempt would give an important opening to those who saw the only solution in the expropriation of the idle latifundios. For this reason and because of the impractical nature of Decree 290 (and of its proposed variants) a comparatively simple proposal was at last worked out in 1959 by a group of "progressive capitalists" and was introduced into Congress. It provided for the levying of a so-called "territorial tax" of 2 per cent on all rural properties. This tax would replace (by multiplying it by five) the old land tax (*impuesto predial*) of 4 per thousand, but unlike the latter it was to entitle the payer to a tax credit against his tax on income from agricultural activities. As a result only those who did not earn a fairly good income from their landholdings would be hurt: the tax would in effect be levied on properties that failed to yield income. Here was a simple proposal which in this form had never been put forward by any foreign expert.

The proponents of this measure realized that it could be frustrated if lands were not assessed at realistic values. They fell back on Villaveces' device of self-assessment combined with the threat of expropriation at the declared value.

In November 1959, President Lleras gave strong support to this proposal with an address to a "National Peasant Congress" held in Bogotá. After having castigated those who merely held land in the hope that public highway construction and other works, paid for by the taxpayer, would make millionaires out of them, he went on to say that there were two solutions to the land problem: "Either the forcible distribution of landed wealth with the natural violence that this method brings with it, or the patient, continuous and inflexible action of the state through taxation which converts the land into a means of production, whose ownership is justified by the income it produces. Faced with this alternative I am sure that Colombians shall not hesitate."[1]

They did! Congress apparently was in no mood to approve a tax that would really hurt, and within the government itself there was resistance. The National Planning Council, which, in principle, was to coordinate not only development planning but economic policy as well, criticized the proposal as insufficiently "technical" and proposed an alternative: to impute to landowners a "presumed income" of the order of 7 to 10 per cent of the value of their land and to tax them in accordance with the normal progression of the income tax.[2] This is indeed an attractive formula: with the territorial tax proposal the accumulation of idle land would not be without cost, but the cost would be far less irksome, in comparison to his other tax burdens, for a taxpayer in the higher brackets (the top bracket rate of the Colombian income tax is 51%) than for middle or low income groups. It will be recalled that this proposal had been advanced some four years earlier by the Bank mission.[3] Intellectually the most attractive of the many variants of the same basic idea that were being discussed, it was least effective in gaining political support; it was not even introduced into Parliament as a proposed bill. The member of the Planning Council who had espoused the "presumed income" scheme actually became Minister of Agriculture for a short period in mid-1960, but at that time an entirely new, major effort was already underway to satisfy the craving for some action on the land problem.

The Handicaps of Land Tax Schemes

If we date the effort at using the taxing powers of the state to force idle lands into production from the original Currie proposal, we can look back

---

[1] *El Espectador*, Bogotá, November 27, 1959.
[2] This program was incorporated into the "Economic Platform" of the government by the Planning Council and officially adopted in February 1960. Cf. *Legislación Económica*, Bogotá, April 18, 1960, p. 102.
[3] See pp. 126–127.

on a ten-year period of intense intellectual activity, abundant legislative experimenting, . . . and rather complete futility, at least if one discounts the
effect that continuous public discussion of the issue may have had on the
incriminated landowners. Why did this ten-year effort have so little to show
in the end?

The most obvious explanation is the one we are already familiar with:
the ruling class is too short-sighted and egoistic to seriously undertake a
program of self-taxation, even though such a measure may eventually reduce the probability of expropriation. However, in the light of this decade
of experience, one cannot find this explanation wholly satisfying. Granting
that the foreign experts who recommended the measures were naïve and
oblivious to the realities of class interests, why would there have been so
much tinkering with such measures? Were not the various Ministers of
Finance or Agriculture who were proposing unacceptable measures or
creating unenforceable ones aware that they were playing with fire, that
the failure of these proposals toward which they seemed to conspire would
lead to demands for far more drastic measures? Moreover, it is simply not
true that inaction and failure were planned in advance by the participants
in what admittedly turned out to be an elaborate non-decision-making
process.

Alternative or additional hypotheses are therefore needed. Let us first
look at the specific characteristics of the task: it is desired to establish
monetary penalties for holding idle or underdeveloped agricultural land.
One trouble with this task is that it allows too much play to intellectual
creativity and ingenuity of a rather low order (therefore sometimes referred to as "gadgetry"). There are so many possible solutions (self-assessment, imposition of additional tax payments for under-utilization somehow
defined, taxation of potential income or of presumed income, territorial tax,
etc.) that decision-makers tend to countermand the decisions of their predecessors in favor of a more "technical," or less "anti-technical," solution or
cannot make up their mind between two equally attractive proposals.[1]

A more important reason for the lack of decisive and consistent action
was that everything depended in the end on the quality of the cadastral

---

[1] It is reported that a British commission, sitting early in this century, had agreed to
adopt the decimal system, but that it could not reach an agreement on the question
whether the pound was to be maintained at its existing value and was to be divided
into 100 new pennies, or whether it was to be redefined as 100 old pennies. A psychologist may of course assert that the trouble with the members of the commission was that
they really wanted to hold on to the British system. But the fact that two equivalent
solutions were available is of some importance in that it permitted them to gratify this
wish while pretending to themselves and to the world to be reform-minded.

survey or of some other method of classifying and surveying land and land values. It is perhaps the feeling that a realistic survey is beyond hope that accounts for the byzantine discussions about various schemes, all of which are worthless without good survey work. A typical vicious circle is faced here: land taxation is ineffective without realistic land values, yet the administrative effort needed to make a reliable survey will hardly be forthcoming unless the prospective yield of land taxation makes such an effort worthwhile for the national authorities. One way in which the vicious circle can be broken is by technical advances in survey work, such as aerial infrared photography at high altitudes which would materially shorten the time within which an accurate survey can be completed. As a result, the effort may suddenly seem worthwhile to policy-makers with a rather short time-horizon.

Perhaps the cardinal weakness of the tax approach lies in the very simple fact that additional taxation is usually found acceptable only when there is an imperious need for specific new expenditures. Taxes are meant to defray expenditures and the decisive political push for them comes from those who have an interest in making the expenditures, whether they be interest groups or the state itself (for example, in the case of war). In our case, the link between the proposed measures and the beneficiaries was indirect and unclear to the group directly involved: the landless peasant, for example, could not perceive that land taxation would tend to make landowners more willing to sell or rent land to him and might also depress land prices. As for the small farmers, they were openly hostile to the various tax projects. In spite of provisions exempting them, they feared additional taxation far more than they were seduced by the vague prospect that land might become easier and cheaper to buy or rent from the large landowners. The 1960 parliamentary elections confirmed the basic unpopularity of the proposals. The victory of the Ospina faction of the Conservative Party over the Laureano Gómez wing was widely attributed to a swing in the vote of owner-cultivators in the coffee-producing Departments out of apprehension — actively fanned by the candidates of the Ospina group — over the land tax proposals that were being proposed by the government whose Conservative members were at that time primarily identified with the Laureano wing.

An Exception: The Cauca Valley Corporation

The maxim that to push through a tax one must first have or invent a good reason for spending the tax proceeds is confirmed by a successful experience with land taxation carried out in Colombia during the fifties in the Cauca Valley. Here a regional development agency, the "CVC," was established in 1954, after having been enthusiastically promoted by a group of prominent citizen-businessmen of Cali who had brought in David Lilienthal as a consultant.[1] The corporation retained the services of three consulting engineering firms, two from the United States and one from Colombia, and an investment program consisting primarily of large-scale hydroelectric installations and irrigation and drainage works was proposed in the hope that financing would be forthcoming from the International Bank and the national government. In the course of 1955–56, however, the fledgling organization saw this hope founder: first, the Bank decided to suspend new lending to Colombia as it lost confidence in the Rojas Pinilla regime; secondly, that regime itself became increasingly hostile to the CVC, partly because it favored the poorer Eastern provinces of the country and partly because the administrators and directors of the CVC were known to be out of sympathy with the Rojas clique.

Faced with a financial vacuum, the corporation had to lower its sights from the originally planned large-scale projects to pilot flood control and irrigation schemes that would require far smaller outlays and whose cost could be recuperated rapidly by assessing the landowners who benefited. Even so, there was need for initial financing and the CVC decided that it would try to obtain authority for doubling the 4 per thousand tax on rural properties and for earmarking the proceeds for its own operations. Normal legislative procedures having been suspended, a decree of the central government was then all that was needed to enact the additional tax. The Rojas Pinilla government acceded to the request, partly because it felt that after having created the CVC with great fanfare it had to do something for it, partly because it enjoyed taxing the Valle "money-bags," and partly because it secretly hoped that through the tax the CVC and the Valle authorities would make themselves thoroughly unpopular with important circles. A determined battle was indeed fought over the tax, with the traditional landowners and cattlemen in strenuous opposition. But support was

---

[1] In Spanish, CVC stands for Cauca, Valle del Cauca, and Caldas, the three Departments over which the authority of the Corporation (its full name is *Corporación Regional Autónoma del Cauca*) was originally supposed to extend. Eventually, in large part because of opposition to the tax measures about to be discussed, both Cauca and Caldas withdrew from the agency so that its authority and activity have been almost wholly restricted to the Valle Department. This Department, however, contains by far the largest portion of the river valley which is to be benefited under the regional development scheme.

forthcoming not only from the progressive business circles (industrialists, sugar interests, contractors, etc.) who were the original promoters of the Authority, but also from the Church, labor groups and public opinion at large where the CVC idea had become popular. The tax was decreed in January 1956,[1] but the battle over it was vigorously renewed after the downfall of Rojas in 1957, since legislative approval was now required for the tax to remain on the books. The enemies of the tax now tried to present it as one more arbitrary act of the Rojas government. The CVC compromised to the extent of acquiescing to a reduction from the 4 per thousand rate to 3 per thousand and of changing the tax partially into a compulsory bond issue. In this form the measure was converted into law in 1959.[2]

As a result of the tax, the CVC had of course acquired a considerable interest in realistic land assessments and it entered into a special contract with the Geographical Institute designed to accelerate survey work in the Valle Department. It thus demonstrated that while a land tax can hardly become effective without realistic assessment, the latter may follow rather than precede the institution of the tax itself. However, the tax can hardly be expected to muster political support unless the public is aware of and sympathetic to the uses to which the money is going to be put. The idea that public funds are usually wasted is deeply ingrained in Latin America; this is also the principal reason for which taxes, and especially new taxes, are so frequently earmarked for special *fomento* purposes, in violation of the rules of orthodox budgetary doctrine.

The Colombian experience is by no means unique. Whatever redistributive effects progressive income taxation has had in the advanced industrial countries has been a by-product rather than the primary motive. The latter was supplied by some compelling need to increase revenue, usually during wartime. External war, or the threat of war, is thus frequently the condition for achieving a *peaceful* redistribution of income within the country. Without such an external threat and the consequent imperious need to increase *total* expenditures, redistribution is far more likely to take place directly, i.e., through the have-nots seizing the belongings of the haves, than indirectly through taxation of the rich.

The peculiar difficulty facing land taxation as a means of improving the pattern of land utilization and ownership is not so much that it is directed

---

[1] Decree 160 of January 31, 1956.
[2] Law 25 of May 30, 1959. Several of these changes had already been made by the military junta (Decree 282 of October 31, 1957) and were merely confirmed by this law.

against the "ruling class" — legislation taking a good slap at the "oligarch" is by no means uncommon in Latin America. The weakness of land taxation is that while it arouses the opposition of the landed interests, it does not hold out an obvious appeal to any other important social group.

Counterpoint: Colonization

As a bland means of improving land use and distribution, land taxation has its symmetrical counterpart in colonization. The former hurts the existing landowners financially without immediately and concurrently satisfying the land hunger of the landless or minifundio peasants, whereas colonization gives land to these peasants without taking it from the existing landowners. In view of these characteristics, colonization may be expected to be amply tried out in a country where the landowners are powerful and where virgin, state-owned lands are plentiful. The success and historic importance of spontaneous Antioqueño colonization from the nineteenth century onward has of course further enhanced the appeal of this line of policy-making in Colombia.

The Colombian state still owns huge tracts of lands, mostly in the largely unexplored and uninhabited plains east of the Andes and in the rain forest along the Pacific Ocean, but also in various more accessible parts of the Magdalena Valley. When the problems of the landless or minifundio peasant became more pressing, the suggestion was invariably advanced that public lands should be used before private property is touched. "The State is by far the largest latifundista" was the stock phrase with which demands for agrarian reform were met.

The sharpening and increasing frequency of social conflicts in the twenties and thirties indicated precisely that this particular solution had ceased to be readily available. Accessible lands with familiar characteristics (i.e., with attractive altitude and climate) had been largely taken up and spontaneous "colonization" turned frequently into occupancy of privately held properties.

If colonization of public lands was to continue and was to provide an alternative to the occupancy of private latifundios, it appeared that the state had to take a more active part than heretofore, by building access roads and by financing the colono during the initial period of settlement, and perhaps even by making additional investments in schools, hospitals, houses, etc. A few colonies were established in the late twenties and in the thirties with financing provided on an *ad hoc* basis by the national budget and official credit institutions.[1] But the first ambitious effort in this field was undertaken in May 1948, only four weeks after the famous Bogotá riots, with the establishment of an Institute of Colonization, Parcelization and Forest Defense.[2] This action was one among several almost reflex-like reactions to that sudden and awesome explosion of mass violence. However, the outbreak was so extraordinary that it was soon dismissed as an inexplicable accident; this is perhaps the reason why it failed to lead to a continuing active search for ways of relieving social tensions in the country.

The Institute of Colonization, once established with the usual fanfare, was left to lead a rather wretched existence, lacking both adequate financing and personnel. Its principal activity was not in colonization, but rather in "parcelization," i.e., in the subdividing of privately held lands that were already under some sort of cultivation or use. Usually parcelization was the attempt to regularize de facto occupations: the Institute purchased the land from the (nominal) owner and resold it in parcels to the occupants. The Institute took over a number of such operations that were already in progress. In the field of colonization the activity of the Institute, which received only a one-time endowment of ten million pesos, was virtually nil.

Perhaps this was all to the good, for the next stage of colonization policy witnessed a burst of activity as sudden as it was calamitous. Again a political event of great moment led to almost immediate legislative action: one month after the coup in which Rojas Pinilla seized power, a new "Institute of Colonization and Immigration" absorbed the sleepy institute created in 1948 and formulated ambitious and expensive plans for setting up "colonization centers."[3] Under inexperienced management, with hardly any prior study, the Institute plunged into several colonization ventures, built airstrips, bought machinery to set up sawmills, brought volunteer settlers to work poor soils in inhospitable climates and . . . met with total disaster. The evidence of failure and of misuse of public funds must have been rapid and overwhelming indeed for the President to consent, only nineteen months later, to have the Institute, one of his favorite creations, dissolved and whatever remained of its unencumbered assets and activities absorbed by

---

[1] Law 89 of November 18, 1928; a history of colonization efforts is given in Romilio Rodríguez A., "La colonización agrícola y algunos problemas de la tenencia y uso de la tierra en Colombia," FAO, 1957, mimeo., pp. 10–24.
[2] Decree 1483 of May 11, 1948.
[3] Decree 1894 of July 18, 1953.

the Caja Agraria, the old-established and respected agricultural credit institution.[1]

But the peculiar fascination which colonization exerts on successive governments, particularly when they are hard pressed, is unfailing. The Lleras government, while unable to agree on, or to have the Congress vote for, its various land tax schemes, had little trouble obtaining, a few months after its inauguration, a law which provided finance for a renewal of both colonization and parcelization, this time under the guidance of the Caja.[2] Finance was secured by channeling 10 per cent of the deposits of the country's savings banks to the Caja where they were earmarked for the twin programs. The law was entitled "Parcelization Law," probably because of the bad name the Rojas Pinilla regime had managed to give to programs of colonization; but the latter were clearly included among the activities to be engaged in. As under Rojas Pinilla, one of the principal purposes of the Caja's colonization efforts was to resettle peasant families that had been displaced by countryside violence and guerrilla warfare and were living wretchedly as refugees in provincial towns. Several colonization centers were established in widely separated and outlying locations; and the limitations and unanticipated difficulties of this kind of effort soon became apparent once again. The Caja avoided the reckless expenditures which had characterized the Rojas Pinilla ventures, but as a banking institution it committed the opposite mistake: it aspired to set up the colonies on a fully reimbursable basis, by apportioning its basic investments in roads and services among the individual settlers. This policy led to difficulties with existing and potential settlers and the new colonization effort soon bogged down; the total number of families that was settled from 1959 on did not exceed 1,000 when in 1962 the Caja decided to abandon its colonization activities altogether and to transfer them to the newly established Agrarian Reform Institute.

As a result of these repeated failures, difficulties and proven limitations of planned colonization, the Institute appeared determined to concentrate its activities in this field to assisting *spontaneous* on-going colonization, through the building of access roads and the provision of technical assistance and credit to settlers.

---

[1] Decree 461 of March 2, 1956, Article 4, reads significantly: "The Caja . . . is empowered to write off totally or partially debts owed to the Institute that are of dubious or difficult recovery and to reduce (literal translation: chastise) the value of the assets by whatever amount the Board of Directors considers advisable."

[2] Law 20 of May 14, 1959.

A close reading of the record of planned colonization in Colombia could underpin the assertion that this particular line of policy-making is particularly *failure-prone,* just like some persons are accident-prone. Perhaps this is so because the idea of planned colonization, of carving a harmoniously functioning community out of the wilderness, has a good chance of attracting the crackpot, the utopian planner and, of course, the prestige-hungry politician, interested in "inaugurating" a model colony. At the same time, because colonization schemes appear to offer an escape from the nasty class struggle, there is a good chance that they will on various occasions be proposed as the best solution to the land problem — and a similarly high probability that such schemes will fail. Hence, this line of policy-making presents many a wandering policy-maker with an inviting alley which, upon turning out to be blind, helps to convince him that the issue of expropriation of privately held lands cannot be eschewed after all. The authors of the preface to the land reform project, which we shall examine presently, issued a remarkably candid and well-balanced statement on this point:

> It is frequently said that the possibility of occupying public domain lands . . . makes it unnecessary to utilize, for the purpose of carrying out the agrarian social reform, lands that are today in private hands. The most superficial analysis would be sufficient to dissipate so erroneous an opinion. . . . the cost of colonization is very high and the obstacles . . . notorious. Only in certain easily accessible regions, incorporated already or almost into the national economy, can colonization be meaningful from the human and economic points of view. We do not ignore the large contribution it can make but it is evident for us that the social-agrarian reform could not be confined within its limits.[1]

THIRD PHASE: LAND REFORM

Adoption of Law 135

The resistance of Congress to the territorial tax combined with the electoral victory of the Ospina wing of the Conservatives in early 1960 had dashed any hopes of attacking the problem of land utilization through fiscal measures. But just when it appeared that government and Congress were unable or unwilling to take any action on the land problem, an entirely new endeavor got underway which was to culminate in December

---

[1] *El Tiempo,* Bogotá, October 25, 1960.

1961 in the signing into law by President Alberto Lleras of Colombia's So-cial-Agrarian Reform.[1]

Thus, after a decade of tinkering with the indirect approach to land re-form via taxation, the country turned away from it and chose the direct ap-proach. In part, this was of course the result of the political resistance to taxation. But at the same time it had become increasingly clear that the conversion of some grazing lands to mechanized crop production, which was one of the principal objectives and likely results of the various tax schemes, would do little to improve the lot of the mass of Colombia's rural population. As we have noted, this conversion had been proceeding apace in some areas during the late fifties; yet the levels of living in the traditional mountainous areas of settlement had rather deteriorated because of the natural increase in population and the consequent further splitting up of al-ready uneconomically small holdings, because of the drop in world coffee prices, and because of the long-continued and widespread insecurity and violence.

In mid-1960, renewed concern over possible peasant movements arose. In the congressional elections of March a newly organized left-wing faction (MRL — Movimiento Revolucionario Liberal) of the Liberal party led by Alfonso López Michelsen, a son of the former President, had made a good showing in the countryside as well as in the capital, and some of the leaders of the old-established, Communist-led peasant enclaves not far from Bo-gotá stood for election — on the MRL ticket — for the first time and won. There were scattered reports about land invasions. In March the widely read weekly *Semana* had carried a special report on "El incendio agrario" (the agrarian blaze) with detailed data about the numerous rural conflicts. Finally, in mid-1960 the attraction exerted — and the fears provoked — by the Cuban revolution were perhaps at their peak.

These factors, together with the proven impossibility of pushing mean-ingful land tax measures through the Congress, were responsible for a com-plete change in scenery: one political leader after another now pronounced himself in favor of some sort of "agrarian reform." A Conservative Senator gave voice to widespread feelings when he declared: "I do not wish to be a prophet of doom: but if the next Congress fails to produce an Agrarian Reform, revolution will be inevitable."[2] And a Catholic trade union leader

---

[1] Law 135 of December 13, 1961. Senado de la República, *Reforma Agraria*, Im-prenta Nacional, Bogotá, 1961. This booklet contains the bill as it came out of the Senate Committee (and as it was finally passed by both chambers), together with a very useful report by Carlos Lleras Restrepo.

[2] Diego Tovar Concha, as reported in *El Espectador*, July 11, 1960.

agreed: "The Agrarian Reform must take place anyway for the people have been realizing the need to break up the present structure of land property and if this need is not satisfied by legal means, a revolutionary movement is likely to do so."[1] The leader of the Liberal Party, Carlos Lleras Restrepo, may have shared this belief or, as an expert politician, he may have sensed a unique opportunity to shake the National Front government out of the *inmovilismo* (inaction) which had begun seriously to undermine its strength and appeal. In any event, he now took hold of the situation with unique determination, tenacity and intelligence.

To begin with, he encouraged the political leaders of the various parties and factions to put in writing their opinions on the agrarian problem and a sort of public essay competition ensued. From the essays which were published by the daily press, an optimist could draw the conclusion that the distance between the various points of view was perhaps not unbridgeable. President Alberto Lleras then decided to constitute a National Agrarian Committee in which all political tendencies as well as the Church, the Army and various interest groups were to be represented. Under the chairmanship of Carlos Lleras, who had just been elected by Congress to be Vice-President, the committee was to propose an agrarian reform law to the Cabinet, which in turn would introduce it into Congress.

The representatives of the Laureano Gómez Conservatives and of Alfonso López Michelsen's MRL decided not to participate in order to be free to oppose the project in the Congress, but a wide spectrum of opinion was nevertheless present in the committee (for example, left-wing opinion was represented by a number of Congressmen with advanced opinions and by Gerardo Molina, the rector of Bogotá's Universidad Libre).

Constituted by decree on August 31, 1960, the committee met for the first time on September 8. Supplied with a constant flow of working papers by the indefatigable Carlos Lleras, it issued its unanimous report and draft law consisting of 101 articles, many of which were lengthy, after barely seven weeks of intensive work, on October 24.

The legislative procedure was far more laborious, and in fact the greatest danger threatening the project was not so much the various concessions to Conservative opinion that became necessary as the possibility that passage of the project would not be completed before the congressional and presidential elections of 1962. Moreover, after December 1961, legislation em-

---

[1] Remarks by Delegate Eugenio Colorado during the discussions of the National Agrarian Committee, in September 1960 — Comité Agrario Nacional, *Acta No. 2* (processed).

powering the Congress to decide the matter by simple vote would expire: thereafter a two-thirds majority would be required and would most likely be impossible to achieve because of the opposition of both Laureano Conservatives and the MRL.

Hence the deadline for the project was December 1961 and it was barely met. The National Agrarian Committee project was presented in November 1960 by the government to the competent Senate committee where it was vigorously discussed and amended during the first months of 1961. The revised project was presented to the full Senate in a lengthy report by Carlos Lleras in April and received a favorable vote in June. It was now essential that the House accept the Senate version as it stood, for any change would have required the return of the project to the Senate and hence would have made it impossible to complete the legislative process in 1961. The House, which, like the Senate, contained a good number of landowners, settled down for lengthy discussions of the project, and it took all the skills of persuasion and pressure of Carlos Lleras to achieve passage toward the very end of the session, in November 1961. The project became law (Law 135 of 1961) on December 13, 1961 when President Alberto Lleras affixed his signature to it at a solemn ceremony.

Bargaining on Expropriation and Compensation

The Reform Law is essentially the outcome of two negotiations: one in the National Agrarian Committee and the other in the Senate. Both times discussion centered around the most sensitive issue of any land reform: who can be expropriated and how is he going to be paid? It was rather easy to reach a consensus on the order of priority which the future land reform was to follow in distributing land to campesinos in any given area: first, easily accessible publicly owned lands were to be tapped, then similarly situated privately owned, uncultivated lands, then poorly cultivated lands and only as a last instance was expropriation of properly cultivated lands to be envisaged. Yet it was also agreed that seizure of such lands could not be avoided altogether as, for example, in areas where minifundio holdings were to be enlarged or when an absentee owner had subdivided his property and rented out individual lots without making any managerial or financial contribution of his own. Those were precisely the cases which had most frequently led to rural conflicts, to refusals to pay rent, etc.[1] More-

---

[1] Cf. Carlos Lleras Restrepo, "Planteamientos de la reforma social agraria," *La Nueva Economía*, Vol. I, No. 1, 1961, p. 27.

over, if it was considered desirable to move farmers from the eroding slopes to the plains, as had been so frequently proposed by international experts, expropriation and splitting up of even properly used level lands might also be necessary in some areas, particularly since for land to be considered as "in economic use" it had traditionally sufficed that it carry no more than one head of cattle per hectare.[1] Since it was clear, then, that any reform had to contemplate the expropriation of properly cultivated lands in certain cases, this issue was not an attractive one on which to make a stand from the point of view of the conservative forces. As a result, the principal fights in the committee and the Senate were over the manner of payment for lands subject to expropriation.

That payment in bonds was permissible for uncultivated or inadequately cultivated lands could be made to follow without undue difficulty from Law 200, which had ordered outright confiscation for lands that remained uncultivated for more than ten years. With so radical a penalty for a serious neglect of the "social function of property" already in existence, the proponents of the reform project could convincingly argue that it was reasonable to apply milder penalties (such as expropriation with payment in bonds) to other, somewhat less serious forms of neglect. But what if there was no neglect at all? Should the constitutional provision[2] that expropriation requires *"prior compensation"* then apply?

Here again, however, the brief but ardent "New Deal" period through which Colombia had passed in the thirties with the first López administration stood the reformers of 1960 in good stead. For the same article that established "prior compensation" as the general rule had a "radical" last paragraph which permitted the Congress, through majority vote of both houses, to expropriate *without* any compensation "for reasons of equity." Hence, Carlos Lleras could argue convincingly that if the Constitution authorizes the Congress to order confiscation, then it certainly permits that body to pass a law which provides for a form of payment that is intermediate between zero and full cash in advance. "Who may do more, may do less" was the legal axiom with which he buttressed his argument.[3]

In the case of this paragraph of the constitution, as in that of the reversion rule of Law 200, a provision that was utopian in the context of the contemporary social structure had been adopted in a moment of exaltation and had perhaps achieved passage largely and somewhat demagogically just

---

[1] Art. 6 of Decree 59 of 1938.
[2] Art. 30 of the Constitution of 1936.
[3] *Reforma Agraria*, pp. 115–116.

because it was never expected to become operative. Later on, however, the
existence of such a provision, even though still largely inapplicable in itself, facilitated considerably the adoption of some less advanced, yet
solidly progressive and more workable measures.

With the constitutionality issue thus disposed of, the battle in the committee, and again later in the Congress, turned around the terms and conditions of deferred payment for the to-be-expropriated lands. The opposition to compensation in long-term, low-interest bonds must of course be
expected to be particularly strong in a country without a developed capital
market and with a chronic inflation (the rate of Colombia's inflation as
measured by various price indexes was close to 10 per cent per year in the
fifties). But in a sense, once the discussion was allowed to get onto this terrain, the principle of the reform had already been accepted[1] and this may
well have been the tactic of the pro-reform forces.

The table shows the three stages of negotiations starting with the proposal of Carlos Lleras Restrepo to the committee, which must be interpreted as an initial bargaining move. As can be seen, the adequately cultivated lands were split in the course of the negotiating process into two
categories that were to be treated quite differently: For lands actually par-
celled out among tenants or sharecroppers and where the absentee owner
merely provides the land and carries no financial risk, Carlos Lleras received from the committee practically what he had proposed. But a real
deadlock developed over the lands whose cultivation is managed and financed by the owner: here the idea of compensation in long-term bonds
which were sure to suffer considerable depreciation in the market was
fiercely resisted and agreement was reached only by providing for part
payment in cash and part payment in bonds *computed at their market
value* — financially a most unsound idea but one which had the virtue of
achieving a temporary compromise within the committee.

Once the project was introduced into the Congress, the bargaining process started all over again, partly because of the very unsoundness of the
committee compromise, but mostly because the principal counterpart of
Carlos Lleras in the committee, the Conservative leader and Presidential
aspirant Gilberto Alzate Avendaño, had suddenly died. The laboriously

---

[1] An old Jewish story makes this point neatly: A customer steps into a shop to en-
quire about the price of a hat in the window. "Five dollars," replies the storekeeper.
"Oh, no that's much too expensive, I might give you two dollars," says the customer.
The shopkeeper now settles down to bargain, but first he triumphantly whispers to his
wife: "The fellow already *has* the hat."

concluded negotiation behind which Alzate had been expected to rally his party was now reopened and further concessions to Conservative opinion became necessary: the cash payments were slightly increased and the terms of the deferred payment were considerably shortened. But some partially compensating gains were achieved by the pro-reform forces: interest rates were lowered and the unsound feature of the committee project concerning payment in bonds computed at their market value was eliminated.

THE BARGAINING PROCESS ON TERMS OF PAYMENT FOR EXPROPRIATED LANDS

	ORIGINAL C. LLERAS PROPOSAL[a]	COMMITTEE PROJECT	LAW 135
Uncultivated land[b]	30-year, 2% bonds; no amortization for 5 years.	25-year, 2% bonds	25-year, 2% bonds
Inadequately cultivated land	20-year, 3% bonds; no amortization for 2 years		
Adequately cultivated land but through tenants and sharecroppers[e]	15-year, 6% bonds[f]	50,000 pesos cash; remainder in 15-year, 7% bonds	20% of value of property in cash, but not more than 100,000 pesos and not less than 75,000 pesos;[e] remainder in 8 equal annual installments (non-negotiable) with 4% interest.[d]
Other adequately cultivated land	15-year, 6% bonds[f]	200,000 pesos cash; next 500,000 pesos in 15-year, 7% bonds computed at market value; remainder in same bonds computed at nominal value.	20% of value of property in cash but not more than 300,000 pesos and not less than 150,000;[e] remainder in 5 equal annual installments (non-negotiable) with 6% interest.[d] Expropriation permissible only in specifically enumerated situations.

[a] *Documento de Trabajo No. 5 of Acta* of National Agrarian Committee.
[b] That cannot be confiscated outright under Art. 6 of Law 200.
[c] Provided, of course, that property is appraised at more than this minimum.
[d] Or 15-year, 7% bonds at option of expropriated owner.
[e] And without managerial and financial contribution from owner.
[f] The Lleras proposal did not differentiate between various kinds of adequately cultivated land.

The objection to payment in bonds that could and would depreciate in the market was countered by a new, purely face-saving formula: in lieu of bonds, the expropriated owners were to receive Treasury obligations which, being non-negotiable, would not *exhibit* any depreciation; at the option of the owners, these obligations could be exchanged into negotiable, longer-term bonds.

One further concession was made by the sponsors of the legislation in the Senate: The committee project had provided that *all* lands were subject to expropriation even though the Institute should turn to properly cultivated, owner-operated lands only as a last resort. But the Senate Committee decided that such lands could only be expropriated in specifically listed circumstances, for example, if they were needed to remedy minifundio conditions in a nearby zone. Actually this concession was not very serious because the listed circumstances under which expropriation remained permissible covered the most important situations under which it was in fact desirable. As a general rule, an expropriated owner was entitled to retain 100 hectares for his own use.

The compromise on expropriation — especially the shortening of the terms of payment to five years for adequately cultivated lands — no doubt made purchase of such lands on any really large scale a rather expensive affair for the Colombian Institute of Agrarian Reform (INCORA), which was to be established. But since the financing of INCORA was rather generous — it was to receive 100 million pesos each year from the budget (i.e., about 4 per cent of total fiscal revenue) plus the income from bonds to be issued in its favor which was expected to double this budgetary allotment — the concessions by no means made it impossible for INCORA to develop some forceful action, the more so since its action could be expected to focus initially on inadequately cultivated land. Moreover, much would depend on the definitions of adequately vs. inadequately cultivated lands and on the prices at which the to-be-expropriated properties would be appraised; in both these respects the regulatory decrees which were issued in 1962 were to be quite helpful.[1]

The Law and the Decrees

To do justice to the Reform it is not nearly enough to consider the terms and conditions on which lands can be expropriated. In fact, it is possible

---

[1] See pp. 151–152.

that the fascination with this particular topic made it possible to speed through Congress a great many highly important new land policies provided for in the law which it might not have been easy to get through Congress had they been presented in isolation. Here are some of the more important of these innovations:

1. An Institute of Agrarian Reform was to be set up, with adequate staff, powers and means to enforce and administer the Law. This was largely the result of experience with Law 200, the ineffectiveness of whose provisions on reversion to the state of uncultivated lands can be traced in part to lack of administrative energy and continuity in the Ministry of Agriculture. Moreover, the creation of an Institute made it possible to write into the law only the general principles of expropriation and thereby to postpone the hardest decisions, i.e., the actual application of those principles to individual holdings.

2. The Law broke new legal ground in an endeavor to avoid either the spread of excessively small (minifundio) holdings or the return to latifundio patterns of properties to be subdivided in pursuance of the Reform. With respect to minifundios, the Law establishes a general rule declaring legally void any subdivision resulting in the creation of properties of less than 3 hectares; it also lays down procedures for consolidation of widely scattered small holdings. On the other hand, when farmers receive lands as a result of reform projects, acquisition of title to such lands is conditional upon performance during a certain period and even thereafter the owners are not free to resell or rent their lands: the Institute retains certain residual property rights and the Law approaches here the Mexican ejido type of property.

3. The Law contained much-needed provisions about expropriation and limitation of property rights in areas in which public irrigation, flood control or drainage projects are undertaken. In the absence of appropriate legislation, irrigation projects had usually failed to change latifundio patterns of land tenure and, in spite of attempts to tax away capital gains, had frequently resulted in making millionaires out of existing landowners in areas where public works financed through the budget or through international loans were undertaken.[1]

---

[1] For example, in the irrigation projects of the Saldaña and Coello rivers, financed in part with Export-Import Bank loans. Arcesio Tovar Andrade, *Problemas agronómicos de los distritos de riego del Coello y Saldaña y su posible solución*, Universidad Nacional de Colombia, Facultad de Agronomía del Valle, Palmira, 1962, mimeo., pp. 21–22.

4. Acreage limits were set to the amount of land that can be adjudicated to private persons out of public lands.

5. Finally the Law attempted to put teeth into the celebrated Article 6 of Law 200 according to which privately owned land reverts to the state if left uncultivated for ten years, principally through the following:

(a) The new Institute itself rather than, as before, the Ministry of Agriculture was empowered to enforce Law 200.

(b) A requirement was established that all owners of large properties — initially those of more than 2,000 hectares — declare their holdings to the Institute with indications as to their use; in case of non-compliance the owners cannot invoke the judicial procedure through which they can appeal against extinction of their property rights.

(c) The judicial procedure itself was simplified and some of the delays provided for in Law 200 were shortened.

(d) It was specified that "physical impossibility" to cultivate, due, e.g., to floods or droughts, cannot be argued as a valid excuse for non-cultivation and hence cannot halt the application of the Law (Art. 68).[1]

All of these are important and progressive stipulations, and some of them are outright revolutionary from the point of view of Colombia's legal and administrative tradition.

All in all, then, the Law had considerable potential strength and if applied with determination could become a powerful instrument for changing Colombia's agrarian structure. This was realized with some surprise by the general public during the first half of 1962 when a strongly pro-reform Minister of Agriculture, Hernán Toro Agudelo, and Enrique Peñalosa, the energetic first General Manager of INCORA, issued a series of regulatory decrees based on the Law and started the first land reform projects (the Minister is the President of the Board of Directors of INCORA and as such wields considerable power over its policies).

In the past, decrees which are to spell out in some detail the general rules laid down by a law had frequently frustrated its reform intentions as various interest groups brought to bear their influence on the officials drafting the decrees with greater efficiency than on an enthusiastic or demagogic Parliament. Now the opposite occurred: a notable effort was made to ex-

---

[1] The regulatory decree No. 1489 of 1962 added disturbances of public order as another excuse that cannot be invoked. Given the wide range of the *violencia*, this provision was absolutely essential if the law was ever to be applied anywhere. Nevertheless it aroused vehement protest (cf. article by Manuel Castellanos in *El Tiempo*, June 27, 1962).

ploit up to their limits the powers to act that Law 135 contained and which frequently lay hidden under its own careful and abundant prose. Naturally the decree-drafters were soon accused of going beyond those limits.[1] While this charge cannot be discussed here, the activist spirit that animated the drafters of the decrees is clearly evident in the following rules:

(a) In expropriating lands the Institute is to follow the priorities established by the Law,[2] but the administration of these rules is to be a matter of internal decision of the Institute.

(b) The Institute was authorized to disregard the order of priorities generally imposed and to expropriate adequately cultivated properties along with others when a person is found to own more than 1,000 hectares in one or several large properties in different parts of the country; in issuing this rule the drafters of the decree interpreted the general mandate contained in Art. 1 of the Law to "eliminate the inequitable concentration of rural property" as limiting and superseding the detailed provisions on priorities in particularly flagrant cases of monopoly over land resources.

(c) Fairly stringent conditions were set down for considering a property to be adequately (rather than inadequately) cultivated; for example, it was required that the yield of such lands in relation to their commercial value should be at least 6 per cent.

(d) The basis for the appraisal of the properties to be expropriated, a most important matter on which Law 135 had been strangely vague, was decided by decree. The Law had merely established a procedure: a corps of expert appraisers was to be organized by the Geographic Institute and appeals against their decision by the owner would lead to a reappraisal, etc., but the Law itself did not provide the appraisers with any guidelines for their delicate work. It probably was generally assumed in the Congress that the appraisers were to aim at the commercial value of the property, for what else could they attempt to "appraise"?[3] Nevertheless, a decree of July 1962, in-

---

[1] An animated public discussion on this topic took place on July 18, 1962 between Guillermo Amaya Ramírez, who had taken an important part in drafting Law 200 of 1936, and the Minister of Agriculture. The principal decrees here commented are No. 1489 of June 12, 1962 and No. 1904 of July 18, 1962. See, for the text of the decrees and for a spirited defense of their legality by their principal author, Hernán Toro Agudelo, *Reforma Social Agraria*, INCORA, Bogotá, Editorial Iris, 1962.

[2] See p. 144.

[3] In his report to the Senate, Carlos Lleras mentions at one point, in an off-hand way, that the Law is generous to the landowners because of the terms of payment and because they are going to be paid the commercial value of their properties. Cf. *Reforma Agraria*, p. 123.

voking the precedent of a law passed in 1959, prescribed that the price to be set by the appraisers could in no case exceed 130 per cent of the assessed (cadastral) value of the previous year![1] In view of the fact that the assessed value of many properties, particularly of the larger ones, lagged traditionally and considerably behind their real commercial value, this provision was perhaps the strongest one of the whole body of new legislation and did much to offset the concessions to conservative opinion that had been made earlier to obtain the wide political and Congressional support needed to pass the Reform Law.

First Reform Projects

While the powers of the new Institute were thus being enhanced and fully spelled out before the new administration of Conservative Guillermo León Valencia took office in August 1962, several agrarian reform projects were being organized. The first was undertaken in the region of Cunday in Tolima where a wide area (altogether some 25,000 hectares), including some valley lands as well as some of the country's remaining large coffee plantations, had long suffered from neglect because of the civil strife that devastated the region between 1954 and 1957.[2] In 1961 groups of pauperized landless peasants of the region invaded several of the haciendas and this pressure, combined with the opportunity to achieve a considerable improvement in economic and social status for a particularly unfortunate group of farmers, determined the selection of this area as the first in which agrarian reform was to become a reality.

Once some of the coffee plantations were expropriated and divided into individual holdings, a first group of 80 titles covering 2,000 hectares was distributed to the beneficiaries in one of the last official acts of the Lleras administration, on July 29, 1962.

At the same time, other projects were being readied. The second one to be officially announced was in the Department of Nariño whose highlands were generally thought to be fully divided up among minifundio holders,

---

[1] This rule was laid down in Art. 1 of Decree 1904 of 1962 and the precedent invoked is Art. 3 of Law 20 (the "Parcelization Law," see p. 140) of 1959. This article had indeed set the same 130 per cent rule and had not aroused much opposition in view of the limited import of Law 20. The provision was not applied in subsequent years since the principal activity that took place under Law 20 was colonization of public lands.

[2] Mons. Germán Guzmán et al., La violencia en Colombia, Universidad Nacional, Bogotá, 1962, pp. 92–99.

so that colonization of lower lying lands on either side of the cordillera seemed the only solution. While the Institute decided on a program of support for spontaneous colonization in some areas, its technicians knew that some large, poorly exploited haciendas continued to be embedded among the minifundios in several municipios. In Consacá, for example, only 25 miles from the provincial capital of Pasto, 89 per cent of the land was in the hands of nine landowners, almost all belonging to the "power elite" of the Department. And here, so says a technical report on that area, "we meet with work conditions which many believe to have been abolished long ago in our country: *agregados* who work on the hacienda during two or three days per week, without any remuneration, in exchange for the right to cultivate a parcel of land of one or two hectares...."[1]

With its Tolima and Nariño projects, INCORA demonstrated that it would give high priority to the immediately pressing, if grubby, task of making owners out of tenants *in situ* and of providing minifundio holders and landless farmers with farmsteads of adequate size by carving up nearby haciendas, both on the hills and in the flatlands.

The Institute was also planning more glamorous operations of large-scale resettlement in conjunction with irrigation, drainage and similar infrastructure investment, but the increase in mechanized farming operations on the country's richest and best located flatlands made it unnecessary and undesirable for INCORA to concentrate on following the old Currie report's sweeping advice to settle these plains entirely with campesinos from the slopes.

At this point, it should be mentioned that in the meantime Currie had come forward with an entirely different, if no less sweeping, formula: since, so he argued, the hilly and mountainous parts of the country could never provide a decent living to those who work them and since the flatlands are best organized as large-scale mechanized farm units, Colombia's peasants really have nowhere to go but to the cities. Currie coined the term "Operation Colombia" for this new mass movement he proposed and for the large-scale investment and industrialization effort required to provide the new city-dwellers with houses and jobs.[2]

Since this doctrine appeared to provide a "positive" alternative to agrar-

---

[1] INCORA, unpublished document.

[2] Lauchlin Currie, "Operation Colombia — A National Economic and Social Program," Bogotá, May 1961, mimeo. Currie's project is evaluated here only from the point of view of its relation to agrarian reform. Its proposals on how to accommodate a larger population in the cities — an undisputable requirement of Colombian development, regardless of agrarian reform — deserve serious attention and have already led to much useful research and public discussion.

ian reform, it had become the intellectual rallying point of the opposition to the reform project even before its adoption. If there were no possibility of improving the Andean peasant's lot as long as he insisted on remaining a peasant and if the semi-idle latifundio was fast becoming or was perhaps already a myth, any justification for basic institutional changes in land tenure would indeed disappear.

But, as INCORA's very first actions were to show, the picture painted by Currie of Colombia's agriculture was much overdrawn. In spite of the increasing subdivision of peasant-owned lands, there continued to exist, in the words of Carlos Lleras, "a very large number of areas where minifundios are surrounded by poorly utilized grazing lands which constitute the only source of additional land for the smallholder and the only way of creating a different agricultural situation."[1]

Correlatively, extensive areas of the country had remained untouched by the modernizing tendencies that could be noted by the casual observer flying over the Sabana of Bogotá or over the Cauca Valley, and even in these privileged areas the traditional extensive hacienda pattern of land utilization had by no means entirely disappeared.

Perhaps the Institute and its promoters realized that the beginning of modernization in the agriculturally richest and best located parts of the country, far from making agrarian reform elsewhere unnecessary, had reduced the original size of the problem and hence had made it more manageable. The opportunity arose to stage a successful attack on the more backward elements of the agrarian structure precisely because they were becoming circumscribed and isolated. But even so, the mopping up of semi-feudal survivals continuing to exist within a modernizing society is by no means an easy task that can safely be left to automatic forces. The history of Germany and of Japan in the past one hundred years sufficiently illustrates this point.

While the extravagant notion that the problem of the idle or underutilized latifundio had suddenly gone up in smoke was of course avidly espoused by the still powerful latifundistas, its intellectual origin is elsewhere: in our opinion, it stems from the inclination to consider a problem as solved, hence as uninteresting and no longer worthy of official attention and action, once spontaneous and decentralized forces making for a solution are perceived to be at work. Perhaps the basis for this strange misun-

---

[1] Speech of Carlos Lleras presenting the project of the National Agrarian Committee to the Congress. *El Tiempo*, October 7, 1960.

derstanding of the role of centralized state action is once again[1] that the state is typically expected to majestically reorder reality, unaided and un-assisted, by the sole virtue of its power and sovereignty. State action is al-most always advocated to produce a total change in a totally perverse situa-tion, hardly ever is it seen in the auxiliary role of supporting progressive forces that are already about in the society, much less in that of mopping up behind them.

Revolution by Stealth?

In mid-1962 all the instruments were ready to make a reality out of agrarian reform in a Latin American country in which the "oligarchy" re-tained considerable economic and political power. Adoption of the Agrar-ian Reform Law is harder to explain than that of Law 200 in 1936. The lat-ter had also been considered as going against the interests of the propertied classes, but it consisted primarily, as we have seen, in the legalization of situations which were the outcome of numerous de facto aggressions on private property staged by peasants in widely scattered actions. The Agrar-ian Reform Law goes beyond this stage since it contemplates the breaking up of existing latifundios. How could so unnatural, so unlikely an event come about?

It is easy to list some of the basic reasons. We have encountered two principal pressures through which the authorities come to the conclusion that some modification of existing land tenure conditions is necessary:

(1) Social unrest in the countryside resulting from living conditions acutely felt as intolerable is continuously signalled by spontaneous internal migrations of landless peasants, by frequent seizures of land by squatters, and by the ease with which guerrilla bands find re-cruits.

(2) Economic policy-makers facing inflationary pressures and balance-of-payments deficits cannot help noticing that low agricultural pro-duction and productivity share in the blame for both these recurrent difficulties.

At the same time, the latifundio owners, though still influential, see their once dominant position in the social power structure weakened as the Colombian society becomes more stratified. Industrialists and even the pro-gressive farm owners and operators cannot always be counted on to stand

---

[1] See pp. 111–112.

up in public for their backward, semi-feudal brethren, as became clear during the discussion of the territorial tax proposal of 1959.

Turning now to the more immediate circumstances leading to the Agrarian Reform Law, we must list for 1959–60 the powerful "demonstration effect" of the Cuban revolution and land reform and for 1960–61 the fact that agrarian reform suddenly became "respectable" and perhaps even financially rewarding as the Act of Bogotá first and then the Alliance for Progress proclaimed by the U. S. government gave it their support.

Furthermore, attempts at solving the problem in a benign, indirect or evolutionary fashion had long been tried and found wanting. The twin failures of, or disappointments over, colonization and taxation schemes in the fifties had prepared the intellectual climate for the acceptance of direct land distribution as the only effective measure.

From the political point of view, land reform does not suffer from the above-noted disability of land taxation. By espousing land reform a politician makes powerful enemies, to be sure, but he also makes numerous friends. Moreover, paradoxical as it may seem, land reform may be more acceptable than land taxation to the landowners themselves. In the first place, with land reform it is easier than with land taxation to provide for a basic exemption (the 100 hectares of Law 135) through which a relatively small group of landowners is singled out as the target. In this fashion, the small and medium-size farmers, who are politically quite influential in some Colombian departments, are neutralized. In the case of land taxation a basic exemption is of course also possible, but it is likely to be smaller, especially for better lands (in the Cauca Valley the exemption for the tax levied by the CVC is set at 100,000 pesos which corresponds to perhaps 20–25 hectares of good valley lands), and the exemption is moreover subject to erosion through inflation. Furthermore, a tax becomes a certainty as soon as voted by the Congress whereas the expropriations envisioned by Law 135 are only set in motion when the Land Reform Institute gets organized and actually makes use of the faculties given to it by the Law. The threat is therefore less immediate and, who knows, it may never become a reality for any one *individual* landowner who in his own mind attempts to decide which of the two, stiffer taxation or expropriation, is the greater evil. This may well appear to him as a choice between taxation for himself and expropriation for his neighbor and he is quite likely to favor the second alternative.

More generally, passage of the Land Reform may have been facilitated by the long tradition of issuing well-meaning and socially advanced laws and decrees which turn out to be ineffective because of lack of enforcement or clever obstruction. This tradition means that politicians, confident that nothing of importance is going to change, will frequently ostensibly favor and vote in favor of "progressive" measures because of the political advantages connected with such a stand. Yet, every once in a while, these politicians outsmart themselves by acting in this way and they find out too late that they have started up a machine which they cannot control. The chances of this occurring increase as a country begins to dispose of an assertive, talented, reform-minded middle class on which the government is likely to draw to administer its laws. Perhaps this is just what is happening in connection with Colombia's Agrarian Reform if the first steps of INCORA are an earnest of future performance.

One remarkable characteristic of the process through which the Agrarian Reform Law was adopted and is being implemented still requires comment: The social group which stood to benefit most from the law — Colombia's small tenant farmers, sharecroppers, minifundio holders and landless laborers — took only a small and indirect part in its adoption. Land invasions continued to occur at scattered points of the national territory in 1960, but they cannot be compared in strength and impact to those which in the thirties led to Law 200;[1] and during the whole period of fifteen months during which the project was discussed in and out of Congress, the future beneficiaries of the bill under discussion hardly made their voices heard.

One pressure was felt strongly, however, by the leadership of the Liberal party: that of Alfonso López Michelsen's Revolutionary Liberal Movement. The MRL success in the 1960 elections meant that, to retain its following, the Liberal Party would have to prove to the electorate that the National Front government stood for more than the defense of the status quo. This was the more important as in 1962 the Liberals would be called upon — according to the National Front formula — to vote for a Conservative President, a most bitter pill to swallow for Colombia's Liberals and one which stood in great need of some sweetening. In becoming the champion of the Reform, Carlos Lleras was thus responding to basic political realities

---

[1] According to information supplied to the writer by the (Catholic) Federation of agricultural workers (Federación Agraria Nacional — FANAL), a constant trickle of land invasions between 1958 and 1962 affected properties covering an area of 90,000 hectares, largely in the northern departments of Magdalena, Atlántico and Bolívar which had remained quiet in the earlier phases of land conflicts. The Federation has of course precise knowledge only of those actions in which it took part itself.

and pressures of mass opinion. Nevertheless, he conducted his campaign for the adoption of the Reform largely on the level of parliamentary party politics, without appeal to active mass or pressure-group support or action even though he did make a number of speeches in favor of the Reform in the provinces and to audiences that included presumably some campesinos.

Carlos Lleras probably felt that he had enough trump cards in his game and he may even have judged that a direct appeal to the "masses" for support might do more harm than good by frightening those in both parties who would vote for the law in the hopeful belief that it would largely remain on paper. As undisputed leader of the Liberals it was rather easy for him to bring the recalcitrant members of his own party — and there were many — in line behind the project. At the same time, he could exert considerable pressure on the Ospina Conservatives who shared in the government and who needed Lleras' support to have their presidential nominee endorsed as the common candidate of both National Front parties.

"Revolution by stealth" — this is almost how one is tempted to describe, with a mixture of admiration and disbelief, the process by which the possibility of effecting basic changes in the country's agricultural structure has been introduced. In the course of the first seven months of 1962, as the regulatory decrees were issued, a society dominated by traditional power groups noticed with shocked surprise that it had introduced into its own midst a Trojan Horse, an infernal machine called INCORA which seemed to take seriously its mission to "reform the social agrarian structure by means of procedures designed to eliminate and prevent the inequitable concentration of landed property or its anti-economic dispersion."[1] A new fight was now in the making and its outcome would depend in large measure on the attitude of Colombia's newly elected President, Guillermo León Valencia. But it became increasingly likely that INCORA, operating in the open and already subjected to increasingly ferocious attacks from those whose interests it threatened, would now need that direct support from public opinion which had not been invoked earlier. The parallel with Brazil's SUDENE, which had suddenly felt the need for mass support when its continued existence and authority was threatened in 1961, is suggestive here. And, in any event, is it not a pity for a country to exclude the public from viewing, applauding and *living* what is surely one of its finest hours?

---

[1] Quoted from Art. 1 of Law 135.

Inflation in Chile

Percentage Increase by Decade, 1880–1960

PERIOD	PER CENT	AVERAGE ANNUAL RATE
1880–1890	57	5
1890–1900	58	5
1900–1910	109	8
1910–1920	74	6
1920–1930	30	3
1930–1940	94	7
1940–1950	412	18
1950–1960	2089	36

Percentage Increase during Year, 1930–1961

YEAR	PER CENT	YEAR	PER CENT	YEAR	PER CENT
1930	—5	1940	10	1950	17
1931	—4	1941	23	1951	23
1932	26	1942	26	1952	12
1933	5	1943	8	1953	56
1934	9	1944	15	1954	71
1935	—1	1945	8	1955	84
1936	12	1946	30	1956	38
1937	10	1947	23	1957	17
1938	2	1948	17	1958	33
1939	7	1949	21	1959	33
				1960	5
				1961	10

Methods and Sources: The data are taken from official cost-of-living indexes for the city of Santiago based successively on 1913, 1928 and 1958. For the period prior to 1913 use has been made of a price index calculated by Adolfo Latorre Subercaseaux in *Relación entre el circulante y los precios en Chile,* unpublished graduation essay, Universidad Católica de Chile, September 1958. The ten-year data are based on the average value of the indexes for the terminal years, while the yearly data from 1930 to 1961 are calculated for twelve-month periods running from December to December.

Inflation in Chile

Introduction

Among the problems which come frequently and forcefully to the attention of economic policy-makers, inflation occupies a prominent place in many Latin American countries. While the most violent inflation of recent years has occurred in Bolivia and the country with the most acute inflationary problem at present is Brazil, Chile has long been the *locus classicus* of inflation in Latin America on account of the length and virulence of the inflationary process. During a period of over eighty years, it has been interrupted by only brief intervals of comparative price stability. Thus the Chilean experience offers a particularly wide variety of reactions, from attempts to live with inflation to dramatic efforts to halt it. Much theorizing about the cause and cure of the disorder has accompanied these reactions. Hence the experience is potentially rich in suggestions for the learning processes which analysts as well as policy-makers undergo in the course of grappling with a persistent difficulty.

As problems facing policy-makers, inflation and a natural calamity such as drought have one basic characteristic in common: when they reach a certain degree of intensity, a strong compulsion to do something is felt and results in a spate of active decision-making.[1] Severe inflation and drought both victimize certain groups in such an abrupt manner as to make them protest and press for help or redress. This is far less true of such problems as "maldistribution of land" or "imperialist exploitation of natural resources," for example, where action follows typically not upon a sudden appearance or aggravation of the condition, but upon a heightened consciousness of it.

---

[1] In a message to Congress, President González Videla declared that inflation "has acquired the characteristics of a real scourge (*flagelo*)," thus using the very term which commonly denotes the droughts in the Northeast of Brazil. *Mensaje 1947*, Santiago, 1947, p. xxviii.

From our point of view, however, there are also important differences between recurring inflation and recurring natural calamity. In tracing policy-making around the latter we can concentrate entirely on the reactions of the decision-makers faced with the prospect or presence of the calamity. Inflation, on the other hand, is viewed as a man-made calamity due to defective functioning of a social institution, the monetary system. Hence we must also be concerned with decisions causing this malfunction to arise and to recur. What is more, the victims of inflation will be so concerned: they will suspect foul play on the part of those who have not suffered or have profited, while the victims of a natural calamity will not ordinarily point an accusing finger at those who have escaped it. Inflation lends itself peculiarly therefore to the search for a culprit, to recriminations among different social groups, and to proposed solutions along strictly partisan or "antagonistic" lines. This will be so whether or not conflict over the dis tribution of the national product is at the root of the inflation; if that conflict is not the cause of inflation, it will certainly be its consequence.

Another characteristic of the problem of inflation is the fact that its fluctuations are subject to month-to-month or even day-to-day observation and measurement. This may account in part for the fascination with the subject, in preference to other economic and social problems which, while perhaps more fundamental in some sense, signal their existence only at long and irregular intervals. The compiling of price and cost-of-living indexes marks an important step in heightening official and public consciousness of the problem. In Chile, for example, cost-of-living data have existed since 1913, and monthly wholesale price and cost-of-living indexes became available in 1928.[1] Even before this, however, the progress of inflation was in fact being observed by the financial community through the fluctuations in the peso-pound exchange rate, and the housewife, of course, has always been able to notice any sufficiently steep increase in prices without the benefit of cost-of-living indexes.

Concerned as it is with the elusive and highly technical subject of money, the problem has not only been fraught with controversy but has

---

[1] See table. Instead of merely reflecting and signalling the problem, cost-of-living indexes can on occasion create it. This happens when the increases are so small or so largely offset by quality improvements or increases in earnings that the change would not ordinarily be perceived or give rise to demands for wage and salary adjustments. A spectacular instance of the signalling system going haywire occurred in Chile in the fall of 1956 when the cost-of-living index suddenly spurted. This was interpreted as proof of the failure of the stabilization program which had been initiated at the beginning of that year, but it later turned out that the increase was mostly due to the seasonal rise in the price of onions, which occupied a wholly unreasonable weight in the index. Cf. *Panorama Económico*, No. 158, December 14, 1956, p. 773.

lent itself to the recurring hope that somewhere there might be an "expert" who, like the specialist in a rare disease, will know just the right prescription or perform just the right operation. For this reason the foreign expert and mission play an important part in the history of inflation in Chile.

Moreover, the problems of inflation, monetary policy and financial organization exhibit a higher degree of formal similarity from country to country than do the other problems considered in this study — land reform and regional imbalance. Hence, for this problem, doctrines with a claim to universal applicability have arisen early, and these doctrines, changing from time to time, have therefore been important actors in their own right, even if they are not physically embodied in foreign advisers.

Putting this characteristic together with some of the previous ones, we find that inflation is a highly technical and at the same time a highly political problem. As a result there is continuous and intensive interplay between economic doctrine and politically charged issues; the expert frequently finds himself projected into the forefront of political battles, as will be abundantly shown in our story.

A final characteristic of the inflation problem, well illustrated by its history in Chile, is that it is easily "oversolved": deflation, the opposite and perhaps even greater evil, can result from an overdose of anti-inflationary remedies whereas the fight against regional backwardness, for example, can proceed without much worry about sudden excessive prosperity occurring in the backward region. This characteristic of inflation has several results: it may inhibit policy-makers for fear that the remedy may be worse than the disease; on the other hand, if anti-inflationary action is taken and does result in a bout of deflation, policy-making could come to exhibit an oscillating pattern moving from one of the evils to the other and back again, for a prolonged period. Policy-making on inflation in Chile frequently exhibits one or the other of these two features.

Early Inflation History, Courcelle-Seneuil and the Fetter Doctrine (1879–1924)[1]

The early phase of the Chilean inflation has given rise to a widely accepted explanatory doctrine, complete with remote and immediate causes. Among the former, the nefarious influence of a French economist who spent some years in Chile as financial adviser around 1860 ranks high,

---

[1] For general background on Chilean political history in English, see Kalman H. Silvert, *The Conflict Society: Reaction and Revolution in Latin America*, The Hauser Press, New Orleans, 1961, Chapter 4, and John J. Johnson, *Political Change in Latin America*, Stanford University Press, 1958, Chapter 5.

while the Chilean landowning elites, supposedly anxious to lighten the interest burden of their mortgages, are usually considered to be the more directly responsible party. We shall deal with both villains in turn.

In contrast to its later strong propensity toward inflation over many decades, Chile long enjoyed a unique reputation among Latin American countries for financial stability. For several decades after independence, the landowning elite, which dominated the country's political life throughout the nineteenth century, was strongly opposed to anything but metallic currency. One Finance Minister exclaimed in 1824 that bank notes convertible into specie would be admitted "only at the point of the bayonet. The person who dared to propose it would be looked upon as a dreamer, a tyrant, even a heretic."[1] The "calamities suffered" by other Latin American countries (which were also politically far less stable than Chile in the period after 1830) because of excessive issues of paper money were important at that time in causing Chilean authorities to show prudence in monetary matters.[2] With the expansion of commerce, the idea of a governmental bank of issue was much discussed in the 1830's and 1840's but it was finally rejected because of widespread fears of mismanagement and inflation. The right of issue granted in 1849 to one bank, the Banco de Chile de Arcos y Cia., was withdrawn the following year upon public protests and an adverse decision by the Supreme Court.[3]

The needs of the growing economy for means of payment and the distrust of governmental economic activities or regulation combined in 1860 to produce a banking law which established the principle of free, almost wildcat, banking. Private banks of issue were permitted to operate subject only to the provision that the right of such banks to issue notes would be limited to 150 per cent of their capital. The legislation "fixed no minimum capital requirement, no limitation on the nature or maturity of loans, no reserve requirement against either deposits or notes, and no provision of any kind for supervision or inspection by the government."[4]

---

[1] Quoted in Guillermo Subercaseaux, *Monetary and Banking Policy of Chile,* The Clarendon Press, Oxford, 1922, p. 62.

[2] *Ibid.,* p. 62. Also *idem, Historia de las doctrinas económicas en América y en especial en Chile,* Santiago, 1924.

[3] Subercaseaux, *Monetary and Banking Policy of Chile,* p. 61.

[4] Frank W. Fetter, *Monetary Inflation in Chile,* Princeton University Press, Princeton, 1931, p. 8. The responsibility of the 1860 Banking Law for the crisis of 1878 had been affirmed by Agustín Ross as early as 1886 in his pamphlet *Los bancos de Chile y la lei que los rije.* For similar later opinions see Subercaseaux, *Monetary and Banking Policy of Chile,* pp. 73–75, and Julio Heise González, "La Constitutión de 1925 y las nuevas tendencias politico-sociales," *Anales de la Universidad de Chile,* Santiago, 1950, pp. 145–146 and 177.

This "extremely liberal and loose" law[1] has a double significance for our story: a good deal of the responsibility for the 1878 suspension of convertibility of bank notes into specie has been attributed to this law *and* it was drafted by the French economist Jean Gustave Courcelle-Seneuil, who had been contracted to come to Chile as professor of economics and adviser to the Minister of Finance in 1855 and stayed on in this capacity until 1863. The figure and role of this early "foreign expert" are of considerable interest.

A fervent partisan of free trade and laissez faire, Courcelle-Seneuil was able to translate his ideas into reality by drafting a series of basic laws in the fields of money, banking, tariffs and financial administration. Furthermore, as the University of Chile's first professor of economics, he instilled apostolic zeal in his students. Chilean writers and historians have traced to his influence a shift from a pragmatic to a doctrinaire economic policy: "Laissez faire was substituted for the political instinct which [up to then] had oriented the march of the Republic."[2]

One of Chile's foremost historians, Francisco Encina, makes the suggestive point that Courcelle-Seneuil himself was quite well aware of the need to temper theoretical principles with realistic considerations but that his Chilean disciples, several of whom were to reach positions of great influence, were far more royalist than the king and lost all sense of reality and of national interest in their desire to remain faithful to the "postulates of classical political economy."[3]

---

[1] Fetter, *Inflation*, p. 8.

[2] Leonardo Fuentealba Hernández, *Courcelle-Seneuil en Chile*, Prensas de la Universidad de Chile, Santiago, 1946. This monograph gives a detailed account of the activities of Courcelle-Seneuil in Chile.

[3] Francisco A. Encina, *Nuestra inferioridad económica*, Imprenta Universitaria, Santiago, 1912, pp. 309–316, and *Historia de Chile*, Edit. Nascimento, Santiago, 1951, Vol. 18, p. 285. Subercaseaux, Chilean economist and first president of the Central Bank created in 1925, ends his disquisition on Courcelle-Seneuil's theories and influence as follows: "Our most intelligent and illustrious statesmen have come until recently under the disturbing influence of these theories; they kept away from the realistic and inductive study of our economic problems, convinced as they were of the soundness of their principles." Guillermo Subercaseaux, *El sistema monetario y la organización bancaria de Chile*, Imprenta Universo, 1920, Santiago, pp. 126–127.

That Courcelle-Seneuil himself was, as Encina intimates, fully aware of the danger of transplanting foreign ideologies to a soil to which they were not suited, appears from the following suggestive passage:

"This revolution [against the Spanish colonial regime], born as it was from the French ideas of the Eighteenth Century, has introduced into the political system of Latin America a theoretical equality completely alien to its actual social structure . . . To introduce democratic government and universal suffrage into societies previously dominated by a landowning aristocracy, necessarily resulted in a succession of military dictatorships, the frequent rise to power of savage tyrants owing to the support of an even more savage population, the utter lack of any regular administration and of se-

The greatest misdeed attributed to these disciples, notably Zorobabel Rodríguez and Marcial González, by their later critics was the surrender of the nitrate mines of Tarapacá to private foreign interests after Chile's victory over Peru and Bolivia in 1882 in the War of the Pacific. The outline of this story is quickly told. Peru had established government ownership and an export monopoly over the mines a few years before the outbreak of the war and had compensated private producers through twenty-year interest-bearing certificates. The Chilean government, advised by a committee dominated by Courcelle-Seneuil's disciples, decided after the war to return the mines to private ownership, i.e., to the certificate holders, and to limit interference to the levying of a specific tax on nitrate exports. The certificates had greatly depreciated during the war and were bought up in Chile and Peru by such speculators as J. T. North, subsequently "King of the Nitrates," and after the Chilean decision were resold at huge profits largely on the London and Continental financial markets. Thus, from the point of view of later nationalist writers, Chile was deprived — through its own fault — of the fruits of victory because of the nefarious influence of a doctrine which held that the greatest of all evils is state management of business enterprises.[1]

Poor Courcelle-Seneuil! His one-man technical assistance mission could hardly have been more successful, according to ordinary standards of performance. His advice was punctiliously followed, the laws he drafted were passed, his bust stands in the University of Chile and his influence as a teacher and publicist came to be widely felt. But just because of that, virtually every serious ill subsequently experienced by the Chilean economy, from inflation to monoexportation, has been traced to him. Monographs

---

curity for either people's lives or their property. The evil was to reach its climax when, as a result of misplaced admiration for the prosperity of the United States of North America, the central power was dismantled and the people were abandoned to a multitude of local tyrannies, in the name of Liberty." J. G. Courcelle-Seneuil, *Traité théorique et pratique d'économie politique*, Guillaumin et Cie, Paris, 1858, Vol. II, pp. 544–545.

[1] This is essentially the version given by Encina, *Historia*, Vol. 18, Chapter 53, and retold by Aníbal Pinto Santa Cruz in *Chile, un caso de desarrollo frustrado*, Edit. Universitaria, Santiago, 1959, pp. 52 ff. Naturally, the Chilean historians are too thoughtful to attribute this denationalization of the nitrate mines to the influence of Courcelle-Seneuil alone. For one thing, they point out that the inept and corrupt administration of the mines under the Peruvian monopoly had done its utmost to impress the Chilean government with the correctness of the master's teachings. Secondly, an important role appears to have been played by the desire of the Chilean elites not only to maintain their good credit rating abroad but to demonstrate to the world, and to the British in particular, that they were "different" and infinitely more civilized than the rest of Latin America.

and even editorials are still being written today to debunk his doctrines and to show that foreign experts are unable to comprehend and give due weight to Chilean "reality" and national interests.[1]

The unkind way in which history has dealt with the well-intentioned Courcelle-Seneuil is nowhere so evident as in connection with his 1860 Banking Law. This law has generally been considered to carry much of the responsibility for the abandonment of convertibility in 1878. There were of course many other perhaps more basic forces at work, such as the adverse balance of payments resulting from the falling prices of copper, silver and wheat in the seventies and increased governmental borrowings from the banks. But unsound banking, the fact that, in view of the highly permissive 1860 law, "the banks were doing business on a very small margin of safety,"[2] has been widely accepted as an important reason for the suspension of specie payments.

On the other hand, it was precisely to prevent such an outcome that establishment of an official bank of issue had been ruled out! The message introducing the 1860 bill said in fact:

> Several times the establishment of a bank by the state has been proposed; but on each occasion the government has rejected the proposal on the ground that it was extremely dangerous since it placed at the disposal of the Executive the means of exerting a powerful influence upon commerce. Not least to be feared are the possible dangers of paper currency fatal, eventually, to the political freedom and industrial prosperity of any country.[3]

Thus the 1860 Banking Law is the ancestor of that whole class of anti-inflationary measures which in the end conspire to bring about more inflation. It may seem surprising that Courcelle-Seneuil, coming from a country that had long had a bank equipped with the exclusive right of note issue, should not have insisted upon transplanting that institution to Chilean soil. But Courcelle-Seneuil was an ardent partisan of "free banking"

---

[1] See the editorial "Back to Courcelle-Seneuil?" in *Panorama Económico* of August 30, 1957 (No. 174) and "Subordination of Chilean Economic Thought" in *Panorama Económico* of March 1960 (No. 212). Courcelle-Seneuil has been accused of so many crimes that his rehabilitation is becoming a tempting task. It had come to be widely believed, for example, that the opening of coastwise traffic to foreign shipping legalized in 1864 through an ordinance drafted by Courcelle-Seneuil was responsible for a subsequent decline of Chile's merchant marine. This thesis has now been refuted in detail by the painstaking research of Claudio Véliz in his *Historia de la marina mercante de Chile*, Edic. de la Universidad de Chile, Santiago, 1961, Chapter IV.

[2] Fetter, *Inflation*, p. 25. See also p. 164.

[3] Subercaseaux, *Monetary and Banking Policy of Chile*, p. 73.

and was strongly opposed to the monopoly of the Bank of France.[1] Here, then, is a characteristic foible of the foreign adviser: usually he is accused of wanting to do over the country he advises in the image of his own; but in reality he often aims far higher and attempts to endow it with those ideal institutions which he has been unable to persuade his own countrymen to adopt.[2]

While Courcelle-Seneuil and his loose banking law have been deemed responsible for the first act in the history of Chile's inflation — the abandonment of the metallic standard in 1878 — the persistence of monetary instability long after that date required and brought forth a different explanation. Long suggested by several Chilean writers, it received sanction and diffusion through the classic 1931 monograph of Frank W. Fetter whose authority was to be invoked henceforth in Chilean literature as the last word on the subject. The doctrine asserts that the landed interests, as the real profiteers of inflation, were responsible for instigating it. In Fetter's words:

> There is something of a paradox in the fact that a country ruled . . . by a conservative aristocracy, with so stable a political history and so excellent a public debt record, should have had so checkered a monetary experience. The explanation is to be found principally in the heavy indebtedness of the landed gentry, and their dominance in governmental affairs.[3]

By placing this "explanation" in his preface, Fetter gave the impression that it was his most important finding and that it applied to the entire half-century (1879–1925) covered in his study. As with every successful theory, Fetter's views were soon to appear in far more sweeping form. Writing on Chile for *Fortune* in 1938 Archibald MacLeish stated:

---

[1] As he argued at length in his *La Banque Libre*, Paris, Guillaumin, 1867.

[2] Some eighty years after Courcelle-Seneuil's mission to Chile, Federal Reserve experts equipped several Latin American Central Banks which they had helped to organize with highly sophisticated tools of monetary control that they had failed to secure from the United States Congress for the Federal Reserve System.

[3] Fetter, *Inflation*, p. vii. Here is one of many similar quotes from a Chilean source:

"[After 1878] there was one and only one economic group which profited from the paper-money regime: the landowners. Eternally in debt because of the system of extensive agriculture practiced in our country, they found themselves in a most favorable position: their products were sold in England against gold while they settled their accounts here in depreciated money. *This prosperity of the landowners which originated in the unbridled issues of paper-money has been the source of all our calamities.*" (Italics in the original.) Alejandro Venegas (Julio Valdés Cange), *Cartas al Excelentísimo Señor Don Pedro Montt sobre la crisis moral de Chile en sus relaciones con el problema económico de la conversión metálica*, Valparaiso, 1909, p. 41.

The Chilean social problem is an economic problem created largely by the monetary shortsightedness, to use no stronger term, of the *hacendados*, the landowners who ruled Chile *from the eighteen thirties down to the World War*. During that period of peace and prosperity the conservative rulers of Chile, unique among the conservatives of history, depressed the value of their own currency by unnecessary paper issues. Their object, however unconscious, was to enable them to repay with cheaper pesos the mortgages upon which they counted for their European journeys.[1]

The explanation proved appealing for various reasons. It satisfied the detective turn of mind that makes us jump to the conclusion that he who has the motive for the crime must necessarily be the criminal. Inflation benefited certain social classes; hence inflation was planned and organized by these classes, a proposition that is even more plausible when it is recalled that these very classes controlled the country's destiny.

Secondly, the theory was bound to be extremely popular among the articulate groups of intellectuals and politicians hostile to the hacendados and ready to accept and circulate any new accusation against the hated oligarchy.

Finally, the theory was most attractive to those who were intent on restoring monetary discipline. Ordinarily backed for the most part by conservative social forces and preaching belt-tightening and sacrifices, they were able by adopting Fetter's explanation suddenly to assume a new role as "champions of the people."

Granted then that the theory was attractive on several counts and to various groups, was it correct? The present writer can do little more than pose this question and call attention to some facts that undermine or restrict the validity of the theory.

In the first place, it is fairly clear from all accounts, including the painstaking one of Fetter himself, that the act of suspending specie payments in 1878 is quite adequately explained by a number of specific difficulties which had nothing to do with the alleged desire of the hacendados to pay off their mortgages at a bargain or to finance their European trips. The whole affair was one of those lapses from virtue which would have been short-lived, just as the earlier suspension of 1865 caused by the War with Spain, had it not been necessary to postpone restoration of convertibility time and again, first with the War of the Pacific (1879–82) against Bolivia and Peru and then because of the Chilean Civil War of 1891.

---

[1] "South America III: Chile," *Fortune*, May 1938, p. 74. (My italics.)

What strikes the observer during the period from 1878 to 1895 is the single-minded determination of almost every government to get back on a metallic standard by withdrawing Treasury notes from circulation and to raise the value of the peso to some "respectable" parity vis-à-vis the pound sterling. This latter intent, of course, made the operation unnecessarily difficult, particularly in a period of falling world prices, and it was an important factor in the repeated postponements. Restoration of convertibility was tackled with particular ardor after Balmaceda's defeat in the Civil War of 1891, in spite of fresh international complications caused by a threat of war with Argentina. With remarkable insistence, one conversion law was piled on another from 1892 on until one adopted in 1895 finally proved workable, at least in the short run. And who was then behind this determined push which not only terminated the debtors' joy ride implicit in currency depreciation, but actually saddled them with heavier obligations as the value of the Chilean peso was increased by some 25 per cent? None other than the landed "hundred families" who ran Chile's government after having successfully revolted against President Balmaceda!

It was Balmaceda who became closely associated during the last years of his presidency with Manuel A. Zañartu, the intellectual father[1] of the *papeleros* or paper money advocates of the early twentieth century. Balmaceda's economic policies and proposals stood for establishment of a government-owned central bank, for an active public works program, for nationalization of the railroads, for increasing participation of Chilean capital in the nitrate industry. In short, Balmaceda voiced nascent aspirations toward state-managed and state-promoted modernization and nationalism. His adversaries, on the other hand, represented the forces of tradition and included quite prominently the large landowners.

In expressing his puzzlement that these groups pushed so strongly for a return to gold and thus did not act in accordance with their own pecuniary interests, Fetter actually put forward what seems the correct interpretation of those events: "The Congressionalists [i.e., the opponents of Balmaceda] regarded their victory as the vindication of the Constitution and the triumph of law and order and . . . they wanted to prove this to the world by their actions."[2]

In 1891, the old order, under which political stability and financial re-

---

[1] Physical as well as intellectual, for Manuel A. Zañartu was the father of Enrique Zañartu Prieto, the most ardent paper money advocate of later years, therefore also known as "Papelito Zañartu."

[2] Fetter, *Inflation*, pp. 67–68.

sponsibility had earned for Chile a place of the first rank among the Latin American countries, was felt to have been badly shaken: there had been the War of the Pacific with its sudden and somewhat disturbing conquest of mineral wealth, the autocratic tendencies and new-fangled ideas of Balmaceda and finally a savagely fought Civil War. And what was at the bottom of these spiraling disorders? Paper money, of course! The suspension of specie payments was treated in the Chilean literature of the time as though it were a fall from grace; in the late Victorian age, a country aspiring to self-respect, dignity and prestige simply could not "debauch" its currency in the way Chile had done since 1878.

The intensity of feeling was noted by one observer in 1894, shortly before the conversion:

> The President of the Republic has paper money in horror. His firmest intention is to restore metallic circulation. He would consider well worthwhile the sacrifices, disappointments and bitter experiences which the exercise of power brings with it if, upon returning to his home [at the end of his term], he had the satisfaction of saying that he has suppressed the inconvertible paper money and *given back to the country the normal monetary system,* lost for the past 16 years.[1]

Such were the convictions of the old (landowning) elites, the guardians of the country's respectability, and little thought was then given to the advantages of cheap, plentiful and depreciating paper money, except by a small group of former partisans of Balmaceda.[2]

----

[1] Francisco Valdés Vergara, *Problemas económicos de Chile,* Imprenta Universo, Valparaiso, 1913, p. 225. (My italics.)

[2] Contemporary Chilean economic historians with a Socialist orientation, such as Julio César Jobet, celebrate Balmaceda as an early protagonist of economic nationalism and industrial development, but are silent about his and his followers' association with the *papeleros;* in that respect they accept and copiously quote Fetter's affirmation of intimate ties between the *papeleros* and the landowners. In addition to Fetter, they are able to quote in support of their views nineteenth and early twentieth century Chilean writers of quite varied tendencies, such as Alejandro Venegas (*alias* Julio Valdés Cange), a schoolteacher who wrote eloquently about the misery of the lower classes, and Agustín Ross, a prominent *orero* and member of the aristocracy. An exception to this strange chorus of agreement is the always perspicacious Francisco A. Encina, who, in his monumental *History of Chile,* stressed the *papelero* inclinations of Balmaceda and who elsewhere criticized Ross precisely for the thesis identifying the *papeleros* with the large landowners that Fetter was to make his own: "The influence [on inflation] Ross attributes to the landowners, bankers and speculators never had the continuity and importance he supposes." The contemporary economist-historian-journalist Aníbal Pinto Santa Cruz quotes Fetter rather approvingly in his instructive one-volume economic history of Chile published in 1958, but appears to have had second thoughts on the subject two years later. In an article he wrote for *Panorama Económico,* Pinto now said that the *papeleros* "had a certain awareness that the productive resources of the country could and should be mobilized more energetically and that the mechanism of the

Thus the country plunged into the 1895 conversion, probably one of the most disastrous monetary operations of all time. In 1893–94 the average quotation of the peso had been 14 d. Revaluation to 18 d., coming on top of a still falling world price level, inflicted a sharp contraction on economic activity. The peso was hardly ever quoted above its gold export point and a specially contracted stabilization loan of two million pound sterling was rapidly dissipated. Moreover, there was continuing heavy domestic demand for gold coin. A run on the banks in 1898 put an end to the unfortunate and futile episode.

The contrast between the depression artificially produced by the return to gold and the prosperity of the preceding period, particularly during the presidency of Balmaceda (1886–90) which had been marked by vigorous programs of railroad building and of public works in general, made a profound impression. Public sentiment now shifted strongly toward the *papelero* side. Not that the aspiration to return to gold was wholly given up. When inconvertibility was declared in 1898, a new date — 1902 — was set for the next return to the path of virtue. But from then on, as the terminal dates approached, further postponements were legislated, sometimes (as in 1904) jointly with the authority to issue more Treasury notes.

One period if any for which the Fetter doctrine should be able to demonstrate its validity is that from 1905 to 1907. This was the heyday of pre-World War I inflation. Currency in circulation, which had remained remarkably stable after the bank rescue operations of 1898, tripled in these three years and, to judge from the increase in strike movements, the cost of living rose rapidly. For the first time new money was put into circulation neither to stave off depression and panic (as in 1878 and 1898) nor to finance international or civil war (as in 1879–82 and 1891). But again it is

gold standard implied a subjection of national economic activity to the erratic fluctuations of foreign commerce." Here is a beginning of a re-evaluation and rehabilitation of the much-maligned *papeleros* whose principal and most fundamental demand was, after all, the establishment of a central bank of issue. Clearly there is need for the whole *orero-papelero* discussion to be thoroughly reassessed, as Bray Hammond has done so brilliantly for a similar chapter in United States monetary history. Sources: Julio César Jobet, *Ensayo crítico del desarollo económico-social de Chile*, Edit. Universitaria, Santiago, 1955, Chapters II and III; Alejandro Venegas, *Sinceridad: Chile íntimo en 1910*, Santiago, 1910; Enrique Molina, *Alejandro Venegas*, Atenea, Universidad de Concepción, 1939, pp. 57–58; Agustín Ross, *Chile 1851–1910*, Imprenta Inglesa Wescott and Co., Valparaiso, 1910; Francisco A. Encina, *Historia de Chile*, Edit. Nascimento, Santiago, 1951, Vol. XIX, pp. 423–426; the passage in quotes is from Encina's foreword to Guillermo Feliú Cruz, *Chile visto a través de Agustín Ross*, Imp. Encuadernación Pino, Santiago, 1950; Aníbal Pinto, *Chile — un caso de desarollo frustrado*, and in *Panorama Económico*, No. 212, March 1960, p. 112; Bray Hammond, *Banks and Politics in America: from the Revolution to the Civil War*, Princeton University Press, Princeton, 1957.

farfetched to put the blame on the hacendados. The immediate cause was the vigorous business boom — one observer calls it the "exaggerated development of the spirit of enterprise" — that got underway in 1904 and led to sudden and strong demands for finance on the part of firms and individuals.[1] It was, so it would seem, a case of the monetary authorities catering with excessive zeal and flexibility to the needs and mood of the business community. Of course, the complete failure of the authorities to exercise some control, to put on the brakes or to "lean against the wind" still requires some explanation. But it is best accounted for by the peculiar political structure which the country had given itself after the Civil War, with its weakened presidential powers and its eternally and rapidly rotating cabinets. From 1891 to 1915 the average tenure was four months for the Cabinet and only three months for the Finance Minister.[2] As a result, lack of initiative was the rule, and the government was run by an amiable clique of decision-avoiders whose attitude has been epitomized by one of its most prominent members, President Barros Luco, in the immortal saying: "There are only two kinds of problems, those that get solved by themselves and those that defy solution." Thus, after the scarring experience with the gold standard the essential characteristic of monetary policy was drift, rather than a carefully hatched plot.

Inflation had been permitted to proceed unchecked from 1904 on and was fueled further by the reconstruction needs arising from the Valparaiso earthquake of 1906. When the boom collapsed, inflation, its creature, came duly to a halt. This time inflation had been visibly responsible for a great deal of suffering among the wage- and salary-receivers. The nascent Chilean labor and trade union movement, which had drawn early strength from the concentration of large masses of workers at the northern nitrate and coal mines and in the two large cities of Santiago and Valparaiso, received further impetus from these hardships. A succession of violent strikes culminated in 1907 in a strike of nitrate mine workers at Iquique which was

---

[1] Subercaseaux, *Monetary and Banking Policy of Chile*, p. 123; also Fetter, *Inflation*, p. 120, Agustín Ross, in *Chile 1851–1910*, p. 24, rates the business boom as a worse disaster than the earthquake of 1906. Enrique L. Marshall similarly relates how "On the stock exchange speculation suddenly ran wild, favored by the ample credits granted by the banks. Large numbers of corporations were founded and many dubious transactions took place which turned into real frauds perpetrated on naive investors or inexperienced speculators." ("Régimen monetario actual de Chile y sus antecedentes históricos," *Revista de la Facultad de Economía*, No. 14, 1945, p. 92.)

From an average of 18 million pesos in 1900–03 stock issues increased rapidly to 74, 342, and 208 million in the next three years and then dropped back to 66 million in 1907. (Julio Zegers, *Estudios Económicos*, Imprenta Nacional, Santiago, 1908, p. 191.)

[2] Feliú Cruz, *Chile visto a través de Agustín Ross*, pp. 96–97.

suppressed only after one of the worst bloodbaths in the history of the labor movement.[1]

The twelve-year period 1895–1907 which had started with a disastrous deflation thus ended with highly disruptive inflation. Sentiment now turned against the *papeleros* and monetary management became conservative, but with both experiences so close together opinion did not swing all the way back in favor of a new commitment to gold. Both *oreros* and *papeleros* having been discredited in turn, a search began for an intermediate solution that would combine stability with "elasticity." A project creating a central bank of issue, elaborated by a commission of experts in 1912–13 and supported by the government, had almost been adopted by Congress when World War I broke out and caused the Senate to suspend final action.

It was after the inflationary bout of 1904–07 that a number of writers pinned the principal blame for the peso's depreciation on the well-heeled and well-mortgaged landowners.[2] Yet monetary developments during World War I were hardly calculated to confirm these views. In response to the strong demand for Chile's exports the peso was then allowed to appreciate freely and substantially, by about 70 per cent from 1916 to mid–1918; surely, if monetary policy had been conducted in the interests of the debt-ridden landowners, such a rise would have been prevented. Once again the simplest explanation for the course of events was the essential passivity of the monetary authorities combined with a floating exchange rate; it now resulted in a strong rise in the peso's external value just as it had earlier led to its fall. The rise was in turn more than erased when the outlook for nitrate sales darkened toward the end of the war.

The unnerving instability of the country's currency was taken as symptomatic of the incapacity of the traditional ruling groups to govern. It contributed to the sweeping victory of the Liberal Alliance, an anti-oligarchic coalition headed by Arturo Alessandri, in the parliamentary and presidential elections of 1918 and 1920.

The new President was pledged to restore the stability of the currency by linking it to gold. On the other hand, he adopted the old *papelero* project of a government-owned Central Bank which fitted in with his conception of the state's responsibility for economic and social order and which

---

[1] The number of victims has been reported variously as 500 or 2,000. See Fetter, *Inflation*, p. 126, and Jobet, *Ensayo crítico del desarollo económico-social de Chile*, p. 135.

[2] Agustín Ross, *Chile 1850–1910;* Roberto Espinoza, *Cuestiones financieras de Chile*, Imprenta Cervantes, Santiago, 1909; Alejandro Venegas (Julio Valdés Cange), *Sinceridad: Chile íntimo en 1910.*

was by now also endorsed by international and orthodox expert opinion. This program was quite popular as the middle and working classes had become convinced that paper money was a capitalist plot. Nevertheless, as the Senate was dominated by a majority hostile to his government, Alessandri was unable to get this or any other substantial part of his program through Congress until exceptional circumstances gave him virtually dictatorial powers in 1925.

Kemmerer and Depression (1925–1938)

Chile's second return to the gold standard in that year is generally credited to the Kemmerer mission. From the point of view of short-run effectiveness and implementation this is probably one of the most spectacularly successful technical assistance efforts in history. The mission arrived early in July 1925 and the three principal bills it drafted were enacted by decree-laws from August to October of the same year. They were:

(1) A monetary law that established the gold exchange standard and fixed the parity of the peso at 6 d., which was close to the average quotation of the preceding three years.

(2) A law that established a Central Bank in Chile for the first time. The composition of its Board of Directors gave more scope to the representation of private, credit-using interests than had been the case in the Chilean drafts of similar legislation. The principal instruments of monetary control of the Bank were to be the discount rate and, hopefully, open-market operations.

(3) Finally, a general banking law that did away with the permissiveness of Courcelle-Seneuil; the law "placed upon the commercial banks restrictions in line with the best banking practice, and provided for the appointment of a Superintendent of Banks, with power and duties similar to those of a superintendent of banks in an American state."[1]

It all reads like a fairy tale: the metallic standard which had been in a deep, almost uninterrupted slumber for half a century was brought back to life by the magic touch of Professor Kemmerer, renowned money doctor, in what was perhaps the crowning achievement of his remarkable career.

Actually it is not too difficult to account for the accomplishment: Alessandri, who had resigned in September 1924 largely because of his recur-

---

[1] Fetter, *Inflation*, p. 178.

ring difficulties with Parliament, returned triumphantly in February 1925 backed by a military junta and armed with full powers to enact a series of fundamental reforms. Among these reforms, monetary stabilization ranked high, for renewed inflation and the resultant discontent of the Army had in part been responsible for the military take-over of 1924. Fetter describes this situation faithfully, if somewhat ingenuously:

> Although [sic] the political situation at the time was abnormal, it was favorable for the prompt acceptance . . . of the Commission's recommendations. The Constitution had been suspended and Congress was dissolved . . . All legislation was in the form of "decree-laws" which required for their promulgation only the approval of the Cabinet and the President.[1]

Clearly, the political situation was favorable for the mission precisely *because* it was abnormal, because the democratic processes were in abeyance. Moreover, the mission, whose general doctrinal convictions were well known from Kemmerer's previous work, had strong advance backing for what it was going to advise. Upon arrival at the Santiago railroad station the North American professor was received by five or six civilians, officials of the Finance Ministry, and about 300 officers in military uniform and formation! This was clamorous notice that the reforms he would propose would be "backed by the sword."[2]

Under these circumstances, the question arises why it was at all necessary to call in foreign experts. With the President all-powerful, why could he not decree the monetary reform that he deemed best? The answer here seems to be that since 1913, when a monetary and banking commission appointed by the government had issued its report, so many reform proposals had been endlessly and fruitlessly discussed that, according to Subercaseaux, "public opinion had reached a stage of confusion amid so much economic literature."[3] Fetter paints exactly the same picture:

> The sentiment of the country seemed to be overwhelmingly in favor of monetary reform, but the stronger the sentiment for reform became, the more diversified were the proposals and the more distant seemed its realization.[4]

Examination of the many proposals that were put forward with ever-increasing frequency in the period 1913–25 makes it clear that the final Kem-

---

[1] *Ibid.*, p. 171.
[2] Ricardo Donoso, *Alessandri*, Fondo de Cultura Económica, Mexico, 1954, Vol. I, p. 409. Cf. also Fetter, *Inflation*, p. 171.
[3] In a farewell article for Kemmerer in *La Nación* of October 6, 1925.
[4] Fetter, *Inflation*, p. 163.

merer bills did not contain any substantial innovations with respect to the crucial topics of restoration of the gold standard and establishment of the Central Bank. The conclusion is therefore inescapable that the mission served principally as an umpire, or perhaps even as a random device: in other words, it was the means for choosing one out of a number of competing proposals.[1]

This conception of the role of the mission naturally does not cast it in a very creative role. Nevertheless it seems to be the only one that fits the facts of the case, and it is conceivable that the role it played was of critical importance in the decision-making process. Actually the idea of a foreign mission had arisen in 1923,[2] in a period when Alessandri's administration was being paralyzed through senatorial opposition and when many monetary reform proposals were being debated. The hope then must have been to bring in "impartial" outside experts whose authority would break the parliamentary deadlock. But even after parliamentary controls were removed there may well have remained some need for the outside experts' nudge since the protracted discussion of monetary and banking issues may have communicated uncertainty and vacillation to the executive branch itself.[3]

While it is frequently the role of parental authority to decide quite arbitrarily certain questions which the squabbling children are unable to settle among themselves, the exercise of this kind of parental authority is humiliating for the children. In the same way the need to resort to a foreign mission must have been rather galling to Chileans who had expended considerable intellectual travail and ingenuity over a long period on the attempt to bring order to their monetary and banking system. This resentment was still apparent twenty-five years later in Alessandri's reminiscences about this period in which he emphatically denied that Kemmerer had brought to Chile either the idea of establishing a Central Bank or the particular

---

[1] Naturally the foreign mission will come forward with a version somewhat different from any of the existing ones. But this does not change the situation. Suppose that at a certain time five variants of a reform proposal exist; it is then quite easy to imagine additional variants formed through a process of permutation and slight modification of the various components of the basic proposal. The mission will then pick one of these conceivable variants rather than any of the existing ones.

[2] Fetter, *Inflation*, p. 170, and Arturo Alessandri Palma, "Las cuestiones económicas, el régimen parlamentario y la cuestión social en Chile desde 1891 hasta 1925," *Atenea*, April 1950, p. 148.

[3] A Chilean economist later remarked that the use of foreign experts to draft important legislation is congenial to dictatorial regimes which are anxious not to have their projects known and discussed by the public prior to promulgation as full-fledged laws (Marshall, "Régimen monetario de Chile," p. 98). While this is an excellent point, it does not seem to cover the Chilean situation of 1925 very well, in view of Alessandri's earlier call for Kemmerer's services.

norms according to which it was to function.[1] Yet, on the whole, there was little *immediate* ill feeling toward the Kemmerer mission, in striking contrast to the treatment accorded the Klein-Saks mission which arrived on the scene thirty years later. What hostility there may have been was probably suppressed by the expectation that a reform bearing Kemmerer's name would provide Chile with access to the New York financial market which was then opening up widely.[2]

In one respect, the return to gold of 1925 represented a definite advance over that of 1895: in line with a number of stabilizations of the twenties, no attempt was made to increase the value of the currency before stabilization and thus deflation was avoided.[3] In addition, Chileans thought that they had improved decisively on the pure gold standard and its lack of "elasticity" by adopting that new invention of the twenties, the gold exchange standard, which allowed the Central Bank to redeem their notes in sterling or dollar drafts rather than in gold.[4] However, in a return visit in 1927, Kemmerer disabused his Chilean friends of any notions that the monetary system to which they had subscribed was lacking in discipline. When asked what kind of monetary policy should be followed in a crisis, he declared: "I do not hesitate to affirm and to reiterate that the Public Authorities must face all the consequences of the crisis before abandoning the gold standard."[5]

This last bit of advice was to be frequently and sarcastically recalled in Chile for it was followed with disastrous consequences. Proud of regaining its monetary stability, Chile was understandably reluctant to return to the slippery path of inconvertible paper money and when the Great Depression came it fought a bitter and exhausting rearguard action to ward off the inevitable.

---

[1] Alessandri, "Las cuestiones económicas," pp. 148–150. Note also the following comment: "The project elaborated by the 1912 Commission which was about to become law and its subsequent drafts make it quite clear that Chile counted with an adequate number of persons qualified to advise the Government on the task that it had set out to do." (Marshall, "Régimen monetario de Chile," p. 95.)

[2] Kemmerer listed this expectation as one reason for the popularity of American-led financial missions in the twenties. "Economic Advisory Work for Governments," *American Economic Review*, March 1927, pp. 1–12.

[3] There also were some conspicuous exceptions, e.g., the pound sterling and the Italian lira, which repeated the Chilean mistake of 1895.

[4] "To avoid the danger that a situation might arise in the future similar to that which in 1898 obliged us to take up again with paper currency, the law . . . establishes the . . . so-called gold exchange standard." Subercaseaux in *La Nación*, October 6, 1925.

[5] E. W. Kemmerer, interview published in *La Nación*, July 31, 1927, reprinted in *Funcionamiento de nuestra legislación bancaria y monetaria*, Balcells & Co., Santiago, 1927, p. 39.

The extraordinarily violent decline in Chilean exports during the depression — their gold value fell by 88 per cent from 1929 to 1932 — is usually advanced as the sole and sufficient reason for the peculiar difficulties Chile experienced during the depression and its aftermath. But the misguided stubbornness in defending the gold standard — the Central Bank's discount rate was pushed up to 9 per cent in the midst of falling prices — must share some of the blame. In contrast to such countries as Brazil, Argentina, Uruguay and Mexico which pragmatically opted for or stumbled on "reflationary" techniques, Chile followed the famous "rules of the game" strictly until mid–1931. At that time the violent economic contraction coupled with the government's total lack of any meaningful response to it gave the opponents of General Ibáñez' thinly veiled military dictatorship their chance. Public protests spearheaded by striking university students led to bloody disorders and forced General Ibáñez (who had already been the power behind the throne during the second Alessandri regime of 1925) to flee the country. Fifteen months of political chaos marked by various coups and counter-coups, including the proclamation of a short-lived "Socialist Republic," were to follow. Yet the futile attempt to defend the parity of the peso was continued until March 1932, six months after the devaluation of the pound!

> In 1930 and 1931, amidst widespread currency depreciation in South America, Chile, thanks to an ample gold reserve and the willingness of the authorities of the Central Bank to use this reserve for redemption purposes, has stayed on the gold standard.[1]

Completing his monograph in mid–1931, Fetter wrote this passage "not without a note of triumph" as was pointed out by a later commentator who, wiser by the depression decade, added: "The character of this defense of the gold standard and its costs, however, give ample cause for reflection concerning the appropriateness of such a defense for a country in the position of Chile."[2] The judgment of Chilean observers was naturally far less restrained. In "those tragic moments of 1931," so writes one of them, "when any delay in decreeing inconvertibility could only aggravate the situation and lead to the pointless drain of our metal reserves, we remained true to the gold standard . . . we have made it a habit in the conduct of monetary policy to sacrifice reality to theory . . . Once more our leaders revealed . . . their complete lack of financial intuition."[3]

---

[1] Fetter, *Inflation*, p. 182.
[2] William Adams Brown, Jr., *The International Gold Standard Reinterpreted, 1914–1934*, National Bureau of Economic Research, New York, 1940, Vol. II, p. 909.
[3] Marshall, "Régimen monetario de Chile," pp. 99–100.

And the principal surviving *papelero* was of course particularly acid:

> Mr. Kemmerer had bequeathed to the directors of the Central Bank
> his unshakable faith in the interest rate device . . . and they were so de-
> voted to [his] teachings . . . that they drowned the country in a crisis . . .
> without avail Congress requested the ministers to take measures which
> would permit the country to get out from the situation ineptly created by
> the real economic policy-makers who were hiding out behind the walls
> of the Central Bank.[1]

In sum, while Chile's second return to gold avoided some of the more
spectacular mistakes committed in 1895–98, the experience again left a
most bitter taste. It displayed once more that propensity, noted by Encina
in his comments on the influence of Courcelle-Seneuil and his disciples, to
take imported doctrines more seriously and to apply them more rigidly and
dogmatically in a foreign country than in their country of origin.

The chaotic eighteen months following the overthrow of Ibáñez in mid–
1931 seemed to justify all the fears that, once deprived of the discipline of
the gold standard, anything was not only possible but was indeed likely to
happen. A period of governmental instability coinciding with the trough
of the depression culminated in the 100-day Socialist government of Carlos
Dávila (July–September 1932). In the light of our doubts about the alleged
collusion between the *papeleros* and the landed oligarchy, it is suggestive
that Enrique Zañartu, the principal *papelero* publicist, became Finance
Minister under Dávila and masterminded the massive inflationary projects,
principally of debt monetization, which resulted in near financial panic and
contributed powerfully to the downfall of the "Socialist Republic."

In 1932–33 Treasury borrowings from the Central Bank took place on so
large a scale that the money supply and wholesale prices doubled while the
cost of living went up by 30 per cent. Thus Chile experienced a sudden inflationary explosion after an unnecessarily prolonged deflation, and was
perhaps the only country in the Western world which in 1933 had to fight
inflation rather than deflation. The new administration of Arturo Alessandri, who had now been elected with right-wing support, undertook a
program of orthodox fiscal management which would ordinarily have
deepened the depression had not the sudden monetary expansion of 1932
created a large amount of excess liquidity which served as the monetary
basis for economic recovery. The inflation of 1932 also had lowered real

---

[1] Enrique Zañartu Prieto, *Hambre, miseria e ignorancia*, Ercilla, Santiago, 1938, p.
98.

wages while many new investment opportunities opened up as a result of the deep import cuts resulting from the country's tight foreign exchange position. Under these circumstances, recovery and industrialization proceeded apace and under conditions of relative price stability in 1933–35, but were accompanied by a minimum of learning on the part of the monetary authorities. This was shown clearly in 1935 by Subercaseaux, now President of the Central Bank, when he affirmed that successful recovery was due entirely to the application of the following principles laid down by Kemmerer in December 1931 at a conference of Latin American Central Banks:

(1) Balance the budget;

(2) Regulate the money supply in accordance with the "needs of business" through discount of short-term paper supplemented by open-market operations.[1]

With these precepts the Central Bank was set to fight the last inflation, the one rooted in fiscal deficits, but was ill-equipped to resist inflationary pressures originating within the private sector which came to the fore in 1936–37 when prices rose by about 10 per cent each year. The doctrine that any expansion of short-term bank credit to the private sector is "self-liquidating," necessarily represents an increase in production, and is therefore non-inflationary, was a particularly dangerous one to rally to at a time when banks were so liquid that they hardly had any need to borrow from the Central Bank as was the case in Chile for several years after the massive injection of liquidity during 1932. Moreover, by adopting this doctrine the Bank cast itself in the "reactionary" role of considering non-inflationary or "organic," as it was wont to say in its annual reports, any support it gave to the needs of the business community while taking a dim view of "inorganic emissions," i.e., of Central Bank assistance to the Treasury or to any state-sponsored development agencies.[2]

The Central Bank held fast to this doctrine for several years during which a lusty inflation largely based on bank credit expansion got under way. A particularly dogmatic way of denying the evidence of the doctrine's clash with reality appears in the annual report of 1940:

---

[1] See Subercaseaux, "La política de regulación del medio circulante en el régimen del papel moneda," Banco Central de Chile, Annex to *Boletín Mensual*, No. 94, December 1935, p. 22.

[2] Subercaseaux speaks of the "need to avoid the temptation to supply more or less immobilized capital for the establishment or the running of industries in mining, manufacturing or agriculture, through Central Bank credits since these would in fact mean increases in the money supply . . ." *Ibid.*, p. 22.

The opinion that the price rise has been due exclusively or in large part to monetary inflation is without foundation. The larger part of Central Bank lending has arisen from effective needs of the market and, therefore, it cannot possibly have had an inflationary character even though there has been a rather considerable increase in such lending.[1]

The 1932–38 period found Chile strangely out of tune with the times in more than one respect. While other countries in the Americas engaged in daring economic and social experiments and reforms — with the important exception of Argentina, which also turned to the Right in the early thirties — Chile's affairs were taken in hand in those years by Alessandri's Minister of Finance, Gustavo Ross, an able international financier absolutely devoid of any interest in social progress or justice. Although his economic policies were rather successful in eliminating unemployment and in promoting manufacturing and construction activity, the middle and working classes became thoroughly alienated from the Alessandri administration. While Kemmerer had on his arrival in 1925 received an enthusiastic welcome from the workers at Valparaiso eager for a stable currency, the orthodox financial and monetary policies were now considered weapons of the oligarchy in its attempt to freeze an unfair distribution of the national income or to enforce an even more unfair one.

The widespread mood of discontent was well expressed by one writer, who, after describing Chile's high infant mortality, alcoholism, illiteracy, low wages and other social ills, commented:

> Faced with this panorama, the government and the parties of the Right declared proudly that the budget is balanced, that there is no lack of money in the Treasury and that all accounts are settled. This manner of looking at the national economy exclusively from the fiscal point of view reveals the incapacity and lack of social outlook of the upper class and its governments.[2]

While earlier the oligarchy was suspected of plotting inflation to serve its own pecuniary interests, it now stood accused of making a fetish out of financial stability.

These stirrings of protest combined with international trends to bring about the formation of a Popular Front Movement in which Chile's tradition-rich and powerful Radical Party, an amalgam of various center and

---

[1] Banco Central de Chile, *Memoria Anual 1940*, pp. 11–12. The distinction between "organic" and "inorganic" emissions is continued in the annual reports until 1946 and remained in use until much later.

[2] Oscar Bermúdez Miral, *El drama político de Chile*, Editorial Tegualda, Santiago, 1947, p. 39.

left-of-center political groups, joined with Socialists and Communists. The Popular Front came to life in the aftermath of the government's violent repression of a 1936 railroad strike motivated by the resumption of the price rise.[1]

In 1938 the Popular Front candidate, Pedro Aguirre Cerda, was elected President over Gustavo Ross, who had been nominated by the right-wing parties because of his reputation as a financial wizard and on the strength of his assurance that he would know how to buy the required number of votes.

The "Radical" Years and 20 Per Cent Inflation (1939–1952)

The Aguirre Cerda administration marks the beginning of the modern phase of Chile's inflation. From the end of 1939 to the end of 1952, prices rose steadily at an average yearly rate of 18 per cent; in no year was the increase below 8 per cent (1945) or above 30 per cent (1947). Then, in 1953, the inflation accelerated substantially.

The fourteen years from 1939 to 1952 are sometimes referred to as the "Radical" years or the years of the "Radical" inflation because Radical Party members — Pedro Aguirre Cerda (1938–41), Juan Antonio Ríos (1942–46) and Gabriel González Videla (1946–52) — occupied the Presidency. Nevertheless, the period is so heterogeneous that the persistence of inflationary pressures of approximately equal strength is in fact traceable to varying combinations of several causative factors. Fiscal deficits, monetization of balance of payments surpluses, massive wage and salary increases in excess not only of productivity gains but often of price increases as well, bank credit expansion, war-induced international price booms, Central Bank credit to state-sponsored development agencies — at any one time at least one and usually a combination of several among these forces were in operation. Perhaps the only common thread running through all the successive stages was the extreme weakness of anything that we would today call meaningful anti-inflationary action. This weakness was reflected in the annual reports of the Central Bank, which only in 1950 came out with a strong statement that something could and should be done about the situation.[2] By that time prices had risen to five times their 1940 level

---

[1] John Reese Stevenson, *The Chilean Popular Front*, University of Pennsylvania Press, Philadelphia, 1942, p. 64.

[2] "There is unanimous agreement that [the inflation] . . . must be controlled and definitely halted." Banco Central de Chile, *Memoria Anual 1949*, p. 9.

and foreign missions were once again called to the rescue.

Why was the reaction so slow, especially after Chile's previous painful experience with inflation? Those who believe in the Fetter theory, who are convinced that the pre–1925 inflations were engineered by the greed of the hacendados, might think that the Popular Front leaders were now determined to show that they too could play at this game of making the dominant group profit from inflation.[1] Actually, this explanation is once again too Machiavellian. Aguirre Cerda and his colleagues had commitments to the middle and working class that were bound to lead to sizable wage and salary increases in a situation of fairly full employment in commerce and industry. They also were committed to give a strong push to government-sponsored development activities. This aspect of the government's economic policy came to the fore particularly after the Chillán earthquake of 1939. Tying controversial projects of state-supported resource development to obvious reconstruction needs, the government persuaded Congress to establish the Corporation for the Promotion of Production (CORFO). Subsequently this agency took the initiative in stimulating and financing such basic industrial activities as steel, electric power and petroleum.[2]

It can be conjectured that the new policy-makers would not have been deterred from pursuing these objectives by the expectation that some inflation would result. However, they had no such expectation, for several new developments made it possible to entertain considerable illusions in this regard. For one thing, the underconsumptionists gained in influence in the thirties, since they were now able to call on modern Keynesian thinking for support, while the applicability of the *General Theory* to the less developed areas had not yet begun to be discussed at this time. Thus Aguirre Cerda held quite sincerely that the best way to increase production was to increase effective demand through wage and salary increases.[3] Even after two years of rapid inflation, he maintained: "As war is restricting our ex-

---

[1] This is the opinion of Ellsworth, who identifies the small producers (the political clientele of the Radical Party), the bureaucrats and the managers of development agencies as the new inflation profiteers and advocates. Paul T. Ellsworth, *Chile: An Economy in Transition*, Macmillan, New York, 1945, p. 114.

[2] CORFO (Corporación de Fomento de la Producción) was financed largely through new taxes and through permission granted to the commercial banks to hold part of their required reserves in CORFO securities. The principal borrowers at the Central Bank were the Agricultural and Industrial Institutes (Cajas), which were combined in 1953 in the present Banco del Estado.

[3] Kalman Silvert, *The Chilean Development Corporation*, unpublished dissertation, University of Pennsylvania, 1948, p. 68.

ports . . . our production finds its principal market right here at home and it has found it thanks to the enlarged purchasing power which the Government has helped create through higher wages and salaries to the middle and working classes who are the consumers *par excellence* since they are unable to save."[1] These underconsumptionist and Keynesian notions incongruously combined with the commercial loan theory of banking inherited from Kemmerer and still strongly entrenched at the Central Bank into a doctrinal mixture with explosive inflationary potential.

Apart from this reasoning, Chile's left-of-center policy-makers of the forties were confident, because of their own *dirigiste* inclinations and under the influence of demonstration from abroad, that the modern state possessed powerful devices such as price stops, subsidies and foreign exchange allocations which would make it a simple matter to control any inflationary tendencies that might appear. These instruments were indeed used profusely throughout the forties; and while price controls and particularly subsidies and exchange controls had important effects on the allocation of resources and the distribution of income, their effectiveness in restraining the rise of the general price level soon turned out to be extremely limited. This experience led at first to attempts at perfecting the controls rather than to the decision to abandon them altogether; and this roundabout course traveled by the policy-makers helps to explain the length of the journey.

Reliance on price controls and the like gave support to the idea that the fight against inflation was largely a problem of enforcing the law against speculators and profiteers. It is significant that the first attempt to control bank credit, made in 1946 under the newly elected González Videla administration, was largely intended not to limit bank credit expansion in general, but to prevent the flow of credit into the wrong channels, i.e., for the use of hoarders and speculators.[2]

Another important line of policy-making on inflation during Chile's "Radical" years was the attempt to live with it — to soften its impact should it come in spite of all efforts at control. Under this heading belong all measures taken to protect various sectors of the population or the purchasing power of various kinds of income against rising prices through more or less automatic readjustment mechanisms. A most important step in this direc-

---

[1] *Mensaje 1941*, Santiago, p. 8.
[2] Banco Central, *Boletín Mensual*, October 1946, pp. 212–213, and November 1946, p. 236.

tion was a 1941 law prescribing annual revisions of the "minimum salary."[1] This law simply established "Mixed Salary Commissions" as administrative agencies in charge of the yearly readjustment (retroactive to January 1), but did not provide the commissions with any clear guidance about the way in which they were to discharge their duties.

Naturally, the movement of the cost-of-living index for Santiago carried much weight with the commissions, but particularly in 1941–42 and again in 1949–50 the prescribed salary increases seem to have overshot the increase in the cost of living by a considerable margin. As a result, the white-collar workers were able to "stay ahead of the game," at least until the acute phase of the inflation. In 1953 the minimum salary was eighteen times the 1936–38 average as against twelve times for the cost of living.[2] Wage earners fared less well. At the beginning of the period under review, in 1939, the new Popular Front government increased all wages by 20 per cent. In the absence of an automatic readjustment mechanism, however, wage earners frequently had to resort to the strike weapon. As inflation persisted, collective contracts, particularly in the mining industry, increasingly provided for automatic wage revisions when the cost of living rose more than a certain percentage.[3]

The ultimate in automaticity was achieved in 1952 for civil servants. In the last weeks of the González Videla administration in 1952 Congress passed a law giving all civil servants in January of each year automatic increases from 25 to 90 per cent of the cost-of-living increase in the previous year.[4] Automatic adjustments were also provided for all retirement and pension payments. The cost of this law in 1952 was estimated at about one-fourth of total revenue. Ironically, the measure was justified on two fairly convincing anti-inflationary grounds: (1) In previous years, pay increases had often *exceeded* cost-of-living increases and to hold them to percentages reaching only up to 90 per cent of such increases was considered helpful;

---

[1] The principle of a minimum salary had been established by the Alessandri administration in a late bid for middle-class support through Law No. 6020 of Feb. 8, 1937. This law was amended by Law No. 7064 of Sept. 15, 1941 primarily to introduce the annual readjustment concept. Both laws were combined in Law No. 7295 of Sept. 30, 1942.

[2] "Exposición del directorio del Banco Central de Chile relacionada con la situación económica y financiera del pais," Annex to *Boletín Mensual* of Banco Central de Chile, No. 327–328, May–June 1955, p. 3. (Also reproduced in Banco Central de Chile, *Memoria 1955*, pp. 41–84.)

[3] Edward M. Bernstein and A. K. Sen Gupta, "Wage-Price Links in a Prolonged Inflation," *International Monetary Fund Staff Papers*, November 1958, pp. 349–351.

[4] Law No. 10,343 of May 28, 1952. The adjustment percentages varied inversely with the level of the salaries.

and (2) the Minister of Finance had been spending such "a grotesque proportion of his time" on resolving continuous salary demands of civil servants that he had been unable to concentrate on the task of fighting the inflation![1]

Evidently these attempts at making inflation bearable had in turn a highly stimulating effect on inflation. In particular, the massive real and psychological effects of the 1952 automatic adjustment privileges for civil servants were very important in ushering in the 1953–55 phase of strongly accelerated inflation, and the first step taken during the 1956 attempt at stabilization was a revocation of that measure.

Thus the attempt to live with inflation eventually collapsed, but for a considerable time it was instrumental in weakening resistance and protest since some strategically located interest groups had achieved inflation-protection. At the same time, the Central Bank doctrine that only "inorganic emissions," i.e., those providing finance to the Treasury or to state-sponsored development agencies, were inflationary left the monetary authorities defenseless against credit demands coming from business.

The prolonged complacency toward inflation in the period 1939–52 can also be explained by the atmosphere of world-wide inflation prevailing during much of this period. During the war and immediate postwar years and again during the Korean boom, the Chilean leaders did not feel too much out of tune with world economic trends and considered themselves the victims of circumstances beyond their control.[2] While wartime inflation in Chile was more acute than almost anywhere else, it was still easy to imagine that stabilization would prevail once the economy stopped receiving the inflationary impulses from abroad. It was only just before the Korean boom and then again from 1952 on that Chileans realized that they were out of step and that their inflation was clearly a home-grown product.

Even more important in restraining forceful action was the fact that during most of the "Radical" years it could be argued that inflation was the price paid for economic and social progress. During the presidency of Aguirre Cerda, under the Popular Front, some redistribution of income in favor of wage and salary earners was clearly achieved. Moreover, the establishment of CORFO in 1939 amounted to a real innovation, and the

---

[1] *Panorama Económico,* No. 50, March 28, 1952, p. 113.

[2] In commenting on the 130 per cent increase in the cost of living during the war years, the Central Bank pointed to the external pressures and added: "It is certain that we have let ourselves be carried by the wind without offering much resistance." Banco Central de Chile, *Memoria 1948,* p. 11.

new agency soon chalked up a good record as an entrepreneur in various basic sectors of the economy. During the war years, under the administration of Juan Antonio Ríos, many new industries were started as a result of wartime shortages. In the early postwar years, under the González Videla administration, industrial expansion continued in a generally euphoric postwar-boom atmosphere and was underlined by advances in electric power, pulp and paper and, above all, steel (the Huachipato plant was inaugurated in 1950). Agricultural mechanization also made strides though food output stagnated on the whole.

The idea that inflation was the price paid for rapid growth was widely entertained, even appearing in a Central Bank document: "Some observers attribute the intensive monetary and credit expansion to the country's excessively accelerated economic development."[1] As a result, more than one Minister of Finance hesitated to take anti-inflationary action for fear of braking economic development.

These circumstances did not preclude all anti-inflationary action in the 1939–52 period, but they did account for the indecisive and ineffective nature of the measures that were taken. This was particularly true of the price control regulations passed during the war by the Ríos administration.[2] For a long time, however, the ineffectiveness of this legislation was attributed to insufficient zeal in prosecuting violators, and much of the anti-inflationary energy of the subsequent González Videla administration was spent on perfecting and enforcing price controls and in asking Congress for ever more repressive measures.

It was under the postwar administration of González Videla that inflation first became an obvious and critical threat to social and political stability. That President's desire, at the beginning of his administration, to form a Cabinet of National Union comprising a wide spectrum of political groups was due not only to his electoral commitments to the Communists whose presence in his first Cabinet he wished to balance by right-wing representatives; it stemmed also from the realization that the disruptive strikes and the particularly rapid inflation of 1946 (the cost of living rose by a record 30 per cent) required some sort of national union and perhaps mutual

---

[1] Banco Central de Chile, *Memoria 1949*, p. 10. Subsequent studies have shown that at no time in recent years has Chile's growth been at all remarkable, even before the almost complete stagnation of the fifties.

[2] Law No. 7747 of Dec. 24, 1943.

sacrifices.[1] But the coalition government of Radicals, Communists and Liberals was itself shot through with so many tensions that it fell apart in a few months.[2] In the end, the strongest measures taken in 1946–47 were exhortations to the banks to refrain from financing inventories, the deportation of some speculators to the extreme south of the country,[3] and the creation of an unwieldy Economic Council[4] whose task it was, among many others, to advise on measures to stop the inflation!

Far more serious was an attempt made in 1948–49. Jorge Alessandri, Arturo's son and present President of Chile, was then González Videla's Minister of Finance in a coalition Cabinet in which the Radicals were collaborating with groups to their Right. Alessandri managed to balance the budget in those years and in 1948 he even achieved a respectable surplus. However, the Treasury left its surplus funds with the commercial banks and thus permitted credit expansion to proceed unabashed.[5] The surplus was due not only to conservative fiscal management but to better yields from export and import taxes made possible by advancing copper prices. With export and import taxes accounting for over half of total revenue and with indirect taxes (mainly turnover and excise) making up another 20 to 25 per cent of the total, the revenue side of the budget was not as vulnerable to inflation as it would have been had more reliance been placed on direct taxes, which normally show a greater lag in collection.

Since the Central Bank had long preached the doctrine — quite a convenient one for the commercial banks which dominated its board of directors — that the budget deficit was the root of the inflation, the policy-makers may well have been surprised that inflation did not come to a dead stop as soon as the budget was in balance. They now turned to foreign advice, in part because even sharper inflation threatened with the prospect of a renewed budget deficit resulting from the decline of copper prices in

---

[1] *Mensaje del Presidente de la República Gabriel González Videla al Congreso,* May 21, 1947, p. xx.

[2] Robert J. Alexander, *Communism in Latin America,* Rutgers University Press, New Brunswick, 1957, pp. 200–303. See also Stewart Cole Blasier, *The Cuban and Chilean Communist Parties, Instruments of Soviet Policy (1935–1948),* unpublished dissertation, Columbia University, 1954, pp. 124 ff.

[3] Banco Central de Chile, *Memoria 1946,* pp. 17–18, and Oscar Bermúdez Miral, *El drama político de Chile,* Edit. Tegualda, Santiago, 1947, p. 161.

[4] Decree No. 1097 of December 28, 1946.

[5] Banco Central de Chile, Annex to *Boletín Mensual,* May–June 1955, p. 8; Jorge Alessandri Rodríguez, *La verdadera situación económica y social de Chile en la actualidad,* Confederación de la Producción y del Comercio, Santiago, September 1955, p. 33.

1949. Even before the foreign missions had handed in their reports, the government, impelled by Alessandri, had decided by January 1950 to request Congress to enact a general wage, salary and price freeze, suspending all existing legal and contractual escalator clauses.[1]

This was of course a most serious step. Possibly the government thought that it had broken the back of any possible resistance by having dealt quite harshly — through imprisonment and deportation — with labor leaders in September 1949 after strikes in the coal and copper mines and riots in Santiago protesting against a rise in bus fares. But now the white-collar workers, who were the most directly threatened, took to the streets. Protest strikes were staged in Santiago by the employees of the telephone and electric power companies, and they were soon joined by the National Union of Employes. The Radical Party, its strength largely rooted in white-collar support, began to have second thoughts about the price-wage-salary freeze and started to negotiate for a way out. The result was the formation, in February, of an entirely new Cabinet which relied on support from various small left-of-center parties in addition to the Radicals. Carlos Vial replaced Jorge Alessandri as Finance Minister in this new so-called "cabinet of social sensitivity." Vial remained in office only six months. While he submitted various proposals to increase taxes and to reduce governmental personnel, the only measure that actually passed was the salary readjustment, which, on its way through Congress, snowballed to raises of up to 44 per cent.[2] Thus, what started out as a serious and unprecedented attempt to bring inflation to a dead stop ended in complete failure and, in fact, resulted in a more massive injection of new inflationary pressures than if the attempt had never been made.

In preparing for its ill-fated actions late in 1949, the government had felt the need for some outside support and perhaps advice. By that time, new international organizations extending technical assistance to member nations had come into existence, and a number of countries, particularly in Europe, had begun to emerge from their wartime and postwar currency disorders through the adoption of monetary reform programs. The first request for a foreign advisory mission was addressed in October 1949 to the United Nations rather than to another available alternative, the International Monetary Fund. The "personalities" of these two organizations had already taken sufficient shape to make it likely that a United Nations mission would attach a somewhat higher priority to the need for development

---

[1] This whole episode is well told in the otherwise extremely partisan *Alessandri*, by Ricardo Donoso, Vol. II, pp. 495 ff.

[2] Law No. 9629 of July 18, 1950; Banco Central de Chile, *Memoria 1950*, p. 18.

and the avoidance of deflation. The preference for a United Nations mission is indicative of the fact that control of inflation still had not become the dominant policy objective of the government.

After the request to the United Nations had been made and agreed to, the Fund let it be known that it was displeased at having been slighted in what it felt was its own area of competence and responsibility. Thereupon, the Chilean government invited the Fund to send a mission also, "by all means"; and a rather unconvincing and unworkable division of labor between the two missions was hastily devised.[1]

Actually, the two missions overlapped in the time of their visits to Chile and in the subject matter of their reports and recommendations. Since the United Nations had recruited such internationally known economists as Professor Lindahl from Sweden and Professor Iversen from Denmark, the Fund felt that it too had to put its best foot forward and asked its Director of Research, Edward M. Bernstein, to head the competing group of experts. Both efforts were thus staged at the highest level of professional competence, yet both were condemned to futility from the start. By the time the missions were organized and made their recommendations in mid-1950,[2] the government's stabilization efforts of January–February had collapsed and both the González Videla administration and the political parties henceforth concentrated on the 1952 presidential election at the expense of any determined anti-inflationary action.

Yet the reports did not go entirely unnoticed. As was to be expected, their emphasis differed considerably. The United Nations mission stressed the need to reverse inflationary expectations through a price stop and proposed to sterilize a portion of consumer money income through a system of forced savings. This last proposal, which was worked out in considerable technical detail, represents the kind of complex miracle drug that foreign money-doctors are often expected to produce. It duly intrigued Finance Minister Vial, who proposed its enactment;[3] but since it was a rather transparent device to achieve indirectly and partially the wage and salary stop which had been so successfully resisted in January, it had no chance of being accepted. As a whole, the recommendations of the United Nations mission were somewhat milder and leaned more in the direction of detailed economic controls than those of the Fund, which succeeded in

---

[1] Report of the Minister of Finance for 1949 in *Mensaje presidencial,* 1950, p. 146.

[2] Cf. United Nations, *Report of the UN Economic Mission to Chile, 1949–50,* New York, 1951, and International Monetary Fund, *A Report on the Process of Inflation in Chile together with Recommendations, 1950,* mimeo.

[3] Carlos Vial, *Cuaderno de la realidad nacional,* Edit. del Pacifico, Santiago, 1952, pp. 103–104.

having the last word and criticized the measures proposed by Lindahl and Iversen as both inadequate and impractical.[1] The Fund report covered a wide area — the budget, price and exchange controls, investment, etc. — but placed its principal emphasis on the need for stringent credit controls. It proposed a ceiling on total outstanding loans of the banking system, a new idea for Chile where the Central Bank had held fast to the commercial loan theory and the government had taken desultory action only against "speculative" credits.[2] The Fund's suggestion was wholly disregarded in 1950, but in 1953 a new Central Bank statute made specific provision for such regulatory powers and they were used soon thereafter. In general, the report's careful analysis of monetary and bank credit expansion had a distinctly educational influence on the thinking of Central Bank and Ministry of Finance officials.[3] The principal usefulness of the United Nations report was in its recommendations on tax and fiscal matters, which led to further technical assistance activities in subsequent years.

On the whole, however, the profit Chile derived from the two foreign missions was disappointingly small and this device, which had been used so lavishly all of a sudden, was now discarded for a while.

No further attempt was made by the González Videla administration to stop inflation; it rocked along at its "normal" annual rate of about 20 per cent until mid–1952 when Law No. 10,343 with its provision for automatic readjustment of all civil service salaries and pensions was passed. As the law was retroactive to January 1, 1952 its provisions led to immediate massive disbursements and to a large budget deficit. As a result, acceleration of the inflation clearly threatened toward the end of 1952.

Inflation Accelerates under Ibáñez (1953–1955)

In September of 1952, in a four-cornered race, General Ibáñez was elected President. He staged this remarkable comeback at the age of 74, twenty-two years after he had been driven from power by his helplessness in the face of deflation. Now his victory derived from the economic emergency gathering around the inflation crisis. Backed only by a few minor

---

[1] A Report on the Process of Inflation in Chile . . . , pp. 94–95.

[2] The U. N. Mission also favored this kind of purely qualitative bank credit restriction. See Report of the United Nations Economic Mission to Chile . . . , p. 13.

[3] Panorama Económico, which later became the fiercest critic of the Fund, said some very kind things about both reports, giving somewhat higher marks to the Fund document in its No. 31 issue of January 1951.

left-wing and extreme nationalist parties, he had no organized movement; yet he received a large independent vote based largely on protest against the traditional parties and their inability to stop the inflation. The long association between inflation and parliamentary government based on ever-shifting coalitions favored the idea that all that was needed to stop inflation was for an authoritarian person in a strengthened Executive to issue a command to that effect; ex-strongman Ibáñez was expected by many to be able to do just that.

These expectations were to be totally disappointed. The inflation gathered momentum rapidly during the first three years of Ibáñez' administration and approached the runaway stage in 1955, the climactic year in which the price level almost doubled. Only toward the very end of that year was a new effort to bring inflation under control attended by partial success.

Another related disappointment of widely held expectations was Ibáñez' unwillingness to assume dictatorial powers.[1] Having learned in his earlier career that dictatorships are unstable, he now sought safety in abiding by the Constitution. But this decision also condemned his administration to virtual impotence since he had only weak and unreliable support in Congress where the traditional parties — Conservatives, Liberals and Radicals — were both dominant and hostile to him. This in brief is the story of the Ibáñez regime during its first three years.

Not that there were no attempts made to stop the process of inflation. While some of the Ministers of Finance appointed by Ibáñez were passive or even added fuel to the fire, several others assumed their office ready to do battle against the scourge. And these attempts were by now far more sophisticated than those of the forties. Confidence in elaborate price or ex-

---

[1] Ibáñez himself showed that he realized this very well when he declared in 1957:
"I have said on several occasions that, on assuming the first office of the nation in the year 1952, I directed the government within the norms of constitutional forms. It is within the general awareness of the country that if I had believed in the existence of a necessity strong enough to break [the Constitution] I would have been able to do it with the acquiescence of the major part of the citizenry, because — to speak with crude frankness — that is just what broad national sectors expected of me. Nevertheless, in obedience to firm conviction and my cool appreciation of what is fitting for the Republic, I have maintained the action of the Government within the respect which is owed to the Constitution and the laws."
An observer who cites this passage adds in comment: "Here is a chief executive admitting that many persons voted for him precisely because he was supposed to be an antidemocratic terror, and now pointing out that he is really allowing free elections, so there!" Kalman H. Silvert, "Elections, Parties, and the Law," *American Universities Field Staff*, New York, April 1957, mimeo., p. 17.

change controls, or in repressive measures against "speculators," had been largely destroyed. The inane distinction between "organic" and "inorganic" emissions was at last dropped by the Central Bank which, impelled by the events and by the foreign missions of 1950, came to realize its responsibility for overall control of the money supply.

Improved instruments for this purpose became available early in the Ibáñez administration as a result of administrative reorganizations for which the President had received special powers from Congress upon assuming office. Thus, the Central Bank received much-needed authority to establish and vary reserve requirements and to control the volume of its own rediscounts and of bank credit in general.[1] Also, the many official credit agencies which had been created since the twenties were combined, with the exception of CORFO, into one large State Bank (Banco del Estado), partly with the thought that the merger would force the coordination of investment and reduce demands on the Central Bank.

At the same time, it became clear that whatever contribution inflation at a rate of 10 to 20 per cent may have made to economic or social progress in the past had ceased entirely in 1953–55. Having by then reached an annual rate in excess of 50 per cent, it had sharpened social conflicts and was causing obvious economic losses, if only because of the increasing frequency of strikes.

Nevertheless, during the first three years of the Ibáñez administration, all attempts to bring inflation under control proved to be abortive. Not realizing the strength of the gathering inflationary storm the President lost valuable time during the first months of the new regime. He did not even use fully the special powers received from Congress for six months, a fact which was to plague him later on whenever he asked for new powers.

The first serious attempt to stem the inflation came in June 1953 with the appointment as Finance Minister of Felipe Herrera, a brilliant young lawyer-economist, now president of the Inter-American Development Bank. Although a Socialist, he had only scorn for old-fashioned, *dirigiste* attempts to repress inflation through price controls and subsidized exchange rates for "essential" imports. Thus he first moved, to the applause of the business community, to unify exchange rates for imports. This meant in effect higher prices for a number of imported foodstuffs and raw materials. To compensate, he provided for increased family allowances and some pay increases to workers and low-salaried employees. Encouraged by

---

[1] Decree-Law No. 106, of July 28, 1953. See also Banco Central de Chile, *Memoria 1953*, pp. 28–35.

the favorable reception of these measures he then decided to ask for a fiscal reform that would increase public revenues and make them more reliant on progressive income taxes.[1] While an increase in taxes was orthodox anti-inflationary policy, the proposal never got anywhere in Congress, especially since the Finance Minister had advocated it with the slogan "Let the powerful also pay." This was in a way the counterpart to the 1949–50 episode when the white-collar workers had been asked — unsuccessfully — to set the example of anti-inflationary belt-tightening. Now it was the turn of the "powerful" or wealthy and they showed themselves equally reluctant. Herrera was attacked as a crypto-Marxist,[2] and after four months in office was replaced in a reorganization of the Cabinet following a serious setback suffered by the Ibáñez forces in a Santiago by-election.

By the end of 1953 the inflation had moved into its acute phase. Felipe Herrera's successor, Guillermo del Pedregal, was a naïve believer in the development-promoting virtues of cheap and abundant paper money, the old *papelero* creed which was now renamed "pedregalismo" in his honor. Having no choice but to grant the massive wage and salary increases that fell due in January 1954, he tried to make virtue out of necessity by reasoning that this disbursement would be disinflationary since it would make for social peace and hence for an increase in production.

This relapse into some of the illusions of the early forties was atypical. Chilean economists had made considerable progress in understanding inflation, and the dominant doctrine during the early years of the Ibáñez administration supplemented purely monetary analysis by an examination of the underlying political and sociological factors. Thus viewed, inflation results from the evermore widespread aspiration toward higher living standards and from the ensuing struggle of each group to improve its position and to increase its share in the national income.[3] In this many-cornered

---

[1] Felipe Herrera, *Desarrollo económico o estabilidad monetaria?*, Editorial Jurídico de Chile, Santiago, 1958, pp. 55–88.

[2] Editorial in *El Mercurio*, July 19, 1953.

[3] As the Minister of Finance stated in an official communication to the Director of the International Monetary Fund on July 31, 1953: "What has so far hampered the solution [of the problem of inflation] is not unawareness of its harmful consequences, but rather the difficulties which countries in the process of development encounter in checking or restraining the desire for rapid progress *of the various sectors of the community* within the limits of the resources existing within the country." (My italics.) The idea that inflation is caused by a seesaw, multi-cornered battle of militant social groups has been propounded on the basis of the French experience by Henri Aujac in "L'influence du comportement monétaire des groupes sociaux sur le développement de l'inflation," *Economie Appliquée*, Avril–Juin, 1950 (translated into English in *International Economic Papers*, No. 4, London, 1954). This article is frequently quoted in the Chilean literature.

struggle, workers and employees use strikes and escalator clauses as weapons to maintain or increase their share, and the business sector enjoys oligopolistic pricing power and access to Central Bank credit. Two conclusions emerged from this analysis: first, inflation is not a purely technical problem to be solved by a highly skilled foreign expert but rather a political and distributional problem requiring an accommodation among Chileans; and secondly, the equitable way to stop the inflation and the only way that promises to avert a violent social conflict is to reduce simultaneously the pretenses of all participants in the struggle. Hence the doctrine of "shared sacrifices," which represents a generalization to all major groups of Chilean society of the earlier theory according to which one group alone — the debt-ridden landowners — was responsible for the inflation. With the guilt thus spread out, the practical solution no longer called for intensification of the class struggle which would punish or liquidate one culprit but for an appeal to all groups to relent and desist from a struggle that had proved futile.

In the light of this doctrine the failure of the 1950 attempt at stabilization was easily explained inasmuch as it consisted in a unilateral exhortation to the white-collar workers alone to forego their salary increase.[1] Felipe Herrera was well aware of this mistake, and attempted to correct it by castigating the "powerful."

The influence of the doctrine of "shared sacrifices" was to be seen fully at work in the next two attempts to bring inflation under control. By mid–1954 the inflation had reached the annual rate of 70 per cent; instead of the social peace promised by del Pedregal, working-class unrest was dramatized by a one-day general strike in May. Realizing that things were not going at all well, Ibáñez began looking for new political support and approached Eduardo Frei, the leader of the Demochristian Party, for help and promised him a free hand. Frei asked for time to work out a program and after a few weeks presented his demands, which included the nomination of an entirely new Cabinet and the replacement of several key economic officials at the Central Bank and elsewhere. He submitted a "com-

---

[1] Because of the possibility that a massive wage increase would set off an accelerated rise in prices, the foregoing of such an increase in January, when due in accordance with the annual adjustment clause, did not necessarily mean that the real wage received *over the year* would be lower than if the escalator clause were applied. This point was discussed by Joseph Grunwald in *El Mercurio* of June 27, 1956. However, a salary or wage stop unaccompanied by any other anti-inflationary measures *may* turn out to be a unilateral sacrifice and, more important, it certainly looks like one to the wage-receiver.

prehensive" plan which required that special powers be granted to the President by Congress. It included not only stringent monetary, banking and foreign exchange measures and an end to automatic wage and salary adjustments, but also fundamental fiscal, administrative, and even agrarian reforms.[1] President Ibáñez balked, either because he doubted the possibility of obtaining the sweeping delegation of powers required or because he felt that Frei had taken his offer of a "free hand" far too literally, for Frei's plan implied that he would be set up as a sort of Premier and Ibáñez was by no means ready for the role of figurehead. Thus, the whole negotiation collapsed and Ibáñez appointed a "technical-administrative" Cabinet (the seventh in his twenty months in office), with Jorge Prat, previously president of the State Bank, as Finance Minister.

Prat's appointment and his first pronouncements revived hopes for stabilization. The plan he announced was another embodiment of the comprehensive, "balanced sacrifices" approach. A promise on the part of the government to practice austerity with regard to its own expenditures was combined with appeals to other groups to follow suit: the wealthy were asked to accept higher taxes and lower dividends; the banks to limit their lending and to contribute to public investment projects; the workers to give up strikes and automatic cost-of-living readjustments (but only after the monetary and fiscal measures had shown some effect). Even the "passive sector" — the beneficiaries of Chile's complex and ambitious social security system — was invited to moderate its claims.

The Prat program did at first restore a climate of greater confidence in the government. In August a law known far too ambitiously as "tax reform" was passed by Congress after having been bottled up for some time.[2] Prat also induced the Central Bank to make use of its new powers to set ceilings on bank credit expansion. Such ceilings had been imposed in September 1953 but were suspended a month later, after Pedregal had taken over as Finance Minister; they were restored in June 1954, when Santiago and provincial banks were enjoined to limit the rate of expansion of their loans to 1.75 per cent and 2 per cent per month, respectively, by no means a very stringent restriction.[3] All of this, while making a "good impression,"

[1] Cf. *Panorama Económico*, No. 102, June 18, 1954. The group of economists editing this magazine, particularly Aníbal Pinto, the principal editorial writer, helped Frei in the elaboration of his program and therefore had inside information on the proposed program which has never been made public.
[2] Law No. 11,575 of August 14, 1954.
[3] Moreover, the measure, as first applied, had many loopholes which were plugged only a year later. Banco Central de Chile, *Memoria 1955*, pp. 125–139.

was far from decisive. The test for the Minister's effectiveness was to come
with the new budget and the massive salary readjustments due in January
1955.

In November the Minister submitted to Parliament a series of projects
making up his program of "economic rectification." Among the measures
he proposed were some concerned with the restoration of incentives for
copper and nitrate companies whose profits were being squeezed as the
exchange rate for their products lagged systematically behind the increase
in internal costs. But principal attention centered on the short-term stabilization measures, including the proposal that for two years wage and salary adjustments should be held to substantially less than the previous year's
rise in the cost of living, i.e., to 60 per cent of that rise in 1956 and to 80 per
cent in 1957. Stabilization was expected to become effective in this period,
during which strikes would also be forbidden. These sacrifices requested
of the workers and employees were to be balanced by a series of compensating benefits and by sacrifices imposed on the wealthy. The benefits included the long overdue extension of minimum salary legislation to the
workers. (Chile is probably the only country in the world that instituted a
legal minimum salary long before a minimum wage.) Furthermore, low-
cost housing construction was to be expanded. The sacrifices to be borne by
the wealthy consisted in higher taxes on luxuries and on gifts and inheri-
tance, but primarily in a dividend limitation which was presented as the
real equivalent of the proposed wage restraint. Dividends were to be limited to 7 per cent of capital and reserves, and any excess profits were to be
either reinvested or taken out in CORFO bonds. There was even a complex
scheme linking wage increases to productivity advances: any relaxation in
the proposed wage restraint was to be conditioned on an increase in the
firm's output and profits and on a scheme for workers' participation in the
latter.[1]

Here was a truly heroic attempt at equitable sharing of the burden of
anti-inflationary austerity. Nevertheless, Prat was unable to enlist Congressional support for his proposals. As it happened, his program of economic
rectification could not have been presented at a worse time. By late 1954,
relations between the President and Congress had deteriorated sharply. To
break a lengthy strike at the copper mines, Ibáñez had proclaimed a state
of siege in September 1954 while Congress was in recess. When Congress
reconvened in special session, Ibáñez asked for additional powers to deal

---

[1] *El Mercurio,* November 22, 1954.

with strikes and agitators; Congress not only refused these powers but, rejecting all Presidential pleas and threats, voted to end the state of siege in December. Obviously the nation was in an increasingly bitter mood, with class pitted against class and the executive branch against the legislative. This was no time for the austerity and shared sacrifices preached by the Finance Minister, who was not retained when Ibáñez reorganized his whole Cabinet in January 1955 to attain somewhat better relations with Congress.

Thus the "sociological" theory according to which inflation is due to the excessive claims of various groups against the national income had not yielded a workable policy. It can be claimed that programs proposing carefully balanced sacrifices by each of the contending groups had not been given a fair test. Yet the whole idea that utter conflict could be replaced abruptly by utter harmony via "shared sacrifices" had the quality of an escapist wish-dream. A more realistic, though more roundabout, strategy for achieving shared sacrifices might have been to plug the inflationary leaks one after another, each time with a different combination of political forces. For example, partial rather than full readjustment for wage and salary workers might have been pushed through by a center-right alliance, and a meaningful tax reform either earlier or later by a combination of center and left-wing groups. In a multi-party system plural objectives are frequently attained in this fashion, sequentially through shifting alliances rather than simultaneously through élans toward national union, which are exceedingly rare.[1] But while a policy of shifting alliances to correct first one abuse and then another is frequently practiced it is hardly ever advocated, for fear of moral reproof. In Chile, therefore, once the head-on attempt to secure shared sacrifices proved to be a failure, nobody had a very clear idea how to handle the constantly worsening situation. In this situation, the country was ripe for another "money doctor" from abroad.

Averting Runaway Inflation and the Klein-Saks Mission (1955–1956)

As before, the unsuccessful outcome of one attempt at stabilization was followed by a relapse into more rapid inflationary drifting. Inflation resumed full force in early 1955 after massive salary adjustments of 60 per cent in January. During the first half of the year the country had three dif-

---

[1] See pp. 263–264 and 294 for further considerations on this point.

ferent Ministers of Finance, and signs of social and political disintegration multiplied rapidly. Strikes became still more frequent and occurred in such vital services as transportation and hospitals; workers involved in illegal strikes against government agencies or essential industries outnumbered by four to one those striking legally. In July a general strike was called by the central trade union organization, Confederación Unica de Trabajadores Chilenos, followed by other serious strike waves in August. Speculation and hoarding was rife as the free market value of the Chilean peso plummeted from an average of 313 to the dollar in January to 752 in August (the rate of 840 was quoted on August 22).

Public order was threatened so repeatedly by strikes and demonstrations that the army virtually camped in the streets of Santiago, and particularly outside the Presidential Palace, for prolonged periods. The President became more strident in his attacks on the hostile Congress, and in his annual message in May he urged a constitutional reform permitting the President to dissolve Congress in certain critical circumstances. This move reinforced suspicions that a military take-over was imminent. Plotting by an officer group known as the *"linea recta"* in favor of assumption of dictatorial powers by Ibáñez was widely reported. In May–June the group appeared to be making considerable headway as a number of senior officers opposed to it resigned, or were arrested or reassigned. In mid–1955 the situation was indeed so chaotic, the breakdown of economic order and the deadlock of the political process were so complete, that only two outcomes appeared possible: either Ibáñez would once again be ousted from the Presidency or he would establish a military dictatorship.

How did it happen instead that both Ibáñez *and* the constitutional regime survived the crisis? For one thing, the anti-Perón revolt of June may have dissuaded Ibáñez from the path of military dictatorship, and as the coup-minded officers were mostly Ibañistas, he was not ousted either. For another, the internal crisis never threatened to turn into external bankruptcy because 1955, the year of Chile's wildest inflation, was also a year of record foreign exchange earnings because of sharply increased copper prices and production. Most important, in the latter part of 1955 a new coalition of forces appeared — a new Finance Minister, a new foreign mission, a new parliamentary majority — which averted the threatening runaway inflation.

It is useful at this point to anticipate and to outline briefly the course of events during 1956–57. In this period the inflationary spiral was not stopped, but it was materially slowed down. The cost of living still rose by

38 per cent in 1956 and by 17 per cent in 1957, but compared with the continuous acceleration of inflation during the preceding period these figures indicated a fundamental change in the economic climate. This was due to a number of decisions taken early in 1956. In January, Congress voted to hold the increase in wages and salaries to 50 per cent of the rise in the cost of living during 1955. However, with the increase in wages and salaries still very large, the budget remained in deficit. The tax increases proposed by the government were emasculated by Congress and the Treasury efforts to avoid recourse to the Central Bank resulted in postponement of public works and investment expenditures in general. This brings us to the darker side of the 1956–57 picture, the marked stagnation in economic activity and especially the decline in construction and the consequent unemployment that began to be noticeable in mid–1956 and persisted through 1958.

To go back, then, to 1955, it is easy to understand that the very danger to the country's constitutional and political stability in mid–1955 activated some counterforces or weakened the determination of those who assailed the government. An inflation that proceeds at a rate of almost 100 per cent a year is qualitatively different from an inflation of 20 per cent, not only in the banal sense that there may be a threshold for forceful action that is being crossed somewhere between the 20 and the 100 per cent rate, but also because certain insights into the inflationary process are gained more easily at the faster rate. This is particularly true for the escalator clauses, which appear as both innocuous and just at one stage but whose contribution to the perpetuation of inflation becomes evident when wage and salary adjustments of 50 per cent or more are up for discussion. Thus, *Panorama Económico*, the rather left-wing economic review, had already in 1954 expressed the view that in the new state of inflation both left-wing and right-wing "fetishes" had to be discarded and that it was ridiculous to pretend that a 40–60 per cent wage rise could be financed out of profits.[1] This evidence of the futility of wage and salary increases helps to account for the strike fatigue that became quite apparent in the second half of 1955, during the August strikes, and then again during the abortive general strike of January 1956.

Among the forces which were activated as a result of the sharpening of the inflation was the long-silent Central Bank. In July 1955 it issued a report on the course of the Chilean inflation with forceful recommendations on the fiscal, credit, foreign exchange, wage-price, and social security meas-

---

[1] *Panorama Económico*, No. 94, Feb. 26, 1954.

ures required to stop it.[1] At the same time, the Institute of Economics of the University of Chile issued a popular pamphlet that was widely distributed, *Chile y la inflación,* which discussed in simple terms the causes of inflation and possible remedies.

More important, however, was the fact that in mid–1955 some of the leaders of the Opposition parties sensed that the deadlock between Ibáñez and Congress must be broken if inflation was to be brought under some sort of control. An opportunity for achieving collaboration arose in August when the Ministry of Economy and, soon after, the Finance portfolio were handed to Oscar Herrera, who, as Education Minister, had established good relations with deputy Enrique Serrano, a skillful Congressional leader of the Conservative Party. Herrera, an "Ibañista" of modest middle-class background, was a man of considerable energy and decision. He was convinced that, to push through an anti-inflationary program, the government needed the political support of some of the parties which had been voting with the opposition since 1953. To accomplish this, however, was no easy task: No party could hope to gain in popularity by associating itself openly with an administration that was increasingly discredited. Ibáñez in turn still thought of himself as a sort of revolutionary nationalist and was not eager for support from "reactionaries" against the left wing.

However, the switching operation was considerably facilitated from September 1955 on by the arrival on the scene of a new foreign advisory mission put together by the Washington consulting firm Klein & Saks. This firm had been contracted by the Ibáñez government in July on the urging and through the intermediary of Agustín Edwards, publisher of *El Mercurio,* Santiago's respected, highly conservative daily newspaper. It is easy to understand the appeal which the idea of bringing in some *deus ex machina* in the person of an illuminated and somewhat authoritarian expert must have had in the chaotic situation that had developed by mid–1955. At that time, in fact, various alternative missions, by the International Bank, by a group of "California professors," and by Pierre Mendès-France, were also canvassed. The choice finally fell upon the Klein-Saks firm, in part on grounds of availability and on the basis of its previous record as advisers to the Peruvian government, but mainly because of its reputed good connections with the Republican administration and its financial agencies in Washington (Mr. Klein had been a member of the Hoover administration). The fact that Mendès-France was under active consideration simultaneously

---

[1] Banco Central, Annex to *Boletín Mensual,* May–June 1955.

with Klein-Saks shows, however, that the government was anxious for any kind of advice, from whatever end of the ideological spectrum. The decision to contract Klein-Saks led to immediate protest, not only, predictably, from the extreme left, but also from such thoughtful observers of the scene as Aníbal Pinto, the editor of *Panorama Económico*. In an article entitled "Mission without Mission"[1] he claimed that the mission did not at all fill the need for "impartial experts" stressed by *El Mercurio* since the laissez-faire, orthodox bias of Klein-Saks was well known from its Peruvian record and, secondly, that in any case Chile's problems were not technical but political and historical. (At that time, Pinto could not have foreseen something which he fully realized later on, namely, that the mission's principal accomplishment was to be, as will be shown, not at all a technical but a political one.)

Headed by Prescott Carter, a retired vice president of the National City Bank with considerable experience in Spain and Latin America, the five-man mission arrived in Santiago in September 1955. It had originally been contracted for six months and, like the United Nations and International Monetary Fund missions of 1950, had been expected to survey the scene and write a "comprehensive" report with recommendations. But several factors conspired to substantially alter its course: One was precisely the failure of the earlier comprehensive reports to have a noticeable effect on policy-making; another was the background of the members of the mission who were monetary practitioners rather than theorists (two of its principal members had been associated with the Federal Reserve Bank of New York); but the most important reason was that the mission was drawn, immediately upon arrival, into the decisive anti-inflationary battle which shaped up toward the end of 1955.

In this battle the usefulness of the mission had various unorthodox but highly significant aspects. In the first place, its arrival produced an atmosphere of expectancy which gave the new Finance Minister a welcome respite, permitting him to lay his plans and to build his new alliances carefully. Once again the most urgent question was whether in January 1956 wages and salaries would be permitted to go up by the full extent of the rise in the cost of living during 1955, in which case they would be almost doubled. Clearly any hope of fighting inflation successfully would be doomed were this to happen, as it would automatically under the existing legislation. Hence the Minister repeated the attempt that had failed the

---

[1] *Panorama Económico*, No. 126, July 15, 1955.

year before and back in 1949–50: to get legislation passed that would end
the automatic readjustment and would limit wage and salary increases to
a portion of the rise in the cost of living. Instead of the 60 per cent recommended by Prat he proposed a 50 per cent readjustment, softening this
blow by an increase in family allowances (à la Felipe Herrera!), by a
somewhat theoretical price stop, and by the long-overdue establishment of
a minimum wage alongside the minimum salary.[1]

Secondly, the presence of the mission acted as a binding agent for the
newly emerging coalition of Ibañistas, Conservatives and Liberals that was
put together by the joint efforts of deputy Serrano and the Finance Minister. While Serrano organized a number of private, almost conspiratorial
get-togethers of the Finance Minister, the principal parliamentary leaders
of the new coalition and some mission members, both the Ibáñez forces
and the two traditional right-wing parties wanted above all to avoid a public embrace.[2] With the mission freely issuing its recommendations, both
parties could and did claim that they were merely following the advice of
El Mercurio's famous "impartial experts." In this fashion the new coalition
could maintain an extremely loose structure: the new supporters of Ibáñez
never entered the Cabinet and talked more to the mission than to their
Ibañista allies whom they found distasteful.

This interpretation of the events is quite consistent with the excellent
retrospective analysis given by Aníbal Pinto in Panorama Económico in the
following terms:

> Oscar Herrera understood the need to create a political platform for
> the action of the government or, more exactly, for the development of
> this action in the crucial area of the fight against inflation . . . For these
> purposes Herrera found the perfect ally: the Conservative Party which
> was won over by some leading parliamentarians of recognized ability and
> perspicacity. In the traditional political game it would have been natural
> for this alliance to be reflected . . . by the participation of that party in
> the Government. But here as elsewhere both promoters of the enterprise
> proceeded with singular skill. Both understood that this step would
> weaken rather than strengthen the enterprise . . .

---

[1] Law No. 12,006.

[2] Note the following comments of Ibáñez, reported by his biographer: ". . . the two
traditional parties [Liberals and Conservatives] which supported the economic plans [of
the Klein-Saks mission] were ostentatious about their political independence. When
elections drew near, their leaders repeated that they had nothing in common with the
Government and that the support of certain economic reforms was not incompatible
with being in the opposition." Luis Correa Prieto, El Presidente Ibáñez, Orbe, Santiago,
1962, p. 182.

But for the broader support other allies were needed, such as the Liberal Party and the business associations . . . At this juncture the Klein-Saks mission began to play its role. Its job was essentially to function as the shepherd of the suspicious, the lukewarm, and the recalcitrant. Its North American origin guaranteed the orthodoxy of its advice and raised expectations of support from the United States. This was without any doubt the cardinal contribution of the Klein-Saks mission — paradoxically not in the technical, but in the political arena.[1]

The greatest triumph of this singular combination of forces — the mission, Finance Minister Oscar Herrera, and the new parliamentary majority — came when the bill limiting wage and salary readjustments to 50 per cent of the 1955 rise in the cost of living was voted on in Congress. It was approved in the Chamber with a comfortable margin on December 22, but in the Senate the voting on January 5, 1956 twice resulted in a tie which was broken only after members of the Klein-Saks mission were able to convince ailing Senator Cruz Coke, a prominent member of the Conservative Party, to make an appearance and cast a favorable vote. A further hurdle was the general strike called in protest for January 9; it fizzled badly, however, not only because of repressive measures ordered by the government but also on account of "strike fatigue." Thus the stabilization program was launched. Along with the wage and salary regulations, new and tighter restrictions on bank credit were issued, and in March the foreign exchange system was simplified. This resulted in financial assistance from the International Monetary Fund and from United States official and private agencies in the amount of $75 million. The program and the mission thus scored an important initial success.

Some further observations should be made, however, about the contribution of the Klein-Saks mission. For one thing, it is clear that the purely *technical* contribution of its "impartial experts" was minimal. A virtual consensus had emerged among Chilean technicians about the measures needed to stem the inflationary tide. Almost all the technical measures applied or proposed in 1956 had been suggested in the Central Bank memorandum of July 1955, and the proposal to decelerate the rise in money incomes by adjusting wages and salaries for only a portion of the rise in the cost of living had been put forward by Jorge Prat a year earlier. Since 1953 the Central Bank had been experimenting with its new powers to restrict credit, and the exchange rate reform had been anticipated in large part by Felipe Herrera in 1953 but had been rendered ineffectual by the continued inflation

---

[1] *Panorama Económico*, No. 145, May 25, 1956, pp. 231–232.

since then. The only new device suggested by the mission in conjunction with the exchange reform was the provision for advance deposits on imports which required importers to deposit a stated percentage of their intended purchase with the monetary authorities some time in advance of the actual obligation to settle with the foreign supplier. This device, however, was at that time coming into widespread use as an alternative to quantitative restrictions of imports: Ecuador, for example, had been experimenting with it rather successfully since 1953.[1]

In its technical aspects, then, the Klein-Saks mission resembled less the 1950 United Nations and Fund missions, which introduced new-fangled proposals or an as yet unfamiliar type of monetary analysis, than the Kemmerer mission, which, as we have noted, also drew on existing plans and ideas. Despite their lack of innovation both missions had a considerable impact. But there the parallel ends. For the Kemmerer mission came to Chile when President Alessandri was holding virtually absolute powers while the Klein-Saks mission arrived when President Ibáñez had lost all of the prestige of his electoral victory and a power vacuum had been created by his prolonged rift with Congress, his resulting inability to define any consistent line of policy and his decision to abide by the constitutional rules. The situation required the exertion of some authority, and the Klein-Saks mission had no compunction about assuming a role inherited by default of the usual carriers of authority. If the statement "Sovereign is he who decides the emergency situation"[2] be true, then the Klein-Saks mission, in cementing the new political coalition, took on the attribute of sovereignty as well for a short period in 1955-56.

This anomalous situation was vaguely sensed[3] and deeply resented. Indeed, some of the widespread criticisms of the mission become intelligible only in the light of this reaction. For example, the mission was attacked for giving piecemeal advice as each problem arose instead of proposing a "general, integrated plan." But when the mission arrived in Chile there was neither the time nor the need for still another comprehensive report on inflation; to have any success at all it had to go into battle on the various is-

---

[1] See Jorge Marshall, "Advance Deposits on Imports," *International Monetary Fund Staff Papers*, April 1958, pp. 239–257.

[2] Quoted from Carl Schmitt by Franz Neumann in "Approaches to the Study of Political Power," *Political Science Quarterly*, June 1950, p. 178, reprinted in Neumann, *The Democratic and the Authoritarian State*, The Free Press, Chicago, 1957.

[3] A cartoon in *Topaze* of November 11, 1955, shows Prescott Carter of the Klein-Saks mission watching with great alarm a storm-tossed launch marked "Chile" from which a carefree and relaxing Ibáñez calls out: "What does it matter to you if the boat founders? Is it yours by any chance?"

sues of wage, credit and foreign exchange policy as each came to, or could be brought to, a head in the real world. It is not easy then to see why the mission should have been so vehemently criticized for acting in this way *unless* the criticism is understood as surprise and resentment at the mission's not having resigned itself to the somewhat frustrating task of writing a comprehensive report for the enlightenment of the real decision-makers. Instead, by its memoranda on specific questions, its lobbying in Congress, and its general manner of operating, it in effect usurped the role of policy-maker.[1] In so doing the Klein-Saks mission followed in the footsteps of that highly successful adviser-operator, Professor Kemmerer, who summarized his experience as follows:

> The expression "Commission's Report" . . . is misleading. With three exceptions none of the commissions with which I have been associated has presented any general report. It has been found more effective to submit specific memoranda on specific subjects. These memoranda do not take the form of the usual government report, but rather of definite projects of law drafted in a form ready to be enacted by the legislature or definite administrative orders ready to be issued by the executive authority.[2]

In criticizing the mission for its performance during these first critical months one must go deeper and question the usefulness of having any overall mission at all in a situation such as the one Chile faced in mid–1955. Even if it is recognized that the "technical" character of the mission was something of a smokescreen and that the real problem facing the country was political, the case for such a mission is frequently argued on the ground that it provides a government which is forced to issue some unpopular measures with a scapegoat that can be blamed for having suggested the measures. The argument is often used in retrospect by the expert and the nations and agencies dispensing technical assistance because it casts them in a posture of self-denying, almost saintly, service. Yet claims to saintliness must be treated with some scepticism. Even if they are warranted, the question arises whether any nation or international agency can, simply from the point of view of self-preservation, afford to be the perennial

---

[1] The mission's report is a collection of memoranda, mostly addressed to the Minister of Finance: *El programa de estabilización de la economía chilena y el trabajo de la Misión Klein & Saks*, Editorial Universitaria, Santiago, 1958. It is preceded by a "comprehensive report" (pp. 1–38) which, however, was written in retrospect, toward the end of the mission's stay in 1958.

[2] "Advisory Work for Governments," *American Economic Review*, March 1927, p. 7.

scapegoat. The United States, for one, appears to be discovering that to become everybody's whipping boy is not particularly clever.

But there is also a real question whether it is in the best interest of the country *receiving* technical assistance to be *handed* a scapegoat, that is, to rely on foreign experts to take things in hand and assume the task of issuing authoritative advice at moments of crisis. A little reflection will show the possible drawbacks of this procedure.

The Chilean inflation had long been explained on the ground that the claims of the various social groups for shares in the national product exceeded the available output at current prices. In this view of the inflationary process, one group after the other engages in actions to enforce its claims and achieves success in the short run. Although it may encounter much protest and *direct* resistance from other groups, the protest is ignored and the resistance overcome. Eventually, however, each group is thwarted in its design by similar unilateral "grabbings" by other groups.

This picture actually fits two, almost opposite hypotheses about underlying social situations and group attitudes. In one situation, *straightforward dissent* is strenuously avoided: it is neither politic nor polite ever to *say* no, and denial of a request after the initial approval is achieved by indirection. In the other, various groups maintain and prize an attitude and phraseology of unbending opposition and hostility: they coexist, but are most anxious to avoid *overt agreement* and compromise. Both situations have one element in common, namely, a certain amount of "faking." In one case the degree of harmony and consensus existing in the society is exaggerated; in the other, contending groups play at being more irreconcilable than they really are. Both modes of behavior are well known to anthropologists;[1] it is even possible for them to exist side by side in the same society —

---

[1] For example, avoidance of face-to-face conflict is a noted feature of the social behavior of the Saulteaux Indians, but pent-up hostility and aggression are indirectly discharged by gossip and particularly by sorcery. Just like inflation, sorcery becomes a means of withdrawing a concession which has been granted in order to avoid overt disagreement. The opposite situation where the parties wish to maintain a hostile stance while in effect transacting some business together is characteristic of *dumb barter*, i.e., barter carried on through leaving the goods intended for exchange at an appointed place so that face-to-face contact is entirely avoided; a somewhat more convenient arrangement serving the same purpose prevails when men belonging to two hostile groups let women largely take over the trading function. A. Irving Hallowell, "Aggression in Saulteaux Society," in *Personality in Nature, Society, and Culture,* in Clyde Kluckhohn and Henry A. Murray, eds., Knopf, New York, 1956, pp. 260–275; E. Adamson Hoebel, *Man in the Primitive World,* McGraw-Hill, New York, 1958, pp. 453–454; Francisco Benet, "Explosive Markets: The Berber Highlands," in *Trade and Market in the Early Empires,* Karl Polanyi, Conrad M. Arensberg and Harry W. Pearson, eds., The Free Press, Glencoe, 1957, p. 205.

for example, there may be ritualized, though spurious, friendliness between government and business while a rigid façade of hostility is maintained between business and labor.

The Chilean situation appears to be weighted more heavily with the avoidance of agreement, with the maintenance of a militant stance on the part of all contending groups.[1] In a sense this stance is the desired benefit and inflation is its cost. As inflation quickens, however, the maintenance of inter-group hostilities becomes increasingly "expensive" and at a certain point can no longer be afforded. The unpleasant effects of accelerated inflation therefore provide a stimulus toward the overcoming or assuaging of these hostilities. But this kind of learning can be effectively stunted by bringing in a foreign advisory mission at the crucial moment; for it is then possible, as happened precisely in the Klein-Saks case, for the various groups to give gingerly support to the mission instead of working out an agreement with each other. *The mission appears in this context essentially as a device permitting the contending groups to evade once again their responsibility to hammer out a workable compromise in face-to-face discussions.* The inflation is tamed temporarily, but a *minimum of learning* is achieved in the crucible of the inflationary crisis, and basic attitudes are unchanged and have perhaps become even more dogmatic. In taking over highly responsible functions of policy advice and policy formulation at a critical juncture, the mission permits other groups to slip into, retain or reinforce the very attitudes of irresponsibility and excessive hostility which are the breeding ground of inflation.

This negative aspect of the Klein-Saks mission's work must be set against its undoubted contribution to the avoidance of runaway inflation. It appears in the ease and lack of discussion with which the principle of automatic readjustment of wages and salaries was reintroduced in 1961[2] as though the momentous fight of 1955–56 against this principle had never taken place at all. It is also easily illustrated by reference to the climate of opinion before and after the mission's arrival. In mid–1955, under the pressure of the emergency, we find the following yearning for pragmatic reasonableness in *Panorama Económico*:

> Our milieu is distrustful of everything that smells of earthy empiricism
> . . . Instead of concentrating energies on stopping the fire which already

---

[1] Avoidance of overt dissent may be the more important ingredient in the case of the Indonesian inflation, perhaps also of the Brazilian one.
[2] Law 14,688 of 1961.

> consumes the first floors, one speculates about the generalities of an
> agrarian transformation which few understand properly . . .[1]

But later on the mission was attacked by the same editorial writer precisely
for following his earlier advice:

> The failure of the mission is not in what it has done but in what it has
> not done . . . experience shows that its strategy of advice in corridors or
> committees, its preference for busying itself, upon the request of influen-
> tial authorities, with specific questions without relating them organically
> to one another has as many or more drawbacks than the preparation of an
> overall plan.[2]

One of the compelling reasons, according to *El Mercurio* and others, for
bringing in foreign "impartial" experts was the alleged partiality of the
Chilean economists, the fact that they all had some dogmatic political axe
to grind. Maybe we have here a self-fulfilling prophecy: if foreign experts
are brought into a country on the ground not that the country has no experts of its own but that its experts are unable to be "objective," some of
the jilted domestic experts will be tempted to snipe at the foreign ones
from the sidelines and to *become* strongly partisan in the process.

Stabilization Stalemate, Stagnation and "Structuralism" (1956–1962)

The bitterness of the criticism of the Klein-Saks mission had its roots in
the deep resentment against the mission for playing a crucial political role
in general and for facilitating the government's switch to the Right in particular. But these early months of the mission's stay were in reality its heyday during which the wage-salary bill, bank credit restrictions and the exchange reform were adopted. Then came the setbacks. Finance Minister
Oscar Herrera was replaced in August 1956, the price of copper dropped,
the government proved incapable of pushing a meaningful tax bill through
Congress, and the Chilean economy developed some serious and stubborn
soft spots, particularly in construction and related activities. Moreover, it
became clear that inflation had only been slowed down; it had by no means
been stopped.

Why Oscar Herrera, the strong man of the stabilization program and the
architect of the coalition which had pushed it through, was eased out by

---

[1] *Panorama Económico,* No. 119, April 1, 1955.
[2] *Panorama Económico,* No. 155, October 11, 1956.

President Ibáñez in August 1956 has never been made clear. The most plausible interpretation is that the President began to resent his increasingly powerful Minister with his solid, though tacit, right-wing–foreign-expert support as soon as the danger of runaway inflation had been effectively conquered.[1] One of the inherent difficulties in an effective fight against inflation in Chile appears to be the need for a Finance Minister who is so strong that he invariably arouses the suspicion and jealousy of the Chief Executive. A somewhat similar relationship of complete reliance followed by sudden dismissal existed in 1949–50 between President González Videla and his enterprising Finance Minister Jorge Alessandri and again in 1960–61 between Jorge Alessandri, then President, and his "strong man" Finance and Economy Minister Roberto Vergara. Ibáñez' decision to back out of the arrangement he had offered Frei in 1954 when the latter asked for what Ibáñez felt was too free a hand is a variant of this situation. Like the Roman general who returns from a victorious war, a finance minister who is waging a successful fight against inflation seems to be an uncomfortable fellow to have around.

Moreover, the emerging slump in the construction and some consumer goods industries and the resulting unemployment and discontent, particularly in Santiago, may have dampened the President's zeal for any vigorous prosecution of the stabilization program. The momentum of the program carried through to 1957 during which prices rose by only 17 per cent, but in 1958 the reins were definitely loosened and the rate of inflation returned to a lively 33 per cent. Throughout this period, moreover, the economy stagnated and per capita income actually declined. Chile seemed to have chosen for itself the worst of several possible worlds, since it had "neither stability nor development," to quote the title of a brochure by one of its most articulate economists.[2]

Much of this thoroughly unsatisfactory performance must be attributed to the weakness and incompetence of the slowly and ingloriously expiring Ibáñez regime. Rumors of official malpractices and graft thickened during these years (specifically in connection with the operation of the Arica free zone), creating an atmosphere singularly unpropitious for convincing other groups to make sacrifices and to adopt programs of discipline and austerity. At the same time, government agencies and semi-autonomous in-

---

[1] A cartoon in *Topaze* (February 3, 1956) shows Herrera as an acrobat hanging from two rings, one marked "Klein-Saks," the other "Right Wing," with the legend: "And this is the strongman of the regime."

[2] Aníbal Pinto Santa Cruz, *Ni estabilidad ni desarrollo,* Santiago, 1960.

stitutes proved unable to conduct anti-cyclical policies tending to offset or to correct the soft spots which had developed in the economy as a result of the credit restrictions and the change in expectations. In fact, the housing slump, which was brought on by the decline in high-cost office and apartment house construction, was reinforced rather than compensated by the public sector. Official construction activity by the government's social security funds and low-cost housing institute declined strongly in 1956 as a result of general financial stringency and responded only very slowly to several attempts at reviving it.[1]

The general social and economic malaise of the 1956–58 period erupted suddenly in the bloody riots of April 1957, which came as a great shock to the ingrained Chilean belief that such things as the Bogotá riots of 1948 "could not happen here." Touched off once again by an increase in bus fares, the riots demonstrated that inflation-induced distortions in the price system were not easily corrected in an environment of economic stagnation.[2]

The unsatisfactory performance of the Chilean economy in 1956–58 provided the critics of Klein-Saks with an excellent target for attack. The mission came to be criticized for a wide variety of failings: for not having resigned when Oscar Herrera was dismissed, for not having been able to get its fiscal reform projects adopted, for not having brought inflation to a complete stop, but, most of all, for having landed Chile's economy in a slump.[3] Once again, it was felt, the granting of exceptional authority to foreign experts had had disastrous results just as in the case of Courcelle-Seneuil and Kemmerer. The time had come, therefore, for a thorough reappraisal of prevailing doctrines on inflation and stabilization in the light of the recalcitrant Chilean reality. The result was the now well-known "structuralist" thesis on inflation, so named in contrast to the "monetarist" position identified with the ideas and policies advocated by the Klein-Saks mission and the International Monetary Fund. One of its great merits and attractions

---

[1] *El programa de estabilización de la economía Chilena y el trabajo de la Misión Klein & Saks*, pp. 12, 20, 209.

[2] For a detailed account and some incisive comments on this episode, see Silvert, *Reaction and Revolution in Latin America*, Chapter 9.

[3] Some of these criticisms are evaluated in David Felix, "Structural Imbalances, Social Conflict, and Inflation: An Appraisal of Chile's Recent Anti-Inflationary Effort," *Economic Development and Cultural Change*, January 1960. For a good example of a violent attack by a highly respected Chilean economist, see Flavian Levine, "Errores que se repiten," October 1957, mimeo.

was that here, for the first time, was a well-reasoned, indigenous doctrine elaborated by Chilean and other Latin American economists in reaction to imported doctrines judged to be inapplicable to Chile.

The tenets of the "structuralist" school have been described elsewhere[1] and will be only briefly summarized here. A basic distinction is made between the "structural" and the "propagating" factors of the inflation. The structural factors are essentially conceived to be the following:

(a) The low productivity of agriculture and its lack of response to economic incentives due to the latifundio pattern of ownership; as a result, industrialization and urbanization tend to lead to rising food prices.

(b) The tendency to a deterioration in the terms of trade, which derives from the fact that the demand for imports (of equipment, semimanufactures and food) increases faster in a country like Chile as development proceeds than does foreign demand for its exports; this results in a tendency for the price of imported goods to rise, usually as a result of devaluation.

(c) Sometimes, the uneven distribution of income is designated as a further structural factor. It is argued that, instead of leading to higher savings and investment, this distribution leads to continuous pressures against the two critical shortage areas: food consumption on the part of the bulk of the population and foreign exchange de-

---

[1] See the papers by Roberto Campos, David Felix and Joseph Grunwald in Albert O. Hirschman, ed., *Latin American Issues*, Twentieth Century Fund, New York, 1961. Grunwald's article carries an extensive bibliographical note (pp. 97–98) to which should be added an article by the late Mexican economist Juan Noyola Vásquez, "El desarrollo económico y la inflación en México y en otros países latinoamericanos," *Investigación Económica* (México), Cuarto Trimestre 1956, pp. 602–648. This article appears to be the first one to have drawn a clear distinction between the "structural" and the monetary or "propagating" factors. This distinction was incorporated into ECLA's 1957 *Annual Economic Survey of Latin America* (pp. 197 ff.) and elaborated by a group of Chilean economists including Jorge Ahumada, Jaime Barrios, Luis Escobar, Aníbal Pinto and Osvaldo Sunkel. Nicholas Kaldor espoused and elaborated the structuralist point of view in his influential article "Problemas Económicos de Chile," *Trimestre Económico*, April–June 1959. The present writer was unaware of this literature when he suggested a rather similar interpretation of inflation resulting from unbalanced growth in his *Strategy of Economic Development*, Yale University Press, 1958, pp. 156–66. A recent contribution is in Dudley Seers, "A Theory of Inflation and Growth in Underdeveloped Countries," *Oxford Economic Papers*, June 1962, pp. 173–95. There are obvious points of contact between the structuralist thesis on inflation in underdeveloped countries and the cost-push analysis of inflation for industrial societies although, to my knowledge, the points of convergence and of difference have not been systematically canvassed.

mands on the part of Latin America's rich with their weak stay-or-reinvest-at-home propensities.[1]

These structural factors exert upward pressures on the prices of specific but important groups of commodities. The pressures are then validated by the extension of bank credit and permitted to affect the general price level, and they are further amplified and perpetuated by wage and salary adjustments and consequent fiscal deficits. The latter elements of the process make up the "propagating" factors, one might say the superficial as opposed to the fundamental, underlying, "structural" ones.

Attempts to hold down the expansion of the money supply through bank credit restrictions, fiscal discipline, or wage and salary stops are in this view directed "merely" at the symptoms of the disease, not at its real cause. They may do more harm than good because, with the structural factors continuing to exert their influence on the price level, a decision not to validate these pressures can lead to a decline in growth, output, employment — and to serious trouble in the streets.

The theory thus turns the tables most effectively on those who had focused attention on the various sources of monetary and income expansion. For these analysts had originally also proposed as fundamental their favorite remedies of fiscal discipline, bank credit restriction and wage restraint in contrast to price controls, subsidies and exchange controls which they decried as stop-gaps, doing more harm than good because of the ensuing distortion in prices, costs and production. With the advent of structuralism, those who had fancied themselves deep thinkers were suddenly told in turn that they were shallow. With inflation (or recession) remaining a problem in spite of the substitution of general monetary and fiscal for specific controls, it was perhaps natural for the "fundamental" remedy of yesterday to be downgraded to today's palliative.

By holding that basic reforms are required to fight inflation effectively,

---

[1] The foregoing factors are frequently described as *the* structuralist position, but they actually should be designated as making up the (dominant) left-wing variety of that position. Different structural inflationary pressures have occasionally been identified by analysts with a right-wing orientation; the principal ones are the Chilean social security system with its large overhead cost and early retirement features, the irrational preference of the labor force for white-collar jobs, parasitic government controls of economic activity, etc. These right-wing views on the basic causes of inflationary pressures have been best formulated by Jorge Alessandri, who, like the left-wing structuralists, says: "It is naïve to think that the problem of inflation in Chile could be solved essentially through credit measures, without an attack on its fundamental causes, unless one wishes to bring about in this fashion . . . the paralysis of many activities and to generate a large volume of unemployment which would put a violent end to wage and salary readjustments." *La verdadera situación económica y social de Chile en la actualidad*, Confederación de la Producción y del Comercio, Santiago, 1955, p. 32.

the structuralist theory also represents a reversal of an earlier — and tempting — line of thinking that attributed virtually all the evils of Chilean society to inflation, as, for example, in the following particularly naïve passage:

> . . . the depressed condition of commerce, the ruinous state of industry and even more of agriculture, the corruption and disintegration of the political parties, the demoralization and inefficiency of our public administration, and finally the profound contempt of the better-off for the poor — all can be traced to the regime of depreciated paper money.[1]

Here it is clearly expected that once inflation, the dominant problem, is solved, all the other manifold evils to which it has given rise will also vanish, so that an independent attack on these evils is hardly worthwhile. Concentration of attention on inflation may thus at times have retarded action on other problems. Structuralism illustrates the opposite relationship: the search for inflation's underlying causes may induce action on other problems of Chilean society.

It should be noted that the structuralist critique of the traditional "monetary discipline" is quite different from the one that views inflation as the consequence of the struggle of different social groups for ever-larger slices of the social product. Those who hold this "sociological" view concede that inflation would stop if the increase in monetary supply and income could be restrained; but they point out to the innocent foreign adviser that this is a far taller order than he realizes, that inflation results not merely from irresponsible profligacy, from some isolated failure of will power, but represents the difficult-to-change outcome of group attitudes and conflicts. *The structuralist, on the other hand, affirms that, to eliminate inflation, not only attitudes but basic economic relationships must be altered.*

Among these relationships the agrarian structure is of special importance. The patterns of land tenure and ownership are held responsible for the lag in agricultural output, for the inadequate response of food supply to technological opportunities, and hence for the constant pressure for increased food prices as well as food imports. Thus Chilean thinking about inflation had come full circle: As half a century earlier, at the times of Agustín Ross and Alejandro Venegas, though now for quite different reasons, the hacendado stands once again accused of causing the inflation.

This time the reasoning was more subtle. Unlike the earlier argument, the link between the hacendados and inflation was not forged through the assertion of an historical fact whose correctness can be questioned — the

---

[1] Alejandro Venegas, *Cartas*, Preface, p. 13.

landowners unloosed the inflation with the intent of improving their financial position — but through two hypothetical propositions, namely: (1) if the present latifundio system were abolished, agricultural productivity could be increased, and (2) if agricultural productivity were increased, inflationary pressures would lessen. These propositions cannot, of course, be refuted although they are perhaps not quite as compelling as their proponents make them appear. One can point to the case of Mexico which despite land reform has nevertheless suffered from inflationary pressures and to pre-Castro Cuba which without land reform did not. Naturally, if we focus on an increase in farm output through land reform as the only conceivable change for the better in the Chilean situation, the argument becomes extremely convincing and attractive. But why should we? Why could Chile not gain foreign outlets for its manufactures and import more food? Why should it not be possible to improve the efficiency of government operations and thereby set aside new resources for productive investment?

As a matter of fact, improving the efficiency of an economy at any point whatever has dampening effects on inflation since it increases the ratio of total output to total input; it is therefore always possible and formally correct to claim that inflation is due to the failure to carry out one particular improvement. Thus it is easy to connect inflation causally with whatever particular social ill or economic inefficiency or evil one is interested in or hopefully capable of correcting; and if inflation persists it will no doubt be so connected by the advocates of social and economic reform.

In other words, persistent inflation will arouse or strengthen demands for basic social and economic reforms; and a society that is unable to make the relatively small inter-group adjustments required to end inflation is likely to find itself faced with strong and persuasive demands for much more fundamental social changes.[1] It is as though the story of the wanderer who, to gain entrance to a sanctuary, must solve progressively harder riddles were being inverted: the harder riddle is being submitted to him who has *not* been able to solve the easy one.

Disappointment over the performance of the Chilean economy in 1956–

---

[1] Here is another illustration of this type of rather paradoxical governmental behavior: when the state is unable to provide a satisfactory quantity and quality of those basic services needed by private enterprise in order to prosper, demands frequently arise for the government to take over *additional* functions, namely, those that are in the event unsatisfactorily discharged by private enterprise. This has been pointed out by Alexander Eckstein in "Individualism and the Role of the State in Economic Growth," *Economic Development and Cultural Change*, January 1958, pp. 81–87.

58 and hostility to the Klein-Saks mission caused most of Chile's economists to rally to some variety of the structuralist position during those years. This reaction was quite different from those observed during several earlier experiences with stabilization efforts that had gone awry in some way. Those experiences — the 1895–98 episode most conspicuously but also the gold standard-cum-depression experience of 1929–31 and the orthodox budget-balancing policies of Ross during the thirties — had always resulted in a willingness to give a new try to markedly inflationary policies in the interests of economic development or of income redistribution. After the spectacular and painful disruptions of 1953–55, naïve inflationism was no longer intellectually respectable.

While representing progress, the structuralist position appeared at first rather utopian. With its "a plague on both your houses" mentality, it rejected inflation, yet was also most unenthusiastic about all the tried methods of fighting it. This attitude of virtual withdrawal from practical policy-making reflected the already noted radicalization of the Chilean intellectuals under the impact of the 1953–58 experience and of the Klein-Saks mission.

From the point of view of the hard-pressed monetary authorities struggling with acute inflation who are told that changes in the pattern of land tenure or export diversification are required to attain price stability (or at least the kind of price stability worth having) the structuralist position seems most unhelpful. Yet this position is not essentially different from that of earlier policy critics — today considered as both orthodox and practical — who maintained that inflation could not be brought under control in the absence of certain institutional innovations such as a Central Bank endowed with ample powers to regulate the money supply. As it turned out, the structuralist thesis did not remain wholly utopian for too long, but had a significant effect on policy-making in 1961–62 when land and fiscal reform projects actually began to be tackled with some energy.[1]

By then, events had reinforced the structuralist arguments as a result of experience with a second attempt at stabilization which took place under

---

[1] The agrarian reform project which the Alessandri administration proposed to Congress and which was passed in 1962 is far more timid than the Colombian law discussed in Chapter 2. In Chile pressure for land reform came almost entirely from analysts concerned with the stagnation of agricultural production; in contrast to its militant blue- and white-collar workers, Chile's landless and tenant farmers (*inquilinos*) have seldom resorted to land occupation or to similar direct action. However, the 1958 elections had shown them to be no longer ready to cast their vote according to the instructions of the landlords.

conditions far more favorable than those prevailing in 1956–58. In the 1958 presidential elections, Jorge Alessandri, running primarily with right-wing support, had won a narrow plurality of the vote (he obtained only 31 per cent of the total vote). Along with the economists, the Chilean masses had also become radicalized during the supremely frustrating Ibáñez years and the Socialist-Communist candidate Allende failed to win the elections only because of the presence of a left-wing splinter candidate.

Alessandri's victory was widely interpreted as the "last chance" for the traditional elites to show that they could solve the country's principal problems among which inflation, proceeding in 1958 at the newly boosted rate of 33 per cent, retained a privileged place. Alessandri was aware of this challenge. Like all upperclass Chileans, he felt overwhelming distaste for the Ibáñez regime and attributed its failures not to any one of its policies but to the overall indecisiveness and incompetence (if not worse) of the administration. Essentially Alessandri felt that stopping inflation was a matter of will power, steady nerves and common sense. Disenchanted with international experts and unwilling or unable to make use of Chile's "radicalized" economists, he put together a Cabinet of *gerentes* or business executives. As "general in charge of the battle against inflation" he appointed the energetic and strong-willed Roberto Vergara, who, like Oscar Herrera, combined the Finance, Economy and Mines portfolios.

The experiment was started under far more favorable auspices than that of Ibáñez in 1955–56. In Congress Alessandri could count, if not on a majority, at least on a strong minority base in both houses. By 1955 Ibáñez had lost one precious half of his six-year term and virtually all of his prestige whereas Alessandri decided to act within the first year of his election. The competence of Alessandri's appointees was universally considered to be higher than that of the Ibáñez appointees. Finally, in 1958 the country had the experience of the almost-runaway inflation of 1955 still fresh in its memory, but the actual rate of inflation was "only" around 30 per cent so that total success in the fight against inflation in the sense of bringing the rate down to zero was easier to achieve than in 1955 when prices almost doubled.

The new attempt at stabilization was launched in earnest in mid–1959. This timing showed some learning from previous attempts including that of Alessandri himself when he was Finance Minister in 1949–50: At that time and in 1955–56 the stabilization effort was started at the year-end and under the circumstances the first move in the effort was inevitably to oppose the raising of wages and salaries in the amount of the previous year's increase in the cost of living. This move aroused considerable resistance which either killed the whole effort as in 1950 or definitely tagged it as unfairly anti-labor from the start. On the other hand it was virtually impossible to launch a stabilization effort with credit restrictions and the like right after a salary increase at the beginning of the year. But by mid-year the annual January rise in wages and salaries would have largely worked itself through the price system; and there remained a few critical months prior to the next January readjustment during which decided anti-inflationary action could take effect, so that the government could *then* point to the attainment of price stability in pleading for moderation in wage and salary demands. This was the strategy of Vergara. Starting in April 1959 the government and the Central Bank revised and strengthened the system of credit control. The government took certain spectacular measures: it announced a new currency unit (one escudo = 1000 old pesos), unified definitively the exchange rate system, and stopped Central Bank rediscounting for the commercial banks, the State Bank and the Treasury while finding various ingenious ways of avoiding any drastic curtailment of bank credit or of Treasury resources. It became clear that the country had at last a government that knew how to act; public confidence, especially among the business community, was restored, international credits were secured in large amounts in July, and for the first time in over twenty years prices virtually stopped rising in August. Largely on the strength of this success, the government was able to hold wage and salary increases to between 10 and 20 per cent early in 1960. It then exerted considerable pressure on the business community to absorb these wage increases, both by direct suasion, which the *gerentes* turned Ministers were particularly well fitted to engage in, and indirectly, through an active, helicopter-spearheaded campaign of consumer education and orientation. Prices continued fairly stable throughout 1960 despite the economic disruption and reconstruction expenditures occasioned by the unprecedentedly severe earthquake in the South. However, industrial production, which in 1959 had staged a strong recovery, based mainly on inventory replenishment, sagged somewhat in 1960. Hence it could be claimed that, just as in 1956–57, stability was again being bought at the price of development.

The left-wing opposition also blamed the government for submitting abjectly to the dictates of the International Monetary Fund, which had been the principal negotiator for the foreign credit package obtained in 1959. Actually this accusation was unjust, for the new government itself "had religion": its thinking on monetary and fiscal policy was more rigid than that of the Fund and it was more convinced than the Republican administration in Washington that, with monetary stability assured, economic growth would automatically follow. This was particularly true for "strong man" Roberto Vergara whose high-handed and self-assured methods of operating recalled the style of Gustavo Ross, the clever but unpopular Finance Minister of Arturo Alessandri in the thirties. Increasing Congressional hostility toward Vergara, even from within the governmental parties, came to the fore when the earthquake reconstruction bill he sponsored was discussed in September 1960. His resignation followed shortly, caused perhaps also by the President's feeling that a new balance between the two objectives of stability and growth, and between *gerentes* and *políticos* in his Cabinet, was required.

Thereafter the economic policy of the government gradually assumed a different physiognomy: monetary and price stability remained an important concern, but was no longer the sole objective of economic policy. In January 1961 a ten-year development plan on which CORFO technicians had long been working was officially adopted by the government, and in the course of that year agrarian and fiscal reform projects were studied in the executive branch for submission to the Congress. At the same time low-cost housing construction expanded sharply and was an important factor in a general strong upturn of industrial production. In August 1961, in response to Congressional election results, came the participation of the Radical Party and with it the appointment of Luis Escobar, Dean of the Economics Faculty of the University of Chile, as Minister of Economy, Reconstruction and Development. With Escobar, the structuralists achieved some representation in the Cabinet.[1] At the same time the government had a stable majority in both houses of Congress, and, thanks to the Alliance for Progress, long-term foreign assistance was to become available in unprecedented amounts. Hence, the chances for improving the performance of the Chilean economy in various "structural" ways while keeping the traditional scourge under some control looked more promising than they had for a long time.

Conclusion: Inflation, Revolution and Civil War

An author attempting to understand a phenomenon normally felt as deplorable — be it pain, death or business cycles — frequently ends up by identifying with it and turning explanation into apology and apology into

---

[1] See Escobar's article, "Desocupación con inflación: el caso chileno," *Panorama Económico*, No. 205, August 1959, pp. 287–293; also "Interpretación nacional del desarrollo económico," *El Trimestre Económico*, Oct.–Dec. 1960, pp. 606–615 and "Problemas actuales del desarrollo económico en América Latina," *Economía*, Santiago, second quarter of 1961, pp. 1–11.

eulogy. The classical way of performing this mutation is to show that in the absence of the evil with which one is concerned an even worse calamity would befall humanity. This exercise has of course been undertaken frequently by the apologists of inflation when they have attempted to demonstrate that under certain circumstances inflation can become the only alternative to stagnation. The Chilean experience does not provide much support for this thesis, but it supplies some basis for a more unusual one: that inflation can serve to head off revolution or be considered as an alternative to civil war. We shall take up these two assertions in turn.

Inflation and Revolution. We noted in the introduction to this chapter that inflation is a particularly conspicuous problem since it is constantly noticed by both housewives and statisticians: consequently, it may engage a disproportionate amount of public attention in comparison to other less immediately harassing, but perhaps more fundamental, problems. From this point of view, inflation has often been held to divert attention from these basic "smouldering" problems. But the Chilean experience suggests that inflation may also serve as a combined fever thermometer and divining rod for these other problems. Persistent inflation, especially when refractory to traditional therapy, encourages a search for those more deep-seated troubles in the economic and social structure which might be held responsible for the inflation. Even though the causal connections established in this way may sometimes be contrived or tenuous, there is considerable *independent* value in having such a search undertaken, especially when other troubles do not ordinarily signal their existence until it is "too late" in some sense. In other words, action to correct them may take place earlier with the stimulus of inflation than without it. It is tempting here to cite the exemplary monetary stability enjoyed by Cuba until 1958; this fact certainly contributed to the impression in some circles that nothing much could be wrong in such a country. No such false sense of security could ever arise in Chile where the inflation has led to a scrutiny of the country's principal institutions from the system of land tenure to social security and from the status of foreign capital to the political structure. If revolution comes to Chile, it certainly will not be for want of warning!

Inflation and Civil War. In line with the "sociological" theory (see pp. 195ff.) the Chilean inflation has been explained by "what the Chileans themselves often call the 'struggle' or even 'civil war' between the country's major economic interest groups."[1] Is this a mere figure of speech or can this

---

[1] Francis H. Schott, "Inflation and Stabilization Efforts in Chile, 1953–1958," *Inter-American Economic Affairs*, Winter 1959, p. 7.

vaguely sensed relationship between inflation and civil war be more precisely defined?

Let us first note one general similarity between inflation and civil war: both frequently result from miscalculation. The provocative nature of the first step or the response is due to the fact that the challenger or the respondent overestimate their strength. Many civil wars have been intended as coups or revolutions, and an inflation is frequently brought underway by a group which wrongly believes that it can get away with "grabbing" a larger share of the national product than it has so far received. An overestimate of strength on the part of at least one group, and usually of several, is thus a characteristic cause of both civil war and inflation. Such miscalculation is in turn likely to be caused by poor inter-group information and communication, a situation typical of rapidly changing societies with hitherto fairly rigid class barriers.

Inflation and civil war both being responses to essentially similar social situations, it is tempting to think of inflation as a substitute for civil war. This goes counter to the Lenin dictum that there is no surer way to revolutionize a society than to "debauch its currency." In this well-worn, though perhaps apocryphal, phrase so frequently and enthusiastically quoted by American bank presidents, inflation is seen as a steppingstone to revolution. No doubt in some cases the disruptions and psychological scars inflicted by prolonged and acute inflation have helped set the stage for revolutionary change. But this should not keep us from realizing that through the device of inflation society gains precious time for resolving social tensions that otherwise might reach the breaking point right away. This would certainly be confirmed by many a Minister of Labor who has settled or prevented a strike by granting inflationary wage increases. How marvelous it would be if we could postpone fighting among nations over territorial issues by some similar legerdemain! That, however, would require a magician who could conjure up for the battle-ready contestants some vast phantasmagorical territory athwart their common frontier which they would then busily proceed to carve up among themselves instead of starting to shoot.[1]

The advocates of monetary stability frequently make it quite clear that what they really want is to do away with all this shadow-boxing implied by successive rounds of "illusory" wage and price increases. Why not have a

---

[1] Elements of such a clash-avoiding diversion are obviously present in the space race between the United States and Russia.

real good fight right here and now? The 1950 report of the International Monetary Fund to Chile says as much:

> The apparent anonymity and impersonality of any action taking place through credit should not be allowed to obscure its real significance. A credit restriction to be effective must force businessmen to sell goods at prices lower than they had anticipated, oftentimes at a loss; *it must make it financially impossible for them to increase wage rates,* and it must cause a certain minimum amount of unemployment.[1]

No wonder that many a government, faced with this kind of advice, prefers the illusion to last and the inflation to continue a while longer!

Inflation then offers an almost miraculous way of temporizing in a situation in which two or more parties who are psychologically not ready for peaceable compromise appear to be set on a collision course. It permits them, as we have seen before, to maintain a militant and hostile stance while playing an elaborate, largely non-violent, game in which everybody wins sham victories. The result is of course that nothing is resolved — no one has attained his objectives except the perhaps not unimportant one of gratifying his hostility. The realization of having been cheated by inflation may then heighten bitterness and hostility, and this could make an eventual clash more likely (Lenin's thesis). But it is also possible that after having played the game a few times, the parties will realize its futility or that a new element will appear which makes a lull, truce or settlement possible. If that should turn out to be the case in Chile, inflation will have provided that country with additional room for social maneuvering during a particularly critical and disruptive period of its development.

---

[1] International Monetary Fund Report, p. 100. (My italics.)

11

Problem-Solving and
Reformmongering

Chapter 4

Problem-Solving and Policy-Making: A Latin American Style?

In this chapter an attempt will be made to present some characteristic features of the policy-making, decision-making and problem-solving techniques and processes described in detail in the individual country studies. At its most ambitious, such an attempt could result in the delineation of a Latin American "style" in handling, learning about, and moving toward the solution of large-scale policy problems. While we are likely to settle for findings that will be both more tentative and more dispersed, the ideally possible result of our inquiry permits us to compare it at the outset to some related concerns of other social scientists.

An attempt to define a national problem-solving style resembles the interest of anthropologists in the study of "culture-and-personality." In fact, the latter concept is sometimes defined as typical or probable "ways of behavior or techniques of solving problems."[1] However, when anthropologists identify cultural "themes," "patterns," "ethos" or "world views," they look for an organizing principle that makes intelligible *established* ways of coping with *permanent* and *basic* problems, such as those of food supply, of interpersonal relations, of man's relation to the unknown. An inquiry into a country's problem-solving style, on the other hand, will concentrate on the *successive* ways in which *newly arising* problems are dealt with from the time they are first experienced. This is a particularly tempting and perhaps manageable task for specific policy problems which move into and out of the center of the stage and which are handled by policy-makers through discrete decisions along one or several well-documented paths.

---

[1] Anthony F. C. Wallace, *Culture and Personality*, Random House, New York, 1961, pp. 6–7.

The feeling that it may be worthwhile to concentrate attention and effort at generalization on this end of the problem spectrum has recently gained some currency. When, in 1957, Walt W. Rostow defined "national style" as the way in which a nation typically deals with its environment and its problems, he had in mind primarily the responses of a nation, as expressed in the actions of its policy-makers, to the principal historic challenges it has encountered. A conference organized to explore the "American Style" proved rather inconclusive, however. Rostow maintained that the "acutely pragmatic national style" of the United States consists in "accumulating experience, feel, judgment, . . . sensing recurrent patterns rather than isolating clean-cut logical connections of cause and effect." This characterization is then used to explain why the United States has been excellent in the arts of "experimental exploration of possible solutions" and baffled when "prompt and radical innovation" is required.[1] Other participants in the conference disagreed sharply with this characterization. They spoke eloquently of our rigid moral absolutism and stressed that, in the United States, a problem has typically been expected to be solved outright rather than to be lived with;[2] and that the advocated solutions, far from being pragmatic, frequently involved attempts at radically remolding reality to make it conform to some simple, universal and ideal formula, such as Free Competition, the Principle of Self-Determination, Prohibition, World-Wide Currency Convertibility, and others.

Clamorous disagreements of this kind cannot fail to arise when the question of national style is discussed without reference to the specific problems in the handling of which one or the other style is supposed to be in evidence, for style is likely to depend as much on the nature of the problem as on the historical and cultural background of the community which is confronting the problem. At the same time and place, two problems may evoke simultaneously the use of quite different styles. If attempts to discuss style are to be more than speculations about national character, style should be made to arise, to the greatest possible extent, out of the characteristics of the problems and of the problem-solving process itself. Different

---

[1] Walt W. Rostow, "The National Style" in *The American Style*, Elting E. Morison, ed., Harper, New York, 1958, pp. 260–261. This conception of what Rostow calls the typical or classical American style is considerably elaborated in his *The United States in the World Arena*, Harper, New York, 1960. The phrase "the acutely pragmatic national style" is from Max Millikan's preface to the former volume.

[2] Abraham Kaplan, "American Ethics and Public Policy" in *The American Style*, particularly pp. 35–51; and Richard Hofstadter, *ibid.*, p. 369, as well as in his *The Age of Reform*, Knopf, New York, 1955, pp. 16–17.

national styles could then still arise from the fact that the principal problems unavoidably encountered by various nations during a prolonged period may have quite different structures and will therefore evoke quite
different reactions, treatments, and learning processes.

To make any progress with the suggestive but slippery concept of style,
it is therefore necessary to develop first some general notions about the different ways in which policy problems are selected for action, and once selected, are attacked and reattacked.

The Selection of Problems and the Function of Ideology

The peculiar character of the problems we are dealing with, e.g., inflation, can best be brought out by comparing them with certain problems
studied cross-culturally by anthropologists, e.g., the disposal of the dead.
After listing the various alternative ways in which the latter problem can
be solved — burial, cremation, exposure or drowning — the anthropologist
will find that any one well-defined culture will have opted in a stable fashion for one of these techniques rather than busily shift from one possible
solution to the other. But this shifting is precisely the earmark and the most
interesting aspect of a protracted fight on inflation! A closely related difference is that the dead are *always* removed in some way from the sight of the
living while the inflation problem is sometimes entirely neglected, sometimes tackled in a half-hearted and perfunctory fashion and then suddenly
attacked with the utmost energy. Hence, before inquiring *how* these problems are analyzed and attacked, it is important to realize that societies may
differ greatly in the *kind* of problems that their policy-makers decide to
tackle seriously.

The mechanisms that citizens and interest groups have at their disposal
for *commanding the attention of policy-makers* differ greatly from one society to another. For example, if the principal mechanism of this kind is the
demonstration of discontent by violence, then it is clear that a great many
problems which affect individual members of the society will not be dealt
with centrally simply because they do not lend themselves to the staging of
violent protest. Thus, the raising of bus fares hurts a large number of people in their pocketbook at the same time and place and thereby invites
demonstrations of discontent while a high rate of infant mortality does not
similarly lend itself to mass protest, even if the provision of adequate health
facilities is felt to be the government's responsibility. Thus, in countries
where violent protest is the principal method open to "problem victims" for

commanding the attention of policy-makers, only a limited range of problems is likely to be attacked at all forcefully. As a result, a sharp split would separate the few privileged problems which the authorities do something about from the many neglected ones. Such a split is one aspect of the *dualism*, i.e., the coexistence of the new and the old, the efficient and the inefficient, the modern and the backward, which has indeed been recognized as an outstanding "personality trait" of the less developed countries.

Up to a point, this variety of dualism is self-reinforcing. Once it has become clear that policy-makers are responsive to threats of violence in one particular area, such threats will be delivered with increasing frequency. Eventually it will become evident, however, that other methods of communication between the ruled and the rulers must be found: a Colombian Minister of Agriculture put this well when he said in 1959 that it is necessary to carry out policies that will "put an end to the [campesinos'] impression that the State will only help those who make trouble."[1]

Differences in pressure account of course everywhere for differences in the extent to which problems are seriously tackled. The fact that problems which lend themselves to mass protest receive preferential treatment is, for example, evident in the priority which unemployment insurance has received in the United States and elsewhere over health insurance. Political development could nevertheless be described in terms of the emergence of a wide diversity of mechanisms and leverages, from elections to lobbying by pressure groups, through which individuals and groups can compel policy-makers to pay attention to their problems. Such multiplicity certainly does not assure *equal* access to the government for all groups and their problems, but it is likely to reduce the huge differences in access that exist when only those that can deliver a credible threat to the stability of the social and political order obtain a hearing.[2]

---

[1] Literally translated ". . . who create problems." It is significant that the term "problem" is often used by politicians in Latin America as a euphemism for trouble and disturbances of public order. The quote is from a speech of Minister Augusto Espinosa Valderrama of February 18, 1959, Ministerio de Agricultura, *Boletín de Información*, No. 89, p. 42.

[2] The concept of "differential access" to government has been developed for the United States, particularly insofar as access to the legislative process is concerned, by David Truman, *The Governmental Process*, Knopf, New York, 1951, Ch. 11. A systematic survey of the various "linkages" existing in the United States between the public and the policy-makers is presented in V. O. Key, Jr., *Public Opinion and American Democracy*, Knopf, New York, 1961, Part 5. Significantly, violence and mass protest are not even mentioned by Key even though they are certainly very much in evidence as a linkage of sorts in the case of both Negro discontent over segregation and White discontent over desegregation.

Yet, to advise countries without a complex web of "linkages" between the public and the government to get to work and develop one is none too helpful, for such a web is the result of a lengthy process which is not easily hurried. Are there possibly any by-ways through which countries lacking such a web can be brought to tackle problems which, having no direct route to the policy-makers' attention, tend to be badly neglected? In our country studies we are actually coming across one promising alternative and indirect way in which such problems may receive attention: In Chile, the repeated and disappointing attempts to stem inflation (without incurring stagnation) led to a search for the underlying causes of inflation and attention was drawn to various "structural" faults of the economy, e.g., to the need for changes in land tenure patterns. In Brazil's Northeast, the lack of success of the dams in strengthening the area's resistance to the periodic droughts led to the examination of other aspects of the region's backwardness, such as lack of research in drought-resistant agriculture, lack of industrialization, education, etc. In Colombia, concern over the balance of payments reinforced the search for means to increase agricultural output.

In all these cases, problems that had tended to be neglected because of lack of *direct* access of the problem's victims to the policy-makers achieved attention indirectly by riding the coattails of the problem which policy-makers were anxious to tackle.[1]

Sometimes, as in Chile, rather elaborate theories were needed to forge a causal link between the privileged and the stepchild problem, and such theories will frequently have a strong ideological flavor. Here, then, is a useful, if latent, function of ideology which is so much in evidence in attempts at problem-solving in Latin America: *ideology sometimes remedies the lack of direct access of certain neglected problems and provides them with indirect access via the construction of theories forging links between privileged and neglected problems.*

The same kind of mechanism results from the emphasis on and commitment to general comprehensive planning. Suppose we have a privileged problem P which commands attention of the policy-makers and a neglected problem N which does not. One way of calling attention to the latter is

---

[1] In the United States much the same mechanism operates when necessary. A particularly important case is aid for foreign economic development. Here the problem victims, i.e., the underdeveloped countries, have little direct access to U. S. policy-makers, hence indirect access had to be secured time and again in various laborious and dubious ways, usually by showing that foreign aid is essential to combat Communism, a problem on which policy-makers were prepared to act.

through a theory showing that the persistence of P is directly due to the existence of N. But a safer, all-purpose and frequently more convincing way of achieving the same result is to claim that P cannot be solved without a Comprehensive Plan and to insert measures to attack N into that Plan. This is essentially the way Celso Furtado operated when he brought the hitherto taboo problems of *zona da mata* cane monoculture within the purview of the SUDENE plan for the Northeast. The Comprehensive Plan is then a generalized device for indirectly achieving recognition for the stepchild problems of a society which lacks in the manifold linkage and access mechanisms of Western-type democracies.

These various ways of connecting neglected problems with privileged ones work only if there exists a privileged problem that stubbornly refuses to give way so that a search for the "real" causes may begin and unearth our various stepchild problems. From this point of view, considerable value attaches for a society with a poor or one-sided signalling system to having a recalcitrant or recurring attention-receiving problem which stimulates a search for other problems that would otherwise go unrecognized and unremedied, perhaps until it is "too late." As in the Arabian tale about the non-existent treasure thought to be buried in a fertile field that has long lain fallow, unexpected benefits are here yielded as a result of the activity connected with the search. In Chapter 3, we make precisely this point when we notice how Chile's inflation problem has drawn attention to various faults of that country's social and economic structure. At the same time, we speculate what might have happened if Cuba had *not* been for so long a model of monetary stability: it is conceivable that some of its smouldering economic and social problems might then have been detected and remedied gradually instead of exploding suddenly in the Castro revolution.

Rather than as superstructure in the Marxian sense, ideology has been viewed in the preceding pages as an "in-between-structure," designed to forge a plausible causal link between two distinct problems. A similar interpretation of the role of ideology may be given in a somewhat different setting which we also encounter in the country studies. Suppose a country is faced, on the one hand, with problems that are continuously exerting pressure but have not responded well to treatment and, on the other, with problems which the present or would-be policy-makers think they can do something about and on which they are anxious to move if only because they feel this will increase their power and popularity. Under these circumstances, a theory will frequently be forthcoming to prove conclusively that action on the latter problems will materially help to relieve the former.

The situation is rather similar to that of a physician who, consulted on an ailment he does not know much about, finds another, better known disorder from which the patient suffers and proceeds to cure this one, assuring the patient that there is a connection between the two. In policy-making this sort of thing happens all the time, for the problems on which the policy-makers are pressed to act are not necessarily those on which they wish to act and on which they have developed or believe to have available special skills. A justification for this kind of *substitution of one problem by another* is usually not too difficult to marshal. In fact a statement such as "no progress can be made on problem A unless we first remedy problem B" frequently is convincing just because it points to an indirect, hitherto neglected and perhaps unsuspected causal nexus. Up to a point, and Occam notwithstanding, such roundaboutness in reasoning carries intellectual prestige not because it is necessarily correct, but because there has been considerable historical association between insight into a problem and roundaboutness.[1] This does not mean that the most roundabout substitution is the most convincing one; decreasing and negative returns are sure to set in beyond some point. But if it is difficult to fashion a *direct* nexus between the problem one wants to tackle and the one which generates the pressure toward action it is again possible to utilize the Comprehensive Program as an intermediate link which makes the connection automatic: Problem A, so it will be argued, can be solved only as part of a Comprehensive Program, and action on Problem B is part of such a Program.

This substitution of one problem for another has this time been made to sound a bit frivolous, but this is not really intended. In the face of ignorance about the "pressing" problem, recourse to substitution is a perfectly legitimate heuristic device. Its use is likely to become particularly marked when the pressure of the "pressing" problems increases and when *the spectrum of possible policy actions* widens as a result of better communications, the development of new policy instruments, or a change in power relationships between social groups. For example, when the possibility of creating a new institution such as a central bank or a common market appears on the horizon, policy-makers and politicians will hopefully assess the possible favorable effects of such initiatives on a wide range of existing problems (which will often include that of their own election or re-election); and the same will occur, at least on the part of some policy-makers, when

---

[1] Just as there has been a historical association between the roundaboutness of production techniques and increases in productivity; the economist will be reminded here of Böhm-Bawerk's theory of capital and its critics.

expropriation of the landowners suddenly becomes a conceivable policy step. This phenomenon accounts for the frequently noted convergence of policy prescriptions: Colombia's balance-of-payments problem, Chile's inflation problem, and the chronic backwardness of Brazil's Northeast suddenly all require the same cure through Comprehensive Programming and Agrarian Reforms. The simple fact is that we have here stubborn policy problems that have hardened in their resistance to the most varied treatments; so it is only natural that, when a new policy instrument becomes available, attempts should be made to try it out. Research on largely unknown diseases, such as cancer, has often proceeded in much the same way by trying out almost at random newly developed drugs. But here there is no strong psychological compulsion to prove *a priori*, through more or less elaborate ideological structures, that the new compound will have beneficial results, if only because it can be tested in the laboratory.

Our inquiry into the process through which problems are selected for treatment by the policy-makers has yielded the following categories:

(a) Problems which the problem victims are able to bring forcefully to the attention of the policy-makers;

(b) Problems which the policy-makers are persuaded to tackle because they have become convinced that progress on them is in some sense prerequisite to progress on (a); and

(c) Problems suggested by a widening of the spectrum of possible actions, that is, on which the policy-makers wish to, and think they ought to, move primarily because new policy actions have become feasible or new policy instruments have become available; it will be hoped and claimed that the resultant progress on these problems will do much to alleviate problems (a).

The overlap between problems (b) and (c) is obvious. The theoretical distinction is that policy-makers hit on (b) as a result of a search for the root cause of (a) whereas they become oriented to (c) independently of (a) and forge the link to (a) as an *ex post* rationalization, out of optimism about the power of the new policy actions. However, in any concrete instance of a non-(a) problem that is taken up it will always be difficult to disentangle the *push* originating in (a) from the *pull* exerted by a newly feasible policy step or a newly invented policy instrument.

In any event, our conclusion that problems (b) or (c) or some amalgam of them will also be taken up by the policy-makers accounts for the observation that Latin American history shows many examples of important actions being taken by the policy-makers themselves without any noticeable pressure from important sectors of public opinion. Recent striking examples are Kubitschek's decision to build Brasília or the attempt to establish a Latin American Free Trade Area; and though our country studies are rather geared to the kind of problems that are tackled under high pressure, we show that the São Francisco Valley Commission (CVSF), the Bank of the Northeast, and to some extent even Colombia's land reform law of 1961 resulted from the policy-makers' more or less autonomous choice rather than from anyone's insistent clamor.[1]

Motivation vs. Understanding in Problem-Solving

This distinction which we have just drawn between the "pressing" problems of type (a) and the more or less autonomously "chosen" problems of type (b) and (c) has its usefulness in considering other aspects of the problem-solving process. Take the learning process: if mistakes are made in handling "pressing" problems, the policy-makers will be told so quite promptly, since the original pressure that led them to act in the first place will not abate and may even increase. On the other hand, if "chosen" problems are mismanaged, corrective forces will be slower to assert themselves since there was no pressure to start with. To illustrate: once inflation had reached an intolerable rate in Chile in the fifties, ineffective anti-inflationary policies became rapidly discredited, while the development plan of the São Francisco Valley through the CVSF, a fairly good example of a "chosen" problem, bogged down during a long period without any strong outcry since the CVSF had not been set up to remedy a specific and strongly felt difficulty. It is of course possible that a "pressing" problem arises or is made worse in the course of tinkerings with a "chosen" one (e.g.,

---

[1] Even in the United States where every conceivable group interest is making its voice heard through active pressure groups, important official actions or programs do not invariably originate in articulate demands presented to public officials. An inquiry into the origins of the spectacular redevelopment plan for the city of New Haven has found that "neither in 1950 nor in later years was there anything like a discernible popular demand for measures to reverse the physical and economic decay of New Haven though citizens were evidently discontented with the city in various ways. . . It would be wrong to suppose, then, that politicians were pressed into action by public demand. On the contrary, they had to sniff out the faint smell of distant political success, generate the demands, and activate the latent consensus." Robert A. Dahl, *Who Governs? Democracy and Power in an American City*, Yale University Press, New Haven, 1961, p. 139.

when the construction of Brasília aggravates inflation); and this may well be an important way in which mistakes made in dealing with "chosen" problems eventually get detected and corrected. In any event, it appears once again that the character of the learning process, an important ingredient of style, will vary with the *kind of problem* that is being tackled and not only with the kind of society that is involved in the process.

But why should any mistakes be committed at all? At first sight this seems a silly sort of question, yet it leads us to the central characteristics of the problem-solving process. Mistakes are likely to occur principally and systematically when the motivation to solve problems outruns understanding of the problem. Let us look at the problem-solving process in terms of these two variables.

A situation which is widely deplored but which is felt not to be subject to change cannot qualify as a problem at all. Examples are the mortality of man and, at least until quite recently, the vagaries and excesses of the weather. Ordinarily we resign ourselves to situations that we feel not to be remotely susceptible of improvement. If we do not make our peace with them, our protest takes on the quality of existentialist "despair" rather than of "discontent."

Thus, no active desire to do something about an unsatisfactory situation is forthcoming when we have no understanding of it, and even less when we are convinced that it cannot be remedied. Let us now imagine that, after some considerable time interval, we take another look at this situation and notice that it has moved to a point where not only has it turned into a problem, but where considerable progress has been made in tackling it: we will then conclude that in the intervening period there must have occurred a considerable advance in understanding and a similar spurt in the motivation to act. But the knowledge of these two terminal points, one where understanding and motivation are low and the other where both are high, does not tell us much about the intervening problem-solving process.

We can, however, immediately define two "ideal type" problem-solving paths or styles: one where advances in understanding tend to induce motivation, and the other where, on the contrary, motivation races ahead of understanding. Naturally, it is also possible to conceive of an ideal or "balanced" path where both understanding and motivation, or to put the matter into somewhat different terms, both the possibility of effecting change and the aspiration to carry it out, expand in step. To look at change in this way may be in fact a fairly satisfactory method when one paints on a very large historical canvas, as Marx was doing when he wrote his famous dictum that "mankind always takes up only such problems as it can solve . . ."[1] Yet as soon as one looks at the process of change in some detail, he perceives the fact that understanding and motivation, or objective and subjective factors of change, are usually out of phase with each other at any one point of time. Lenin, that practitioner of change, knew this very well when he distinguished sharply between objective and subjective conditions required to create a revolutionary situation.

As between the two unbalanced paths which have been defined, the more natural and relaxed one is clearly that where understanding paces motivation. Societies following this path will tackle only problems that appear to be more or less manageable as a result of a change in underlying conditions or an advance in understanding. Or, in a somewhat different formulation, ends are chosen as means become available to achieve these ends. For example, the eradication of malaria has become a feasible goal and has been seriously pursued only with the discovery of DDT. Hence, "perception of a problem or definition of a goal often *follows* and is stimulated by the identification of a possible policy."[2]

This particular problem-solving style is likely to be characteristic of societies which pioneer in technical progress and which chart their own course in matters of political organization and social advance without looking to others for values and tasks. Such "leading" countries would then have the pleasant experience of meeting with much success in their undertakings since they tackle problems only after they have become soluble.

The alternative path is marked by the tendency of motivation to pull ahead of understanding. It may be typical of "latecomer" societies which are anxious to attack a variety of problems regardless of whether their resources, abilities and attitudes are in harmony with the tasks they are undertaking. Perhaps we can place into this category most of today's underdeveloped countries with their "revolution of expectations" and their compulsive desire to solve all problems of economic, social and political backwardness as rapidly as possible. In this case the lag of understanding behind motivation is likely to make for a high incidence of mistakes and

---

[1] The sentence continues: "since, looking at the matter more closely, we always find that the problem itself arises only where the material conditions necessary for its solution already exist *or are at least in the process of formation.*" (My italics.) With this last phrase Marx opens the door slightly to the possibility that matters may proceed in a disjointed or unbalanced way. The sentence is the climax of the summary exposition of historical materialism in the Preface to *A Contribution to the Critique of Political Economy* (Marx-Engels, *Werke*, Dietz, Berlin, 1961, Vol. 13, p. 9).

[2] C. E. Lindblom, in a letter to the author.

failures in problem-solving activities and hence for a far more frustrating path to development than the one that characterizes the industrial leaders.

In our country studies, the motivation-outruns-understanding style of problem-solving is reflected in the endlessly repeated calls for a full, integrated, definitive and rapid solution of the difficulties that are being encountered. This style is also conspicuously evident in the frequent creation of new institutions: in the absence of advances in understanding, the sharpened motivation to do something about a problem finds a welcome outlet through the establishment of an agency to which the problem-solving task is delegated. Our studies permit us to differentiate between agencies which were created with hardly any prior advance in understanding of the problem, such as Colombia's Institutes of Colonization and Brazil's São Francisco Valley Commission, and those, like Brazil's SUDENE and Colombia's INCORA, that resulted from new insights or from meaningful and hard-won battles for changes in institutional and social structure. The contrast between the unsatisfactory performance of the former and the promising beginnings of the latter is surely related to these differences in origin.

La Rage de Vouloir Conclure[1]

While the scheme we have presented may have some value as a first approximation and exploration of our topic, it is unlikely that the complex reality of problem-solving processes can be compressed into such simple terms. Take first the understanding-outruns-motivation style. One pitfall that lies in wait for the "leading" countries using this style is that their very success in problem-solving could breed the overconfidence in the solvability of *all* problems which Hofstadter finds to be characteristic of the United States.[2] Such overconfidence would then lead them soon to tackle problems that are inherently or at least temporarily insoluble, i.e., to the opposite style. But then there are other difficulties. The new understanding which leads to action is usually restricted to a quite limited aspect of the problem; and the other aspects of the problem come into view only after irreversible steps have been taken to apply the new understanding: hence the tendency of the advanced countries constantly to "create more

---

[1] A marvelously apt expression used by Flaubert for a trait he often ridiculed. See *Correspondance*, Conard, Paris, 1929, Vol. V, p. 111. In clumsy translation it becomes "the mania for wanting to conclude."

[2] See p. 228, note 2.

problems than they solve." Examples are the problems created by the automobile, the wonder drugs, atomic fission and fusion, etc. Thus the path of the leading countries is itself strewn with a good number of frustrations.

But let us turn to the latecomers whose problem-solving style was said to be characterized by the tendency to let motivation race ahead of understanding. How does this style affect the problem-solving process in the case of what we have termed "pressing" problems such as the desire of Colombian campesinos for land, the refusal of Nordestinos to die of hunger in the drought-stricken areas or of Chilean workers to remain passive in the face of rapid increases in the cost of living?

In these cases, the policy-makers are strongly motivated to act, at first merely to pacify (or occasionally to suppress) the protest: subsidies are given to the drought victims; the peasants are either permitted to buy on easy terms the lands they have occupied or they are forcibly evicted; wages are allowed to go up or an attempt is made to stop prices from rising further through exhortations, imprecations against speculators, or price controls. In short, the *first* reactions to "pressing" problems are of a stopgap, remedial character, taken with a minimum of understanding of the problem. This is Schumpeter's "adaptive response" which he opposed to the "creative response" that somehow takes advantage of a problem's emergence to galvanize energies and achieve a variety of breakthroughs.

Actually the process of responding to a problem appears to be far more complex than is implied by this alleged one-time choice between adaptive and creative response. In the first place, some adaptive response is bound to take place if the problem is of the pressing type, but given the low initial level of understanding it is also likely to be faulty; hence the problem will remain or recur, perhaps in aggravated form. Secondly, this persistence or recurrence of the problem will send some policy-makers on a scouting expedition in search of a "fundamental" solution and since we are speaking about latecomers, they will not return empty-handed. Rather, they will be supplied with a great many ideas, suggestions, plans, and ideologies, frequently of foreign origin or based on foreign experiences. The Northeasterners will come to believe that they ought to set up a Brazilian counterpart of the U. S. Bureau of Reclamation (or later of the Tennessee Valley Authority), the Chileans will organize a Central Bank according to the most advanced monetary doctrines, and the Colombians will be advised to introduce a highly "technical" land tax scheme. Genuine learning about the problem will sometimes be prevented not only by the local policy-makers' eagerness to jump to a ready-made solution but also by the insistent offer of help and advice on the part of powerful outsiders worried, from the point of view of their own interests, about the consequences of prolonged crisis. The contracting of the Klein-Saks mission to Chile is a good example of such practices which tend to cut short that "long confrontation between man and a situation" (Camus) so fruitful for the achievement of genuine progress in problem-solving.

The new schemes with which policy-makers return from their expeditions can hardly qualify yet as truly creative responses. In analogy to Frazer's definition of magic as pseudo-science, we are rather tempted to call them "pseudo-creative" because of the exaggerated and hasty claims they make to supply a basic explanation and cure. This headlong rush toward the pseudo-insight which Flaubert called *la rage de vouloir conclure* marks a distinctive phase of the problem-solving process engaged in by latecomers. Urged on by pressing problems and by the desire to catch up, and liberally supplied with recipes communicated to them by the advanced countries of both East and West, their policy-makers are only too ready to believe that they have achieved full understanding and to act on the basis of this belief.

As we have seen, some non-pressing problems are taken up in precisely this fashion, partly as a result of the desire to find a remedy for a pressing problem, partly through the attraction of new devices and the perception of new directions in which it is possible to move. In some respects, the process resembles the one described by Lindblom where means take precedence over and determine the ends: the availability of a new instrument, such as the TVA idea, gives rise to a new policy and to the determination of a new objective. However, this activity, which was viewed earlier as being pregnant with success, is now rather failure-prone because of the lack of congruence between the hurriedly borrowed devices and the improvised goals, on the one hand, and reality, on the other.

Policy Shifts and the Failure Complex

Pseudo-insights of the kind we are talking about here have frequently blocked learning. For example, beliefs in the healing power of magic have often been remarkably resilient in the face of what seems obvious disproof to outsiders. The saving grace of the pseudo-insights with which we are dealing here is that, on the contrary, they are readily exchanged for new, if similarly ambitious, constructs especially if they were largely borrowed from abroad and hence are not only unable to command unswerving loyalty but are even resented unconsciously.[1]

Nevertheless, the abandoning of a policy which once was hailed as a guarantee of salvation is quite a different matter from a change in fashions or from the discarding of a tentative hypothesis in a laboratory. When such a policy has proven disappointing, it will be emphatically cast off, ridiculed, described as an utter failure and abomination; and the denial that it was ever anything but a palliative and a muddle, if not a conspiracy, may well set the stage for the commitment of policy-makers to the next Comprehensive, Fundamental, Integral Solution.

This pattern of learning makes it likely that policy-making will exhibit wide swings. A sort of *ideological escalation* may even take place, particularly when rival ideologies compete for the policy-makers' attention. Wide swings in policy-making are in fact strongly in evidence in all our stories. In Brazil, the reservoirs turned from panacea into the laughingstock of the Northeastern experts. In Colombia, land tax measures were tinkered with for a decade and then totally passed over in the agrarian reform bill of 1961. In Chile, the determination to restore and defend the gold standard at all cost was followed twice by its total discredit.

Frequently, of course, the swings in official ideology are far wider than actual swings in policy. Reservoirs continued to be built in the Northeast even after confidence in their efficacy in dealing with the drought had decisively waned. In Colombia, land taxes continue to play an important role in regional development schemes even though the nation-wide approach of Decree 290 has been given up. The fact that the "structuralist" school has won many adherents in Chile does not mean that the Central Bank fails to use and perfect what monetary control instruments it possesses.

Inasmuch as policy really exhibits wide swings as a result of sudden shifts from one "comprehensive" solution to another, three points should be made. First, when understanding of a problem is low, it may be useful successively to try out widely different approaches. Ironically, this method of learning about the problem is not, in our case, a strategy deliberately engaged in because of initial ignorance, but results rather from a succession of diagnoses each of which is put forward with a great air of authority and claims to full understanding.

Secondly, to "zero in" on the correct policy may require wider initial

---

[1] Hirschman, *Strategy*, pp. 138–139.

swings in some societies than in others. If those who experience the result of mistakes are different from the policy-makers (i.e., the mistake-makers), correction depends on the latter being properly and rapidly informed by the former. If two-way communication between these two parties is poor, mistakes may have to be of large proportions to come to the notice of the policy-makers. Sharp policy changes may be justified on this ground until sufficient experience has been amassed or until better two-way communication between those who experience mistakes and those who make them has been established.[1]

Thirdly, a utopian phase of policy-making which is a probable concomitant of wide swings can turn out to have its usefulness because it frequently leaves behind certain marks in the form of legislation, unenforced yet "on the books," which comes in most handy at a subsequent phase during which a practical, reform-minded government finds to its delight that it already *has* the authority to do the things that it wants to do. In Colombia, for example, the question of whether it was constitutional to compensate expropriated landowners in cash or in bonds could be resolved in this fashion, by calling attention to a long-forgotten article in the Constitution of 1936 which in certain circumstances permitted expropriation without *any* compensation. In this manner, the utopian phase of policy-making helped the reform over the constitutional hurdle and thereby facilitated considerably its peaceful advent.

Thus some benefits may after all be reaped from a policy-making style which during an early stage of the problem-solving process is based on successive "pseudo-creative responses" with its characteristic jumps from one policy to another. The style becomes harmful only if it is persisted in after knowledge about the problem has accumulated and progress has been made in attacking it. The disregard of knowledge and the dismissal of progress implicit in the style then become wasteful. Naturally it is not easy to tell when this stage is being reached.

---

[1] In exploring ways of attaining virtue which for him lay at some intermediate point between two opposite vices, Aristotle noted the heuristic role played by deviations from the mean *and by their perception;* and he all but said that the poorer the perception the wider must be the deviation. "The man who deviates little from goodness is not blamed . . . , but only the man who deviates more widely; for *he* does not fail to be noticed. But up to what point and to what extent a man must deviate before he becomes blameworthy it is not easy to determine by reasoning . . . and the decision rests with perception. So much, then, is plain, . . . that we must incline sometimes toward the excess, sometimes toward the deficiency; for so shall we most easily hit the mean and what is right." *Ethica Nicomachea,* translated by W. D. Ross, Oxford University Press, 1925, 1109[b].

A closer look at one ingredient of the style, namely, the insistence on berating past efforts, confirms our somewhat surprising finding that the style is on some counts well suited to the early stages of the problem-solving process, but turns eventually into an obstacle to further progress.

An almost morbid insistence on declaring past policy-making to have been a series of half-hearted, piecemeal efforts, doomed to failure, is one of the most pronounced common characteristics of our three stories.[1] It is extremely marked in the case of land reform in Colombia. This country could legitimately have taken some pride in its success in reconciling various conflicting demands through Law 200 in the thirties; but this law is universally known as a failure largely because the most rhetorical of its articles, the one that looked toward expropriation of land in case of nonuse for ten consecutive years, was not applied in practice. The next important effort, Decree 290 of 1957, which established penalties for non-cultivation, was pronounced a failure before it was even given a chance to show what it could accomplish.

In Chile, it is true that for a prolonged period the fight against inflation rather lacked in seriousness. But then, instead of lamenting the failure of anti-inflationary policies, it would be just as correct to say that the determination of a majority of Chilean policy-makers to pursue certain lines of policy untrammeled by sound money disciplines has been remarkably persistent and successful. Moreover, it was left to a Mexican economist to point out that Chile had done far better than other countries (in particular Mexico of course!) in neutralizing the regressive effects of inflation on income distribution;[2] while one also could legitimately marvel at the uncanny ability of Chile to avoid both dictatorship and runaway inflation in the mid-fifties, since both evils were freely and widely predicted at the time.

But it is most of all in recounting the Brazilian experience that one is struck by the apparent lack of memory of the policy-makers and by their insistence on proclaiming the futility and almost the inexistence of previous efforts. Each time a new agency is proposed or a new program is launched with high hopes and the best of intentions and with success being freely

---

[1] On the tradition of self-incrimination in Latin American thought, see the writer's "Ideologies of Economic Development in Latin America" in Hirschman, ed., *Latin American Issues*, pp. 3–42.

[2] Juan Noyola Vásquez, "El desarrollo económico y la inflación en México y en otros países latinoamericanos," *Investigación Económica*, México, Cuarto Trimestre, 1956, pp. 602–648.

predicted, the fact that similar hopes and predictions animated earlier efforts seems to be all but forgotten. Few attempts are made to canvass either
what went right or why disappointments were met with. For example, in
proposing the creation of SUDENE, Kubitschek said repeatedly that aid
to the Northeast had consisted thus far of little more than improvised relief
measures, dealing with the symptoms rather than the causes of the evil.[1]
Such a statement, echoing almost word for word those of Presidents Penna,
Pessôa and Vargas fifty, forty and thirty years earlier, seems almost ludi-
crous in view of the huge effort and long and earnest search with which one
becomes acquainted upon studying the record in some detail. Yet this
"amnesia," this insistence on the lack of seriousness of previous policy-making and the resulting systematic depreciation of what has been done before,
may itself have its uses.

In the first place, the widely accepted idea that governmental policies
are uniformly ineffectual may have considerable importance for the strategy of reform. Reform legislation that would be fought tooth and nail if it
were really expected to be enforced and enforceable may be passed either
demagogically in the expectation that it will remain largely on paper or
diabolically in the hope that its failure, or the hostilities it will arouse, will
serve to discredit its authors. Passage of Colombia's agrarian reform and
perhaps also of the SUDENE legislation owes much to the former phenomenon, while the acceptance by Rojas Pinilla of the CVC legislation in
Colombia has been traced to the latter.[2]

Moreover, from the point of view of the policy-maker himself, the insistence on the poor quality of previous efforts at solving the problem may
serve an energizing function. This appears to contradict flatly a fairly convincing point that has been made by some writers on economic development. For entrepreneurship to be stimulated in an underdeveloped environment, so they say, it is important that the pioneer entrepreneurs be
successful, in fact be even more successful than they had expected to be.
"The initial entrepreneurs must have a more than satisfactory experience,"[3]
writes one economist; he even italicizes the sentence, as well he might, for
it is not an easy prescription to follow. For if the environment is underdeveloped, this means rather that many entrepreneurs will fail or will achieve
results far *inferior to* their expectations. The prescription is therefore some-

---

[1] Juscelino Kubitschek, *Discursos 1959*, Impresa Nacional, Rio de Janeiro, 1960, pp.
54–55, 352.
[2] See also pp. 272 and 283.
[3] Harvey Leibenstein, *Economic Backwardness and Economic Growth*, Wiley, New
York, 1957, p. 129.

what unhelpful, and in this respect resembles that of balanced growth.[1] What we need are mechanisms that permit entrepreneurs to carry on *in spite of* the inevitable initial disappointments. After all, a child goes on trying to learn how to walk in spite of the fact that its first attempts yield anything but "a more than satisfactory experience."

Our stories teach us one such mechanism so far as governmental entrepreneurial activities are concerned. Suppose many different serious efforts to tackle a problem are staged over long periods of time, each time with high expectations, but on balance with indifferent or negative results. Ordinarily, this experience might prove deadly to further action. If one is interested in the latter, it may therefore be best to repress and deny this experience and to convince himself that no serious effort whatever has yet been undertaken. To dismiss one's predecessors' unsuccessful attempts at a "comprehensive" solution by claiming that no such attempt has yet taken place is the equivalent, in the public sphere, of what is achieved among private entrepreneurs by the writing down of assets: it permits the "buyer" of the asset (i.e., the successor government) to forget about the "sunk cost" and travail that has gone into it without having yielded a commensurate income flow or social benefit.

The practice becomes dangerous only when and to the extent that the experiences dismissed or repressed contain useful information and elements of incipient and partial success. To deny the existence of past efforts is quite a different matter when these efforts have yielded positive (rather than, as we have so far assumed, indifferent or negative) results; it means to shut oneself off from newly emerging cues and insights as well as from the increased confidence in one's capabilities which should otherwise arise. Naturally if a group has long learned to dismiss and deny the seriousness of any prior attempts in order to be able to go on with new problem-solving activities, it is unlikely to reverse its mode of behavior overnight and to scrutinize its own experience for any hopeful clues as soon as they appear. A *lag* in adjustment is likely. Countries that have long struggled with certain problems, initially without much success, will therefore present the disconcerting and distressing spectacle of not taking cognizance of their own advances until a considerable time after they have occurred.[2]

At that stage, the old, deprecatory style of policy-making will clearly

---

[1] See Hirschman, *Strategy*, pp. 50 ff.

[2] The lag appears to be an international phenomenon, affecting the intellectuals with their vested interest in acquired ideologies more than the man in the street. For interesting evidence from present-day Japan, see Herbert Passin, "The Sources of Protest in Japan," *American Political Science Review*, June 1962, pp. 391–403.

have outlived what usefulness it may have had. The principal task of technical assistance may then be not so much to bring in *new* knowledge but to acquaint the policy-makers with their own successes. Actually, at this stage a new tendency may appear among the country's policy-makers: instead of denying the progress that is being achieved, some of them may inflate and extrapolate that progress to the point where the problem is considered to be wholly liquidated and no longer in need of public attention. Thus progress and success may paralyze action instead of stimulating it! This strange reaction to the appearance of progress was apparent in Colombia where the undeniable but limited advances in mechanized crop production were interpreted by some to mean that the latifundio problem had ceased to exist.

The tendency to consider problems as either wholly unsolved or as totally solved results from conceiving the role of the policy-maker as that of a demiurge who is called upon to create singlehandedly order out of chaos or progress out of backwardness. With this self-image, the policy-maker has no use for partial advances achieved through previous policy actions or as a result of decentralized decision-making. Hence he will either deny or inflate such advances for he is unwilling to share the center of the stage with them: either he is the prima donna or he leaves the stage entirely.

It may be hoped that the latter reaction represents only a short station in a long journey. At its happy end, now not far away, our policy-makers will at last be fully appreciative and aware of their country's past achievements, mindful of the unfinished business at hand, and confident in their own problem-solving capabilities.

The Semantics of
Problem-Solving

The literature attacking past and advocating new policies is extraordinarily rich in laudatory and derogatory epithets. Which of these epithets are hurled back and forth in different situations can be quite revealing for the style or the successive styles that are used in handling a given policy problem. The following table distinguishes between two basic approaches to problems: one assumes that a certain and definitive solution to the problem exists, the other professes no such certainty. Each of these two approaches can earn either attack or praise. In this fashion we obtain the four-fold arrangement of the table.

The wealth of terms expressing condemnation of the remedial approach (cell A) and commendation of the ideological one (cell D) is impressive.[1] Just as significant is the comparative paucity of terms denoting approval of the remedial approach.

A universally practiced polemic posture is contained in a phrase such as: "Let us replace the stopgap measures that have been used up to now by a fundamental attack on the problem!" In other words, the proposed policy is dressed in the shining garments of cell D and the to-be-discarded policy in the shabby ones of cell A. In itself, this use of cell D terms does not tell us much about the underlying problem-solving style. It may reflect, for example, a pardonable sense of pride and exultation on the part of policy-makers who have in fact achieved a substantial advance in understanding, but it may also represent the yearning for and pretense at such understanding that comes when the desire to solve a problem runs far ahead of the ability to do so. The next step in the semantic sequence will sometimes give

---

[1] Not to lengthen the table unnecessarily I have refrained from placing adjectives with a negative prefix (e.g., "*incoherent*") in the appropriate cells, when the positive adjectives are already listed.

us a clue as to which one of these two quite different underlying situations we are dealing with. For if there has been a real, though limited, advance in understanding, the new policy will yield some benefits; and when it is noted that it too leaves some problems unsolved or creates some new and unexpected ones, it will be modified and adapted, rather than wholly abandoned. As a result, it will slowly move from the adolescence of cell D to the maturity of cell C. But if the use of the terms of cell D originated essentially in impatience and "pseudo-creative" responses, the results of the new policy are likely to be quite unsatisfactory. The vaunted "fundamental" solution will now be unmasked as a false "panacea," and thus the policy will be moved from cell D to cell B.

There is, however, a third possibility. If the "fundamental" approach is not a spectacular failure, but is merely ineffective and otherwise disappointing, it is quite conceivable that it will be attacked as a muddle rather than as a utopia. In other words, the policy's claims to be "fundamental"

THE SEMANTICS OF PROBLEM-SOLVING

	REMEDIAL APPROACH	IDEOLOGICAL APPROACH
DEROGATORY TERMS	**A** stopgap, piecemeal, hodge-podge, haphazard, makeshift, palliative, patchwork, crazy-quilt, treating the symptoms, muddling through, provisional, improvisation, purely temporary relief	**B** dogmatic, doctrinaire, panacea, cureall, utopian, gadget, gimmick, recipe, slogan, nostrum
LAUDATORY TERMS	**C** realistic, flexible, pragmatic, adaptive change, feet on the ground, *jeito*,[a] *criollo*[b]	**D** integrated, fundamental, revolutionary, coherent, balanced, systematic, comprehensive, coordinated, overall planning, cause and cure, definitive solution, root and branch

[a] Difficult-to-translate Brazilian term meaning unorthodox way out of a difficulty; close in meaning to "Yankee ingenuity," but different in that it refers not only to successful mechanical improvisation, but also, like the French *se débrouiller*, to extricating oneself from man- and society-made trouble. See the perceptive article by Roberto de Oliveira Campos, "A sociologia do jeito," *O Senhor*, July 1960.

[b] Home-grown, native. The term is often applied in Spanish America to ways of doing things that result from a long process of adaptation to local circumstances and do not correspond to any preconceived intellectual scheme of foreign origin.

and "integrated" will be deflated by moving the policy right back into cell A. The "fundamental" approach of yesterday becomes today's "palliative" or "piecemeal" approach and a new "definitive solution" is proposed, only to be similarly downgraded tomorrow. This perpetual, and apparently sterile, cycle is much in evidence in all our stories. It requires that ability to forget and write down yesterday's claims and efforts on whose possible use we have just commented.

Just as it is often a matter of temperament whether a given contribution is presented by its author as a revolutionary discovery or as a marginal addition to the existing store of knowledge, so it can be a matter of national style whether a given policy is advertised primarily as "pragmatically realistic" (cell C) or as "wholly new and comprehensively integrated" (cell D). In the United States, the former course is not infrequent. A particularly good example is the following quotation from Woodrow Wilson's First Inaugural Address:

> We shall deal with our economic system as it is and as it might be modified, not as it might be if we had a clean sheet of paper to write upon; and step by step we shall make it what it should be, in the spirit of those who question their own wisdom and seek council and knowledge, not shallow self-satisfaction or the excitement of excursions whither they cannot tell.[1]

It would probably take a long search to find a similar passage among utterances of responsible Latin American policy-makers, who seem overwhelmingly inclined to present their policies under the flamboyant banners of cell D. The usefulness of cell C terms, such as "flexible," "realistic," etc., is discovered only as it is found desirable to amend a newly adopted policy. At the same time, long exposure to problem-solving efforts using the ideological terms of cell D has produced widespread feelings of scepticism about the constantly renewed and extravagant claims of policy-makers. Hence, we find in both Spanish and Portuguese (or rather Brazilian) terms such as *criollo* and *jeito* which bestow approval on pragmatic innovations as well as on adaptations and evasions of policies originally heralded as "fundamental" and "definitive."

---

[1] Quoted in David Braybrooke and C. E. Lindblom, *The Strategy of Decision*, The Free Press, New York, 1963, Chapter IV.

Chapter 5

The Contriving of Reform

At one point in the preceding chapter, the problem-solving process was described in terms of concurrent or sequential advances in understanding and motivation. For an important group of problem-solving situations these two elements are overshadowed by, and indissolubly linked with, a third condition for advance: the ability to enact and carry through certain measures, remedies, or *reforms,* in spite of the resistance which they evoke. We now turn to such situations; they are of special interest in Latin America today and occupy a prominent place in each one of our country studies.

The Reformer's Initial Handicap

Faced with the claims of the Cuban revolution on the one hand, and with the demands and promises of the Alliance for Progress on the other, Latin Americans appear to have been placed squarely before the familiar, if stark, alternative: change through violent revolution or through peaceful reform?

On the basis of the country studies it will be argued in the following pages that this traditional dichotomy does very poorly at catching the reality of social and economic change. But first it should perhaps be explained that, contrary to what might be expected, a strong initial advantage for the advocates of revolution results from formulating the choice facing the developing countries of Latin America in this bipolar fashion.

Social reform and social revolution are usually distinguished by the manner in which a given change is brought about as well as by the extent of that change. But they have in common the nature of the change, since both propose a shift in power and wealth from one group to another. Hence they are varieties of what we shall call *antagonistic* solutions to problems in contrast to *nonantagonistic* solutions which consist of measures that are expected to leave each group better or at least as well off as before.

A proposed change can be thought of as non-antagonistic by its advo-cates, but may turn out to be antagonistic and to be perceived as such. In fact, any "progress," however non-antagonistic it was meant to be, will al-most always hurt the absolute or relative position of *some* social group, at least initially. Anthropologists have shown that all aspects of the status quo, even those that seem wholly undesirable, have their defenders and profiteers who are going to fight the proffered improvements. Unrealistic expectation of universal cooperation with measures which in the mind of their sponsors had no antagonistic component has spelled the failure of many a technical assistance project. Such disappointments have been well documented even in the ostensibly most non-antagonistic field of public health.[1] Thus we tend consistently to *underestimate* the difficulties of change in the case of (subjectively) non-antagonistic measures and we are constantly surprised and chagrined by the resistances which they en-counter.

The opposite bias — overestimate of the difficulties of change — fre-quently affects measures which are openly and avowedly antagonistic. We know and expect that land expropriation, nationalization of industries or progressive income taxation will be strongly opposed by well-entrenched groups.[2] Hence, when it comes to such measures, the revolutionary who is out to ridicule the peaceful reformer has an easy task indeed. He will show that a basic transformation of existing power relationships is a prerequisite to adopting and enforcing any measure that threatens the interests and privileges of the ruling class. He will deride the argument that the estab-lishment of democratic institutions and of universal suffrage will allow basic reforms to be adopted legally since, so he will argue, democratic trap-pings will be discarded as soon as the real powerholders find them no longer convenient.

This argument was first deployed at the beginning of the century by orthodox Marxists who disputed the emerging belief of the so-called Revi-sionists among the German Social-Democrats that the conditions of the

---

[1] Oscar Lewis, "Medicine and Politics in a Mexican Village," in Benjamin D. Paul, ed., *Health, Culture and Community*, Russell Sage Foundation, New York, 1955.

[2] It is usual, but no longer justified, to limit discussion of such measures to those that are antagonistic to the interests of the older and wealthier ruling groups. More and more frequently, some Latin American countries such as Argentina and Brazil have found it imperative to tackle pressing problems of efficiency and financial solvency by curtailing the privileges of certain strategically located groups among the middle or working classes. What experience we have with this variety of antagonistic measures shows that they are no less difficult to push through than those directed against the older ruling groups.

working class could be improved through the trade union movement and exploitative capitalism evolve peacefully into a more acceptable economic system. Pitted against Eduard Bernstein, the founder of Revisionism, Karl Kautsky, then the guardian of Marxist purity in the Social Democratic Party, exclaimed: "Does anyone believe that this victory [of the proletariat] is possible without catastrophe? I desire it, but I don't believe it."[1]

This point of view was eloquently and unremittingly reaffirmed by Harold Laski in the thirties when he predicted that even though the Labor Party might come to power legally, it would be unable to carry out its program of nationalizations:

> The central weakness [of the orthodox Labor position] is due to the refusal of the Labor Party to recognize that the state is the instrument of that class in society which owns the instruments of production and that it cannot utilize that state for its own purposes so long as that class remains in possession of those instruments . . . Unless a Labor government is prepared to meet a crisis of the first magnitude the forces it will encounter will persuade it rather to operate the capitalist system than to move to its transformation.[2]

More recently the argument, a bit battered from successful experience with reform in the industrial countries of the West, has migrated to the less developed areas. Here, it retains greater plausibility, and, on occasion, considerable validity, for these areas frequently lack a solid tradition of progressive political and economic change. John Kenneth Galbraith was perhaps the first to refurbish the argument for its new use:

> Unfortunately, some of our current discussion of land reform in the underdeveloped countries proceeds as though this reform were something that a government proclaims on any fine morning — that it gives land to the tenants as it might give pensions to old soldiers or as it might reform the administration of justice. In fact, a land reform is a revolutionary step; it passes power, property, and status from one group in the community to another. If the government of the country is dominated or strongly influenced by the land-holding groups — the one that is losing its prerogatives — no one should expect effective land legislation as an act of grace.[3]

---

[1] Quoted in Peter Gay, *The Dilemma of Democratic Socialism*, Columbia University Press, New York, 1952, p. 65.

[2] Harold J. Laski, *Parliamentary Government in England*, Viking, New York, 1938, pp. 159–161.

[3] J. K. Galbraith, "Conditions for Economic Change in Under-Developed Countries," *Journal of Farm Economics*, November 1951, p. 695.

At almost the same time the argument, as applied to underdeveloped countries, was put back into traditional Marxist terms by Paul Baran:

> The alliance of property-owning classes controlling the destinies of most underdeveloped countries, cannot be expected to design and to execute a set of measures running counter to each and all of their immediate vested interests. If to appease the restive public, blueprints of progressive measures such as agrarian reform, equitable tax legislation, etc., are officially announced, their enforcement is wilfully sabotaged. The government, representing a political compromise between landed and business interests, cannot suppress the wasteful management of landed estates and the conspicuous consumption on the part of the aristocracy; . . . Set up to guard and to abet the existing property rights and privileges, it cannot become the architect of a policy calculated to destroy the privileges standing in the way of economic progress and to place the property and the incomes derived from it at the service of society as a whole.[1]

This point of view is readily accepted in Latin America where a non-Marxist Chilean writer and politician put the same thought quite succinctly some fifty years ago.

> Nobody would believe in a law which would injure the interests of the privileged class. It would be the same as if in Russia a law were passed which ordered the Czar to be shot: nobody would believe in the law.[2]

Compared to these reminders of what is and is not credible and feasible when power is distributed in a certain way, the routine of present-day international experts in blandly proposing year-in, year-out essentially antagonistic measures of every description regardless of political realities seems singularly inane or naïve. In fact, the experts themselves, after having absorbed a critical amount of frustration, frequently become converts to the view that, in this or that country, "everything" has to change before any improvement at all can be introduced.[3]

The idea of revolution as a prerequisite to any progress draws immense strength from the very limited human ability to visualize change and from

---

[1] "On the Political Economy of Backwardness," *The Manchester School,* January 1952, reprinted in A. N. Agarwala and S. P. Singh, eds., *The Economics of Underdevelopment,* Oxford University Press, Bombay, 1958, pp. 88–89.

[2] Alberto Edwards speaking in the Chilean Congress in 1909, quoted by Fetter, *Inflation,* pp. 126–127.

[3] An extreme illustration of this mood is the Rio cabdriver who, caught in that city's famous rush-hour jam, remarked to us: "What we need here is a Fidel Castro!" He was obviously convinced that traffic flow cannot be improved in Brazil without a prior social revolution.

the fact that it makes only minimal demands on that ability. All we are asked to imagine by the revolutionary is the tumbling down of the old regime in a total upheaval which will give birth to the new order. Revolution thus conceived is essentially a quite brief, though cataclysmic interlude between two static societies: one, unjust and rotten, which is incapable of being improved, and the other, rational and harmonious, which has no further need to be improved upon. Sorel, the apostle of the violent general strike as an energizing myth, clearly had this concept of revolution in mind when he wrote:

> . . . the general strike must be considered as an undivided whole; consequently, no detail about ways and means is of the slightest help for the understanding of socialism. It must even be added that there is always danger of losing something of this understanding, if one attempts to split this whole into parts . . . the transition from capitalism to socialism must be conceived as a catastrophe whose process defies description.[1]

Sorel thus understood perfectly the dual function of the idea of revolution: to gratify the desire for change and to dispense with the need to visualize the process of change in its intricate and perhaps unpleasant details by telescoping it into an "undivided whole."

The neat trick involved in this operation, while intellectually not very respectable, goes far toward explaining the drawing power of the idea of revolution. But the reformers are also to blame. They have made themselves particularly vulnerable to the charge of being unrealistic by failing to explore how social change short of cataclysmic revolution actually happens. Thus they have permitted the revolutionists to set up a caricature of "change via reform" where the latter follows smoothly (and unbelievably) upon the 51 per cent election victory of the Reform Party or, more modernly though even more naïvely, upon the recommendations of international experts or the offer of finance. Actually there are a good many intermediate stations between this kind of effortless and painless reform at one extreme and total revolution at the other and our studies permit us to map out a few of these stations.

Events of recent years have created a somewhat similar continuum between total peace and total war (cold, phony, brushfire, limited war), and political scientists have identified various types of political regimes (tute-

---

[1] Georges Sorel, *Réflexions sur la violence*, 11th ed., Marcel Riviere, Paris, 1950, pp. 185, 217.

lary democracy, modernizing oligarchies) filling the void between West-ern-type parliamentary democracy and totalitarian autocracy.[1] In contrast to these efforts, our observations do not lead to the firm establishment of a typology. Rather, we shall attempt to show how elements of both reform and revolution are present in the sequences of policy-making which we have studied. In the process we hope to provide basic materials for what may eventually go into a "reformmonger's manual"; perhaps it is time that such a text be written and offer some competition to the many handbooks on the techniques of revolutions, coups d'état, and guerrilla warfare.

This section stands in need of an important postscript. Our argument, as developed so far, does not mean to imply that any reform whatever can al-ways be introduced without revolution, i.e., without the prior, violent, wholesale overthrow of the current power holders. Certainly many situa-tions have existed and still exist in Latin America as elsewhere in which power is so concentrated, opposition to change so fierce, and the social and political structure so rigid that any non-revolutionary change is, short of a miracle, impossible, *besides* being inconceivable. The point we have been trying to make is that there are many other, less rigid situations in which change by methods short of revolution is or has become possible, but where, because of the force of habit or some similar cultural lag, change is still visualized primarily as something that requires a prior revolution. This contrast between reality and the widely entertained image of reality seems to the writer to prevail in much of Latin America today. A similar contrast with opposite content characterizes the present intellectual and political climate in the United States where, as a result of positive experience with gradualism, a majority appears to have come to the unwarranted conclu-sion that any progressive change whatever can and must be achieved ex-clusively by a succession of moderate reforms or cannot be achieved at all.[2] This can be just as much an illusion as the opposite belief of many Latin Americans that any "real" change can only come through revolution.

Violence as an Ingredient of Reform

Our statement that reform and revolution are not nearly as far apart as language would make us believe holds up well when we consider the role

---

[1] Edward Shils, *Political Development in the New States*, Mouton & Co., The Hague, 1962.

[2] The exasperating slowness of racial desegregation in the United States has led to considerable soul-searching on this score, most forcefully expressed in the writings of James Baldwin. See also Eric F. Goldman, "Progress — By Moderation *and* Agitation," *The New York Times Magazine*, June 18, 1961.

of violence. The received idea is that revolutions are violent and reforms peaceful. But if we applied this criterion for distinguishing between reform and revolution to the history of land tenure problems in Colombia, we would immediately have to conclude that Colombia has passed not through one but through several agrarian revolutions. Yet the historical record knows of no such revolution.

On reflection it will be realized that even if violence is a necessary condition for revolution it is not a sufficient one, and that it is also a common element of reform. To qualify as revolutionary, violence must be *centralized;* it must attack and conquer the central seats of political and administrative power. In Colombia violence has been scattered, local, decentralized. For the past hundred years, peasants have occupied and are still occupying today lands that are not theirs. Sometimes they have used force and force has occasionally been used against them by those who claim ownership. But eventually forcible appropriation of large areas has been sanctioned by the state through *ad hoc* intervention or general legislation. Thus, the willingness of the peasants to occupy uncultivated lands — a kind of entrepreneurial spirit — has powerfully contributed to reform legislation. Without the past experience of mass squatting and the threat of more to come, neither Law 200 of 1936 nor the land reform of 1961 would ever have been passed by the Congress.

In Brazil's Northeast, decentralized violence appears in a different guise. It is first unloosened by nature itself which, through its droughts, periodically chases hundreds of thousands of nordestinos from their homes in search of food, water and work. Relief shipments and the organization of emergency public works are an automatic response to the overriding need of social and physical survival so that it may well be said that, whenever a drought strikes, minimal needs of subsistence are "appropriated" by the Northeastern refugees. When the relief funds are not forthcoming with sufficient promptness, looting of food stores in the cities by the drought refugees serves as a reminder. This sudden and forcible appropriation of public monies by the Northeast leads subsequently to a whole chain of attempts to disburse the monies in such a way as to limit the damage that will be wrought by future droughts.

Since violence has in part the function of signalling protest to the central authorities, an improvement in the signalling mechanism serves to increase pressure as much as an intensification of the problem. Something of this kind happened in the Northeast when better and more numerous highways (built largely during droughts) and the availability of trucks permitted the miserable drought refugees to reach the coastal cities more rapidly and in greater numbers and thereby increased the threat to public order consequent upon the droughts.

As though the violent immediate reactions to the violence of nature were not enough, Northeasterners have been casting around for additional stimulants to action in the form of threatened violence. The traditional threat has been that of secession. Yet the threat of this particular violence always remained a bit rhetorical and ineffectual for lack of credibility. For one, it seemed an irrational move since it would cut off the Northeast from the principal source of relief and investment funds. Secondly, the threat is really one of an all-out centralized clash; it cannot be graduated since a region cannot secede "just a little bit." In both respects the Colombian squatter's kind of violence is more efficient, and its Brazilian counterpart has recently come into prominence in the Northeast through the activities of the peasant leagues. The creation of the new development agency in the Northeast (SUDENE) was originally rather a response to the 1958 drought, but the threat implicit in the rise of the peasant leagues strengthened the agency, which could now claim that its reform program represented the only alternative to a violent and disorderly change in the existing power structure in the Northeast.

In addition to being decentralized rather than centralized, the violence we have encountered in Colombia and Brazil is distinguished from revolutionary violence by the fact that it is not immediately countered by the aggrieved party. The violence one meets with is unilateral, sequential, *temporarily unrequited*. Land is "grabbed" by peasants, but ordinarily no immediate resistance follows. There may be action in the local courts and eventually forcible eviction of the squatters by the police and occasionally the army. Or again nothing may happen for a long time; and when the state believes it important that uncertainty be removed, but does not wish to use force to evict the peasants, it may buy the property from the owner and then attempt to sell it back to the peasant who already holds it, but still is ready to pay something for the much-coveted title which, among other advantages, makes it possible to obtain credit.

Thus the violence that is compatible with reform and frequently appears to be part and parcel of it is not the kind of decisive clash — force meets force in the principal square of the capital — which is usually associated with revolutionary violence. Rather it is a violence akin to guerrilla warfare, with the ability of the groups practicing it to now advance, now retreat, now lie low and now come forward with a new thrust.

As shown in the chapter on Chile, the economic behavior underlying inflation is rather similar to the temporarily unrequited violence practiced by squatting peasants and retaliating landlords. Inflation results typically when demands for additional money income on the part of one social group are not resisted immediately and fiercely, but are countered indirectly and after some time interval by similar demands on the part of other groups. In this perspective, inflation appears as a device for the coexistence of several groups who are not hostile or do not feel strong enough to engage in out-and-out revolutionary battles or civil war over the distribution of the social product, yet are not friendly enough either to agree on any one pattern of dividing up the product among themselves. There is reluctance to agree, but also reluctance to disagree to the point of revolution or civil war. This is at least one interpretation that can be given to the Chilean inflation of the last twenty years.

At the same time inflation is sufficiently unpleasant to lead to a search for its cause and cure, and since nothing is easier than to establish a causal nexus between one social evil (such as inflation) and another (such as maldistribution of land), inflation has served the function of putting additional pressure behind a variety of reforms which were suddenly found to be desirable not only on their own merits but also because they would help set an end to inflation. Just as the squatting actions of Colombian peasants put more "steam" behind agrarian reform projects and the droughts in the Northeast regularly led to new initiatives in favor of that area, so inflationary pressures have served as a kind of generalized, all-purpose "steam" behind any improvement in Chile's economic and social structure that caught the eye of the reformers.

A final characteristic of the violence we have met in our studies is that it is not only *protest* and *pressure* on problem-solving authorities, but also *direct problem-solving activity*. The Colombian peasant satisfies his craving for a piece of land when he squats and the Northeastern drought refugee solves his immediate problem of hunger when he loots food stores in the coastal cities as does the Chilean worker when he wins higher wages through strikes. Hence, these individual decentralized actions not only signal a problem to the central decision-makers, but they reduce the size of the problem that remains to be solved by the authorities. In effect, they therefore make at least this problem more manageable, hence more amenable to reform moves (while quite possibly creating new problems elsewhere). In Colombia, for example, it would have been unthinkable for any non-revolutionary government in the twenties or thirties to carry out through centralized action the splitting up of the large estates which actually took place as a result of decentralized, spontaneous peasant movements. But once these events had taken place the New Deal government of Alfonso López was able after a long fight to convince Congress to legalize the peasants' actions through Law 200 of 1936. Instead of the sequence: revolution (centralized violence) → redistribution of land under conditions of revolutionary legality, the Colombians invented a highly disorderly sequence: decentralized violence and illegal redistribution of land → legalization of redistribution through Law 200. Disorderly though it was, this sequence permitted an improvement in the distribution of land.

The Latin American scene thus appears to be replete with mechanisms and sequences which permit the exertion of powerful pressures and the venting and adjudication of conflicts by means equally far removed from traditional concepts of either reform or revolution. Policy-makers usually act as a result and in the midst of such situations. To paraphrase Marx, decentralized, unrequited violence is frequently found in the role of indispensable midwife to *reform*. To advocate reforms in Latin America without tolerating, accepting and sometimes even welcoming and promoting the only kinds of pressures which have proven to be effective in getting reforms through is to risk being accused of hypocrisy and deception: now that the United States has declared itself in favor of a variety of reforms in Latin America, it should perhaps be apprised of the circumstances and hazards usually associated with such an enterprise.

Crisis as an Ingredient of Reform

From violence we now move on to a more general concomitant of reform, namely, crisis. Violence is frequently an important cause and a conspicuous element of a crisis situation (a) because the fact of violence shows that a serious problem exists that requires immediate action, and (b) because the violence itself is felt as dangerous by the constituted authorities who will act to suppress it directly.

Crisis has been defined as a "situation in which there is a great stress toward action, toward the resolution of conflict"[1] and, we might add, toward the solution of problems. The reasons for which a developing emergency or crisis is favorable to problem-solving have not received much at-

---

[1] H. D. Lasswell, "Attention Structure and Social Structure" in *The Communication of Ideas*, Lyman Bryson, ed., Harper, New York, 1948, p. 262.

tention perhaps because the matter seems so self-explanatory. "Crisis concentrates attention," says Lasswell,[1] and it may well be that some problems simply fail in ordinary times to get attacked effectively, not for lack of knowledge, nor even for lack of motivation, but simply for lack of attention. Experience also shows that crisis may make it possible to take required actions against powerful groups which are normally well entrenched and invulnerable; finally, crisis may stimulate action and hence learning on a problem on which insight has been low and which for that very reason has not been tackled as long as it was in a quiescent state.

Yet, can we take it for granted that crisis-induced anxiety about a problem will help insight? Psychological findings hardly permit us to be confident in this regard. Experimental evidence rather appears to indicate that the injection of pressure and tension is not at all certain to improve performance in problem-solving activities. It apparently helps to speed up routine tasks, but turns into a hindrance with problems whose solutions require reflection and insight.[2]

How can the apparent contradiction between the findings of the psychologists and the commonplace attitude of the politician who relies on crisis to produce solutions be resolved? To a large extent by showing that in this case, as in many others known to economists, propositions about individual behavior cannot be extended uncritically to society at large, however suggestive they may be.

In the first place, it is easy to understand that, in a nation, the *quantity* of decision-making, i.e., the total motivation to act, will be increased as a result of the intensification of the problem: certain decision-makers will pay attention to 50 per cent inflation when they were not particularly dis-

---

[1] *Ibid.*, p. 262.

[2] "Results have indicated that the quality of performance in complex learning situations is inversely related to the subjects' degree of anxiety." I. E. Farber, "Motivation in Verbal Learning and Performance," *Psychological Bulletin*, V. 52, 1955, p. 323. For a cautious summary of experimental results, see Kenneth W. Spence, *Behavior Theory and Conditioning*, Yale University Press, New Haven, 1956, Chapter 7. The following is a very strong statement intended by the author, a psychologist, for generalization to societal problem-solving situations: "The basic psychological notion here is that, beyond some optimum level for facilitation, increased motivation serves not only to energize the organism but also to restrict its capacity to select among alternatives at all levels of behavioral organization. The result is that heightened emotion and drive tend to produce stereotypy . . . [which] reduces capacity to solve problems . . . A normally intelligent raccoon trying to get out from under a stinging shower will persistently bang its head against a locked door that used to be open, completely ignoring free passageways to left and right." Charles E. Osgood, "Reciprocal Initiative," in James Roosevelt, ed., *The Liberal Papers*, Anchor Books, New York, 1962, p. 190.

turbed by 10 per cent inflation; more important, new dangers or problems — loss of elections, revolution, secession — arise as a consequence of the aggravation of the old problem and some decision-makers will be sensitive to these threats when they were indifferent or opposed to proposed actions on the problems of land tenure, inflation or Northeastern backwardness as such. In other words, new, hitherto indifferent or hostile forces will join to support actions, hence new alignments become possible and the possibility of new moves is perceived. All of this has no counterpart in individual problem-solving.

But what about the *ability* to solve problems, or the *quality* of this quantitatively augmented decision-making? Is there any reason to think that the intensification of the problem will tend to raise the level of insight? In this regard, we can have no certainty and the findings of the psychologists may well hold: we may merely get a spate of decision-making more or less in line with "the state of the arts," i.e., with whatever views are already held at the time about the way in which the problem should be tackled. And since the very fact that we had to wait for widespread violence to take any action makes it likely that insight into the problem is at a low level, such decision-making may not improve matters very much.

Yet, here also the parallel with individual problem-solving can be misleading: in experiments on individual problem-solving anxiety is injected artificially from the outside while the problem itself remains the same whereas in societal problem-solving, anxiety is induced *by a change, an aggravation of the problem itself,* and frequently this very aggravation makes it possible to understand it better. For example, as inflation accelerated in Chile from the 20 per cent rate of 1939–52 to the 50–90 per cent rate of 1953–55 it became quite clear, as one commentator put it, that wage and salary increases in line with escalator clauses could not be financed out of profits but were bound to lead to further inflation. Similarly, each successive drought in the Northeast brought out one or several ways in which preceding efforts at strengthening the region's resistance to the scourge had gone awry. The 1958 drought, for example, highlighted and exposed the drastic decline in both technical competence and ethical standards which had been suffered by the agency (DNOCS) traditionally in charge of drought relief and public works in the area; this experience was partly responsible for the establishment of a new agency (SUDENE) with a different approach and organization.

The intensification and aggravation of a problem, frequently accompanied and signalled by certain forms of violence, is therefore one way in which reformers strengthen their own motives, gather new allies and gain new insights. Frequently it will not be possible to distinguish clearly which came first, the new motivation, the new allies or the new insights. The appearance of potential new allies will make the reformmongers change the character of their reform proposals so as to accommodate those allies and the emergence of new ideas leads to a search for groups that may support them.

In spite of the fact that this interplay opens up a wide range of possibilities, one particular way of contriving reform holds a privileged place in the popular imagination: the perception of common dangers resulting from the aggravation of the problem is expected to bring the warring parties "to their senses" and result in an equitable solution of the problem "just in time," i.e., just as the revolution was about to take over. Reformers are in this case counting on the danger, the crisis, the emergency, the "brink" to panic everyone into action and their expectations are rather similar to those of revolutionaries: for the latter, the problem is solved by jumping over the brink into an unknown but that much more "transparent region"; for the reformers, the look down the brink is to lead to national reconciliation and rededication through which the overdue reforms are consummated and the problem is finally solved. Both conceptions characteristically assume that a total solution exists, but is sabotaged and held back, either by the "ruling class" which must be destroyed or by misunderstandings, inertia, selfishness and "politics-as-usual" which must be swept away in a great movement toward national union. The idea that national union born out of national emergency is sufficient to solve the country's problems in a comprehensive and integrated fashion is almost as tenacious and powerful a myth as that of "total" change via revolution.

The myth is constantly invoked by policy-makers of every kind, but in only one of our studies did reform or important policy decisions come about approximately in this way. In Colombia in 1960, after renewed concern about unrest and the heritage of violence in the countryside, an attempt was made to bring together all factions of opinion for the purpose of formulating an agrarian reform project once preliminary statements by party leaders had shown a convergence of opinion on the subject. Yet even here "politics-as-usual" was resumed in short order and so vigorously that the Agrarian Reform Bill, elaborated in the fall of 1960 by a special nonpartisan National Agrarian Committee, was bitterly fought in Congress by the opposition, found itself in serious jeopardy several times and had to be considerably watered down before it was finally approved in December 1961.

If we look at the important decisions that were taken in the fight on inflation in Chile or the establishment of SUDENE in Brazil, we find even more that they were marked by bitter and protracted battles, unexpected switches, and narrow margins of victory rather than by the miracle of sudden national unanimity. The reason is precisely that situations do not suddenly change from normal to emergency or crisis. Rather, we have here a gradual ascent in the course of which a *succession* of new reform ideas and possible alliances come into view. Besides, there is always disagreement among different groups as to how serious the crisis really is. Even the kind of violence so noticeable in Latin America, being decentralized and unrequited, does not create immediately a situation of utter emergency, but can rather be compared to what is accomplished in the United States by the sending of protest mail to the White House.

Thus, storms and emergencies gather for a long time and various groups in turn become alerted and sensitized to them gradually and unevenly. Hence, a series of attempts at dealing with the problem through changing coalitions is more likely than a Unique Comprehensive Reform.

This conclusion is strengthened by the fact that a problem such as land reform is in fact a collection of problems each of which is likely to fascinate a different clientele: those who favor, say, aid to progressive farmers in the form of tax incentives are not likely to be the same as those who wish idle estates to be broken up. By combining such measures into a "comprehensive" program, one frequently risks combining the enemies of both into a majority of the decision-makers. In Colombia the former measure was taken in 1957 under one government, and progress was achieved on the latter in 1961 with a quite different combination of political forces.

The Emergence of New Problems as an Aid to Reform

Moreover, Colombia, Chile and Brazil obviously faced other issues besides the ones we chose to analyze. What does this mean for the possibilities of contriving reform on "our" problems? A first thought could be that, since the energies of decision-makers are limited, the raising of other problems is bound to distract them and to hold back action in the areas of our special interest. However, this kind of distraction, or substitution of one problem by another, is not at all conspicuous in our stories unless one considers the lack of action on our three problems during the second World War as an instance.[1] To the contrary, the arising or aggravation of an "extraneous" second problem B is frequently seen to help decision-making on problem A, as though action on A were stimulated not only by its own intensification but also by the injection of any new concern.

One way in which such reinforcement can happen is through the familiar mechanism of logrolling. The advocates of land reform might enlist additional support for their project from, say, the advocates of urban low-cost housing projects by promising to support the latter cause by their vote and influence. There is evidence of this kind of mechanism in the story of Brazil's Northeast. We noticed that Kubitschek's support of the SUDENE project was not unrelated to the support for Brasília and Kubitschek's expansionary monetary policies on the part of the SUDENE backers. Inversely, President Epitacio Pessôa attempted to placate opposition to his large-scale spending in the Northeast by undertaking railroad and other projects in the Center-South as well.

Another type of coalition-building is more prominent in our empirical material. It arises not when two problems merely coexist and the backers of reform trade their votes, but when one problem is seen to be interrelated with the other so that to solve or attenuate one is expected to improve the other. If this can be shown to be the case, the backers of one reform will support the other *in their own interest* rather than merely in the expectation of having the favor returned to them.

A good example of this way of acquiring new allies is the junction of the land tenure and the balance-of-payments problems in Colombia. Ordinarily those who are interested in improving the conditions of the peons and their access to land ownership or secure tenure are entirely distinct as a pressure group from the officials in the Central Bank and the Ministry of Finance who are concerned with the balance of payments. But since balance-of-payments improvements (smaller imports or larger exports of agricultural products) can presumably be realized through better land use we have a potential community of interests between the two groups which came to the fore in Colombia when the country faced a difficult balance-of-payments problem after the end of the Rojas Pinilla regime in 1957. One of the more important steps in the sequence of policy-making around the land

---

[1] This may be so because the three problems we have analyzed have all been crucial, dominant problems in their respective countries at least during certain periods. A dominant problem could be defined as one that holds back action on a series of other problems because of the general expectation that the latter will largely vanish once the dominant problem is solved. The chapter on inflation in Chile quotes a particularly clear, if naïve, illustration of such alleged dominance (p. 215).

problem (Decree 290 of 1958) can largely be traced to this confluence. Thus new allies are secured not only by the aggravation of the central problem which is the target of reform but also by the aggravation of another problem, if it can be plausibly argued that the cure of the latter is connected with that of the former.

The Northeast of Brazil provides us with another, somewhat more complex instance of this relationship. The natural claimants for federal aid to the Northeast were of course the political representatives of the area itself. They traditionally secured the appropriation of relief funds and were responsible for the establishment of the first federal agencies and for the large public works programs in the area. But in the late fifties an interest arose in reorganizing and reorienting these agencies and programs. This move had only limited support in the Northeast since it was directed against some of the local power-holders. But at the same time the apparent inefficiency of the way in which federal funds had long been spent in the Northeast led to concern *outside* of the Northeast. And on the basis of this interest, Northeastern reformers were able to build a coalition with groups in the Center and South. The problem of waste of public funds in the Northeast mobilized groups quite different from those who were traditionally the advocates of federal subsidies to the region. But support of the former groups became most valuable when an attempt was made to attack the Northeastern problem through new approaches which were opposed by a number of traditional Northeastern interest and pressure groups.

The possibility of solving local and regional problems by mobilizing forces outside the region is of particular interest to the reformer who wishes to attack problems by methods short of revolution. When, within a sovereign country, the pro-reform and counter-reform forces are solidly arrayed against one another and the latter are solidly entrenched, it may well be difficult to achieve reform without resort to revolutionary violence. But if the same situation is characteristic of a region within a country, the reform forces can form alliances with groups outside of their region and overcome in this fashion the local diehards. This freedom to maneuver serves to offset two important disabilities under which regional reform movements labor: the threat of revolution is not available to them since they cannot seize the central seats of power and the threat of secession is usually none too credible.

Reformers would do well therefore to be on the lookout not only for symptoms of aggravation of their own problem. By keeping a watch for the emergence of other concerns they may well be able to pick up new allies and to dispense with some old ones who are no longer available or wanted.

The Switch to the Antagonistic Perspective

As we survey the successive attacks on our problems, as well as the many proposed measures, remedies and solutions, the distinction between measures perceived and intended as either antagonistic or non-antagonistic provides us with one way of organizing that plentiful and seemingly disparate material. Do our country studies give us any clue about the sequence in which each category makes its appearance? Does this sequence depend exclusively on the political situation or also on the evolution of the problem itself?

Such questions are of particular interest to reformmongers, for reform, if conceived as an alternative to revolution, is not just any attack on a problem but one that has at least some antagonistic content: the power of hitherto privileged groups is curbed and the economic position and social status of underprivileged groups is correspondingly improved.

It may be helpful, before entering into this matter, to set out schematically the varieties of conceivable policies or events to which the antagonistic or non-antagonistic label might be attached. The policies or events shown in the cells of the table are purely illustrative and are drawn from our studies. For example, land tax schemes, a mildly antagonistic measure, belong in the third column because they affect landowners adversely, and in the second row because the landless peasants do not perceive them as immediately beneficial to them. Thus they are distinguished from expropriation (first row, third column), that antagonistic measure par excellence, which simultaneously hurts the rich and benefits the poor. The other conceivable varieties of antagonistic outcomes — those that hurt the poor while benefiting or leaving indifferent the rich — are never actually advocated; but they happen, as when during an inflation or a drought the rich get richer and the poor poorer. In the following discussion we shall have occasion to refer to most of the possible policies shown in the table.

One striking observation which emerges from our studies is that frequently the horizon of policy-makers seems to be limited to either antagonistic or non-antagonistic remedies to the near exclusion of the other. Policy-makers act typically as though they were either completely oblivious of the possibility of redistribution of power and wealth or completely fascinated by it. Not that all policy-makers, after having long dealt in non-an-

tagonistic remedies, suddenly favor antagonistic measures; but these measures suddenly "steal the show," become the dominant theme around which
conceivable solutions of the problem are discussed. The situation reminds
one of the well-known psychological experiments where a subject is shown
a composite picture in which he perceives either an elegant woman or an
old witch (or: either seven or eight cubes) and can perhaps learn to switch
from one to the other and back, but can never perceive both together.

Now, to a considerable extent, the change in outlook which makes
people suddenly switch from, say, a non-antagonistic to an antagonistic
perspective is tied to general political and historical developments. No
doubt the Cuban revolution contributed powerfully to placing the land reform issue in its most antagonistic form on the agenda of Latin American

ALTERNATIVE REFORM POLICIES AND EVENTS
ACCORDING TO THEIR PERCEIVED IMPACT
ON DIFFERENT SOCIAL GROUPS

		Impact on the upper-income groups, as perceived by them		
		BENEFICIAL	INDIFFERENT	DETRIMENTAL
Impact on the lower-income groups, as perceived by them	BENEFICIAL	NA Northeast: Alloca-tion of Federal funds. Colombia's agriculture: Special credit facilities and technical as-sistance.	NA Colonization of public lands.	A Expropriation of privately held lands and parceling out to peasants.
	INDIFFERENT	NA Tax rebates and special credits to large landowners introducing mech-anized cropping.	—	A Land tax designed to force landowner to cultivate or rent or sell.
	DETRIMENTAL	A Profiteering during drought. Ordinary course of events in early stages (spe-cially 1904–07) of Chilean inflation.	A Ordinary course of events during Northeastern droughts.	NA (?) Mutual sacrifices in inflation.

A = antagonistic   NA = non-antagonistic.

policy-makers. But, while such overriding influences must be recognized, an exploration of the inner dynamics of the problem-solving process can give us a fuller understanding of such switches in perspective.

Take, as a particularly clear example, the droughts in Brazil's Northeast. Here is a natural calamity gravely affecting all the people making their livelihood in a certain region, and among possible remedies thought will quite normally be given first to the securing of relief and investment funds from the rest of the country and to public works which might attenuate the effects of the next calamity and improve the regional economy in general. The region secures a supplement of consumption and investment resources from the outside, and the intention, presumption and general impression are that all major groups in the region will stand to profit in some measure from the transfer. However, as the problem is tackled in this non-antagonistic fashion over a long period and yet remains as far as ever from a satisfactory solution, renewed analysis turns up some antagonistic factors: the differential impact of the drought on the large landowners and the sharecroppers or rural laborers, the enrichment of some groups and the profiteering that come with drought relief and public works, and, perhaps most important, the impossibility of putting to productive use the waters dammed up in the expensive reservoirs because of the obstacles to irrigation under existing systems of land tenure. Some policy-makers become aware of these factors before others, of course; in fact, in the Brazilian case, we encounter the extraordinarily farsighted and crafty Arrojado Lisboa, the first director of DNOCS, who, just because he realized the antagonistic implications of irrigation, decided to soft-pedal that aspect of the problem and to concentrate on the non-antagonistic task of dam construction in the expectation that, once in place, the dams themselves would "cry out" for progress in irrigation.

Such calculating foresight is rare indeed and generally the various facets of a problem are revealed to the surprised policy-makers, or to some of them, as their labors advance. But if, in a first phase, such labors are entirely concentrated in the non-antagonistic area, and if the problem does contain an antagonistic component, then at some point this component will appear as the principal task. Since antagonistic tasks will ordinarily appear after non-antagonistic policies have long been in use, the attraction of the new is reinforced by the discredit of the older set of policies or perhaps simply by boredom with them. Here lies one explanation for the thoroughness with which non-antagonistic policies may suddenly give way to an antagonistic perspective.

The Brazilian sequence is broadly repeated in our Colombian and Chilean stories: in 1959–60 antagonistic proposals moved to the center of the stage in both countries. In Colombia, the theme of outright land reform became dominant in 1960 after experiments with colonization and land taxation had turned out to be unsatisfactory and after entirely non-antagonistic policies, such as agricultural credit, storage, extension, etc., had long been in more or less intensive use. In Chile, the idea that deep "structural" changes, largely of an antagonistic kind, were required to deal with inflation, rather than "merely" monetary measures that would leave the relative power and income positions of various social groups largely intact, appeared around 1958–59 with the strength of a fundamental new insight.

It could be asked why our stories seem to move primarily from the use of non-antagonistic to antagonistic remedies. Is it because the latter are intrinsically more persuasive? This is hard to believe. The discovery that non-antagonistic remedies are available after antagonistic measures have held sway should in principle be greeted as just as stunning an intellectual discovery as the opposite feat. It requires at least as much imagination and sophistication to perceive that two groups whose interests were universally assumed to be wholly divergent actually have some important interests in common as to notice an opposition of interests between groups that were hitherto thought to be, and thought of themselves as, partners traveling along the same road toward common objectives. To illustrate, we recall the sweeping victory of Free Trade with its doctrine that foreign trade is mutually beneficial over mercantilism's dogma that one trading partner's gain is the other's loss. The similar discovery that Russia and the United States actually share one overriding interest, namely survival, while it has not created international harmony, has nevertheless had a profound effect, not only on the debates about nuclear strategy and disarmament, but on the behavior of the two super-powers as well.

Some elements of our stories can also be quoted here. In Colombia, Currie's 1961 proposal to accelerate industrialization and urbanization was favorably received in some sectors of public opinion largely because it opened up a non-antagonistic perspective, a way of sidestepping land reform and its traumatisms. In Chile during the early fifties, the long-continued, desperate and futile struggle of each group to secure a favored position for itself in the course of inflation endowed with considerable intellectual prestige the idea of "mutual sacrifices." This is a special kind of non-antagonistic remedy (see the table, third row and column): it proposes that all parties undergo an immediate loss, proportionate to their economic position, to solve the problem of inflation; but such a remedy is likely and turned out to be particularly difficult to put across.

The difficulty of finding in our material really good and effective examples for a shift from the antagonistic to the non-antagonistic perspective is easily explained. We are dealing with societies where the existing social order had not been seriously disturbed or questioned at the point of departure of our stories. The remedies then proposed were those advocated by the well-entrenched upper classes who had no doubts about the identity of their own interests with those of society at large. Only later was this assumed harmony questioned, and the discovery that an antagonistic treatment might be required came as a blinding insight after so long a period of firm belief in, and practice of, the non-antagonistic therapy. This must be understood if the depth of antagonistic feeling in Latin America today is to be correctly gauged.

The Reformer — Naïve or Wily?

In principle, the turn toward the antagonistic perspective should give their chance to both revolutionaries and reformers. Revolutionaries will maintain, as we have seen, that the needed changes cannot be effected without a *prior* overthrow of the "system"; reformers, on the other hand, behave like the country or the chessplayer who exasperatingly fights on when "objectively" he has already lost — and occasionally goes on to win! The reformer sets out after his reforms blissfully unaware that the ruling class will never allow this or that antagonistic measure to pass or to become effective. He is a naïve and pathetic figure at the start, an easy target for the revolutionary's sarcasms, but since he *acts*, he learns from his mistakes and from the resistances he encounters, and he frequently ends up as a wily individual from whom the revolutionary may well learn a trick or two.

This education of the reformer is well brought out in our stories. In Colombia, for example, reformers attempted in the fifties to achieve better land utilization through the mildly antagonistic measure of penalty taxation combined with the non-antagonistic measure of colonization of public lands. But they soon found out that planned colonization can make at best only a marginal contribution to the solution of the agrarian problem and that penalty taxation arouses opposition without generating support, since it is fiercely resisted by the landowners but is not perceived as a direct benefit by the landless farmers. The turn to land reform can in part be explained by these negative experiences; even though it is a more antagonistic measure than taxation, its proponents are sure of support from the campesinos, they do not incur the hostility of the small and medium-sized landowners, and the large ones may actually not fight the reform very hard because any individual owner is liable to think that the reform will either not be applied at all or will not reach down to him. Taking full advantage of such constellations, our "naïve" reformer has by now turned into a master tactician who manages to slip through a workable reform to the surprise and dismay of both landowners and revolutionaries!

A similarly a priori improbable feat is the establishment of SUDENE with its group of determined reform-minded top officials, equipped with considerable finance and power, in the middle of a Northeast still dominated by its traditional elites. Again, this achievement was due to learning from prior non-antagonistic attempts at solving the Northeastern problem and to a judicious exploitation of a crisis atmosphere combined with a remarkable talent for forming temporary alliances.

The reforms which take place in Latin America today are anything but manifestations of sweet reasonableness. Nor are they accurately described as resulting from a "recognition by the ruling class that it has to give up something in order not to lose everything," as the cliché would have it. Rather they are extraordinary feats of contriving in the course of which some of the hostile power groups are won over, others are neutralized and outwitted, and the remaining diehards often barely overcome by a coalition of highly heterogeneous forces.

"Divide and reform" tactics are usually found to be one important ingredient of the maneuvers making these feats possible. The reason why such tactics may be successful has been well put by one of Latin America's most acute political thinkers:

> The social conflicts existing at present in our country express essentially not so much irreducible class struggles as conflicts that divide, within the domain of each class, its dynamic and static sectors, or the productive and parasitic forces.[1]

When economic development has been underway for some time it may be possible to limit the purely antagonistic portion of one's program to, for

---

[1] Hélio Jaguaribe, *O Nacionalismo na atualidade brasileira*, Instituto Brasileiro de Estudos Brasileiros, Rio de Janeiro, 1958, p. 50. For a further systematic development of the theme of increasing differentiation of Brazilian society, see his recent *Desenvolvimento económico e desenvolvimento político*, Editôra Fundo de Cultura, Rio, 1962, particularly pp. 169 ff. Differences in the rigidity of class barriers and traditional power structures in Brazil are also stressed by Celso Furtado in "Brazil: What Kind of Revolution?," *Foreign Affairs*, April 1963, pp. 526–535.

example, the "parasitic, reactionary, routine-ridden" landlords while neutralizing and perhaps even enlisting the collaboration of the progressive,
modernizing group. This is admittedly an extremely delicate operation
both because of the long-standing commitment of the pro-reform forces to
comprehensive change and because of traditional fears of property owners
that any one reform may be followed by another, more radical one. In fact,
at the present time it is still uncertain whether a limited, rather than cataclysmic, reform can be successfully carried out in the Northeast of Brazil
where the collaboration of the more progressive cane growers and sugar
mill owners is sought in diversifying agriculture in the coastal belt or in Colombia where the reform law tends to exempt efficient large-scale producers from the projected land redistribution.

These considerations qualify our earlier remarks on the way in which action on a problem is stimulated. No doubt this happens most regularly as a
to-be-remedied condition is aggravated or intensified. The histories of the
Chilean inflation and of the Northeastern droughts abundantly illustrate
this point. Yet, under certain circumstances, the opposite relationship will
also be found: action of either a reformist or a revolutionary nature may be
stimulated when the problem begins to *recede!* In recent years the most
conspicuous example of this relationship is the fight against colonialism
which has increased in ferocity the more clearly colonialism was seen to be
doomed. Action intensified because the task to be accomplished by the
anti-colonial forces suddenly looked manageable and a favorable outcome
of their fight appeared probable. Similarly the generalized fight for agrarian reform in Latin America today may have been stimulated by the fact
that old-style latifundismo has not only been eradicated in the countries
which have experienced agrarian revolutions but is being eroded elsewhere
as well.[1] In Colombia, as we have seen, modern commercialized and mechanized agriculture has been expanding in some erstwhile latifundia while
others continue to be broken up by spontaneous colonization and squatting. Thus the problem has become smaller and more manageable: in a
way, the animal is already cornered and wounded and the agrarian reformers, as elsewhere the anti-colonialists, are moving in for the kill. In such a

---

[1] A counter-example that comes to mind is "poverty in the affluent society." Action
on the problem of poverty, once it has shrunk in size, becomes more difficult as the
remaining poor tend to belong to a *hard core* of sick, old, "unemployable," etc.; action
also becomes less compelling because the problem victims are increasingly scattered or
isolated. Whether action on a problem is stimulated or slackens as the problem recedes
may well depend on these two questions: (1) Does the problem have a hard core? (2)
Are the remaining victims of the problem capable of joint action?

situation, the reformers do not face a wholly hopeless task, and what would have required a major social upheaval thirty years ago may be achieved today by methods short of revolution.

Action is actually stimulated when a problem recedes, not only by the fact that it begins to look more manageable and "lickable," but also because revolutionaries are likely to redouble their energies when they notice that the problem on which they had counted to revolutionize society is fading away. Lenin had exactly this reaction in the face of the transformation of Russian agriculture consequent upon the Stolypin reforms and was clearly worried lest the land measures "so transform the countryside that it would no longer be a revolutionary force."[1]

In fact, it is quite possible that revolutionaries have one of their best chances when some policy-makers begin to convince themselves that the problem is well on the way out and that it can safely be left to fade away. This may happen either because, as outsiders, the policy-makers do not experience the problem in their everyday lives or because they are not interested in policies that "merely" help existing trends along instead of majestically initiating new ones.[2] Thus they will judge that patience is in order at precisely the time when those who do experience the problem will become desperately impatient. Interestingly, patience of the outsiders and impatience of the insiders increase for the same reason, namely, that "the end is in sight."

Much has been made in the preceding pages of the opportunity to gain new allies which becomes available to today's reformmongers in Latin America. But even with those allies, the margins with which the battles for reforms are won are narrow indeed. It is therefore easily understood why reformmongers dare not cut themselves off from any actual or potential

---

[1] Bertram D. Wolfe, *Three Who Made a Revolution*, Beacon, Boston, 1948, p. 360. The following passage quoted by Wolfe (*ibid.*, p. 361) from Lenin's writings is revealing:

"The Stolypin Constitution and the Stolypin agrarian policy mark a new phase in the breakdown of the old, semi-patriarchal and semi-feudal system of tsarism, a new movement toward its transformation into a middle-class monarchy. If this should continue for very long periods of time . . . it might force us to renounce any agrarian program at all. *It would be empty and stupid democratic phrase-mongering to say that the success of such a policy in Russia is 'impossible.' It is possible!* If Stolypin's policy is continued . . . then the agrarian structure of Russia will become completely bourgeois, the stronger peasants will acquire almost all the allotments of land, and agriculture will become capitalistic . . ." (My italics.) *Proletarii*, April 29, 1908, reprinted in *Collected Works*, Third Russian Edition, Vol. XII, p. 193. This passage also shows Lenin to be far less dogmatic concerning the possibility of reform than today's "Marxist-Leninists."

[2] See p. 154 for an episode in our Colombian story which invites this interpretation.

group support of substantial size even though they may disagree with the final objectives of that group. Clearly it would be foolish for them to gain allies on the Center and Right at the cost of losing the Left.

This need to spread his net as wide as possible will make the reform-monger appear to be quite naïve once again, this time about the dangers of Communist infiltration. Often this is so because the most effective reformmongers are to be found amongst erstwhile revolutionaries who notice, much to their own surprise, that some of the social changes they have been seeking can be achieved without that "prior" revolution in whose necessity they had long believed. To turn such private insights into the collective experience of a group that has long remained in a position of pure protest against the established order is perhaps even more important than the achievement of any single reform in itself if Latin American societies are ever to become "integrated." From this point of view also, the effective reformmonger must delay as long as possible, and perhaps avoid altogether, any break with his radical followers. Frequently this will not require any special effort or dissimulation on his part since he is himself still doubtful — quite rightly so until the returns are in — that it is possible to dispense with revolution.

At his best, our reformer-revolutionary will therefore retain the trust of his old followers even as he enlists aid and support from new quarters. He will now have to play to several quite different galleries; he will contrive change by negotiating for new allies while not ceasing to agitate for it. These two tasks are of course so different that they are best performed if they can be dealt out to *several* principal actors who feel quite independent of each other, in the manner of the struggle for Italian unification which was able to draw on the highly diverse talents of Cavour, a master contriver, and of Mazzini and Garibaldi, who filled the roles of conspirators and agitators. But sometimes there is only one chief actor who, to be successful, must combine both roles, appear in the guise of Necker and Stolypin one day and in that of Danton or Lenin the next — a highly risky assignment, though perhaps also rather an entertaining one!

In fine, the roads to reform are narrow and perilous, they appear quite unsafe to the outside observer however sympathetic he may be, *but they exist*. Having become acquainted with their twists and turns throughout this book, we emerge with a heightened consciousness of the difficulties facing Latin American policy-makers; but also and foremost, with a new appreciation of the many unsuspected and unorthodox opportunities for maneuver and advance.

Models of
Reformmongering

Having taken, in the last chapter, a certain pleasure in showing the enormous complexity of the problem of reform, we are tempted to simplify and to probe — rather diffidently — whether formal reasoning can make a contribution to the understanding of our subject.

To begin with, we may point out that the conventional idea of the alternative between reform and revolution can indeed be represented by a very simple model based on the following assumptions:

    (1) a constitutional group of decision-makers — a town meeting, a parliament, a bureaucratic organization with a somewhat dispersed power structure — has before it a proposed change in the status quo on which only a 'yea' or 'no' vote is possible;

    (2) in the absence of a 'yea' vote on the part of the constitutional body of decision-makers an extra-constitutional attempt to secure the proposed change will be staged;

    (3) this is not known to the decision-makers at the moment of their vote.

Under these assumptions, the alternative is as stark as it is simple: if a majority of the constitutionally established decision-makers favor positive action, "peaceful, legal reform" will be achieved; if not, "violent revolution" will break out. A presumption that revolution will in fact win over reform — "the reformer's initial handicap" of the preceding chapter — results from a *fourth* assumption, namely, that the constitutional decision-makers are in their majority wedded to the status quo.

Those who put their hopes on reform generally accept this last assumption but reverse the third one: by supposing that the decision-makers know all about the impending revolution they conclude that self-preservation will impel the decision-makers to "give up something in order not to lose

276

everything." This kind of reform is also known as "revolution from above" which, being imposed by the ruling class, is thus neatly opposed to revolution from below. There is no room in the model for intermediate forms of getting the reform through.

It is perhaps sufficient to present the primitive structure of the traditional reform-vs.-revolution models to establish a presumption that the cases in which they are an approximately valid representation of reality will be rare indeed.

In the following we shall complicate matters slightly:

(a) by allowing for the *uncertainty* that affects future events such as anticipated revolutions and by showing that (in part because of this fact) the choice between status quo, reform and revolution lends itself to a great variety of preference patterns and hence alliances;

(b) by allowing for the existence of *more than one issue* on which varying stands may be taken by the decision-makers and by pointing out the diverse opportunities that arise in this situation for "reformmongering."

In this fashion, we hope to approach reality while not losing the opportunities for manipulation and analysis that come with model-building. The numerous points of contact between the properties of the models which will be developed in the following pages and the events which have been chronicled in the country studies are left to be appreciated by the reader. Suffice it to say that Model I has been largely inspired by the Colombian experience with land reform and Model II by the Chilean experience with inflation, while the story of Brazil's Northeast contains illustrative material for both models.

MODEL I: *Engineering Reform with the Help of the Perspective of Revolution*

Let us take as starting point a situation in which reform can be achieved legally only if parts of both "conservative" and "progressive" groups in the constitutional decision-making body — we shall call it Parliament from now on — join forces to vote for it.[1] We suppose that the reform can be graduated, that is, can be more or less sweeping and we assume at this stage that progressives prefer the more sweeping to the less sweeping reforms, *all the*

---

[1] This may be so either because Parliament is evenly split or because a qualified majority is required or because of the presence of some extremist opposition of Right and Left that votes systematically "no."

way, while the opposite holds of course for the conservatives. How much reform can be achieved without prior revolution may be subject to considerable differences of judgment, but we may assume the existence of some "degree of sweepingness" which *undoubtedly* requires prior revolution. Our definition of progressives implies then that they are unafraid of revolution and that they in fact welcome it, not for its own sake, but because it permits the realization of the more sweeping reforms that are inconceivable without revolution (e.g., expropriation of land without any compensation).

We now introduce the following symbols:

a for a moderate reform which is being proposed to Parliament;

$\bar{a}$ or non-alpha, for the status quo; and

β for the sweeping reform that would result from revolution.

The preference patterns or orderings of our two groups of decision-makers will look as follows (the most preferred alternative being placed at the top):

Progressives	Conservatives
β	$\bar{a}$
a	a
$\bar{a}$	β

If one works in this situation with the usual assumption on voting in collective choice models, namely, that only two alternatives are pitted one against the other at any one point of time,[1] then the chances for progressives and conservatives to come to any agreement are nil: their preferences are opposite whichever pair out of the three available alternatives is voted on.

Yet we feel intuitively that to reach agreement on alpha should not be wholly impossible. One way of engineering this agreement is for some reformmonger to appear on the scene and to rig the voting in such a way that progressives think they vote between a and $\bar{a}$ while conservatives are made to believe that they vote between a and β. Unanimous agreement on a will be the result! To achieve it, pairwise voting must be abandoned. The decision-makers must scan all three possible outcomes simultaneously and a reformmonger must manage to convince progressives that no matter what

---

[1] See Kenneth J. Arrow, *Social Choice and Individual Values*, Wiley, New York, 1951, p. 20; Duncan Black, *The Theory of Committees and Elections*, Cambridge University Press, Cambridge (England), 1958, p. 3.

they do the chances of revolution and hence the possibility of realizing beta are zero so that their only real choice is between the status quo and moderate reform; at the same time, he must feed exactly the opposite information to the conservatives and persuade them that their real choice lies between moderate reform and revolution.

While this kind of tactic is familiar enough to anyone who has participated in the engineering of compromise, it is not necessary to view agreement in this situation as resulting from at least one party to the agreement, and perhaps both, being fed the wrong information. The fact is that when the reformmonger talks to conservatives about the imminence of revolution, and to progressives about its remoteness, he does not give out information but makes prediction about future events, and the future is uncertain. By taking uncertainty into account we may actually be able to dispense with the services of our reformmonger as we shall show presently.

For almost 200 years now, the *possibility* of revolutionary overthrow of the existing order has been present in the minds of decision-makers, conservatives and progressives alike, not to speak of the revolutionaries themselves. Hence, important policy choices can be expected to be influenced by the probable effect of that choice on the chances for revolution: In other words, politicians do not decide the issue reform vs. status quo only on its merits; each of the ostensible alternatives has another silent dimension that has its weight in the final choice. On the one hand, we have a *and* the subjective probability that revolution will break out, i.e., that beta will follow with alpha in place; on the other, there is $\bar{a}$ *and* the corresponding probability that revolution will break out if the status quo is kept.

Suppose it is generally believed that the probability of revolution will decline if reform gets adopted. Denoting this estimated decline as Δ we can now state that the real choice before our decision-makers is between the status quo, $\bar{a}$, on the one hand, and (a, Δ) i.e., the reform *and* the consequent estimated decline in the likelihood of revolution, on the other.

It is then perfectly conceivable that some conservatives who prefer $\bar{a}$ to a nevertheless prefer (a, Δ) to $\bar{a}$ provided Δ is of a size sufficient to justify the switch. Some progressives, on the other hand, who preferred a to $\bar{a}$ to start with, may well continue to favor (a, Δ) over $\bar{a}$ *provided Δ is not too large*. A very large Δ means that the revolution is practically certain if the status quo is maintained just a little longer; in that case our progressives would rather wait for the revolution to break out and thereby secure β instead of settling for a and thereby spoiling β's chances. There may exist, then, a *range* for Δ which rallies a majority of both conservatives and progressives behind a. If Δ falls within this range, then agreement on reform alpha does not rest on differences of information and probability judgments, nor does it necessarily involve any misrepresentation or other chicanery on the part of a crafty reformmonger. Naturally, the more successful the reformmonger is in making conservatives believe that Δ is large while encouraging the opposite belief among progressives, the better the chances for agreement on a. But our point is that this activity of the reformmonger may not be indispensable for agreement on a to be reached. Such an agreement may not express the feeling of the majority on alpha when alpha is pitted strictly on its merits against the status quo, but it may do so when the effect of the choice on the likelihood of an uncertain future event is taken into account.[1]

So far, the task of introducing reform has been made to look unduly easy. All we have to do, so it seems, is to introduce the specter of revolution or radical reform (beta) and consensus on reform (alpha) will be rapidly forthcoming. But we have neglected the fact that a wide variety of preference orderings will appear once reform beta enters the field.

To obtain a fuller view of the principal possibilities we return for a moment to the situation in which the adoption of reform is the only conceivable alternative to the status quo. At that stage only two positions exist, namely, that of the progressives who prefer a to $\bar{a}$ and that of the

---

[1] The situation here described conflicts with one frequent assumption of collective choice models, namely, that preferences between any two alternative courses of action are unaffected by the presence or absence of additional alternatives. This assumption, which is closely related to the previously mentioned assumption of pairwise voting, is known as the principle of the independence of irrelevant alternatives. (Cf. Arrow, *Social Choice*, pp. 26–28 and R. D. Luce and Howard Raiffa, *Games and Decisions*, New York, Wiley, 1957, pp. 288, 335–338.) In our context, the existence of alternatives outside of the immediate question at issue is highly relevant to the way that question is going to be decided. If decision-makers preferring A to B perceive that choosing A will increase the probability of C occurring eventually, some of them may well vote for B rather than A. This kind of situation hardly ever exists in economic choices. A person choosing between apple pie and cherry pie, and preferring the latter, does not usually have to consider the possibility that if he chooses cherry pie, lemon meringue pie may well be the only item on the menu next time (whereas such a change in menu is much less likely if he chooses apple pie)! But such considerations are fairly common in and even characteristic of a wide range of political choices. Policy-making is a continuing, never-ending process, in which today's choices are known to affect tomorrow's events. Policy actions must therefore be in part influenced by these expected repercussions. Issues are often decided not "on their merits," but with an eye to the decision's effect on changes in the likelihood of some highly feared or highly desired event. The very example chosen by Arrow to illustrate the independence postulate can easily be turned around to show that the postulate is *not* plausible: "Suppose that an election is held — so writes Arrow — with a certain number of candidates in the field, each individual fil-

conservatives who have the opposite preference. If the progressives are in the minority and are therefore unable to make any headway with their demands for alpha, some of them may turn into revolutionaries and in this fashion the possibility of beta will appear on the horizon.

Both progressives and conservatives will now split into various subgroups. As already mentioned, some "staunch" progressives may simply favor beta on the ground that it improves upon alpha. Then there will be some who feel that beta is going "too far" or is too costly to obtain; they may or may not prefer the status quo to beta, but definitely prefer alpha to either. Finally the progressives that turn into revolutionaries will be of two varieties: there will be those (R1) who now turn against alpha altogether because they have convinced themselves that alpha is not worth fighting for, that the "genuine" alpha is not obtainable without prior revolution, or because they fear alpha's possible blunting effect on their followers' revolutionary zeal. These revolutionaries will behave in effect as though they preferred the status quo to alpha. But there may be other revolutionaries (R2) who do not have much use for alpha either, yet who feel that the achievement of alpha is worthwhile because it will "sharpen the internal contradictions" of the to-be-overthrown social order and hence represent an easier jumping-off point for the revolution than the status quo.

The conservatives, in turn, will divide into the following categories: the "staunch" conservatives who, in spite of any information about the danger of revolution, continue to prefer the status quo to reform alpha while of course detesting beta even more than alpha; the reformers who, threatened with beta, will develop a more or less sincere preference for reform over the status quo;[1] and the diehards (D1) who will oppose alpha even more than

---

ing his list of preferences, and then one of the candidates dies. Surely the social choice should be made by taking each of the individuals' preference lists, blotting out completely the dead candidate's name, and considering only the orderings of the remaining names in going through the procedure of determining the winner." (*Social Choice*, p. 26.) If we suppose, however, that the candidate who died was a dangerous demagogue aspiring to dictatorship, the orderings of the remaining names may have been profoundly affected by the would-be dictator's existence — for example, his opponents may have given first choice to some other powerful politician whom they would not support under more normal circumstances. Hence the only way of finding out about the community's real preference after the death of one of the candidates would be to repeat the election. Our objection to the independence postulate is different from, and perhaps more basic than, the usual criticism which has been leveled at it on the ground that it leads one to discard valuable information about the intensity of preferences. (See Luce and Raiffa, *Games and Decisions*, pp. 335–337.)

[1] The difference between these two groups of conservatives may be due either to a stronger original preference for the status quo by the "staunch" group and/or to a more optimistic appraisal on its part of the chances to avoid revolution.

beta because — like some of the revolutionaries — they feel that alpha leads inevitably and rapidly to beta and represents cowardly appeasement to boot. Some diehards (D2),[1] however, may make common cause with the reformers, because they trust that alpha is either unenforceable and hence will not really change anything or because they hold alpha to be unworkable and hence well designed to prove the wisdom of the status quo.

Thus, we obtain the following preference orderings:

Progressives split into:			Conservatives split into:		
(1) Staunch Progressives and Revolutionaries R2	(2) Reformers	(3) Revolutionaries R1	(4) Staunch Conservatives	(5) Reformers and Diehards D2	(6) Diehards D1
β	α α	β	$\bar{\alpha}$	α	$\bar{\alpha}$
α	β $\bar{\alpha}$	$\bar{\alpha}$	α	$\bar{\alpha}$	β
$\bar{\alpha}$	$\bar{\alpha}$ β	α	β	β	α

We are now able to discuss further the effect of an emerging revolutionary perspective on the chances of reform. Since, in accordance with our earlier assumption, conservatives (contained in columns 4 to 6) outnumber progressives (columns 1 to 3), a pro-reform coalition can gather a majority only if some conservatives reverse their previous preferences, i.e., if a sufficient number of conservatives switch to preference ordering (5). At the same time, however, we are losing some support for alpha among our progressives, namely, the revolutionaries who come to hold the preference pattern indicated in column (3). Hence, for reform to become possible, those who come to hold preference pattern (5) must be more numerous than those who become partisans of (3).

Can one say anything about the chances of this occurring? Revolutionaries of pattern (3) will emerge as time passes without any reform being achieved while conservatives will become reformers of pattern (5) as they become concerned about the revolutionary threat. Hence, the chances for reform *worsen* at first as the reform forces lose some of their strength to the revolutionaries. If reform is to become a reality the number of conservative reformers must thereafter begin to grow *more rapidly* than the number of revolutionaries. It is conceivable that this condition will be fulfilled only for a certain period of time and that, thereafter, the number of

---

[1] So designated mainly to correspond to the revolutionaries R2 whose counterpart they are on the conservative side since both support reform for ulterior purposes.

revolutionaries will again show faster growth than that of the reformers. This constellation, which is of course only one of many possibilities, is behind such frequently used figures of speech as "the time for reform is running out."

In addition, the preceding table reveals some highly unorthodox and frequently unsuspected possibilities of pushing a reform through. Revolutionaries (and diehards) may differ about the effect of reform on the likelihood of revolution (or on the status quo) and such differences in judgment may have an important bearing on the course of events. Thus, once an important group of revolutionaries has come into existence, a reform coalition could win the day because some revolutionaries come to support the reform as a stepping stone to revolution (i.e., because there is a switch from the R1 to the R2 position). Similarly a reform coalition could draw initial strength from the feeling of conservatives (the diehards D2) that a projected reform is going to be meaningless or abortive and can therefore be supported without any risk.

Let us then take a closer look at the coalition we may have to put together in order to get the reform through. Enumerating all those who, in the preceding table, prefer a to $\bar{a}$, we obtain the following highly heterogenous list of characters:

(1) the revolutionaries R2 who have little use for alpha as such, but expect the turmoil following upon alpha to result in revolution;

(2) the staunch progressives who are willing to settle for alpha for the time being even though they prefer beta;

(3) the reformers among the progressives who, while against the status quo, dislike beta or find that it is not worth a revolution;

(4) the reformers among the conservatives who consider alpha as a real sacrifice but hope to prevent beta by conceding alpha;

(5) the diehards D2 who accede to alpha in the expectation that it will prove an unworkable, disruptive measure which will lead to a restoration and firmer establishment of the status quo.

To put together such a coalition will take quite some expert juggling. In contrast to the earlier situation where we considered only how conservatives may turn into reformers, some of the parties do entertain this time perfectly opposite motives and expectations. Naturally, the less they realize this the better, for the coalition may otherwise fail to materialize: each group would fear for the validity of its own judgment as it saw another group vote for the same measure from radically different motives. In this situation, clarification of goals would prevent rather than facilitate agreement.[1]

The difficulty of forming a coalition favoring reform alpha and the brittleness of such a coalition thus depend on the strength of our various "parties." Reforms will clearly be impossible if we have excessively large numbers of revolutionaries and diehards of the first category. Yet it cannot be said that the smaller the number of such extremists the better. For it is only the presence of the revolutionaries that makes it possible to obtain support for alpha among conservatives along the lines explored above; and the progressives are similarly induced to settle for alpha by the presence of a solid group of staunch conservatives and diehards who are unwilling to yield anything. Any elimination of these groups may render agreement between progressives and conservatives impossible.[2]

The composition of the reform coalition will be of importance for the character of the reform. When the pro-reform groups are heavily weighted with revolutionaries R2 and diehards D2, who favor the reform only as a stepping stone either to achieving revolution or to putting the status quo more firmly back into the saddle, the reform is likely to be designed in such a way as to reflect in some measure the intended instability. Furthermore, the reform coalitions which it is possible to put together will vary considerably as experience with reform is accumulated. Where traditional ruling groups have never been seriously challenged or where reforms have frequently been abortive, reformmongers may be able to count on the neutrality of diehards D2 who feel sure that the newly proposed reform will come to the same innocuous end as all the previous ones. For the very same reason it may be difficult *initially* to enlist active support on the Left where scepticism about the possibilities of real reform without prior revolution will be strong. If the reform nevertheless turns out to have or to acquire some teeth, the reform coalition will thereupon attract active hostility from the Right, but may compensate for this loss by enlisting part of

---

[1] Charles E. Lindblom, "Tinbergen on Policy Making," *Journal of Political Economy*, Dec. 1958, p. 534.

[2] It may be interesting to contrast this finding with those of Duncan Black's *Theory of Committees and Elections*. Black showed that if alternatives can be arranged along a unilinear scale and if preferences among those alternatives have a single-peaked profile, then there is always one most preferred alternative. What prevents the convergence of democratic opinion on one solution are the U-shaped or multi-peaked preference curves. In our view, on the contrary, it is the emergence of U-shaped preference orderings (such as that of the revolutionaries who prefer both status quo and revolution to reform) which bends around the preferences of others so that a consensus on reform becomes possible.

the revolutionary Left which, as a result of the experience with the possibility of reform, will be going through a process of "agonizing reappraisal" of its beliefs. The likely result is a shift in the center of gravity of a reform coalition toward the Left while the Left itself becomes more willing to work within the existing — and, lo and behold, changing — society.

MODEL II: *Engineering Reform through Logrolling and Shifting Alliances*

The preceding section has examined how agreement on reform can be engineered when only *one* issue is up for discussion, but when a widespread consciousness exists that this issue can be dealt with in *three* distinct ways: through maintenance of the status quo, through a reform (a) which may not require prior revolution, or through a more sweeping reform (β) which clearly requires revolution.

We shall now complicate the simple reform-vs.-revolution model in a different way: we largely revert to the assumption of that model according to which the danger (or promise) of revolution is not perceived by the decision-makers so that voting on the proposed reform measures may be assumed to be untainted by worries over (or hopes of) such a contingency. As in the primitive model, it is understood that if action on reform is not forthcoming, revolution will break out; but this fact is not now allowed to influence the proceedings, except in one situation to be explained below. On the other hand, we complicate the original model in the direction of *pluralism* by supposing that decision-makers will have to take a stand on at least two issues rather than only on one.

The simplest way of describing the ensuing constellation in our decision-making body[1] would be to indicate in a two-by-two matrix how the decision-makers can be divided into four categories, namely:

(1) those who are in favor of some specified proposed reform actions on both issues;

(2) and (3) those who are in favor of the specified actions in the case of one issue but against them in the case of the other, and vice versa; and

(4) those who are against the proposed actions on either issue.

For reasons that will become clear we shall introduce a more compli-

---

[1] Exclusively to simplify exposition we shall again talk about "Parliament" as the decision-making body and about "Members of Parliament" or "Members" as those who share in the decision.

cated model by taking intensity of feeling into account. We assume that, faced with the proposal for action on an issue alpha, Members can be divided into the following four categories:

(1) those who are strongly in favor (A)
(2) those who are weakly in favor (a)
(3) those who are weakly against (ā)
(4) those who are strongly against (Ā)[1]

The same subdivision applies to stands on issue beta, with the corresponding symbols. We can now establish the matrix set out in the accompanying table, which shows the voting strength of every possible combination of stands on the two issues. For example, the symbol aB̄ (fourth row, second column) stands for those members who are weakly in favor of action on issue alpha (for the sake of brevity we shall say from now on "in favor of alpha"), but strongly against beta. The total number of members is n and, if we assume voting by simple majority, we need $m = \frac{n}{2} + 1$ votes to carry any motion.

The chances of getting action on alpha and beta depend on the distribution of Members among the sixteen cells of our matrix. We shall now distinguish five basic constellations:

1. *Majority in Favor of Both Reforms.* If the occupants of the four cells in the northwestern quarter (AB, aB, Ab, ab) who favor both alpha and beta make up a majority, our whip's task is simple: he can bring both measures to a simultaneous vote and victory on both issues is assured and effortless.

In our next three constellations we move away from this simple situation and assume that neither the four northwestern cells nor the corresponding southeastern cells (whose occupants oppose both alpha and beta) contain a majority. The reformmonger's task is now to maneuver in such a fashion as to enlist the support of some Members in the remaining eight cells who favor one of the two measures, but are either weakly or strongly opposed to the other. His strategy will depend on the distribution of voting strength among these eight "for-and-against" cells. The principal or typical strategies will be taken up in order of increasing difficulty.

2. *Majority Formation through Logrolling.* If the additional votes needed for the formation of a majority can be found in the cells āB and Ab̄,

---

[1] Most of the propositions that follow could be derived from a three-way split: in favor — indifferent — against. The four-fold division seems slightly better at bringing out some characteristics of the model.

POSITIONS AND DISTRIBUTION OF VOTING STRENGTH
IN RELATION TO TWO ISSUES

Positions taken on issue alpha

	STRONGLY IN FAVOR	WEAKLY IN FAVOR	WEAKLY AGAINST	STRONGLY AGAINST
STRONGLY IN FAVOR	AB	aB	āB	ĀB
WEAKLY IN FAVOR	Ab	ab	āb	Āb
WEAKLY AGAINST	Ab̄	ab̄	āb̄	Āb̄
STRONGLY AGAINST	AB̄	aB̄	āB̄	ĀB̄

Positions taken on issue beta

n

Note: Symbols represent numbers of decision-makers taking the indicated position.

i.e., amongst the Members who are strongly in favor of alpha, but weakly against beta and vice versa, an obvious tactic to pursue is the one known as logrolling. The āB's will make a deal with the Ab's through which they commit themselves to vote in favor of alpha which they know to be highly desired by the Ab's, who in exchange promise to vote in favor of beta. As has been pointed out by Buchanan and Tullock, both parties gain in the process since they give up opposing a measure which they really do not care much about to obtain passage of another which is of considerable importance to them.[1] Note that it is the self-interest of the parties concerned

---

[1] J. M. Buchanan and Gordon Tullock, *The Calculus of Consent*, University of Michigan Press, Ann Arbor, 1962, Chap. 10.

which will make for success in getting action on both alpha and beta; the reformmonger has little more to do than to indicate the advantages of logrolling to those who do not see the point by themselves.

Thus, if a majority can be formed by aggregating the occupants of āB and Ab̄ to the four northwesternmost cells, the task of getting alpha and beta through can still be handled fairly easily.

The symmetrically opposite situation to the one just described obtains when the opponents of both measures in the southeastern corner of the matrix are able to form a majority by adding the occupants of cells aB̄ and Āb. "Negative" logrolling between these Members is just as likely as "positive" logrolling between Ab̄ and āB. Members with the aB̄ persuasion are sure to vote against alpha which they favor only weakly if in exchange they can get some other Members to block beta to which they object strongly.

3. *Shifting Alliances.* Next, let us assume that majority formation through positive logrolling is not feasible (because of the lack of strength in Ab̄ and āB), but that majorities could be formed by either the first two columns or the first two rows of our matrix. In other words, we have a parliamentary majority which favors alpha and another which favors beta but each majority has a different composition. The solid northwestern core must ally itself with the southwesterners to get alpha through and then it must shed these allies and tie up with the northeasterners for a vote in favor of beta. Logrolling is not feasible in this situation because Members in the AB̄ and aB̄ cells whose vote is required to get alpha through will not give up their opposition to beta even if they are assured that by doing so they will be able to secure passage of alpha: they hate beta far too much for that. By far the most practical way of getting *both* measures through is to tackle one issue at a time and to shift the basis of one's political support in between.

In this fashion it may even be possible to frustrate the formation of a potential all-round negative coalition. Suppose that in a Parliament of 100 Members we have 45 Members for and 35 Members against both alpha and beta, while the twenty remaining are subdivided equally between cells aB̄ and Āb. If negative logrolling between these Members is allowed to take place, any action on either alpha or beta will be stalled ($35 + 10 + 10 =$ majority). But there still remains the possibility for the 45 AB's to push alpha through by forming a coalition with the 10 aB̄'s provided the latter do not suspect that the AB's will later on make similar common cause with the Āb's in order to obtain the passage of beta.

4. *Mutual Sacrifices*. The final step in complicating the task of our whip or political strategist is to assume a voting distribution such that the only way of forming a positive majority is to mobilize the voting strength of all ten cells outside of the diehard opponents of both measures (and the "negative logrollers") in the southeastern corner. In this situation, neither alpha nor beta can be gotten through separately by having the pro-alpha forces team up together first (regardless of whether they are for or against both) and the pro-beta forces next. Once again, as in the logrolling case, we need to have anti-alpha and pro-beta forces in the northeastern corner vote in favor of alpha as well as of beta and the anti-beta and pro-alpha forces in the southwestern corner in favor of beta as well as of alpha. However, the possibility of arranging a "private" deal of the logrolling type is not now present because much of the needed voting strength is assumed to be concentrated in cells $A\bar{B}$ and $\bar{A}B$ so that the parties cannot gain by swapping votes. There is, nevertheless, one maneuver through which Members who are strongly opposed to beta might be induced to vote for beta as well as for alpha: it consists in tying up alpha and beta together and in proclaiming a national emergency in which mutual sacrifices of various groups are required to avert revolution.[1] The essential ingredient is simultaneity of action on alpha and beta in some great élan of virtual national unity, with the exception of the bitter-enders in the southeastern corner — yet who knows, they may not be able to resist the general enthusiasm!

Admittedly only a remote chance exists that the maneuver will work, that southwesterners and northeasterners will engage in this sacrifice-sharing ceremony and will forget about their contrasting interests and traditional hostilities. But it is certainly worthwhile to play this last card if the prospect is — and our reformmonger will certainly point this out to the more reluctant Members — that action on alpha and beta will otherwise be taken by:

5. *Revolution*. This is the last of our possible outcomes which in accordance with our basic assumption (action on alpha and beta must be taken —

---

[1] Here is the exception to the assumption which we are otherwise making in this model, namely, that the possibility of revolution does not influence Members' voting. It should be noted that the threat of revolution is brought in as a *deus ex machina* which carries the day for reform only as a last resort, after other ways of finding a pro-reform majority have been exhausted. Moreover, the threat of revolution intervenes only to sway Members such as $A\bar{B}$ and $\bar{A}B$ who are virtually indifferent toward the joint adoption of reforms alpha and beta, since they are strongly in favor of one and strongly against the other. The situation remains therefore quite different from that described in Section I of this digression where the possibility of revolution is permanently on the Members' mind and is allowed a far more decisive influence on their voting.

or else) becomes a certainty when a solid majority of decision-makers occupies the southeastern corner of our matrix, i.e., is made up of Members
who oppose both alpha and beta.

Before passing to comment on these various constellations it should be
noted that each of the intermediate strategies (2), (3) and (4) are of
course open also to the opposition, as has already been pointed out in
connection with logrolling; also, as was shown in the case of shifting alliances, these reformmongering or reform-blocking strategies can frequently be countered through skillful use by the opposition of these
same strategies.

Comment

We now have some knowledge about the basic properties of our model
and can evaluate its usefulness.

A first comment should be made on the remarkable difference between
a one-issue model and a two-issue model. The one-issue 'yea' or 'no' model
as described at the beginning of this section allows for only two basic outcomes, namely, peaceful, pleasantly easy reform, on the one hand, and
revolution, on the other. In comparison to the unrealistic simplicity of this
model, the two-issue model which we have been analyzing, while still exceedingly simple, does a far better job at accounting for various types of
intermediate outcomes which stop short of revolution but entail considerable amounts of risk, adroit maneuvering, and bargaining. These intermediate outcomes strongly resemble real-life situations with which one is
well acquainted. It is therefore worthwhile to examine these situations and
the specific differences between them in greater detail.

*Majority Formation through Logrolling versus Majority Formation
through Shifting Alliances.* Let us imagine two types of societies, one of
which is able to get its reforms through by logrolling and the other in
which reforms are achieved by means of shifting alliances: clearly the
politics of these two entities will be quite different. With the unmaking and
rebuilding of coalitions required by shifting alliances, a society relying on
this mechanism is likely to exhibit political instability, a tendency toward
multi-party systems or toward very weak party discipline. Logrolling, on
the other hand, is compatible with considerable continuity in the executive
branch and with a system of two parties, each of which (one pro-, the other
anti-reform) is grouped around a strong central nucleus. Yet, as we have
seen above, only a seemingly small shift in voting strength from cells Ab

and āB to cells AB̄ and ĀB, respectively, makes it necessary to substitute shifting alliances for logrolling. What, then, is the nature and meaning of this shift?

Logrolling is likely to emerge as an important form of politics when large numbers of decision-makers feel — and know they feel — far more strongly on one set of issues than on another. Those who take positions such as Ab (or any other position combining a capital with a small letter) reflect this disposition: they are content to act frankly as partisans, lobbyists and specialists worrying far more about those matters that are of direct concern to them than about those which they sense as a bit remote from their interests, region, or field of competence. This type of political behavior is frequently encountered in the United States[1] where logrolling is in fact a widely practiced art (even though switching alliances is by no means unknown).

The "logrolling society" may now be contrasted with another ideal type of society whose members and decision-makers are apt to feel quite strongly on virtually every issue that comes up. This behavior, which seems strange to North Americans, can usually be traced to one or more of three underlying situations:

(a) the decision-makers are a small upper-class group and every one of them is or has been actively involved in almost all phases of the country's political and economic life;

(b) each issue that comes up is immediately connected with some overriding political schism and stands on it are taken strictly and strongly along party lines (it looks as though shifting alliances were not possible in this situation, but this is not necessarily so — see p. 293);

(c) the typical member of the society, even though he is far more affected in his own immediate interests by one issue than by the other, feels honor-bound to acquire and propound strong opinions on both, either because it is *macho* (manly) to hold forth authoritatively on

---

[1] George Gallup has said that "the amazing thing about opinion in this country . . . is that people readily disqualify themselves from giving an opinion when it concerns something in which they have no information. It has been assumed that people want to be regarded as well informed on every issue. In the 25 years we've been polling, we've never found this to be true." *Opinion Polls*, Fund for the Republic, Santa Barbara, Calif., 1962, p. 24. This finding may be related to the fact that, according to a 1952 study of the Michigan Survey Research Center, only 35 per cent of Americans identify themselves strongly with either of the two principal parties. Alfred de Grazia, "Research on Voters and Elections" in *Research Frontiers in Politics and Government*, The Brookings Institution, Washington, 1955, p. 120.

every subject or because a moral obligation is felt to ferret out and support the "right" answer to every question.

Once more we have described traits of political behavior that can be found in the real world — particularly in Latin America. The author has even come across a term which has been specially and whimsically coined to describe this behavior: he was told once by a Colombian that "here in Colombia *somos todos 'toderos'* — we are all 'allists' (specialists in everything)"[1] — the implication being both that "we" — i.e., the people that count — have a finger in every pie, and also that even in the absence of this particular infrastructure, we like to acquire and exhibit strong opinions on every issue. Naturally the very fact that this attitude is being adverted to and ridiculed by the invention of an absurd term may indicate that it is beginning to be eroded by a more "modern" specialist-lobbyist type of attitude. Yet, for the time being, it is still strongly entrenched.[2]

It should be noted that in addition to the prevailing ethos and the stage of economic development (development brings with it specialization and heterogeneity of interests) the mere size of a country may be an important factor in determining the comparative strengths of "todero" and sectionalist sentiment. In a large country it is far more difficult to have a strong opinion on all important public issues than in a small one. This makes logrolling between various regional groups attractive and important in large countries such as the United States and Brazil.

Political behavior in a society where decision-makers are "toderos" rather than sectionalists is not amenable to majority formation through logrolling. With much strength being concentrated in cells $A\bar{B}$ and $\bar{A}B$, such a society will frequently have to resort to shifting alliances and changing majorities if it wishes to get action on the various issues confronting it. This is an interesting result: the more uncompromising, ideological, strongly committed the individual decision-makers are, the more likely it is that the government will have to draw in turn on different groups for support. Or, to put it starkly, *the more principled the individual decision-makers, the more un-*

---

[1] *Todero* is an ad hoc creation formed by *todo* — everything — and the suffix *-ero*, which usually denotes a specialized craftsman as in *panadero* (baker), *platero* (silversmith), etc.

[2] A comparative study of attitudes of university students in the United States and Argentina has found that Argentines consistently take more extreme positions of either strong agreement or strong disagreement with statements of opinion on which they were tested than United States students (Adolfo A. Critto, dissertation in progress, Columbia University, Department of Sociology). For considerable evidence on variable intensity of feeling on public issues in the United States see V. O. Key, Jr., *Public Opinion and American Democracy*, Knopf, New York, 1961, Chapter 9.

principled will be governmental political behavior, with yesterday's allies being jettisoned today and yesterday's enemies suddenly being honored in startling turnabouts.[1] And it also follows that greater political stability, according to this analysis, requires *less rather than more interest in public issues,* more willingness on the part of the decision-makers to act as representatives of sectional interests, hence more proneness to logrolling deals.[2]

One plausible objection to the foregoing argument should be briefly noted: is it not likely that with a dogmatic, ideologically all-around committed, "todero" type of individual political behavior all issues would cluster around one overriding division (e.g., of the left vs. right type) so that our decision-makers would be found entirely among the stand-patters $A\bar{B}$ and the all-out reformers AB with nobody left in the $A\bar{B}$ and $\bar{A}B$ cells of our matrix? Surely this is a possibility and in certain very simple, bipolar societies may even become a likelihood. However, as soon as development and differentiation set in, the possibility of taking different stands on various newly arising issues appears. To give only one example, in almost every country the question of priorities of regions and sectors will cut across established left-right divisions. Moreover, it is possible that the need to shift alliances arises in spite of bipolarity if the decision-makers are predominantly arrayed in $A\bar{B}$ and $\bar{A}B$ rather than in AB and $\bar{A}\bar{B}$. This is frequently the case if a society faces two issues on one of which, say, abusive social security or featherbedding, action is supported by the Right but opposed by the Left whereas the situation is reversed on, say, land reform. In this case, obviously, the few who favor both reforms must team up alternately with the forces of the Left and the Right to obtain action.

Respectability of the Various Outcomes and the Hankering after Simultaneous Solutions. Recent writings of political scientists and political economists in the United States have pointed out that logrolling is not necessarily a conspiracy against the public interest. Our reasoning shows similarly that the logrolling mechanism can be utilized with great advan-

---

[1] Breaking our rule against casual empiricism we cannot refrain from pointing out that our model contributes here nicely to the understanding of the politics of the Frondizi administration in Argentina.

[2] In the United States, where there is danger of apathy on important issues that do not touch people's lives directly, organizations such as the League of Women Voters or the Committee for Economic Development (CED) have given themselves the task of alerting various groups to public policy problems and of having them take a stand on the issues. These organizations assume of course a universal attachment to the constitutional system and its stability as such. What may be needed in Latin America, where this assumption is frequently unwarranted, are opposite efforts to encourage interest groups to act overtly, unashamedly, and exclusively as interest groups.

tage by the reformmonger (as well as, of course, against him). But it goes further: in Machiavellian fashion, it asserts that, in certain circumstances, the price of progress and reform is the betrayal of one's friends — for what else is this maneuver which we have blandly termed "shifting of alliances?"

No wonder, then, that this particular solution, while receiving abundant practice, is hardly ever advocated. In a situation in which it is a possible way of getting action while the out-and-out reformers, even with assistance from positive logrolling, are unable to carry the vote, a clamor will rather arise for our fourth solution, majority formation through mutually shared sacrifices. This modus operandi has no moral stigma attached to it; on the contrary, it represents a deep aspiration in countries which have long been rent by partisan strife, somewhat like the former aspiration toward the nation-state among the fragmented German and Italian principalities. Those who do not pin their hopes on revolution in these countries frequently dream of an emergency situation — perhaps the threat of imminent revolution or disaster of some kind — which would suddenly bring the parties to their senses and reveal the essential unity of the nation. Each country's history knows of such privileged moments in which old hostilities are forgotten, a sense of national unity is restored and important, long-delayed decisions are taken. However, such occasions are exceedingly rare and even when they occur, they can be deceptive and short-lived, like the famous session of France's Legislative Assembly known as "Lamourette's Kiss," during the Revolution.[1] The excessive burden placed on such situations in the political thinking about problem-solving is perhaps explained by the reluctance to include other available mechanisms such as shifting alliances and logrolling among the possible alternatives.

The omission of these potential, if somewhat tortuous, roads to reform from the range of policy alternatives consciously discussed and openly advocated may be due not only to moral revulsion but also to *intellectual* antipathy against a solution that precludes a grandiose simultaneous victory on both issues. Both logrolling and shifting alliances imply that the several problems that are before the country are to be tackled *sequentially* rather than simultaneously. This is obvious for shifting alliances but re-

---

[1] It is worthwhile to quote an eyewitness account of that episode: "The Assembly by a sudden spontaneous movement, rose as one man, and passed the resolution [against any alteration in the Constitution] amid universal acclamations. Immediately members gathered together from all parts of the hall, and, exchanging reciprocal tokens of fraternity, they merged for a moment all other feelings in the sole love of their country." Quoted from the official minutes of the session by A. Aulard, *The French Revolution*, translated by B. Miall, T. Fisher Unwin, London, 1910, Vol. 1, p. 366.

quires a word of explanation in the case of logrolling, where nothing appears to stand in the way of simultaneity. However, logrolling is a *private*, sometimes secret transaction between these two parties and it does not affect the order in which the two reforms are brought to a vote. In the normal course of events, one issue will simply be voted on after the other. This is also required by elementary prudence on the part of the reformmonger who may not be privy to the logrolling agreement and hence may be worried about a possible double defeat if both issues are brought up together.

The situation is quite different in the case of majority formation through mutual sacrifices: here, the promises of the $A\bar{B}$ and $\bar{A}B$ Members to vote for beta and alpha are not private deals but public commitments. The solemnity of the occasion actually requires here a simultaneous consummation.

A simultaneous solution is intellectually far more attractive, especially once the reforms are perceived to be interdependent in some sense. An argument can then be made that a comprehensive, integrated program is required and that the introduction of one reform without the other may be impossible, useless or worse. A simultaneous solution is "organic" and "balanced," a sequential one "messy" and "unbalanced." These differences of our various roads to reform are brought out in the following schematic presentation:

Alternative roads to two reforms	Timing of action on two reforms	Usual intellectual and moral judgment
1. Majority in favor of both reforms	Simultaneous	Strong approval
2. Majority through positive logrolling	Close together, but not simultaneous	Weak disapproval
3. Majority through shifting alliances	Sequential	Strong disapproval
4. Majority through mutual sacrifices	Simultaneous	Strong approval
5. Majority hostile to both reforms, hence revolution	Simultaneous	Approval[a]

[a] On grounds of "historical necessity" and "blindness of ruling class."

Although approval certainly does not hinge exclusively on whether the two problems are tackled jointly or sequentially, the correspondence between simultaneity and approval is striking. In any event, this synoptic view brings out the fact that the intermediate solutions of logrolling and

shifting alliances are likely to lack intellectual appeal and moral respectability, even when they are the most rational ones in terms of getting results.

In effect, therefore, policy-makers are likely to concentrate on the extreme situations (1) smooth, simultaneous reform or (4) and (5) which
are alternative results of revolutionary brinkmanship: in the case of (5)
the brink is overstepped and revolution results whereas with (4) the specter of revolution brings about a near-miraculous last-minute assertion of
sense and energy in favor of needed reforms.

Intermediate solution (2), majority formation through logrolling, is often likely to be assimilated, in the minds of policy-makers, with (1) or
what we have called smooth reform. This confusion is the easier since the
logrollers, once they have voted for a measure they were originally against,
are in a state known to psychologists as cognitive dissonance.[1] This state is
the result of one's acting in a way contrary to his stated beliefs; it is unpleasant and our logrollers may well attempt to reduce dissonance by convincing themselves that the measures in favor of which they have voted
were really rather opportune. Solution (2) thus may shade over into Solution (1) and it will often be difficult to distinguish between the two, especially upon looking backward.

No such fusion or confusion is possible between Solutions (3) and (4).
On the contrary, it is hard to imagine a sharper contrast than between the
élan toward national unity of Solution (4) and the reversal of alliances of
Solution (3). Here again it is likely that the policy-makers will consciously
plan, perhaps we should say "dream about," Solution (4), but finding that
shared sacrifices are out of reach the logic of numbers will make them turn
to (3), i.e., to shifting alliances. Those who do that will naturally be
branded as turncoats and traitors, the more so since they merely stumbled
on (3), having consistently pursued and advertised previously the image of
national union and shared sacrifices.

The contempt and disapproval in which Solution (3), shifting alliances,
is held results in one further risk. It is conceivable that the AB people, i.e.,
those who are strongly in favor of both reforms, are so strongly convinced
that both reforms must be enacted *together* that they are strongly set
against "partial" reform or "half-measures." Convinced that half a loaf is

---

[1] Leon Festinger, A *Theory of Cognitive Dissonance,* Row, Peterson, Evanston, Ill.,
1957. Also Jack W. Brehm and Arthur R. Cohen, *Explorations in Cognitive Dissonance,*
Wiley, New York, 1962.

worse than none, they prefer $\bar{A}\bar{B}$ to $\bar{A}B$ or to $A\bar{B}$ while their first choice is still AB.[1] In this somewhat special, but by no means unthinkable, situation, it will not be possible to form a temporary coalition first of the AB's with the $A\bar{B}$'s and then of the AB's with the $\bar{A}B$'s. Revolution may then be the entirely avoidable result of a commitment of the reformers to an integrated, comprehensive, simultaneous solution. Later on, the revolution may be ascribed to the "blindness of the ruling class" when in actual fact it was due to the reformers' reluctance to try out a sequential solution.

---

[1] They bear a strong resemblance to revolutionaries R1 of Model I.

Index

C